D0331740

Lapland

the Bradt Travel Guide

James Proctor

edition
4

www.bradtguides.com

Bradt Travel Guides Ltd, UK
The Globe Pequot Press Inc, USA

Lofoten and Vesterålen islands: rugged mountains and sandy beaches make this island chain Lapland at its most spectacular
page 94

Tromsø: *the* place in Lapland to enjoy some urban sophistication with great bars and restaurants
page 186

Prehistoric rock carvings: marvel at the vivid prehistoric rock carvings that adorn this part of the Arctic Ocean coast
page 203

Ofotbanen train journey: jaw-dropping vistas from the train window on this scenic ride between Sweden and Norway
page 84

Inlandsbanan: ride the Inlandsbanan through some of Swedish Lapland's most remote landscapes
page 69

Icehotel: do it once in your life – spend a night in sub-zero temperatures inside the world-famous Icehotel, snuggled up in a thermal sleeping bag
page 77

Staloluokta: take a helicopter flight to this remote Sámi summer camp beside Swedish Lapland's most beautiful lakes
page 63

Lappstaden: get an insight into Lapland's Sámi culture at this traditional church town of gnarled wooden cottages and storehuts
page 55

Norwegian Sea

Sørøya

Hasvik

Gar

Skjervøy

Ringvassøy

Tromsø

A

Storfjord

Finnma

1326m

Andenes

Gryllefjord

Finnsnes

W

Vesterålen

Risøyhamn

Harstad

R

Sortland

Stokmarknes

Narvik

Riksgränsen

T

Svolvær

Lofoten

Stamsund

Bognes

Kebnekaise
2102m

Jukkasjärvi

Å

Reine

Kiruna

Værøy

Stora Sjöfallet
National Park

N

Bodø

Fauske

Ritsem

Svappavaara

Vittangi

Ørnes

Padjelanta
National Park

2090m

Laponia
World Heritage
Area

Junosuand

Staloluokta

Sarek
National Park

Gällivare

Kvikkjokk

Porjus

Muddus
National
Park

N

S

W

E

D

E

Arctic Circle

931m

Jokkmokk

Kåbdalis

Boden

Arjeplog

Boden

Arvidsjaur

Älvsbyn

Luleå

Strömsund

Sorsele

Slagnäs

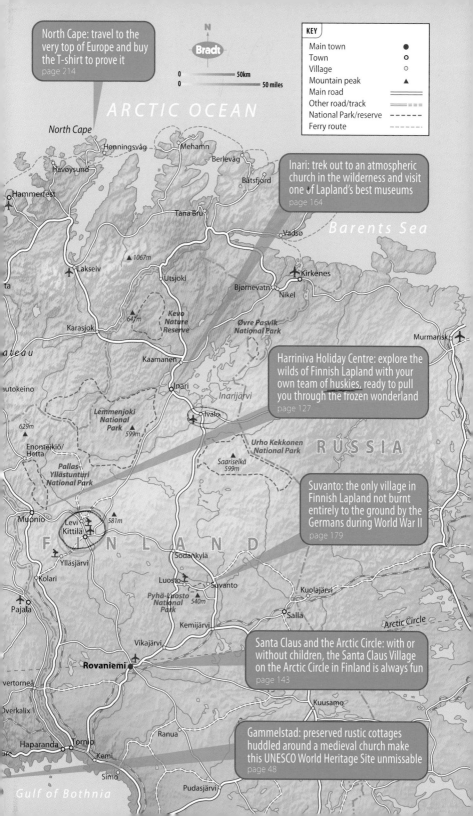

North Cape: travel to the very top of Europe and buy the T-shirt to prove it
page 214

KEY

Main town	●
Town	○
Village	○
Mountain peak	▲
Main road	
Other road/track	
National Park/reserve	
Ferry route	

N

Bradt

0   50km

0   50 miles

ARCTIC OCEAN

North Cape

Honningsvåg

Mehamn

Berlevåg

Havøysund

Båtsfjord

Hammerfest

Tana Bru

Vadsø

Barents Sea

▲1067m

Lakselv

Utsjoki

Kirkenes

Bjørnevatn

Nikel

Inari: trek out to an atmospheric church in the wilderness and visit one of Lapland's best museums
page 164

641m

Kevo Nature Reserve

Øvre Pasvik National Park

Karasjok

Murmansk

Kaamanen

...ateau

...utokeino

Inari

Inarijärvi

Lemmenjoki National Park

599m

Ivalo

629m

Urho Kekkonen National Park

R U S S I A

Enontekiö/Hetta

▲ Saariselkä 599m

Harriniva Holiday Centre: explore the wilds of Finnish Lapland with your own team of huskies, ready to pull you through the frozen wonderland
page 127

Pallas-Yllästunturi National Park

Muonio

Levi Kittilä

581m

Suvanto: the only village in Finnish Lapland not burnt entirely to the ground by the Germans during World War II
page 179

F I N L A N D

Ylläsjärvi

Sodankylä

Kolari

Luosto

Suvanto

Kuolajärvi

Pyhä-Luosto National Park

540m

Pajala

Kemijärvi

Salla

Arctic Circle

Vikajärvi

Santa Claus and the Arctic Circle: with or without children, the Santa Claus Village on the Arctic Circle in Finland is always fun
page 143

Rovaniemi

...vertorneå

Kuusamo

...verkalix

Ranua

Gammelstad: preserved rustic cottages huddled around a medieval church make this UNESCO World Heritage Site unmissable
page 48

Haparanda

Tornio

Kemi

Simo

Pudasjärvi

Gulf of Bothnia

Lapland
Don't
miss...

Northern lights
The phenomenon everybody wants to witness: the enigmatic northern lights, or aurora borealis, can be seen right across Lapland
(KK/NNTB) page 4

Santa Claus
If you are looking for Santa Claus, you will find him most readily on the Arctic Circle in Finnish Lapland
(RTM) page 143

Lofoten islands

The Lofoten islands (named 'lynx foot' by the Vikings after their supposed resemblance) really are something special

(JM/S) page 105

Icehotel

Around 4,000 tonnes of ice and 30,000 tonnes of snow go into the construction of the Icehotel every year

(AK/IAS) page 77

North Cape

The Sámi call Norway's northernmost island Máhkarávju or 'steep barren coast'

(K/S) page 214

Lapland in colour

above	Explore 430km of pristine wilderness on foot along the spectacular Kungsleden trail in Swedish Lapland (JO/S) page 85
left	The Pielpajärvi wilderness church was built beside Inarijärvi in the 1750s (JP) page 168
below	Hiking near Rovaniemi, Finland – the surrounding forests make the perfect escape from the tourist hubbub of the town (LM) page 136

above   A stay in Abisko allows you to get up close to the vast open expanses of Swedish Lapland and Torneträsk Lake (BZ/S) page 81

right   The Finnmark Plateau is one of the last wilderness areas of northern Lapland (DT) page 135

below   Riding the coastal ferry through impossibly narrow Trollfjorden with its sheer rock walls is one of Lapland's great adventures (TFAS/NNTB) page 105

AUTHOR

James Proctor first visited Lapland in 1983 on board the legendary train, the *Lapland Arrow*, from Stockholm. The thrill of crossing the Arctic Circle proved irresistible and James has been back and forth ever since. While working as the BBC's Scandinavia correspondent, he produced reports on everything from the reindeer races at the Jokkmokk winter market to the effects of the Chernobyl nuclear disaster on the Sámi community. James now divides his time as a travel writer between the south of France and his forest retreat in Sweden. A
self-appointed Nanook of the North, he has also written Bradt's *Faroe Islands* and *West Sweden* guides as well as co-writing and contributing to guidebooks about the Nordic countries for other major travel publishers.

AUTHOR'S STORY

Ever since mistakenly studying Swedish at university (I actually signed up to do Spanish but went to the wrong lecture room), I have been fascinated by Scandinavia. It's still an area of Europe which is little known and little discovered. Yet, that is precisely its charm. In today's world there are few places where you can travel for hours through vast areas of untouched nature without seeing a soul. When I lived in Sweden during the mid 1990s, I travelled frequently to Lapland, in both winter and summer, and soon understood that this was a very special part of Scandinavia. Lapland remains, however, a vague concept to most people. In compiling this guide, it has been my aim to lift the lid off this remote Arctic region and to bring its attractions to a wider audience.

The book you have in your hands is the only English-language guide to Lapland, and also the first guide to Scandinavia that is not country-specific. Lapland is a region that spreads across three, arguably four, countries and travel here is determined more by routes than by national borders. Hence, I have organised the chapters of this guide by route, rather than country, to save you constantly flicking backwards and forwards when you cross a border to find the next town account. In *Lapland: The Bradt Travel Guide*, one town account follows another, irrespective of whether you are in Norwegian, Swedish or Finnish Lapland. Don't underestimate distances up here: Lapland is truly huge and, accordingly, there's plenty to fill a holiday of two weeks or more – after all, Lapland has much more to offer than being the home of Santa Claus.

The range of landscapes you'll encounter is enormous, everything from barren treeless upland plateaux, to densely forested river valleys, to jagged mountain peaks and sea cliffs. As a Scandinavian specialist, it is with great pride that I recommend a visit to Lapland – it's a chance to experience nature in the raw like nowhere else in Europe. Listen to the whisper of the wind through the birch trees and breathe the crisp air heavy with the scent of pine, and you're well on the way to understanding what Lapland is all about.

Fourth edition published January 2022
First published 2007
Bradt Travel Guides Ltd
31a High Street, Chesham, Buckinghamshire, HP5 1BW, England
www.bradtguides.com
Print edition published in the USA by The Globe Pequot Press Inc,
PO Box 480, Guilford, Connecticut 06437-0480

Text copyright © 2022 James Proctor
Maps copyright © 2022 Bradt Travel Guides Ltd; includes map data © OpenStreetMap contributors
Photographs copyright © 2022 Individual photographers (see below)
Project Manager: Carys Homer
Cover research: Marta Bescos

ISBN: 978 1 78477 589 6

British Library Cataloguing in Publication Data
A catalogue record for this book is available from the British Library

Photographs Awl-images.com: Jürgen Weginger (JW/AWL); David Tipling (DT); Discover The World (DTW); Dreamstime.com: Neil Burton (NB/D); Heart of Lapland (HL); Icehotel Art Suite: Asaf Kliger (AK/IAS); James Proctor (JP); Lapland Marketing (LM); Mark Churn (MC); Northern Norway Tourist Board: Espen Mortensen (EM/NNTB), Jørn Tomter (JT/NNTB), Konrad Konieczny (KK/NNTB), Kristin Folsland Olsen (KFO/NNTB), To-Foto AS (TFAS/NNTB); Rovaniemi Tourism & Marketing Ltd (RTM); Shutterstock.com: Bildagentur Zoonar GmbH (BZ/S), BMJ (BMJ/S), canadastock (c/S), Frank Fichtmueller (FF/S), James Percy (JP/S), Jan Miko (JM/S), Jens Ottoson (JO/S), Kartouchken (K/S), Mikhail Varentsov (MVa/S), Michele Vacchiano (MV/S), Ondrej Prosicky (OP/S), Pecold (P/S), Soili Jussila (SJ/S), V. Belov (VB/S); Superstock.com (SS); Visit HaparandaTornio (HT)

Front cover Husky sledding (JW/AWL)
Back cover The northern lights over Norwegian Lapland (JP/S); Tromsø city views, including the cathedral (MVa/S)
Title page Trollfjorden (TFAS/NNTB); Sámi woman crafting (MV/S); lynx (JP/S)

Maps David McCutcheon FBCart.S; regional maps compiled from Philip's 1:1,000,000 Europe Mapping; relief map base by Nick Rowland FRGS

Typeset by Ian Spick, Bradt Travel Guides
Production managed by Jellyfish Print Solutions; printed in India
Digital conversion by www.dataworks.co.in

Acknowledgements

As I've updated this guide over the years, I have come into contact with people too numerous to mention here, who have shared their intimate knowledge of, and passion for, this remote part of Europe with me. It is their help that has enabled me to write and update the book you have in your hands and it is they who deserve my sincere and heartfelt thanks. Share my thanks to the people who make the northernmost fringe of Europe home and benefit from their first-hand knowledge, which I present in these pages, to explore this fascinating and much-overlooked destination.

Contents

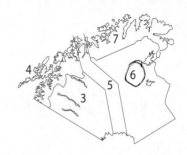

Levi – p. 148

Introduction

Jooti lea buoret go oru
'Better to keep moving than to stay in one place'

Sámi proverb

For a place that doesn't officially exist, Lapland is famous the world over. Children know this snowy winter wonderland as the home of Santa Claus and his illustrious red-nosed reindeer, Rudolph, who take to the starry skies over Lapland every Christmas Eve to deliver presents and goodies to homes across the globe, a truly remarkable feat of aviation, timetabling and largesse that leaves even the world's favourite airlines lost for words. However, beyond the popular image of Lapland, little is known about this mysterious region lost somewhere on the very fringes of Europe. It's the aim of this guidebook, the only one in English dedicated solely to Lapland, to unlock some of the secrets of this vast, forgotten corner of the continent, larger in size than the entire United Kingdom.

First-time visitors are often astonished at the sheer variety of Lapland's landscapes: classic Norwegian fjords amid some of the most awe-inspiring mountain scenery anywhere in Europe; sweeping forests of pine and spruce that cloak the great inland plateaux of Swedish Lapland; and austere, treeless fells surrounded by steely grey lakes and unforgiving marshes that give Finnish Lapland its very individual character. This is Scandinavia at its most elemental. Thanks to good road, rail and air links, travel between the different regions of Lapland is straightforward, making it perfectly possible to visit Santa Claus in Finland, spend a night at the Icehotel in Sweden and go island-hopping in Norway all on the same trip. True, winter temperatures can plummet to −30°C and below, but public transport in Lapland is reliable, accommodation is warm and snug and eating out offers up a variety of options; reindeer, a local source of low-fat nutrition that's been consumed by generations of Laplanders, could even be on the menu.

Inevitably, the indigenous inhabitants of Lapland, the Sámi (who dislike the name 'Lapps', which was imposed on them by insensitive southerners) are today a minority in their own land and make up barely 7% of the total population. The promotion of Sámi culture is widespread and efforts to save the seven (or arguably nine; page 17) different dialects of the Sámi tongue from extinction have met with some success. Travel across Lapland and sooner or later you'll see Sámi in their brightly coloured traditional dress – this is sometimes put on for tourists, but at key festivals in the Sámi calendar wearing these clothes is a sign of pride and fraternity. The nomadic lifestyle may have all but disappeared but there's still a strong sense of community, which reaches across national borders.Inextricably drawn to last places, I first travelled to Lapland in 1983 and have been a regular visitor ever since. There's quite simply something about the sheer austerity of the nature – and, at times, the gruffness of the people who choose to live high inside the Arctic Circle – that fascinates me. Lapland may be at its most magical during the long winter months when daylight is in short supply and snow lies thick on the ground – it's certainly the perfect time to head out on a snowmobile tour or a dog-sled safari, or, indeed, to curl up with a good book beside a wood-burning stove inside a log cabin – but it's equally alluring in summer when the midnight sun and the quality of the light in the northern sky are perhaps two of the most difficult things about Lapland to qualify on paper. Visit Norwegian, Swedish or Finnish Lapland and you'll take away much more than Santa Claus could ever give you.

THE BRADT DEFINITION OF LAPLAND – AND ITS ORIGIN

Spanning no fewer than four countries, Lapland is different things to different people. For the sake of this guidebook, we have determined Lapland to be roughly contained by the Arctic Circle in the south, the Arctic Ocean in the north and the Russian–Finnish border in the east. Strictly speaking, Lapland is found in Norway, Sweden, Finland and Russia. However, due to tiresome visa restrictions and a lack of tourist facilities in Russian Lapland (effectively, the Kola peninsula west of Murmansk), we have limited our coverage of Lapland to those areas that lie within the aforementioned Nordic countries. Travel across borders here is easy and trouble-free and a visit to Lapland, therefore, can feature anything up to three countries.

THE NAME 'LAPLAND' The exact origin of the name 'Lapland' is not known. The term entered English, and other languages, from Swedish, where the wild, untamed lands of the north have always been known as Lappmark (later Lappland), where '*mark*' simply means 'land' (compare the country name Den*mark*). However, it's likely that Swedish itself inherited the word from Finnish where the northern parts of Finland have always been known as 'Lappi'. The meaning of the '*lapp*' element is not clear, though one suggestion is that the Swedish word refers to the *gakti* or traditional dress of the Sámi (in Swedish '*lapp*' is a piece of cloth or a patch, which requires mending), while another possibility is that it is a term of contempt related to the Middle High German word '*lappe*', meaning 'simpleton'.

Part One

GENERAL INFORMATION

LAPLAND AT A GLANCE

Location Lapland is the northernmost part of Scandinavia. The region spreads across Norway, Sweden, Finland (and the Kola peninsula in Russia, not covered in this book) and is generally considered to lie between the North Cape at 71°N and the Arctic Circle at 66°N. However, Lapland's indigenous population, the Sámi, consider their homeland to stretch as far south as central Sweden and Norway, an area they call Sápmi.

Size/area Lapland covers approximately 300,000km² (115,000 square miles), an area bigger than the whole of the United Kingdom

Climate Subarctic with sparse vegetation. See page 4 for more information.

Status Lapland is composed of Finnish, Norwegian and Swedish provinces, which answer to national governments in Helsinki, Oslo and Stockholm. The Sámi parliaments in Finland, Norway and Sweden aim to promote Sámi culture though they have limited political power.

Population Approximately 900,000 people live in Lapland of whom around 66,000 are indigenous Sámi (40,000 in Norway, 20,000 in Sweden and 6,000 in Finland; exact numbers are hard to ascertain since self-identification as Sámi varies considerably)

Main towns Finnish Lapland: Ivalo, Rovaniemi, Tornio; Norwegian Lapland: Hammerfest, Narvik, Tromsø; Swedish Lapland: Luleå, Gällivare, Kiruna

Language Finnish, Norwegian, Sámi and Swedish

Religion Traditionally, the Sámi believed in animism whereby everything in nature from animals to minerals has a soul. Today, though, Sámi and non-Sámi alike are Evangelical-Lutheran.

Currency/exchange rate Finnish Lapland: euro (£1 = €1.18, US$1 = €0.86); Norwegian Lapland: Norwegian krone (£1 = 11.60NOK, €1 =9.86NOK, US$1 = 8.52NOK); Swedish Lapland: Swedish krona (£1 = 11.91SEK, €1 =10.12SEK, US$1 = 8.75SEK) (October 2021)

International telephone codes Finland +358, Norway +47, Sweden +46

Time Winter: Norwegian and Swedish Lapland GMT + 1 hour, Finnish Lapland GMT + 2 hours; summer: Norwegian and Swedish Lapland GMT + 2 hours, Finnish Lapland GMT + 3 hours

Electrical voltage 220V; European two-pin plugs

Weights and measures Metric

Flag The Sámi flag is based on the motifs of a shaman's drum and the sun. It features a yellow and green stripe crossed by a red and blue circle, all overlaid against a blue and red background.

Public holidays Finnish Lapland: 1, 6 January, Good Friday, Easter Sunday, Easter Monday, 17 May, Whit Sunday, 23 June, 3 November, 6, 25, 26 December; Norwegian Lapland: 1 January, Maundy Thursday, Good Friday, Easter Sunday, Easter Monday, 1, 17 May, Whit Sunday, Whit Monday, 25, 26 December; Swedish Lapland: 1, 6 January, Good Friday, Easter Sunday, Easter Monday, 1, 17 May, Whit Sunday, 6, 23 June, 1 November, 25, 26 December

Bus information Sweden: w resrobot.se and w ltnbd.se; Finland: w eskelisen. fi and w matkahuolto.fi; Norway: w snelandia.no

Train information for Swedish Lapland w sj.se

1

Background Information

GEOGRAPHY AND CLIMATE

GEOGRAPHY Western and northern areas of Lapland, predominantly in Norway, comprise fjords, deep valleys and mountains, whereas further south and east, in Swedish and Finnish Lapland, the land is flatter and made up of countless marshes and lakes, the largest of which is Inarijärvi in Finland. The highest mountain is Kebnekaise (2,102m), near Kiruna in Swedish Lapland. The geography of Lapland falls roughly into three main categories. The **coastal fringe** of Norwegian Lapland and its immediate hinterland is characterised by countless rocky islands and skerries, deep fjords that penetrate considerable distances inland and a chain of mountain and lesser peaks, predominantly found in northwestern areas between Narvik and Tromsø. Moving east and south away from the coast, the terrain of Swedish and Finnish Lapland is characterised by low mountains and **sweeping plains** blanketed with boreal coniferous forest, subduing its irregularities and eliminating colour variation through the constancy of its greenery. The mountains here, unlike those in Norwegian Lapland, are widely dispersed and rise sharply above the surrounding country. Several of the north's great rivers, such as the Luleälv, Tornionjoki and Kemijoki, drain these vast areas and empty into the upper reaches of the Gulf of Bothnia. Between these two main zones lies Lapland's third geographic category: the Finnmarksvidda or **Finnmark Plateau**. Stretching south of the Norwegian town of Alta for around 200km to beyond the Finnish border, this barren upland plateau is carpeted with dwarf birch forest and is criss-crossed by rivers and small streams.

The Arctic Circle: polar night and midnight sun The imaginary line drawn around the earth at roughly 66°N, known as the Arctic Circle, marks the southernmost extent of the polar night in winter and the midnight sun in summer. At the Circle, there is one day of total darkness each winter on the **winter solstice** (albeit the period around midday is edged with blue or grey since the sun is only just below the horizon) and, conversely, one day of 24-hour daylight at the **summer solstice**. As you travel north, so the length of the polar night and period of midnight sun increases.

Location	Polar night	Midnight sun
Kilpisjärvi	25 Nov–17 Jan	22 May–25 Jul
Kiruna	22 Dec–16 Jan	30 May–15 Jul
North Cape	18 Nov–23 Jan	13 May–29 Jul
Tromsø	25 Nov–16 Jan	20 May–22 Jul
Utsjoki	25 Nov–17 Jan	16 May–27 Jul

Incidentally, the Arctic Circle is actually moving north by 14–15m every year due to the earth's uneven orbit. In ten to twenty thousand years' time this northward drift will stop, when the Arctic Circle will be roughly at 68°N, and it will start to drift southwards again.

Northern lights: aurora borealis One of the most spectacular sights in Lapland is the aurora borealis, as it is known in Latin, or the northern lights. During the darkest months of winter, the sky is often lit up by these shimmering arcs of green, blue and yellowish light, which can disappear as fast as they appear. The science behind their existence is complex but essentially the displays are caused by solar wind or particles charged by the sun, which light up as they reach the earth's atmosphere: blue is nitrogen and yellowy-green is oxygen. In order to see the northern lights, the night sky must be clear of cloud. It is said that the colder and stiller the conditions the better the chances of a display, and the further north you travel the more impressive the lights will be. If you're flying to Lapland during the hours of darkness, be alert as you look out of the plane windows because the aurora borealis can also be seen clearly when you are in the air above the cloud.

CLIMATE Although Lapland's climate is **subarctic**, there are considerable variations between milder maritime regions and those further inland, which suffer the full brunt of the Arctic winter chill. The coastal areas of Norwegian Lapland are considerably milder and wetter than the inland plateaux of Swedish and Finnish Lapland, where, for example, January mean temperatures are commonly below –15°C, and in some areas as low as –30°C. Large parts of Lapland receive less than 500mm of precipitation per year.

The flow of the warm North Atlantic Drift is the factor of greatest importance in modifying the climate of coastal stretches of Norwegian Lapland. Here there is no great excess of either cold or heat; winter temperatures fluctuate a couple of degrees either side of freezing, and in summer they reach 10–12°C. As distance from the sea increases, so, in general, winter temperatures decrease and summer temperatures increase; maritime influences seldom find their way over the mountain chain dividing Norway from Sweden and the Finnmarksvidda from Finland.

That said, the effects of climate change are having a dramatic impact on Lapland: temperatures are currently rising at twice the global average, impacting

AVERAGE DAILY TEMPERATURES/PRECIPITATION

	Tromsø (Norway)	Sodankylä (Finland)	Jokkmokk (Sweden)
January	–6°C/104mm	–14°C/33mm	–14°C/30mm
February	–6°C/87mm	–13°C/28mm	–14°C/27mm
March	–4°C/82mm	–8°C/26mm	–9°C/24mm
April	–1°C/64mm	–2°C/29mm	–2°C/30mm
May	4°C/49mm	5°C/35mm	4°C/35mm
June	8°C/58mm	12°C/61mm	11°C/48mm
July	12°C/68mm	14°C/70mm	14°C/78mm
August	11°C/79mm	11°C/63mm	11°C/74mm
September	6°C/102mm	6°C/57mm	6°C/55mm
October	1°C/133mm	–1°C/48mm	–1°C/41mm
November	–3°C/100mm	–8°C/41mm	–8°C/36mm
December	–5°C/101mm	–12°C/33mm	–14°C/32mm

the migratory routes, habitats and behaviour of the animals that live there. Official statistics from the Finnish Meteorological Institute, for example, show that Finland's annual mean temperature has risen by 2°C since the mid 19th century. At certain times of the year rain is now more prevalent than snow, which, when it falls on snow-covered ground, forms a hard ice crust, making it difficult for reindeer to reach lichen and other food below the snow's surface.

Equally, operators within the tourist industry across Lapland have been consistently reporting a late onset to the winter season – with the snow arriving later and melting sooner. This is combined with highly irregular and unstable weather patterns during the winter season when, traditionally, temperatures were consistently low and stable for months on end.

During the **winter** months, most precipitation falls as **snow**, often resulting in considerable depths. In Sodankylä, for example, just inside the Arctic Circle in Finnish Lapland, snow can lie at depths of at least 60cm from October to mid-March. The annual duration of snow cover is determined by air temperature and precipitation. Much of Lapland is covered with snow for more than 200 days per year; in the mountains of Swedish Lapland this figure rises to 220 days per year whereas the Lofoten islands have only 120 days with snow.

The long winters naturally have an impact on the growing season in Lapland, which lasts less than 130 days on average, extending roughly from mid-May to mid-September, a full two months shorter than that of southern Sweden and western Norway. During the short **summer** months, Finnish Lapland, far away from the cloud-producing mountains of the coastal fringes, is one of the sunniest regions in the whole of Scandinavia, whereas rain clouds crossing the mountain range make Riksgränsen in Swedish Lapland one of the wettest spots in the entire country. Conversely, Abisko, barely 35km to the east, lies in a rain shadow and is the driest place in Sweden.

NATURAL HISTORY

For more on wildlife in Lapland, check out Bradt's 52 European Wildlife Weekends. *Get 10% off at* w *bradtguides.com/shop.*

Lapland's unique geographical position has produced a highly distinctive natural history. The range of flora and fauna is not huge but it is certainly impressive. Whether it is whales or reindeer, eagles or the three-toed woodpecker, you are likely to encounter some unusual wildlife as befits the unusual terrain. The landscape varies from tundra to lush river valleys with heavily forested hills, fells and swamps in between. Despite – or perhaps because of – the fact that much of it is still a virtual wilderness, it is little surprise that Lapland has always been a favourite destination for nature-lovers.

FLORA The main dividing line in terms of what vegetation to expect is the treeline. Above it is mostly tundra, literally 'treeless plains' where all plants struggle to survive. Below it there is much greater variety and, at certain times of the year, a colourful display of plant life, most spectacularly in the early autumn as leaves turn red and gold on the trees.

Tundra The principal feature of tundra is the absence of any trees, but otherwise it can be very varied. Although based on permafrost, depending on the natural drainage available the terrain can be wet, in the form of peatland, or dry. The bogs tend to be characterised by many tall hummocks encrusted with a wide variety of lichens, some of which have been living for more than a hundred years, as well as plants like **crowberry** and **cloudberry**. **Cotton grass** and **sedge marshes** (the Sámi have traditionally used sedge grass to line their shoes) cover large areas and there are huge varieties of moss, but in some parts of Finnmark in Norwegian Lapland the terrain is so rocky that plant life is minimal.

Where moisture seeps down into hollows and depressions you will find willow scrub, which can grow to impressive heights of 2m or more in places. **Northern willow** is the most common, followed by **downy willow** and, where there's a lot of chalk or lime in the soil, **woolly willow**. The amount of snow and the rate of thawing make a big difference to plant life. Where the snow lingers long into spring and even summer, the wetness encourages **liverworts** and small herbs as well as **bilberry** and **mat grass**. Certain varieties of **buttercup** grow among the snow beds and **dwarf azalea** can provide some additional colour, too.

Forests Lapland's coniferous forests are known as '*taiga*' and have very few tree types. The principal ones are the **Scots pine** and the **Norway spruce**. At higher altitudes the tougher **downy birch** often provides a border strip to the forests that can go on for many kilometres. In places you will find a lot of aspen, alder and rowan, but these tend to be in more isolated patches. When the deciduous trees change colour in September to October the displays of reds, golds and yellows are awe-inspiring.

Under the tree cover **juniper** is the most common shrub, although even this can be quite sparse. The generally poor, acidic soil in much of the region means that at the forest-floor level plants struggle to survive. You are most likely to see crowberry, cowberry and bilberry, while certain heathers reach well into the north of Lapland, even as far as the North Cape. **Ferns** do well in some forest areas, along with the inevitable **lichens**, **mosses** and **liverworts**. This is especially true where there is a lot of fallen, dead wood, which breaks down into forest-floor humus. Thistles grow in patches.

Watch out for the spectacular large **monkshood**, with large leaves and tall purple spikes. It looks impressive where it grows, mainly in southern Lapland, but it is highly poisonous. **Forget-me-nots**, **sorrel**, **cow parsley** and various worts are among the herbs that are commonly found. Surprisingly several types of **orchids** also do well, including the common spotted orchid, frog orchid and lady's slipper. On dry heaths the **mountain aven** can make a beautiful display and the **Lapland rhododendron** prospers on the fells.

FAUNA The reindeer is emblematic of Lapland and is undoubtedly the most eye-catching of the region's animals. But it is far from the only one. Regrettably perhaps, insects are to be found everywhere, including midges, mosquitoes, blowflies and wasps. More happily, butterflies can brighten up the terrain in summer.

Birds As many as 175 breeds of birds have been identified as breeding in Lapland. Most take advantage of the summer sun to nest and raise their young before flying south again. A few stick it out for the harsh winters, notably **grouse**, **crows**, **woodpeckers** and **owls**. You will find the biggest variety of birdlife and the largest numbers in the more temperate coastal areas. The long hours of daylight in summer can make birdwatching in Lapland particularly rewarding. There are large populations of breeding **ducks**, **sandpipers**, **greenshanks** and **dotterels**.

Inland there can be a disappointing lack of birds. If you're lucky, you may see the **snowy owl**, especially when rodent numbers are high, as well as **rough-legged** buzzards and eagles. More common are the **meadow pipit, wheatear** and **willow warbler**. **Snow bunting, willow grouse** and the **Siberian jay** are often seen, and on fell heaths you might encounter **golden plover**. The **brambling** and the **three-toed woodpecker** are quite common, but don't expect to get close enough to start counting digits. On fast-flowing rivers the **water ouzel** likes to dive for fish. In swamp areas the **sandpiper, ruff, crane** and **bean goose** are happy to get their feet wet.

Mammals

Land mammals Having originated from the wild caribou, Lapland's **reindeer** are now domesticated and semi-tame. They are plentiful – literally running into hundreds of thousands – and hard to miss, although they move about depending on the season and the available grazing. Every square millimetre of their bodies is covered in fur and to provide extra insulation each hair is hollow.

The Sámi have traditionally depended on the reindeer for meat, hides, bones and oil, and also materials for clothing, tents, fuel and tools. The herdsmen round up their reindeer in summer into specially made corrals, where the fawns are marked with the same mark as their mothers'. These round-ups can make for impressive photo opportunities if you're lucky enough to catch one. There's a second round-up every autumn when the reindeer that are to be slaughtered are separated from the herd. This is also the time for a stock-take and to treat the animals for parasites.

The rutting season, when the males fight for supremacy, is September to October and the bulls can weigh up to 150kg at this time of year. They then shed their antlers in November, unlike the females (cows), who keep theirs all year round. Reindeer herds attract predators, notably **bear, lynx** and **wolverine**, but visitors are extremely unlikely to spot any of them. They generally hunt at night and are very timid. The brown bear can weigh over 300kg, but it is the much smaller wolverine that poses the biggest threat to the reindeer, killing the deer by biting into its neck and hanging on with its teeth until death.

Elk are also prone to attack. These huge, antlered, herbivorous creatures are usually found close to the pine forests. Unlike reindeer they prefer to be alone, although in winter small clusters can be seen. The **Arctic fox** is well adapted to the harsh climate as it has small extremities, apart from a huge tail, which it can wrap around itself for extra warmth. Even the soles of its feet have fur on them and when the outside temperature drops as low as −30°C it can keep its body temperature at a comfortable +40°C. Arctic foxes are fearless and inquisitive, and about the size of a small dog.

Smaller still is the **lemming**, whose reputation for mindless self-destruction is undeserved. In fact lemmings do not get together in large numbers and jump off high cliffs in acts of mass suicide. Rather they potter about on the tundra, dig burrows and eat a lot. The Norway lemming is particularly colourful but not famous for its friendliness. The myth probably came about because of the cyclical overpopulation of lemmings. At these times they seem to panic that the food is going to run out and head off in large numbers to find more fertile territory.

Marine mammals On the face of it, the **killer whale** has little in common with the Norwegian lemming, but it too suffers from an unearned reputation. A name like 'killer whale' creates an image of a huge bloodthirsty monster prowling the deep on the lookout for anything to kill. In fact, they are very intelligent, social and surprisingly gentle. They are also one of the most common whales off the coast of Lapland and very impressive to watch. They generally live in large pods of around 20 animals, have distinctive black-and-white bodies, and the males have large dorsal fins.

Minke whales are much smaller, sleeker and not at all carnivorous. They are mostly grey in colour and generally less striking to watch. But fortunately for them the whale's only predator, man, has shown limited interest in them and their numbers are plentiful. The white-beaked **dolphin**, though small, is actually a close relative of the orca whale. They travel in large groups and go surprisingly far north for animals that can't cope well with ice. Although they are protected by a thick layer of blubber that keeps them warm, it is not unusual for dolphins to get trapped in pack ice and die.

CONSERVATION The natural environment of northern Scandinavia is extremely sensitive. Harsh climatic conditions are responsible for poor soil cover in many parts of Lapland and vegetation regeneration is hampered by the short summer growing season and long, dark winter. It is therefore essential that travellers reduce their impact on the natural environment as much as possible. Nature conservation is best achieved by sticking to trails when out hiking or snowmobiling; camping where possible only in designated areas; and always taking rubbish with you. In Lapland it can take years even for organic rubbish, such as orange peel and banana skins, to break down; always err on the side of caution and don't leave anything behind after your visit. All three countries are world leaders in recycling – you'll find automatic machines in most supermarkets and food stores which will accept used plastic bottles and aluminium cans. They're a doddle to use: you simply feed your recyclables into the slot, one at a time, and then press the receipt button when you're done and trot off to the tills to get your deposit refund. It doesn't matter whether you have shopped in the store or not; you'll get your money back either way. The return deposit is included in the price of the bottle or can you bought. Hence, if you don't recycle you'll not only be out of pocket, but you'll also be unnecessarily burdening the environment. Throughout Lapland, when you go food shopping, you have to buy plastic carrier bags at the tills, so it makes sense to re-use your bags wherever possible. When it comes to car hire, consider renting a car which runs on ethanol (widely available from the main rental companies in Scandinavia), which is not only more environmentally friendly in its production, but also leaves minimal pollution as you drive.

HISTORY

Over the centuries the history of Lapland has been characterised by countless struggles by greater powers, notably Denmark–Norway and Sweden–Finland, for domination. Lapland's rich natural resources proved alluring as early as the Viking period. However, it is perhaps in more modern times – particularly during and after World War II, when large tracts of Lapland were destroyed and seemingly every building burnt to the ground as occupying Nazi forces implemented their scorched earth policy as they retreated south – that the world became aware of Lapland and its fate. The resettling of refugees who had fled the fighting only to return to discover their homes reduced to piles of rubble and the rebuilding of an entire region's infrastructure after the war proved some of the toughest challenges Lapland has ever faced. This, and the repeated abuse of the rights of an indigenous people, the Sámi, has greatly influenced the face of today's Lapland.

EARLY SETTLERS The first real signs of life in what we now call Lapland can be traced back around 7,000 years when the ice cap that once covered Scandinavia slowly began to melt and retreat. Primitive signs of human habitation have been found around Alta in Norwegian Lapland dating back to this period, though it is not clear whether these first Laplanders were Sámi or not. Prehistoric **rock carvings** here, created between 2,500 and 6,000 years ago, clearly show how people hunted reindeer and other animals for survival. Their tools and jewellery show influences from other peoples living further south, providing proof that they didn't exist in a cultural void.

The first written accounts of life in the far north date from the late 9th century. Ottar of Hålogaland, a chieftain and farmer from central Norway, not only told the English king, Alfred the Great, about his expeditions along the Arctic Ocean coast and around the Kola peninsula, but he also gave details of his trade with the Sámi from whom he collected taxes in the form of skins, feathers and whales' teeth. According to Ottar, other merchants settled around the head of the Gulf of Bothnia were also journeying north to trade and collect taxes from the Sámi at this time.

Another source of detail from this period is contained in the **Icelandic saga** of Egill Skallagrímsson, which recounts events during the reign of the Norwegian king Harald Fairhair. The king's representative in what is now Swedish Lapland, Torolv Kveldúlfsson, conducted trade with the Sámi, collected taxes and plundered and killed anyone who crossed his path. According to the saga, he accepted an invitation to fight on behalf of King Faravid, who presided over an area of land at the head of the Gulf of Bothnia under siege from harrying tribes from what is now central and southern Finland. If the saga is accurate, King Faravid is the first leader from Finnish Lapland to be mentioned in any written account of Lapland's history.

THE GREAT POWERS During the Middle Ages, Lapland's rich natural resources, in particular skins, furs and fish, led to rivalries between the great powers of the time, Denmark–Norway, Sweden–Finland and Russia. The Sámi were often subject to taxes from all three countries as a result of the lack of national borders in the north. In an attempt to control the valuable fur trade with Lapland, the Swedish king, Magnus Eriksson, passed a law in the mid 14th century which ensured that all goods for export had to be handled by either Stockholm or Turku in Finland. A similar law followed in Denmark–Norway giving Copenhagen and Bergen sole export and import rights. As a direct result of both laws, trade and development in Lapland stagnated.

During the 16th century Sweden cranked up its attempts to control Lapland – not just fiscally but now politically as well. Following victory over the Russians at Narva in 1584, which effectively ended Russia's maritime access to the Baltic Sea, Sweden was keen to squeeze its enemy further by taking control of Lapland, which lay along Russia's only other sea route to the west from Arkangelsk.

It was around this time, too, that missionaries were dispatched to Lapland in an attempt to strengthen the position of the Swedish crown in the far north. Churches were built across the region and trade became centred on these new places of worship attracting inhabitants from regions further south. However, further conflict between Sweden and Denmark, which culminated in the peace agreement of Knäred in 1613, led to an agreement by Sweden to relinquish control over Lapland. A visit to northern Norway and the Kola peninsula by the Danish king, Christian IV, in the 1790s was a clear sign to Sweden and the rest of Europe that Denmark–Norway considered itself to have won control over Lapland.

THE RUSSIAN INVASION In February 1808, Russian troops loyal to Tsar Alexander I attacked Swedish positions in Finland as part of a secret pact between the tsar and the French emperor, Napoleon. The Swedish king, Gustav VI Adolf, fell foul of the plot by refusing to assist the French in blockading England's seaports. Poorly equipped and badly trained Swedish troops retreated to Umeå and Tornio as the Russians advanced, leaving Finland undefended. In March 1809, the Russians pushed forward again towards Tornio driving the Swedish forces to withdraw westwards. Finland's fate was sealed and as part of the peace agreement of Fredrikshamn of September 1809 Sweden was forced to cede Finland to Russia. A new border was drawn from the head of the Gulf of Bothnia along the rivers Tornio, Muonio and Könkämä towards Kilpisjärvi (the current border between Sweden and Finland), splitting former villages and parishes in two and setting Finnish Lapland firmly within the Russian sphere of influence.

Although large numbers of Finns had begun leaving their homeland for neighbouring Norwegian Lapland in the 1700s, this migration continued and intensified after the Russian takeover; in all it is estimated that 10,000 people fled to escape the harsh economic conditions that prevailed in Finland at this time and to look for prosperity across the border. Indeed, the rich fishing grounds of the Arctic Ocean attracted many Finns who chose to settle in Vadsø on the Varangerfjord, a town which became more Finnish than Norwegian and even today carries its own Finnish name, Vesisaari.

As so often in Lapland's history, the Sámi bore the brunt of this new colonisation and as the Finns moved north they took land which had previously been used for reindeer herding. Over the centuries it has been a common Finnish agricultural practice to clear large areas of forestland for farming by burning down the trees and then planting crops such as rye in the rich ashes that then cover the ground. This practice destroys the land and forests which the Sámi need to tend their reindeer.

During the **Crimean War** in the mid 1850s a wind of change began to blow through the Swedish capital, Stockholm, where the king became suspicious of Russia's expansionist intentions in Finland (until 1809 Finland had been part of Sweden). He turned to England and France for support should Russia lay claim to yet more Swedish or Norwegian territory (after centuries of Danish domination, Norway entered a union with Sweden in 1814).

The newly created border between Sweden and Russia–Finland was closed and Sweden refused to grant Russia grazing and fishing rights on Swedish territory. This agreement, contained in the November Treaty of 1855 of the Crimean War, remained in force until 1908. The Russians retaliated in 1855 and made it illegal for Norwegian Sámi to drive their reindeer across the border into Finland. Norway followed suit in 1889, closing its border with Finland. The border closures hit the Sámi hard and effectively made it impossible for their reindeer to follow their traditional patterns of migration. As a direct result, many families abandoned their homes and sought new pastures, notably in Swedish Lapland. Meanwhile, across the border in Norway, the fear of Russian aggression was deemed so real that farmers from the south of Norway were encouraged to move north to foster a greater sense of Norwegian nationalism in these remote northern outposts. The Finnish migrants felt the full brunt of this Norwegianisation policy and were openly regarded by the authorities in Oslo as a danger to the state.

INTO THE 20TH CENTURY At the turn of the last century, Lapland was on its knees economically. **Poverty** was widespread in all parts of the region and a shortage of food was a fact of life for most families. In Norwegian Lapland, although ever-decreasing fish catches and the falling price of fish on world markets were the key causes of the problem, the fishing community's total dependence on middlemen who set unrealistic terms for loans and debt collection only served to compound matters. In Swedish and Finnish Lapland things were little better. A series of failed harvests due to drought and severe winters meant that many families were on the brink of starvation during the winter of 1902–03.

However, some of the greatest geopolitical changes ever to affect Lapland were now only a matter of years away. In 1905, the union between Sweden and Norway, which lasted just short of a century, was peacefully dissolved and Norway came of age taking on all the trappings of a modern independent state for the first time in its history.

Although Lapland wasn't directly involved in **World War I** (Norway and Sweden had declared themselves neutral states), the Russians made Finnish Tornio, on the Gulf of Bothnia, their main port to the west since the Germans controlled the entrance to the Baltic Sea, the Öresund Strait. Between 1914 and 1917, the population of Finnish Lapland benefited financially from Tornio's new prominence and many people became involved in the transport of goods and refugees in and out of Russia. One person who transited through Tornio at this time was none other than Vladimir Ilich Lenin who returned to Russia from exile in April 1917 ahead of the **Russian Revolution**. Profiting from the general confusion in St Petersburg, Finland lost no time in declaring its independence from Russia on 6 December the same year, bringing an end to its existence as a grand duchy under the tsar. With the outbreak of the revolution, Russia withdrew from World War I and Finnish Lapland was, for the first time in its history, under direct rule from Helsinki.

However, between late January and mid-May 1918 **civil war** raged in Finland between the Social Democrat-led Red Guard and the White Guard, a right-wing private army, over the future direction of the newly independent country. Finnish Lapland came under the control of the Whites whereas the Reds dominated in Helsinki and the industrial cities of the south. The victorious Whites regarded the civil war as one of (Russian) liberation, something that set the tone for the policy of Finnish nationalism, which later followed. The Russian–Finnish border was not fixed until the **Treaty of Tartu** of October 1920 when, in return for the areas of Repola and Porajärvi, north of Lake Ladoga, Russia ceded a strategic arm of land to Finland, which gave the Finns ice-free access to the Barents Sea at Petsamo (Pechenga in Russian).

Following the discovery of nickel in the area, mining began a year later and a road linking Sodankylä via Ivalo to the Petsamo fjord was completed in 1931 making Petsamo an unlikely Lapland tourist destination; it was the only port on the Barents Sea that could be reached by car. The Petsamo strip remained Finnish territory until 1944 when it was ceded to the Soviets as part of the armistice agreement.

WORLD WAR II Three months after the start of World War II, Stalin's troops attacked Finland on 30 November 1939 after Helsinki refused to accept Soviet demands to cede Finnish territory on the Karelian isthmus in order to protect Leningrad; Moscow wanted the Finns to move the border 25km to the west. At this time the Soviet–Finnish border was just 32km from Leningrad and Stalin feared Germany, despite having signed a non-aggression pact with the Soviet Union just three months earlier, would use Finland as a bridgehead from which to invade. Outnumbered four to one, the Finns initially had the upper hand in the campaign, which became known as the **Winter War**. They moved adeptly on skis, dressed in white camouflage against the snow, and the harsh winter conditions with temperatures down to −40°C coupled with local knowledge played to their advantage – they managed to hold out against the superior enemy until March 1940.

Under German representation the Finns agreed to negotiate the terms of a peace agreement with the Soviet Union. The **Moscow Peace Treaty** inflicted a grievous wound on Finland: the loss of around 10% of its pre-war territory. In the south, the Karelian isthmus, including the country's second city, Viipuri (Vyborg in Russian), a large part of Karelia and the whole of Lake Ladoga were handed over to protect Leningrad. In the north, large parts of the Salla area of Lapland (now referred to as Old Salla) were given to the Soviets in order to move the Finnish border away from the sensitive Leningrad–Murmansk rail line; at one point the frontier came within 80km of the Soviet rail network.

The Finns also agreed to construct a new rail route on their own territory from Kemijärvi, northeast of Rovaniemi, to the new border. The aim of this was to provide the Soviet Union with a direct route between the port of Kandalaksha (Kantalahti in Finnish), on the White Sea, and the head of the Gulf of Bothnia at Kemi. Finland ceded part of the recently acquired Petsamo area of Lapland, four islands in the Gulf of Finland and agreed to lease the Hanko peninsula, in the far southwest of the country, to the Soviets for 30 years so they could establish a naval base there to control the sea approaches to Leningrad.

On 9 April 1940, Germany attacked and invaded Norway in order to take advantage of the country's strategically important Atlantic coastline, thwarting the British, who had the same plan. Although the Norwegians were unprepared for the surprise attack, resistance lasted for two months, and the month-long **Battle of Narvik** became one of the first major confrontations of the war between Britain's Royal Navy and the German Kriegsmarine. Narvik provided an ice-free harbour for the export of valuable iron ore from the mines at Kiruna and Gällivare in Swedish Lapland and was therefore a prized possession for both sides. Following the fall of France, the Norwegians surrendered on 8 June 1940.

During the five years of Nazi occupation, the Norwegians mounted a campaign of civil disobedience and resistance. It became common practice, for example, to pretend not to understand German when addressed by a soldier and not to sit next to German troops when travelling on public transport; the Germans retaliated by making it illegal to stand on a bus if seats were available. However, at the same time, around 400 Norwegians worked as guards in the concentration camps which the Nazis set up across Norway; there were five such camps in northern Norway including Beisfjord (see box, page 94) and Karasjok (page 173). Both Norwegian and German guards were involved in the torture and massacre of hundreds of prisoners.

During World War II, Sweden followed a policy of questionable **neutrality**. Surrounded by German forces all around, the Stockholm government agreed to German requests to transit troops and war equipment through neutral Sweden to occupied Norway – something the Norwegians still to this day find hard to accept. Firmly in control of the port of Narvik, the Nazis bought Swedish iron ore from the mines in Kiruna and Gällivare and transported it to Norway for export to steel plants in Germany where it was critical to war production.

Following Germany's attack on the Soviet Union under Operation Barbarossa, Finland joined World War II on 25 June 1941 against the Soviets, provoked by bombing raids by Moscow on several Finnish cities including Helsinki and Turku. Finland had previously given Germany permission to move troops across its territory and to use Finnish air bases to launch attacks on the Soviet Union. Although the Finnish leadership and people never shared the Nazis' ideology, they did subscribe to the common goal of defeating the Soviet Union – an attempt to rectify the injustice, as they saw it, done to them in the Moscow Peace Treaty and to regain what the Soviets had taken from them.

In late July 1941, the British bombed the ports of Petsamo and Kirkenes, which were being used by the Germans as supply bases from which to attack Murmansk; damage was limited, however, since the harbour in Petsamo was almost empty of ships, though 15 British aircraft were shot down. On Finnish Independence Day

6 December 1941, Britain declared war on Finland. Despite this, the Finns succeeded in retaking Karelia though they refused requests by the Germans to continue eastwards and attack Leningrad, just as they objected to their involvement in blowing up the Murmansk railway line.

By early 1943, Finland began actively to seek a way out of the war following the disastrous German defeat at Stalingrad. Intermittent negotiations stalled and Stalin opted to force Finland's hand, bombing Helsinki in February 1944. The Continuation War came to an end with the signing of the **Moscow Armistice** on 19 September 1944; the conditions for peace were similar to those laid down by the **Moscow Peace Treaty** of 1940, namely that Finland had to cede parts of Karelia, Salla and islands in the Gulf of Finland. However, Finland lost Petsamo and was forced to lease Porkkala (west of Helsinki) to the Soviets for 50 years, though this was returned in 1956. **War reparations** totalling US$300 million were payable to the Soviet Union and Finland was bound to drive German troops out of its territory, which led to the Lapland War.

THE LAPLAND WAR Since summer 1943, the German command had been making preparations for the eventuality that Finland might sign a separate peace accord with the Soviet Union. Plans were laid to withdraw forces northwards to protect the nickel mines of Petsamo and, accordingly, roads between Finnish and Norwegian Lapland were greatly improved by the use of prisoner of war labour. In late 1944, there were still around 200,000 German troops in Finnish Lapland who, despite years of fighting and fatigue, had no intention of capitulating before their former allies. Caught in a pincer movement between advancing Soviet troops pushing west and Finnish forces moving north, the **Germans retreated**. Particularly fierce battles were fought at Tankavaara and Kaunispää, south of Ivalo, as the Germans headed for Norway.

As they retreated the Germans employed a **scorched earth policy** in retaliation for the betrayal by their former colleagues, the Finns. The order was given directly by the German commander in Lapland, General Lothar Rendulic, who was convicted of war crimes by the Allies after the war and sentenced to 20 years' imprisonment, though his sentence was later reduced to ten years. The Germans burnt the provincial capital, Rovaniemi, to the ground leaving just 13% of the town's buildings remaining. It is estimated that around half of all structures in Finnish Lapland were destroyed; all but two bridges in the region were blown up and roads were mined. From the other side of the border in Sweden, relatives watched helplessly as one village after another went up in flames; the smoke could be seen for miles around. Indeed, north of the Arctic Circle, nine out of every ten buildings were burnt.

In response to a request by the Helsinki government in September 1944, Sweden opened its border to 50,000 Finnish **refugees** who crossed the frontier at several points between Karesuando in the north and Haparanda in the south, bringing with them everything they could carry. In total, around 100,000 refugees fled Finnish Lapland at this time.

Nor was Norwegian Lapland spared: between the Varangerfjord in the east and Skibotn, southeast of Tromsø, everything from hospitals to telegraph poles was destroyed. Hitler himself ordered the evacuation of the region's population ahead of the approaching Soviet troops from the east. Some 45,000 people were forced out of their homes, which were then systematically destroyed, but it is estimated that one in three inhabitants of Finnmark, the northernmost province in Norwegian Lapland, escaped the evacuation by hiding in caves and tents in the countryside. In Kirkenes, for example, many people sought refuge in a bomb shelter under the town.

The scale of the reconstruction required after World War II, particularly in Finnish Lapland, was immense. Not only did Finland have to pay US$300 million to the Soviet Union in war reparations, but it had also lost roughly 10% of its land area, including important industrial centres such as Viipuri, and the northern third of the country had been laid to waste. Despite investment in new industries in the south of Finland, which attracted new workers from across the country, Finnish Lapland's economy remained essentially agricultural. Between 1950 and 1980, around 55,000 people left the region in search of a better life abroad, predominantly in Sweden, where they sought work in the iron-ore industries in Kiruna and Luleå.

The problems facing Norwegian Laplanders on their return to their former homes were no different from those that people in northern Finland were dealing with; over the decades thousands of people, here too, decided to leave the area to find work in southern Norway. It is estimated that about 170,000 people emigrated from Lapland in the 30-year period to 1980.

THE CHERNOBYL DISASTER AND ITS AFTERMATH In the early hours of 26 April 1986, the most far-reaching disaster ever to hit Lapland occurred a thousand miles away at the Chernobyl nuclear plant in Ukraine (then part of the Soviet Union). Regarded as the worst accident ever in the history of **nuclear power** generation, a plume of radioactive fallout, carried by winds and rain, fell over large parts of eastern Europe and, in particular, northern areas of Scandinavia.

The radioactivity was first detected by Swedish scientists two days after the accident, forcing tonnes of fresh produce to be destroyed. Lichen, the reindeer's main food source, acted like a sponge and absorbed large amounts of **radiation**, which, in turn, was consumed by reindeer grazing in Lapland's forests. At the time of the explosion, it was estimated that reindeer meat could not be safely consumed for at least 40 years.

However, since Chernobyl, radiation levels have fallen and original estimates have been downsized, though soil across Lapland remains contaminated. The Swedish National Food Administration authority declared that reindeer meat with a high becquerel per kilogram level was unfit for human consumption. In the 1986 slaughter, 80% of Sweden's **reindeer population** was killed, a move that devastated the Sámi community since their livelihood depends, to a large extent, on the production of reindeer meat for the domestic market. Amid continuing uncertainty over the effects of consuming infected meat, becquerel levels were later lowered in Norway and Sweden, and compensation payments were made by central governments to Sámi who slaughtered their animals.

It is still too early to state accurately what the true health consequences of Chernobyl have been on the Sámi and other inhabitants of Lapland, since the incubation period for cancer following exposure to radiation varies widely, and studies are still ongoing. The accident has forced the Sámi to adapt their herding practices and their uses for the reindeer's carcass – the Sámi have traditionally used every part of the deer from its hooves and blood to its entrails. Radiation-free lichen is now imported and added to reindeers' feed to avoid further contamination. Several weeks before slaughter animals are fed special pellets, which prevent radioactive caesium from entering the bloodstream, and can reduce radiation levels in the meat of slaughtered animals by 50–75% and in milk by 80%. Despite these measures, average contamination rates in Lapland's reindeer are expected to remain high for the next 20 years or so.

LAPLAND TODAY Through the founding of the three **Sámi parliaments** in Lapland, the voice of the region's indigenous population has become louder. First Norway in

1989, then Sweden in 1993 and finally Finland in 1996 passed legislation to set up these elected bodies whose task it is to maintain and develop Sámi language and culture. Although real political power is limited, the existence of the parliaments is a sign by national governments in the south that the Sámi have a right to be heard in matters that directly affect them.

Attempts have been made in recent years to increase cross-border **economic co-operation** in Lapland. The idea of developing an economic base in Lapland, independent of that in southern Scandinavia, is perfectly sensible when you consider distances: the southern Swedish city of Gothenburg, for example, is closer to Venice in Italy than it is to Kiruna in Swedish Lapland. However, there are ongoing efforts to improve links with Russia, too.

To that end, the Finnish government has declared that Finland needs rail access to the Arctic Ocean in order to benefit from new transport opportunities linked to the opening of the Northwest Passage. From Rovaniemi, a new rail link is proposed to connect the Finnish rail network to the ports at Kirkenes or Murmansk. For more on this, see the box on page 145.

Perhaps the greatest challenge facing Lapland today, though, is how to stem the increasing number of people who are choosing to leave the region to find better job prospects in the south of their respective countries. The lure of bigger salaries and urban sophistication available in the south is too strong for many to resist. The result is that Lapland is haemorrhaging valuable expertise and talent which it sorely needs to keep: the **population density** in Finnish Lapland, for example, is just two people per km², compared with the national average of 17 people per km².

GOVERNMENT AND POLITICS

The three parts of Lapland covered in this book, Norwegian, Swedish and Finnish, come under direct rule from Oslo, Stockholm and Helsinki respectively. All areas send MPs to their national parliaments. Finland is a republic, but Norway and Sweden are constitutional monarchies, with a king as the head of state. Finland and Sweden are members of the European Union, both joining on 1 January 1995, whereas Norway, despite holding a public referendum on EU membership at the same time as its Nordic neighbours, elected to stay outside the union.

However, in order to maintain the long-standing Nordic passport union, whereby Nordic citizens enjoy the right of travel across the region without passports, Norway was allowed to join the EU's Schengen zone (a group of countries that allow passport-free travel) alongside Sweden and Finland despite its non-membership of the European Union. As a result there is free movement of people, goods and services between the different parts of Lapland and it is extremely unusual to be asked to show your passport when crossing national borders, even on entering and leaving the EU.

Although there is no political body that wields power over Lapland as a whole, the three Sámi parliaments located in Kiruna (Sweden), Karasjok (Norway) and Inari (Finland) are all charged with protecting the rights, culture and language of northern Scandinavia's indigenous population, and often work together on cross-border issues which affect the entire Sámi community.

SÁMI ECONOMY

REINDEER HUSBANDRY The reindeer has been at the centre of Sámi life and culture for thousands of years. Despite the devastating effects of the Chernobyl nuclear disaster in 1986, which contaminated vast tracts of key grazing land (see opposite),

1

many Sámi still follow a semi-nomadic lifestyle determined by their deer. But the days when entire families followed the seasonal movement of the animals across the plains are long gone. Instead, reindeer husbandry today is subject to advances in modern technology just like any other industry; herders travel by snowmobile in winter rather than by sled, live in modern houses rather than traditional *kåtor* (round wooden huts that resemble tepees), and communicate by mobile phone.

Since their access to food varies from season to season, the mountain and forest reindeer are migratory animals. Mountain reindeer are especially susceptible to irritating insects, such as mosquitoes, and move up on to the mountaintops during summer days where there are cool patches of snow and fewer insects. The **Mountain Sámi** follow their animals from the forest up to the treeline by the time spring comes, then on into the mountains for summer; in August they start making their way down.

Forest reindeer, on the other hand, prefer open, more marshy areas when there is no snow on the ground, moving deep into the forest when tormented by insects; the **Forest Sámi** consequently move with their herds within the forests. Come September, many animals are slaughtered in corrals dotted across the region. Then, following the mating season in late September and October, both species are to be found in the forests during the long winter months where it is easier to dig for lichen in the snow. The reindeer's gestation period lasts for around 225 days; calves are born in May and suckle throughout the summer months.

Reindeer husbandry requires vast tracts of land because of its migratory nature and sparse food resources. Over the centuries, the reindeer industry in all three countries has had to learn to co-exist with other forms of industry and land use, which has naturally led to a number of conflicts between the Sámi and non-indigenous groups in Lapland. For example, Sámi have accused Swedes of stealing their land; Swedes have accused Sámi of scrounging off the state. Sweden didn't officially recognise the Sámi as an indigenous group (and consequently acknowledge their rights) until 1977. In 1988, the Minister for Agriculture and Sámi Affairs asked the Sámi, on behalf of her government, to forgive the way the Swedish state had treated them throughout history.

FISHING Fishing is the oldest, though now smallest, branch of Sámi industry and has long traditions in Lapland culture. In Norway, the Sámi carry out sea and inland fishing, whereas in Sweden and Finland the Sámi only fish inland, in lakes and rivers. Lawyers and the Norwegian Sámi parliament have asserted that Sámi who live along the coastline have age-old rights to exploit the coastal waters, though this has yet to be laid down in national legislation. When reindeer herders tend their animals from remote highland settlements during the summer months, their diet consists mainly of fish. The right to fish in many mountain lakes has been asserted by many Sámi with the result that some have been set aside for the sole use of reindeer-herding Sámi. This decision has given rise to envy not only among the non-indigenous population, but also among non-reindeer-herding Sámi.

PEOPLE

As the definition of 'Sámi' is ambiguous and varies from one country to another, population experts have found it difficult to quantify exactly how many Sámi live in Lapland. However, generally accepted figures show that there are around 70,000 Sámi living across the region: 40,000 in Norway, 20,000 in Sweden, 6,000 in Finland and a further 4,000 in Russia. The total population of Lapland, when we apply this book's definition, is around 900,000, making the Sámi about 7% of the total. The overwhelming 93% is made up of non-indigenous Norwegians, Swedes and Finns. Although there is a high degree of co-operation between the two communities, there still remains a great deal of mistrust and misunderstanding; indigenous Sámi culture is strikingly different from that of mainstream Scandinavia. Consequently, we have given information about the minority Sámi people and their culture.

LANGUAGE

Norwegian, Swedish and Finnish are the majority languages in Lapland, but the Sámi also speak their own language known as **Sámegiella** (Sámi). It belongs to the Finno-Ugric family and its closest relatives are Finnish and Estonian (neither is mutually intelligible with Sámi), and, much more distantly, Hungarian. The distance between Sámi and Hungarian, though, is as great as that between English and Persian, which are languages of the same family. Having said that, Sámi is not a single language. Instead, seven (or arguably nine) **dialects** of Sámi are recognised, which fall into two main groups, western and eastern; not all dialects are mutually intelligible and only six of the nine dialects have written forms.

Within the western division, the dialect known as **northern Sámi** is spoken by around 15,000 people across the provinces of Finnmark and Troms in Norwegian Lapland and northern areas of Swedish and Finnish Lapland. Its core area, both with regard to number and concentration of speakers, as well as cultural and linguistic vitality, is found around Karasjok and Kautokeino in Norwegian Lapland.

The largest of all the nine dialects, it accounts for around three-quarters of all Sámi-speakers and is regarded as the standard Sámi language; it is therefore the variant we use in this guide.

DISAPPEARING LANGUAGES The eastern group of dialects is spoken in northeastern parts of Finnish Lapland, including in and around Inari, as well as on the Kola peninsula in Russian Lapland. In 2010, one of these dialects, Ter Sámi, had just two elderly female speakers left; it's unclear whether the speakers are still alive. Western Sámi dialects are spoken in areas of Sweden stretching from Kiruna down to the province of Dalarna. However, here, too, the number of speakers is dwindling; it's estimated that Ume Sámi has barely ten speakers (it also had no written form until 2010) and is considered a dead language along with Ter Sámi. Pite Sámi, spoken around Arjeplog and Arvidsjaur, is critically endangered and has around 25 speakers.

SÁMI TODAY Sámi is a legally recognised language in the northern and eastern municipalities of Finnish and Norwegian Lapland respectively, and was granted the status of one of Sweden's five minority languages in 2002.

It is thought that Sámi and Finnish originate from the same proto-language but became separated around 1000BC. At this time it is unlikely that there were any notable differences in pronunciation or grammar between speakers in different areas. However, by the 9th century AD, linguists believe that the major subdivisions that now exist between the various Sámi dialects had taken shape. The differences between the various dialects spoken in the areas covered by this guide developed due to the nomadic nature of the speakers' lives and the intermittent contact they had with people from other areas.

Sámi first appeared as a written language in the 17th century in Sweden since missionaries dispatched to Lapland by the crown required information to be written in the local language; spelling was based on the southern dialects. North of the border in Norway emphasis was given to northern Sámi and the first Sámi grammar appeared in 1748. The clergyman Nils Vibe Stockfleth produced another grammar almost a hundred years later in which he employed artificial orthographic characters to portray Sámi sounds that were not present in Norwegian. Although a unified spelling system was in place for northern Sámi by 1951, the Finnish Sámi continued to use a different system based on their own conventions. It wasn't until the 1970s that all three countries managed to agree on a single orthography, which was a compromise between all those in use; spelling in northern Sámi was finally standardised in 1978 and is based largely on Stockfleth's system, which has contributed some unusual consonants to the Sámi alphabet of today.

Only one in three Sámi people can actually speak their native tongue and all Sámi-speakers are bilingual, speaking the national language of the country they are resident in (Finnish, Norwegian or Swedish) alongside their indigenous tongue. This is because the language was harshly suppressed until recent years (particularly so in Norway), so many parents failed to speak Sámi to their children and thus transmit it to the next generation as they regarded knowing the language to be a social handicap.

In Norway, from the second part of the 19th century, the authorities carried out a policy of assimilation, depriving Sámi of its function in primary education. The reason was partly nationalistic: Norway was newly independent and the idea of 'one nation – one language' played a prominent role in the philosophy of some nationalists in Oslo. The fear of Finland, too (page 10), helped to create a unified purely Norwegian front in these northern frontier areas. In addition, a law existed in Norway from 1902 to 1963 forbidding the sale of state-owned land in the province of Finnmark to anyone who couldn't write, speak or read Norwegian. Although this law was aimed primarily at immigrating Finns, it had a negative effect on the development of Sámi in Norwegian Lapland. Only in 1959 did the Norwegians reintroduce Sámi as the language of instruction in schools.

In Sweden, Sámi was never forbidden in school as it was in Norway, though Swedish also took a dominant role. Things began to change in the late 1970s, when parliament passed a law allowing linguistic minorities the right to instruction in their home language. The situation was largely similar in Finland, where Sámi has only recently been given an equal status with Finnish in areas where most Sámi live.

For a glossary of Sámi terms, see page 232.

RELIGION AND MYTHOLOGY

In common with many other indigenous peoples, living in harmony with nature is key to the Sámi's existence. Their view of the world was **animistic** by nature, with some shamanistic features, and there's evidence that elements of these ancient beliefs were practised until the late 1940s. Animism holds that every element in nature, be it a stone, the wind or an animal, has a soul and, accordingly, the Sámi still believe today that human beings should move through the countryside without making a noise or disturbance.

Alongside the material world was an underworld where everything was more defined than in the material world and where the dead continued their lives. A *noaidi* or **shaman** was the link between the underworld and the present. A shaman was generally a young man who received a calling from the spirits to enter a period of learning in order to move between the two worlds. On particularly demanding trips into the underworld, the shaman would use a *goavddis* or **drum** and would probably also perform a *joik*, a form of throat singing (also known in Mongolia), to help him achieve a state of ecstasy and reach out to the spirits. Outsiders considered the goavddis to be charged with magic and therefore a satanic instrument of evil; owners of drums were paraded before the courts and fined, flogged or killed and their drums burnt.

Perhaps the element of Sámi belief most tangible today is the practice of leaving an offering at a *sieidi*, or sacred image, such as a tree, rock, mountain, lake or even waterfall situated at strategic points for the reindeer-herder or hunter. It was common practice, particularly at the beginning of the hunting season, to leave a coin or some other object of value. Indeed, as recently as 1994, coins and reindeer antlers were found at a sieidi in the province of Finnmark. It is not known whether this represents an offering or simply a continuing tradition.

Although the animistic elements of the ancient beliefs live on, today's Sámi are Christian. Many adhere to the conservative religious movement known as **Laestadianism**, which is known across the north of Scandinavia. The Swedish revivalist preacher Lars Levi Laestadius (1800–61) saw it as his mission to rid Lapland of the scourge of alcohol. Posted to the parish of Karesuando in Swedish Lapland in 1826, he saw the effects of alcohol abuse at first hand; not only was most of the congregation drunk during his church services, but children were left to fend for themselves and reindeer were allowed to drift aimlessly, risking attack by wolves and other predators, as the herders lay drunk in their huts. When he met a young Sámi girl, Mary of Lapland, in 1844, Laestadius was inspired to renew his efforts to steer the Sámi towards a life of total purity and teetotalism.

After Laestadius died, the movement split into opposing factions: a conservative western group in Sweden and Norway, and a more liberal eastern one in Finland. Today, followers lead their lives according to a strict set of rules: contraception, make-up and hair dye are forbidden, so too are dancing, watching television, wearing a tie and playing rhythmic music; drinking, of course, is totally out of the question.

CULTURE

Today, one of the best-known features of Sámi culture is the *joik*, or chanting, akin to that of some North American Indian cultures which was once outlawed because of its alleged association with paganism. Sung *a cappella* or occasionally accompanied by a drum, the joik is not a song about a person or a place, rather an attempt to transfer the essence of someone or something into song; the Sámi, therefore, joik their friends, rather than joik about them. A joik is often personal and may even be composed for an individual at the time of birth. In recent years, the joik has found an appreciative audience outside Lapland, thanks in part to the group Enigma, which had a hit with the joik-influenced 'Return to Innocence' in 1994; Sámi singer Mari Boine, who hails from Karasjok in Norwegian Lapland and enjoyed international recognition with her début album, *Gula Gula*; and more recently through the haunting melodies of Kautokeino-born Máddji – her album *Dobbelis* (*Beyond*) is an excellent introduction to Sámi folk music. Sámi rapper and joiker Fred Buljo, also from Kautokeino, co-represented Norway in the 2019 Eurovision Song Contest with a Sámi-influenced song and finished in sixth place.

Until the early part of the 20th century, there was precious little written cultural material available to the Sámi; for generations, people had relied on the **oral tradition** of storytelling, and tended to write in Norwegian, Swedish or Finnish, if at all. Only at the beginning of the 20th century did Sámi authors begin to compose literature in their mother tongue. Writing in northern Sámi, Johan Turi (1854–

1936) is regarded as the first modern Sámi author. His *Muittalus sámiid birra*, which appeared in 1910, dealt with everyday life in Lapland, language and beliefs, and was translated into several languages including English. Probably the best known of Lapland's contemporary authors is Nils-Aslak Valkeapää (1943–2001), from Enontekiö in Finnish Lapland, who also worked as a singer; he won the Nordic Council's prize for literature in 1991.

One of the most tangible elements of Sámi culture is **handicrafts**. As you travel around Lapland, you will see examples of Sámi handicrafts seemingly everywhere you turn: everything from cups made of hollowed-out birch wood, which were traditionally used for drinking from rivers and lakes while reindeer herding, to exquisite wallets and purses made of reindeer hide. Although targeted at the modern tourist trade, most elements of Sámi handicraft have a long tradition of fabrication. Their shapes have been honed over centuries: there are no sharp edges, for example, to Sámi knives or other similar tools to avoid getting caught in knapsacks or trouser pockets while out on the fells.

LAPLAND ONLINE

For additional online content, articles, photos and more on Lapland, why not visit w bradtguides.com/lapland?

2

Practical Information

WHEN TO VISIT

Undoubtedly the most magical time to be in Lapland is **winter**. Snow is thick on the ground, activities are in full swing and it's the only time you can see the northern lights. However, this is the busiest time of year for the tourist industry and accommodation is at a premium during the winter months; it always pays to book well in advance to ensure a bed for the night.

In general, the winter season starts in late November/early December, peaks at Christmas and New Year, and runs through to around Easter, though destinations such as the Icehotel in Swedish Lapland stay open for several weeks beyond the end of the peak season. It's worth remembering that daylight is in short supply during winter and that Christmas and New Year are the darkest time of the year – the sun barely skims the horizon at the Icehotel. Snow cover helps considerably in brightening things up by reflecting the little light there is. See page 31 for suggestions of what to bring if you travel at this time of year.

The snow usually melts in May (or mid-June in more mountainous areas). **Spring** in Lapland, though short-lived, is glorious: trees burst into leaf seemingly overnight, flowers emerge from their enforced period of winter hibernation, carpeting the plains in a mêlée of reds, yellows and blues and the birds start to return – and sing. Within a matter of weeks the short but hectic Lapland **summer** is in full swing, with the midnight sun adding to the attractions of this time of year. In tourist terms, summer is usually counted as mid-June to mid-August, the period when everything is open and there's a marked spring in people's step. After the middle of August certain museums and other services start to close down. If you're thinking of hiking or canoeing, summer is the perfect time of year to visit Lapland, though be prepared for swarms of Scandinavia's infamous mosquitoes (Finnish *hyttynen*; Norwegian and Swedish *mygg*) and lesser-known though arguably more painful horseflies (Finnish *paarma*; Norwegian *klegg*; Swedish *broms*; all useful words when at the pharmacy), which are present from the beginning of June until early August.

By August, the first frosts are generally felt somewhere in Lapland, marking the beginning of the slow return to winter. However, the frost is responsible for one of the most breathtaking spectacles of the Lapland year: the Finns call it *ruska*, nature's last stand before winter, when the leaves on birch, aspen and mountain ash trees turn bright yellow or scarlet red, bathing the hillsides in an orgy of colour. It's hard to predict the exact time this happens, though generally the sight is at its most spectacular between mid-August and mid-September. **Autumn** is the time to come to Lapland to enjoy nature's fruits – this is when the region's forests are bursting with berries, mushrooms and various herbs ripe for picking. The exact time of the first snows varies from year to year but there's usually snow cover somewhere in Lapland by October.

Distances between attractions in Lapland are always greater than you think and it's important to bear this in mind when planning a trip. The distance from Karesuando, for example, at the very tip of Swedish Lapland, to the North Cape is still a whopping 500km. It makes sense, therefore, on a short trip to concentrate

WHERE SHOULD I GO IN LAPLAND TO SEE THE NORTHERN LIGHTS?

It's the question I'm asked most frequently when the subject of Lapland pops up in conversation: 'where's best to see the northern lights?' Annoyingly, there's no definitive answer to the question – in large part, the choice of where to go to see the aurora depends on what else you want from your Lapland holiday. **Tromsø**, for example, is a good choice; it's accessible (there are direct flights from London), the average winter temperature is only around –4°C and clear skies are relatively common (the surrounding mountains help keep the sky cloud-free in winter). Plus, there's plenty to keep you occupied when you're not hunting for the lights – the town's wide range of museums, bars and restaurants probably, therefore, makes it the best destination to head for in Norway. However, Norway's high prices are legendary and you may decide you're better off in Sweden or Finland where everything is significantly cheaper. In Sweden, **Abisko** (page 81) is perhaps geared up for the lights better than elsewhere, offering a trip by chairlift to observe the aurora from the top of Nuolja Mountain. Of course, you don't need to go up the mountain to see the northern lights – if the sky's clear, you can see them anywhere – the chairlift ride is simply part of the experience. Another option in Sweden, if your pocket can face it, is **Icehotel** at **Jukkasjärvi** (page 77). If you plump for Finland, maybe because you want to combine seeing the lights with Santa Claus, then consider **Rovaniemi**, **Luosto** or perhaps **Torassieppi** – there's really no right or wrong place (pages 136, 177 and 128 respectively). Across Lapland you'll find activities operators offering snowmobile tours or husky safaris to hunt for the northern lights. Once again, you don't need to be on a husky sled or a snowmobile to see the lights – it's simply a way of creating an experience around the adventure. What's much more important is the weather. The aurora can't be seen on cloudy nights so, remember, that, statistically, the longer you stay in Lapland the greater the chance of spotting the lights – no matter where you are. You'll find a reliable forecast of northern lights activity at w gi.alaska.edu/auroraforecast/europe.

Since the first edition of this guide was published in 2007, the popularity of Lapland as both a winter and summer destination has increased exponentially. Over the past decade or so, tourism trends have undergone significant change; increasingly, people are searching for that elusive niche destination which remains off the beaten track. Lapland is still just that. Of course, during the winter months, a small handful of places are inundated with planeloads of visitors seeking Santa Claus or a close-up of the northern lights. But this area of northern Scandinavia is so vast that a short sidestep will soon take you to places untouched by tourism.

For more on the northern lights, see *The Northern Lights: A Practical Travel Guide* by Polly Evans, also published by Bradt.

on one particular area of Lapland and explore that thoroughly rather than hurtling from town to town and spending all your time on the road.

In **winter**, Lapland's two blockbuster attractions are **Icehotel** at **Jukkasjärvi** near Kiruna in Sweden and **Santa Claus** at either **Rovaniemi** on the Arctic Circle or **Kakslauttanen** near Ivalo, 260km further north. The main draw in Norway is the **North Cape**, which is accessed via Alta. One day is enough for the attractions at Icehotel, though, if you visit Kiruna as well you should add in one or two more; it's perfectly feasible to visit Icehotel over a **weekend** and be back at work on Monday morning.

For trips to Santa Claus, allow two to four days depending on how many activities you want to include. Although there are plenty of one-day charter flights to Lapland during the winter months specifically aimed at visiting Santa Claus, such a flying visit will give you the briefest glimpse of Lapland (it will already be dark when you get there); remember, too, that a direct flight from Britain to Lapland is around 4 to 5 hours one-way.

Although it is possible to visit all of these destinations on one trip, it will entail driving 1,800km in icy conditions and isn't recommended for first-time visitors. If you're looking for a two-centre break of a week in Finnish Lapland, a good option is to combine a visit to Rovaniemi or Kakslauttanen with a husky safari out of **Muonio**; the distance between Rovaniemi and Muonio is 230km, Kakslauttanen to Muonio is 300km.

In **summer** the main place to head for is undisputedly the **North Cape**. Consider starting your adventure at Alta, the main airport closest to the cape, and perhaps also visiting the Sámi settlements of **Karasjok** or **Kautokeino**, to make a week's holiday. Alternatively, make the journey directly to the cape starting from either Kiruna or Rovaniemi; once again, you should allow a week for this trip. Another option for a week's holiday would be to combine a visit to Kiruna with an excursion to the **Lofoten islands** in Norway. With a couple of weeks at your disposal you could extend this journey to include the North Cape by flying into either Luleå or Kiruna in Sweden, then heading via Narvik across to the Lofoten islands en route to the cape and then return from there via Karasjok or Kautokeino to Rovaniemi in Finland. From here you could fly home or continue back to Kiruna or **Luleå** to complete your circuit.

SUGGESTED ITINERARIES

In addition to those listed above, here are some ideas for routes which will take in some of Lapland's other highlights. A trip to Lapland will vary between winter and summer, hence, we've given a few suggestions for both times of year.

WINTER
One week Fly to Kiruna and stay at Icehotel. Rent a car or travel by train south to Luleå, crossing the Arctic Circle, to see Gammelstad. Then cross the border into Finland and take a trip on the *Sampo* icebreaker in Kemi. Then either head for Muonio for a few days' dog-sledding or make straight for Rovaniemi to see Santa Claus and a chance to go snowmobiling.

Two weeks As above, but extend your journey north from Rovaniemi or Muonio into Norwegian Lapland and include a visit to the North Cape, stopping in Karasjok and Alta on the way. Consider flying south from Honningsvåg to help reduce the long journey south from the North Cape.

SUMMER

One week Fly to Luleå to see Gammelstad. Then take the train north via Kiruna to Narvik to experience the fantastic views of the Ofotbanen railway. From Narvik head out to the Lofoten and Vesterålen islands before returning back to Evenes airport for your flight south.

Two weeks As above but extend your journey from Lofoten by flying to Tromsø and then continuing to the North Cape. Return from the North Cape by bus south to Rovaniemi, perhaps stopping in Karasjok or Inari on the way south.

Three weeks The ultimate tour of the whole of Lapland. As the two-week summer tour, but continue east from the North Cape to Kirkenes, either by Hurtigruten ferry or by plane. From Kirkenes head south into Finland to visit Utsjoki and Inari. Consider canoeing on the Ivalojoki River before you head south for Rovaniemi. From Rovaniemi take the train south to Kemi and cross back into Sweden to return to Luleå. From Luleå you could also extend your travels to include Arvidsjaur and Jokkmokk, returning to Luleå for your flight home.

TOUR OPERATORS

Although Lapland is geared up for individual travel, with a full range of accommodation and transport options to ensure a trouble-free stay, there are a number of tour operators who also specialise in holidays to the region. The main ones are listed below.

CANADA
Great Canadian Travel Company
☎ +1 800 661 3830; e info@gctravel.ca;

w greatcanadiantravel.com. Trips to Sweden's Icehotel as well as the classic Norwegian coastal voyage past the North Cape.

DISTANCES IN LAPLAND (KM)	Alta	Arctic Circle	Hammerfest	Honningsvåg	Ivalo	Kautokeino
Alta		859	142	210	347	131
Arctic Circle	859		1,000	1,013	1,205	985
Hammerfest	142	1,000		180	370	273
Honningsvåg	210	1,013	180		338	342
Ivalo	347	1,205	370	338		282
Kautokeino	131	985	273	342	282	
Kirkenes	572	1,422	541	562	239	452
Kiruna	449	505	590	603	491	322
Murmansk	797	1,655	768	736	286	680
Narvik	519	331	661	729	926	647
North Cape	238	1,044	208	35	369	370
Rovaniemi	500	1,359	656	624	286	373
Sortland	638	388	782	849	1,028	766
Tromsø	405	597	548	616	797	533

UK

Canterbury Travel ✆01923 822388; e info@ canterbury-travel.com; w canterbury-travel. com. With over 40 years' experience, the market leaders in 1–4-night trips to see Santa Claus, plus skiing holidays at Luosto in Finnish Lapland. Can arrange weddings in Lapland, also at Luosto.

Discover the World ✆01737 888141; e travel@discover-the-world.co.uk; w discover-the-world.com. The only company selling the direct flight from London Heathrow to Kiruna (page 27). Experienced & well-respected specialist operator with 37 years of experience in arranging independent holidays to Lapland. Options include summer & winter breaks to Finnish, Norwegian & Swedish Lapland, including northern lights tours, husky safaris, self-drives, stays at the Icehotel & log cabin holidays & even bear-watching tours in Finland.

Inghams ✆01483 791111; w inghams.co.uk/ lapland. Offering 7-night activity holidays from Dec to Apr, as well as their popular 3- & 4-night Santa breaks in Dec to the resorts of Levi & Ylläs. You can experience a wide choice of activities including husky & snowmobile safaris, cross-country or downhill skiing, northern lights excursions & even stay in a thermal glass igloo. Non-stop direct flights from a selection of UK airports.

Nordic Experience ✆01206 708888; w nordicexperience.co.uk. Northern lights & Icehotel tours, as well as holidays to the snow hotel in Kirkenes.

Nordic Visitor ✆0800 066 4730; w nordicvisitor. com. Iceland-based tour operator with an office in Scotland which can arrange any number of classic Lapland activities from stays in Sweden's Icehotel or Finland's Snowhotel to tours to see the northern lights & trips to meet Santa Claus. Also offers a range of 4-day/3-night breaks to Swedish & Finnish Lapland.

Regent Holidays ✆0117 4534203; e regent@ regentholidays.co.uk; w regent-holidays.co.uk. Specialising in Finnish, Swedish & Norwegian Lapland, Regent Holidays can offer a range of winter breaks, including trips to Tromsø to see the northern lights. Stay in a glass igloo, opt for a hotel with a glass-roofed room & enjoy excursions such as snowmobile, husky & reindeer safaris in the Arctic wilderness at Harriniva & Kakslauttanen.

Taber Holidays ✆01274 875199; e office@ taberhols.co.uk; w taberhols.co.uk. A wide range of Lapland holidays from this Yorkshire-based tour operator – everything from wilderness log cabins in the Luleå archipelago, holidays using local transport, snowmobiling, dog-sledding & the Treehotel or Icehotel in Sweden.

Kirkenes	Kiruna	Murmansk	Narvik	North Cape	Rovaniemi	Sortland	Tromsø
572	449	797	519	238	500	638	405
1,422	505	1,655	331	1,044	1,359	388	597
541	590	768	661	208	656	782	548
562	603	736	729	35	624	849	616
239	491	286	926	369	286	1,028	797
452	322	680	647	370	373	766	533
	769	243	1,090	590	473	1,210	977
769		756	175	635	337	329	382
243	756		1,325	767	551	1,450	1,196
1,090	175	1,325		757	512	202	259
590	635	767	757		655	877	644
473	337	551	512	655		569	577
1,210	329	1,450	202	877	569		378
977	382	1,196	259	644	577	378	

Where The Wild Is ↳0117 450 7980; e info@ wherethewildis.co.uk; w wherethewildis.co.uk. Whether you're looking to go whale-watching in Tromsø, stay in Sweden's Icehotel, or hunt for the northern lights in Finnish Lapland, this versatile young company has got it covered. Bringing her valuable experience in the travel industry to the fore, Emma Durkin's new venture is fast becoming a well-respected name in Lapland tourism.

USA
5 Stars of Scandinavia ↳+1 800 722 4126; e info@5stars-scandinavia.com; w 5stars-scandinavia.com. The American specialist in holidays to the region including a wide range of Arctic adventure specials covering Norwegian, Finnish & Swedish Lapland; naturally the Icehotel & the northern lights are included in the extensive programme.

CRUISE OPERATOR In addition to the tour operators listed above, Norwegian ferry company, **Hurtigruten** (↳+47 81 00 30 30; e booking@hurtigruten.com; w hurtigruten.com), is the main cruise operator in Lapland. They operate regular ferry services along the Norwegian coast between Bergen and Kirkenes and, in terms of Lapland specifically, the main ports of call, from south to north, are: Svolvær, Sortland, Harstad, Tromsø, Hammerfest, Honningsvåg (for the North Cape), Vardø and Kirkenes. All vessels are comfortable and well appointed and cabin accommodation ranges from comfortable to luxury. While it's certainly possible to travel all the way along the coast by these ferries in one go, it's arguably more relaxing and fulfilling to break your journey along the way. Full details of all the package options available can be found online, as, too, can the regular passenger fares for shorter hops between settlements.

RED TAPE

European Union, American, Canadian, Australian and New Zealand nationals need only a valid passport to enter Finland, Norway or Sweden – and, hence, Lapland – for a maximum period of three months. All other citizens should contact the appropriate embassy for visa information.

After the UK leaves the European Union, documentation requirements for UK citizens may change. Check before travelling.

EMBASSIES Since Lapland crosses national borders and is not an independent country, it has no embassies or consulates of its own. Instead, the national governments of Finland, Norway and Sweden are the point of contact for all affairs relating to Lapland. For full lists of embassies in each of Lapland's countries, visit w embassypages.com/finland, embassypages.com/norway and embassypages. com/sweden.

Australia
🇪 **Finland** ↳02 6273 3800; e sanomat.can@ formin.fi; w finland.org.au
🇪 **Norway** ↳02 6270 5700; e emb.canberra@ mfa.no; w norway.no/australia
🇪 **Sweden** ↳02 6270 2700; e ambassaden. canberra@gov.se; w swedenabroad.com

Canada
🇪 **Finland** ↳613 288 2233; e embassy.ott@ formin.fi; w finland.ca

🇪 **Norway** ↳613 238 6571; e emb.ottawa@ mfa.no; w norway.no/canada
🇪 **Sweden** ↳613 244 8200; e sweden.ottawa@ gov.se; w swedenabroad.com

UK
🇪 **Finland** ↳020 7838 6200; e sanomat.lon@ formin.fi; w finemb.org.uk
🇪 **Norway** ↳020 7591 5500; e emb.london@ mfa.no; w norway.no/uk
🇪 **Sweden** ↳020 7917 6400; e ambassaden. london@gov.se; w swedenabroad.com

USA

E Finland ✎202 298 5800; **e** sanomat.was@
formin.fi; **w** finland.org

E Norway ✎202 333 6000; **e** emb.
washington@mfa.no; **w** norway.no/usa
E Sweden ✎202 467 2600; **e** ambassaden.
washington@gov.se; **w** swedenabroad.com

GETTING THERE AND AWAY

Given the tremendous distances involved in reaching Lapland, even from elsewhere in Scandinavia, the only feasible way of getting there is **by air**. Naturally, it is possible to drive to Lapland as part of a greater European tour, but consider just how far it is: London to Kiruna, for example, is 3,000km one-way.

BY AIR The main airports to aim for in Lapland are Kiruna (KRN), Luleå (LLA), Narvik/Harstad (EVE), Tromsø (TOS), Rovaniemi (RVN) and Ivalo (IVL), but flying to Lapland will generally entail first reaching one of the Nordic capitals and then changing planes for a domestic flight to one of the airports listed above. The best transit airports to aim for when heading for Lapland are Stockholm Arlanda (ARN), Oslo Gardermoen (OSL) or Helsinki Vantaa (HEL). Copenhagen's Kastrup airport, although the biggest hub in Scandinavia, has no direct flights to Lapland and is worth avoiding for that reason. The duration of the flight from one of these hubs up to Lapland is roughly 1½ to 2 hours, depending on destination. If bought in advance, it is possible to pick up a single domestic ticket from around £50/US$75.

From the UK The UK has direct winter flights to Lapland; **Norwegian** fly four times weekly from London Gatwick (LGW) to Tromsø (TOS) and Rovaniemi (RVN) three times per week, while easyJet also fly to Rovaniemi from both Gatwick and Manchester (MAN) twice weekly, though the season for Manchester only runs from late November to early January. Reaching Lapland otherwise entails changing planes in Stockholm, Oslo or Helsinki for a connecting flight north. A return ticket usually costs from £250/US$330.

In addition, British tour operater, Discover the World, runs a direct charter in co-operation with **SAS** from London Heathrow (LHR) to Kiruna (KRN) over several dates between mid-December and early March; seats are sold as part of a package from DTW but close to each departure date – if there are seats left they are sold for around £500 return; contact Discover the World for details (page 25).

Useful websites are:

✈ **British Airways** **w** ba.com (LHR to ARN, OSL & HEL)
✈ **Easyjet** **w** easyjet.com (LGW & MAN to RVN)
✈ **Finnair** **w** finnair.co.uk (LHR & MAN to HEL)
✈ **Norwegian** **w** norwegian.com (LGW to TOS & RVN, ARN, HEL & OSL; also EDI & MAN to ARN & OSL)
✈ **Scandinavian Airlines** **w** flysas.co.uk (LHR & MAN to ARN & OSL; also EDI to ARN)

From the USA and Canada The best fares from the USA and Canada to Scandinavia are from the east coast. Norwegian is constantly changing its service to North America and can throw up some good value tickets. Airlines change their routes at an alarming rate, though, in general, the direct flights listed here can be depended on. High-season fares are in the region of US$1,300, falling to US$1,000 in the shoulder season and as low as US$750 in low season.

✈ **Finnair** w finnair.com (JFK to HEL)   ✈ **Scandinavian Airlines** w flysas.com (ORD,
✈ **Norwegian** w norwegian.com (EWR to OSL)   LAX & EWR to ARN; EWR to OSL)
                                                   ✈ **United** w united.com (EWR to ARN)

From the rest of the world Getting to Lapland from elsewhere in the world naturally involves reaching one of the Scandinavian gateways first, from where connections are available as described below. If you want to buy a through ticket to Lapland, the best options are Scandinavian Airlines and Finnair, which will be able to offer connections through their Stockholm and Helsinki hubs respectively from several destinations in Asia and Australia, sometimes using codeshare flights with their partners. A good place to start your research is an online travel website such as Kayak or Momondo.

HEALTH *with Dr Felicity Nicholson*

HEALTH RISKS The health risks while travelling in Lapland are minimal and healthcare is of an excellent standard. Visitors should be up to date with childhood vaccinations, including MMR. Rabies is only present in bats in Lapland – although contact with them is highly unlikely – but a bite from any mammal should be followed by a trip to the doctor.

Language (except occasionally in Finland) is rarely a problem and health workers are generally proficient in English. Under reciprocal health arrangements, European Union citizens (plus those of EEA countries) can take advantage of Finland and Sweden's healthcare services under the same terms as residents of those countries. All that's required is a European Health Insurance Card (EHIC), which is available via the post office in the United Kingdom and Ireland; the EHIC has replaced the old E111 form. Note that when the UK leaves the European Union, British visitors may need to take out separate medical travel insurance in order to be covered while travelling in Finland and Sweden. Check before travelling. Citizens of non-EU/EEA countries are liable to pay for healthcare, hence, it is probably sensible to make sure you have health insurance before leaving home. Rules for Norway are slightly different since the country is not a member of the European Union: EU/EEA citizens are entitled to discounted medical treatment within the national public healthcare system; citizens of other countries receive no discount. All citizens may therefore want to consider taking out health insurance to cover any health bills while in Norway.

TICK-BORNE ENCEPHALITIS Caused by a virus in the same family as yellow fever, tick-borne encephalitis is spread through the bites of infected ticks which are usually picked up in forested areas with long grass, and it can also be transmitted through the unpasteurised milk of infected livestock. Anyone liable to go walking in late spring or summer (when the ticks are most active) should seek protection. A vaccine is available against the disease and initial immunisation ideally consists of three injections. The second is given one to three months after the first and the third five to 12 months later. If time does not allow for the third dose, around 90% protection is given by the first two and, if time is shorter still, then the second dose can be done two weeks after the first. There is a different vaccine for children aged one to 15 (Ticovac Junior) but the schedule is the same. Taking preventative measures is also very important. When walking in grassy and forested areas, ensure that you wear a hat, tuck your trousers into socks and boots and your shirt into your trousers, have long-sleeved tops and use tick repellents. Ticks can more

European ticks are not the prolific disease transmitters they are in the Americas, but they may spread Lyme disease, tick-bite fever and a few rarities. Ticks should ideally be removed complete, and as soon as possible, to reduce the chance of infection. You can use special tick tweezers, which can be bought in good travel shops, or failing this with your finger nails, grasping the tick as close to your body as possible, and pulling it away steadily and firmly at right angles to your skin without jerking or twisting. Irritants (eg: Olbas oil) or lit cigarettes are to be discouraged since they can cause the ticks to regurgitate and therefore increase the risk of disease. Once the tick is removed, if possible douse the wound with alcohol (any spirit will do), soap and water, or iodine. If you are travelling with small children, remember to check their heads, and particularly behind the ears, for ticks. Spreading redness around the bite and/or fever and/or aching joints after a tick bite imply that you have an infection that requires antibiotic treatment. In this case seek medical advice.

easily be seen on pale clothing and can be flicked off before they get a grip on you, so consider your clothing carefully. It is important to check for ticks each time you have been for a long walk – this is more easily done by someone else. If you find a tick then slowly remove it (see box, above), taking care not to squeeze the mouthparts.

TRAVEL CLINICS AND HEALTH INFORMATION A full list of current travel clinic websites worldwide is available on w istm.org. For other journey preparation information, consult w travelhealthpro.org.uk (UK) or w wwwnc.cdc.gov/travel (USA). Information about various medications may be found on w netdoctor. co.uk/travel. All advice found online should be used in conjunction with expert advice received prior to or during travel.

SAFETY

Two particular hazards to bear in mind when travelling in Lapland are the heightened risk of road accidents as a result of the large number of wild animals on the road, especially reindeer, and the effects of cold during the winter months.

WOMEN TRAVELLERS Women travelling alone are unlikely to encounter any problems. Nordic males are generally well mannered and far too shy to create trouble. On Friday and Saturday nights, though, when the beer starts to flow, it's obviously sensible to keep your wits about you, but, once again, you are unlikely to become the target of abusive behaviour.

LGBT TRAVELLERS Gay travellers will have to forego the pleasures of gay bars and clubs while in Lapland – quite simply, there is no gay scene whatsoever. Attitudes towards homosexuality are generally tolerant, though the views of unmarried lumberjack types may not be the most enlightened. The sight of a same-sex couple walking hand in hand through a remote Lapland village, particularly with a large Sámi community, is likely to cause quite a stir, so it's probably best to keep outward displays of affection to yourselves.

TRAVELLING WITH A DISABILITY Finland, Norway and Sweden, as you might expect, are model countries when it comes to meeting the needs of disabled travellers. Throughout Lapland you'll find hotels with rooms specifically designed for disabled access and trains with special hydraulic lifts which are designed to get wheelchairs in and out of carriages with a minimum of fuss. Buses, too, are often fitted with a divide which allows the front of the vehicle to drop down closer to the ground to ease disabled access. The Hurtigruten ferry in Norway is also geared up to disabled travel with special lifts and cabins for disabled users. Winter, though, can be a tough time for wheelchair users as pavements are rarely completely free of snow and ice and can be extremely difficult to negotiate.

TRAVELLING WITH CHILDREN Naturally, Lapland is a magnet for children, enchanted by the wonders of Santa Claus and Rudolph. Travel companies, particularly in and around Rovaniemi in Finland, understand that many travellers come to Lapland purely because of their children. Accordingly, they have made sure that there are plenty of activities on hand to keep younger travellers busy and contented. Public transport, too, is well equipped and provides easy access for pushchairs and prams. Many trains have separate family carriages where there's a play corner for children, making it possible to supervise children at play from your seat. However, it's important not to underestimate the severe climatic conditions which you are more than likely to encounter when you disembark the plane or train on arrival in winter; it is not uncommon for temperatures to stubbornly hover around the –30°C mark which poses a serious challenge to outdoor exploration. Hence, you should make sure you have plenty of warm clothing, hats, gloves and scarves to protect against the extreme cold. Remember, too, that children may find the 24-hour darkness of winter Lapland disorientating, not to say boring. Conversely, in summer, it may be hard to get children to sleep when it never gets dark!

WHAT TO TAKE

Obviously, what to take on a holiday to Lapland depends on when you're going. In winter, for example, you'll need to be properly kitted out with cold-weather gear and the like. In summer, the relatively mild climate doesn't require any particular items of clothing, though it can be useful to have a decent **waterproof jacket** since the heavens can open at any moment. If you're considering hiking, a good pair of **sturdy waterproof boots** and **trousers** are essential, and it is worth taking a

COTTON KILLS – WHAT NOT TO WEAR IN LAPLAND

Clothing keeps you warm by trapping warm air near your skin. However, once cotton becomes wet – when you sweat – it ceases to provide insulation. Instead, the air pockets in the fabric fill up with your perspiration, acting like a sponge. Cotton takes a long time to dry and conducts heat away from your body 25 times faster than air. Since the air around you is colder than your body temperature and the cotton is no longer insulating, you instantly feel cold. This situation is potentially very dangerous and can quickly lead to hypothermia in Lapland's extreme cold conditions. Instead of cotton, you should choose layers of clothing made of polyester or microfibres, such as fleeces, which are designed to insulate while shedding moisture.

waterproof cover for your rucksack if you have one. Use the **alarm clock** on your mobile phone for early-morning buses and ferries.

The Finnish, Norwegian and Swedish electricity supply is 220V and all plugs are the northern European two-pin standard, for which **adaptors** are readily available at major airports. If you're taking a **laptop, tablet** or **mobile**, you'll generally be able to connect to the internet wirelessly in most hotels for free.

TRAVELLING IN WINTER The Lapland winter is not to be taken lightly and in order to enjoy a visit between October and May, when the cold is at its most intense, it's essential to come prepared. The key to surviving the chill is to wear **several layers of clothes**, though not ones made of cotton (see box, opposite) which act as an effective insulator; jeans are not a good idea, but if you must wear them, be sure to wear effective long johns underneath or you'll freeze to death.

In addition to a warm and snug winter coat, you should bring a thick woolly hat, scarf, gloves and the thickest socks you have. If you fail to keep your head and feet warm, you risk losing up to 50% of your body heat.

Hiking boots or other stout shoes are an absolute must – preferably the type that have a deep tread to help you walk on the compacted, polished snow that covers city streets in winter. Don't expect roads and streets to be cleared every time it snows – it is simply impractical. Instead take extreme care when walking on snowy or icy pavements and roads, even those that have been treated with salt or sand, because they can still be extremely slippery.

MAPS The best maps of Lapland are Pohjoiskalotti by Finland's Genimap (1:800 000), or the more detailed Nordkalotten (1:700 000) by either Norway's Cappelen or Sweden's Kartförlaget.

These maps are best bought in the countries concerned. If bought abroad, for example in the UK, they are much more expensive.

MONEY AND BUDGETING

MONEY Annoyingly, three currencies circulate in Lapland: Norway uses the **Norwegian krone** (plural *kroner*; official international abbreviation NOK); Sweden, the **Swedish krona** (plural *kronor*; official international abbreviation SEK); and Finland, the **euro** (EUR). The currencies are not interchangeable, ie: you cannot spend Norwegian kroner in Sweden, for example. Notes and coins are in circulation in all three countries. We have given prices in the local currency of each country.

Across Scandinavia in general, more and more places are becoming cash-free. The use of **credit cards** such as Visa and Mastercard is widespread, even for small amounts, and in many cases is the preferred means of paying for goods and services. AMEX is also accepted though less widely.

If you really must have cash, the best way to get money in Lapland is by using a Visa **debit card**. This makes it possible to withdraw money from cashpoints/ATMs much as you would at home. Although there is a small charge levied by banks for this purpose, it is much less than you would pay in bank commissions when exchanging travellers' cheques. Cashpoint machines are no longer as widespread as they once were, so make sure to withdraw cash before you leave the beaten track. **Banking hours** in Norway are usually 08.30–15.30 Monday–Friday (17.00 or 18.00 on Thursday); in Finland banks tend to be open 09.15–16.15 Monday–Friday; in Sweden service hours are 09.30–15.00 (till 17.30 on Thursday). Banking facilities, either a bank or a cash machine, can generally be found in most larger towns.

BUDGETING Costs in Lapland vary widely from country to country. The most expensive part of the region is Norwegian Lapland where prices are punitive. Norway has long had a reputation as one of the most expensive countries in the world to visit – sadly, this is still very much the case. Even something as basic as a pizza can easily cost upwards of 180NOK. You should expect to pay two or three times more than at home for just about anything you want to buy. A main course in a restaurant, for example, will cost around 300–400NOK; a beer is in the region of 85NOK.

Mercifully, Swedish and Finnish Lapland are different. Sweden is the cheapest of all the Nordic countries and in some circumstances you'll pay less for things than you would at home. The filling daily set lunch (*dagens rätt*) available in restaurants everywhere, for example, costs around 85–95SEK and includes a main dish, salad, bread, a soft drink and coffee – that's a fantastic deal for around £8/US$10. Alcohol is cheapest in Finland, where half a litre of beer, for example, costs around €6; in northern Sweden it's normally around 75SEK. Tipping and bargaining are not expected in Lapland, though you may wish to round up a restaurant bill to the nearest large number, for example, 280SEK becomes 300SEK, as a sign of your appreciation.

Accommodation in Finland and Sweden costs significantly less than in Norway. Transport costs are roughly the same throughout Lapland and, given the huge distances involved, represent good value for money.

When budgeting for a trip calculate that you should be able to get by on £50/US$65 per day in Sweden and Finland (£70/US$90 in Norway) staying in hostels, eating lunch and seeing the sights; having the odd drink and staying in hotels will push prices up to around £100/US$170 in Sweden and Finland (£150/US$190 in Norway).

GETTING AROUND

Although distances are often long and journeys between towns can take several hours (if not all day in some circumstances), travel around Lapland is straightforward. The public transport system in all three countries is efficient, and more often than not runs on time. In Sweden **trains** run from Luleå northwest to Gällivare, Kiruna and Riksgränsen before crossing the border to Narvik in Norway; when bought in advance a single ticket from Luleå to Narvik costs around 455SEK – not bad for a 7-hour journey. There are trains between Gällivare, Jokkmokk and Arvidsjaur running on the privately operated single-track **Inlandsbanan** (w inlandsbanan.se) between June and August; irrespective of when you buy the ticket, a single from Gällivare to Arvidsjaur, for example, costs 514SEK. For more information, see the box on page 69. In Finland rail services effectively expire at Rovaniemi although there is an occasional service as far north as Kolari via Tornio Itäinen and east to Kemijärvi.

In Norway, all transport north of Narvik is by **bus**; services run all the way to Kirkenes in the far east of the region and are described in the text; a single ticket from Narvik to Tromsø costs 443NOK. Both Finland and Sweden have a comprehensive bus network, and in the summer months there are cross-border services between Finland and Norway, which can help you get around the region as a whole; once again details are given in the text; a single from Kaaresuvanto, for example, to Tromsø costs around €51. In Norway, the Hurtigruten coastal **ferry** (page 26) provides a relaxing (if expensive) way of travelling up and down this highly indented coastline, as do the Hurtigbåt express ferries that operate over shorter distances; the Hurtigruten from Tromsø, for example, to Kirkenes costs from 2,700NOK, including a cabin. Note that a second company, Havila Kystruten, will begin services on the coastal route from 2021, operating four of the eleven ships which ply the route between Bergen and Kirkenes. Your day of departure will determine which company operates your service; full details of the new company's services are available at w havilakystruten.no.

Flights too can be particularly useful, especially to cover some of the grinding distances between towns in Norwegian Lapland; the key airline to look out for here is **Widerøe** (w wideroe.no). During the summer months (generally late June to late August), the airline sells the amazingly useful 'Explore Norway' ticket ('Norge Rundt' in Norwegian). This great-value air pass allows you to fly as much and as often as you like within a fixed time frame; see the company's website for details and click the 'Explore Norway' button. However, getting around **by car** is always going to be the most convenient way of seeing Lapland. Not only are you free of the tyranny of timetabling, but you can also get well off the beaten track beyond the reach of most buses. **Car hire** though is pricey and you may find it cheaper to arrange car hire before you go; airlines sometimes have special deals. Once again, Sweden and Finland are considerably cheaper than Norway, where even the Sultan of Brunei would think twice before hiring anything larger than a Nissan Micra. On the whole, expect to pay upwards of £350/US$450 a week for a small car. For a list of car-hire agencies, see below.

Across Lapland the rules of the road are strict: there's a **speed limit** of 30km/h in residential areas, 50km/h in built-up areas and 80–90km/h on other roads. Speed cameras exist and penalties are high, particularly in Norway where on-the-spot fines can reach over 11,000NOK and include an unconditional jail sentence.

At the time of research, **fuel prices** (petrol/diesel) were cheapest in Finland, around €1.53/1.36 per litre; and in Sweden at 16/15.60SEK (euro equivalent €1.55/1.48); but considerably more in Norway, around 16.70/15.30NOK (euro equivalent €1.73/1.59). For up-to-date prices, check w fuel-prices-europe.info.

CAR-HIRE AGENCIES The main car-hire agencies represented in Lapland are:

Avis Norway 81 53 30 44; Finland 010 436 2200; Sweden 0770 82 00 82; w avis.com
Europcar Norway 81 55 18 00; Finland 0200 12 154; Sweden 0770 77 00 50; w europcar.com

Hertz Norway 22 10 00 00; Finland 020 011 2233; Sweden 08 657 3000; w hertz.com

Gas ≈ $6⁰⁰/gallon

ACCOMMODATION

Inevitably, accommodation is going to be your biggest expense, particularly in Norway, where staying in **hotels** can be extremely pricey. However, they are of

ACCOMMODATION PRICE CODES

The hotels and guesthouses in the guide have been graded according to price, based on the cost of the least expensive double room in high season. Where two prices appear after an entry the first refers to high season, the second to low season and/or weekend rates (ie: €€€/€€).

Luxury	€€€€	1,000SEK/1,200NOK/€110>
Top range	€€€	751–1,000SEK/901–1,200NOK/€81–110
Mid-range	€€	501–750SEK/601–900NOK/€41–80
Budget	€	<500SEK/600NOK/€40

a universally high standard and have free Wi-Fi access. In Sweden, in particular, much-reduced weekend (Friday and Saturday night) and summer prices (generally mid-June to mid-August, every day) can bring the cost of a night tumbling down. Unfortunately, many hotels suffer from an identity crisis – there are countless mundane concrete blocks across Lapland that have little character to charm the visitor. More pleasing are the ubiquitous **guesthouses** dotted across the region, which are often family-run and much more homely alternatives to the anonymous hotels. It's also worth looking on **Airbnb** (w airbnb.co.uk), where you'll find a good number of accommodation options, particularly in Finnish Lapland. **Youth hostels** can be found in several towns offering double rooms and accommodation in dorm beds, as well as access to a communal kitchen and sauna. **Campsites** generally have **cabins** sleeping two to six people and can be an economical (and infinitely more cosy) alternative to a guesthouse giving you self-catering facilities.

EATING AND DRINKING

FOOD In the bigger towns and cities across Lapland you will find a wide range of eateries. In addition to the regular Nordic restaurants serving **traditional specialities** such as Arctic char and reindeer in its various guises (see box, below), over recent years there has been a profusion of Thai restaurants, which can make a tasty change to the ubiquitous pizzerias that line the streets of northern Scandinavia. Chinese restaurants and burger bars are common. In smaller towns, hotel restaurants are generally the best place to find quality food. Cafés can be a good place to pick up an open sandwich piled high with various toppings such as prawns or meatballs, though they are generally closed on Sundays. It is generally not necessary to book a table in a restaurant in Lapland.

Breakfast is a perfect way to fuel up for the day. Hotels and guesthouses in all three countries provide a generous help-yourself buffet (included in the room rate) with yoghurt, cereals, ham, cheese, bacon, egg, herring, coffee

KNOW YOUR REINDEER

While non-Scandinavians are sometimes wary about eating reindeer, it is without doubt the dish of choice for most people of the far north. In taste it resembles beef, though with a more gamey flavour. It's extremely low in fat and comes in several varieties:

- thin slices of sautéed reindeer meat (a bit like kebab meat to look at), usually served in a deliciously creamy mushroom sauce with mashed potatoes and lingonberries, are known as *poronkäristys* in Finnish, *finnbiff* in Norwegian and *renskav* in Swedish;
- *suovas* (Sámi for 'smoked') is salted reindeer meat, which is cold-smoked and served in small rounds;
- the other main alternative is a regular steak of reindeer meat, mouthwateringly tender and very lean, known as *poronpaisti* in Finnish, *reinsdyrstek* in Norwegian and *renstek/renytterfilé* in Swedish.

Remember that by ordering reindeer from the menu you're choosing to support a strategic part of the Lapland economy.

and juice. You simply take what you want and return to the table as many times as you like.

Lunch varies from country to country. In Norway (*lunsj* in Norwegian) it consists mostly of a sandwich bought from a café, whereas in Sweden and Finland you should look out for the set lunch special (*dagens rätt/dagens lunch* in Swedish; *lounas* in Finnish), which offers an extremely economical way of enjoying a good meal. Served from 11.00 to 14.00 between Monday and Friday, it generally consists of a choice of two or three main dishes, plus salad, bread, a soft drink or a low-alcohol beer and coffee – all for around 85–95SEK/€8–9. By switching your main meal of the day to lunchtime, you'll save a packet.

Eating **dinner** à la carte in the evening is a more expensive undertaking, although much more so in Norway than in Sweden and Finland. Many mid-range restaurants in Lapland serve local specialities, in particular **reindeer** (see box, opposite).

DRINK Finland is the cheapest country in which to buy alcohol, closely followed by Sweden, with Norway off the scale. All three Nordic countries operate a restrictive system of **alcohol** sales aimed at limiting the amount of alcohol people consume. State-run stores known as *vinmonopolet* (Norway), *alko* (Finland) and *systembolaget* (Sweden) are open office hours Monday–Friday and generally on Saturday morning and are found in the larger towns and villages across the region. They are never open in the evening, on Sunday or on public holidays. These shops are the only places to buy wine, strong beer and spirits – the only alcohol available in supermarkets is beer with a maximum alcohol content of 4.5°, in the case of Finland and Norway, or a watery 3.5° in Sweden.

Naturally, alcohol is available in restaurants and bars at higher prices than in the stores. In Norway you should expect to pay 85–100NOK for half a litre of beer in a bar; in Sweden around 75–85SEK; and in Finland about €4.50–6.50.

PUBLIC HOLIDAYS AND FESTIVALS

Despite the restricted sale of alcohol throughout Lapland, there's certainly no shortage of the stuff during the **midsummer** celebration, the most important public holiday of the year, which takes place between 21 and 23 June in Sweden and Finland. Festivities centre round the maypole, an old fertility symbol, which is erected at popular gatherings across the north of Scandinavia. There's much dancing and drinking into the light night – and severe hangovers the next morning. The biggest **Sámi festivals** in the region are the Kautokeino Easter Festival (page 158) and the late August Storstämningshelgen Festival in Arvidsjaur (page 55). Other public holidays are as follows:

FINLAND

1, 6 January	
April	Good Friday, Easter Sunday, Easter Monday
1 May	Ascension Day, Whit Sunday
23 June	Midsummer Day
1 November	All Saints' Day
6 December	Independence Day
25, 26 December	

NORWAY

1 January	
April	Maundy Thursday, Good Friday, Easter Sunday, Easter Monday
1, 17 May	National Day, Whit Sunday, Whit Monday
25, 26 December	

SWEDEN

1, 6 January	
April	Good Friday, Easter Sunday, Easter Monday
1 May	Ascension Day, Whit Sunday
6 June	National Day
23 June	Midsummer Day
1 November	All Saints' Day
25, 26 December	

SHOPPING

Across Lapland you'll be presented with dozens of opportunities to pick up locally produced **handicrafts** of Sámi design and origin: attractively carved wooden knives and forks (with or without engraving), hollowed-out birch knots in the shape of drinking cups, leather goods in various shapes and sizes made of reindeer skin and jewellery are just some of the items on sale. It's possible to pick up a **reindeer skin** (most reasonably priced in Finland), though you should make sure when you buy it that the animal was slaughtered in the autumn since it will moult less; take care not to get the skin wet since that can cause the hair to fall out. Try to buy any of the above-mentioned items directly from Sámi-run stalls or businesses and you'll be sure that the money is going back into the local community. This is a much more satisfying experience than giving your money to a national chain store, for example, that sells mass-produced trinkets for the tourist market. Although Norway operates a system of tax-free shopping, as it is not part of the European Union, you will always find prices higher than in Sweden and Finland, even taking your return tax into account.

Given the considerable distances between settlements in Lapland, you will find shopping opportunities in all but the smallest hamlets. Naturally, choices may not be extensive but there will always be one or two shops selling the essentials and often a few souvenirs to boot. For serious retail therapy, you will need to head for Luleå, Tromsø and Rovaniemi, Lapland's three largest settlements. Remember though, that Lapland is not the place to come to indulge your cravings for the latest designer goods and trend-setting clothing. Shops tend to be more of the practical kind, selling vital everyday goods to local people, rather than catering for the exotic tastes of fashion-conscious shopaholics.

In bigger towns across Lapland you will find all the facilities you're accustomed to at home: banks, supermarkets, pharmacies, clothes shops, bookstores and the like. In smaller villages, however, services are likely to be a little more limited, but, in general you will always find a shop selling groceries and a filling station. Distances between settlements in Lapland are often great which quite simply means that places have to be self-sufficient when it comes to the bare essentials. In the very smallest places, it may be that the filling station also sells a few groceries and basic pharmacy items such as mosquito spray. The exception to this general rule is alcohol. In Finland, Norway and Sweden, alcohol (wine, spirits and premium-strength beer) is not sold in food stores or at filling stations. Supermarkets do sell beer, but its alcohol content is low. The sale of alcohol is regulated by the state and only available in special liquor stores known as *alko* (Finland), *vinmonopolet* (Norway) and *systembolaget* (Sweden). Only larger settlements have one of these stores – in smaller villages, alcohol can usually be ordered through the local food store which acts as an agent – but this is a lengthy operation and involves a wait until your goods are delivered. Better to stock up when you come across an alcohol outlet and take it with you if you're heading out into the sticks.

Payment by credit card is commonplace across Lapland and you're unlikely to have problems should you choose to pay this way: both Mastercard and Visa are widely accepted, AMEX a little less so.

ARTS AND ENTERTAINMENT

In Sámi the words for 'art' and 'artist', as they are perceived in Western cultures, are relatively new. However, traditional Sámi arts and crafts, which include music, storytelling and handicrafts, are all key pillars of the indigenous culture of Lapland, which has a history spanning several millennia. The prehistoric rock carvings dating from 4200BC, for example, discovered in the 1970s near Alta in Norway, are an artistic impression of man's inseparable link to nature – a characteristic of Sámi art when seen from a non-indigenous perspective. Art for art's sake has rarely existed in the Sámi community since utensils and other items were created for their practical rather than aesthetic value. However, in the modern age, Sámi artists have begun to express a Western conception of art, drawing on the ancient culture of their indigenous heritage for inspiration, which has helped the wider community create an identity for itself.

When it comes to non-indigenous art, it's Norway that has the most developed scene. Northern Norwegian artists such as Axel Revold are well represented in exhibitions across Norwegian Lapland, particularly in Tromsø and Henningsvær in the Lofoten islands. There are specialist museums dedicated to paintings produced in the north at the turn of the last century, a period widely regarded as the golden era of contemporary art from this part of the country. A key recurring element in these paintings is the powerful nature of Norwegian Lapland.

For more information on culture in Lapland, see page 19.

PHOTOGRAPHY

Perhaps the most challenging aspect of taking photographs in Lapland is the winter cold; quite simply, extremely low temperatures are not conducive to taking good photographs. Try to keep extra batteries warm in your pockets, since low temperatures tend to drain batteries rather quickly. Remember too, that cold conditions can make electric cables and film (if you're using it) brittle, and prolonged exposure to cold may even cause them to snap. Also bear in mind that bright snow scenes tend to cause the camera to underexpose. If you're using an SLR camera, be sure to overexpose by one or two stops to compensate. When shooting in overcast conditions, an overcast sky can create a bluish hue to photographs. You can get round this by using a warming filter which will take the snow back to its original white. Condensation on the lens can also be a problem when you come into the warmth from outdoors. Wipe the lens carefully to remove the moisture before going back outdoors or it will freeze. Try to wear gloves when shooting in cold conditions or your fingers are likely to stick to any metal part of the camera.

MEDIA AND COMMUNICATIONS

RADIO Although there are now radio stations in all three countries transmitting in Sámi, it's unlikely you'll have anything to do with them, other than tuning in perhaps for curiosity's sake. The best source of English-language radio news is **Radio Sweden**, which produces a daily news podcast at 16.30 for download at w radiosweden.org. Alternatively, tune to FM and locate the Sveriges Radio P2 network (P6 in Stockholm; 89.6FM) for a weekly news summary broadcast at 16.30 on Thursdays and repeated on Mondays on both networks.

TELEVISION National television carries a short daily bulletin of Sámi news. State-run, licence-fee-funded television (NRK in Norway, SVT in Sweden and YLE in Finland) all operate a couple of channels in their respective countries, complementing the offerings of commercial stations TV2 (Norway), TV4 (Sweden) and MTV (Finland, though not the music channel you're no doubt familiar with). Many programmes are imported from Britain or the US and shown with subtitles.

NEWSPAPERS All countries support a number of national and regional newspapers, though unless you speak one of the Scandinavian languages it's unlikely you'll have much call for them. In larger libraries it is sometimes possible to find English-language newspapers and in some towns they are also available for sale, though this is the exception rather than the rule.

TELEPHONES In the land of Nokia and Ericsson, there's little call for public telephones and all have now disappeared. Mobile phone coverage is virtually 100% and you will find it useful to have one with you. If you're in Lapland for a prolonged period of time, consider buying a local SIM card to reduce calling costs. They are available from telephone stores and newsagents in all three countries.

POST In Sweden the **post office** has ceased to exist. Instead you buy stamps from supermarkets, filling stations or hotel receptions. In Norway and Finland the post office lives on, offering the range of services you're accustomed to. Stamps can also be bought from newsagents.

INTERNET Most accommodation places, tourist offices and cafés offer free Wi-Fi, which is great if you're travelling with your own laptop, tablet or mobile. Internet cafés never really made their mark in Lapland, since everyone has internet access at home or on their phone.

TIME

Time in Norway and Sweden is the same. It is always 1 hour ahead of Britain and Ireland (ie: GMT +1 in winter and GMT +2 in summer); and 6 to 9 hours ahead of the continental US. Finland is 2 hours ahead of the UK and 7 to 10 hours ahead of the continental US. Daylight saving is in operation, as in Britain and Ireland, from late October to late March.

CULTURAL ETIQUETTE

Scandinavians in general, and Laplanders in particular, are perhaps the most taciturn of all Europe's peoples. A harsh climate limits social interaction, and accordingly conversations are often short and matter of fact. Lapland is not the

GOING NUDE – SAUNA ETIQUETTE

No visit to Lapland is complete without experiencing a genuine Scandinavian sauna – any sauna you've come across at home will be a poor imitation. It's as well, therefore, to know some of the dos and don'ts before you set foot in the real thing. Firstly, it's important to dispel the myth that saunas are linked with sex in Scandinavia – nothing could be further from the truth. Instead, they are seen (particularly in Finland, which gave the world the sauna) as a cultural marker – somewhere to relax, enjoy the heat and steam and perhaps to ponder – though not talk. In general (and especially in Finland), saunas are silent places. For many foreigners, though, it's the awkward question of nudity which is at the forefront of their minds: do I have to go completely nude to have a sauna? In short, yes. Remember that saunas are generally separate-sex affairs and full nudity is quite normal in the sauna and in the showers – wearing a swimming costume or wrapping yourself in a towel is not the done thing. Instead, follow the rules often posted up in a sauna: undress in the changing room and leave all your clothes there, then, walk naked to the showers and wash thoroughly before entering the sauna. Scandinavians don't suffer from the same body guilt as many other nations and it's quite normal for people to walk freely around in the nude in a sauna environment; covering up will not only make you look prudish and but will also single you out immediately as a non-sauna-savvy foreigner. Leave your towel either in the changing room or the shower room. Sometimes, most commonly in Finland, there are seat mats (either hard plastic or strong tissue) for sitting on in the sauna, close to the sauna entrance. Use one if they're provided. If not, don't take anything into the sauna – above all, do not sit on a towel or a swimming costume. Being naked in the sauna is considered much more hygienic than allowing sweat to soak into towels or swimming gear. When it's time to cool off, head for the showers and rinse or wash – or, even better, in the midst of the Lapland winter, roll in the snow outside; the amazing tingling sensation you'll experience on your skin is sensational! It's a good idea to pause a while between visits to the sauna to allow your body time to cool down. Once again, there's no need to cover up – simply sit and relax and leave your modesty where it belongs in the sauna – at the changing room door. The only exception to the nudity rule is in mixed-sex saunas, sometimes found in smaller hotels and spa complexes, where the wearing of swimming costumes is obligatory and strictly observed.

2

Mediterranean and it is most definitely not the place to expect wild gesticulation and florid outpourings of emotion; quite simply, during the bleak winter months people close up and withdraw into themselves, talking little and socialising even less. However, it's important not to confuse this with rudeness. Honesty and straight-talking are important to the people of the north, so be prepared for few 'pleases' and 'thank yous', but, instead, cherish the sincerity and openness which pervades conversation in Lapland, social ingredients which vanished long ago in many other cultures. On meeting strangers, people in Lapland tend to shake hands, while often saying their name. Friends will hug, rather than kiss, which is considered an altogether southern affectation!

Part Two

THE GUIDE

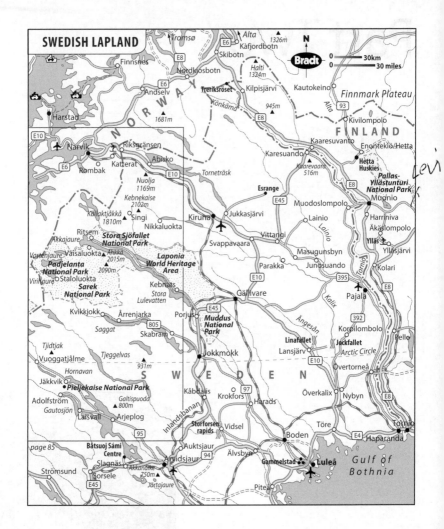

SWEDISH LAPLAND

3

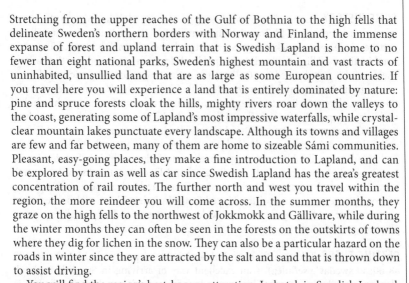

Swedish Lapland: Luleå to Riksgränsen

Stretching from the upper reaches of the Gulf of Bothnia to the high fells that delineate Sweden's northern borders with Norway and Finland, the immense expanse of forest and upland terrain that is Swedish Lapland is home to no fewer than eight national parks, Sweden's highest mountain and vast tracts of uninhabited, unsullied land that are as large as some European countries. If you travel here you will experience a land that is entirely dominated by nature: pine and spruce forests cloak the hills, mighty rivers roar down the valleys to the coast, generating some of Lapland's most impressive waterfalls, while crystal-clear mountain lakes punctuate every landscape. Although its towns and villages are few and far between, many of them are home to sizeable Sámi communities. Pleasant, easy-going places, they make a fine introduction to Lapland, and can be explored by train as well as car since Swedish Lapland has the area's greatest concentration of rail routes. The further north and west you travel within the region, the more reindeer you will come across. In the summer months, they graze on the high fells to the northwest of Jokkmokk and Gällivare, while during the winter months they can often be seen in the forests on the outskirts of towns where they dig for lichen in the snow. They can also be a particular hazard on the roads in winter since they are attracted by the salt and sand that is thrown down to assist driving.

You will find the region's best-known attraction, Icehotel, in Swedish Lapland. It is built of blocks of ice hewn every winter from the frozen Torne River and stands tall until the spring thaw in May. Nearby Kiruna is as good a gateway as any to this part of Lapland and provides easy access to Abisko which, thanks to its clear skies, is the best place in Lapland to view the northern lights. Tucked away on the border with Norway, Riksgränsen is a popular ski destination and the start of the terrific train journey down to Narvik. On the Arctic Circle, Jokkmokk is the location for the region's oldest and most enjoyable market, a mammoth event which attracts tens of thousands of visitors every February. Southeast of here, the quirky Treehotel draws an ever-increasing number of visitors to this unspoilt corner of Swedish Lapland. Arvidsjaur, further south, has a strong Sámi history and culture, witnessed by its impressive collection of Sámi church dwellings, Lappstaden. To the northwest, up in the mountains beyond the village of Arjeplog, some of the finest hiking Lapland has to offer is to be found along one of the quietest sections of the Kungsleden trail. Down on the coast, Luleå, on the other hand, is a modern, thoroughly Swedish city, with an impressive bar and restaurant scene, top-notch accommodation and excellent transport links. Yet it is also the site of Gammelstad, a UNESCO World Heritage-listed collection of 400 knotted wooden cottages neatly gathered around the most stunning medieval church in Lapland.

LULEÅ

With a population of 44,000, Luleå (pronunciation: 'LOO-lee-oh'; Julev in Sámi; Luulaja in Finnish) is the biggest city in Lapland, and thrills in billing itself as the capital of Swedish Lapland, although arguably Kiruna has a stronger claim thanks to its location north of the Arctic Circle. Either way, Luleå is one of the best gateways to Lapland thanks to its busy airport and good bus and train connections. It is an excellent place to rest either side of a trip further north; its restaurant and bar scene is the best for miles around, prices are reasonable (unlike in Lapland's second city, Tromsø) and the impressive UNESCO World Heritage Site, Gammelstad, is just down the road.

SOME HISTORY Founded by Swedish king Gustav II Adolf in 1621 on the site of nearby Gammelstad (Old Town) with its medieval church and attendant church cottages, Luleå grew quickly thanks to its superb though small harbour. However, a combination of falling sea levels and rapid land elevation soon rendered the harbour useless and it was decreed in 1649 that the entire town should up sticks and move to its current location at the mouth of the Lule River. Barely 200 years later, virtually the entire place was burnt to the ground in a devastating fire; only a handful of buildings escaped the flames. Things improved with the arrival of the new railway line, Malmbanan, in the late 1880s, which enabled iron ore from the mines at Kiruna and Gällivare to be transported to Luleå by train for shipping via the Gulf of Bothnia. Today Luleå is a likeable, vibrant, go-ahead sort of place, which is fast developing into a world-renowned hi-tech metallurgical and IT centre, thanks to its research programmes and expansive steel industry. Even Facebook is here now, opening its first data centre outside of the United States in Luleå. There is also a technical university here, which lends the city's wide, open streets and airy public squares a pleasant, youthful air.

GETTING THERE Taking a flight to **Luleå airport** (airport code LLA; ✆010 109 48 00; w swedavia.se/lulea) is an excellent way of arriving in Swedish Lapland. The airport, which, incidentally, has the longest runway anywhere in Sweden, is just 10km southwest of the city and is served by regular flights from the south: Stockholm (SAS and Norwegian) as well as Pajala (Jonair) in the Torne Valley. The bus into town (#4) costs 35SEK (no cash; pay the driver by credit card); a taxi costs about 350SEK. The **train** and **bus** stations are barely 5 minutes' walk from each other, at the eastern end of the town centre. Luleå has direct trains from/to Stockholm, Gothenburg, Kiruna and Narvik. All public transport timetables and connections in Sweden are available at w resrobot.se.

TOURIST INFORMATION The **tourist office** (Skeppsbrogatan 17; ✆0920 45 70 00; e turistcenter@lulea.se; w visitlulea. se; ⏰ 10.00–17.00 Mon–Fri; mid-Jun– mid-Aug 09.00–18.00 Mon–Fri, 10.00–

LULEÅ
For listings, see from page 46

⌂ Where to stay
1 Amber
2 City Sleep
3 Clarion Sense
4 Comfort Arctic
5 Elite Stadshotell
6 Park
Off map
  First Camp Luleå

✖ Where to eat and drink
7 Baan Thai
  Bishops Arms (see 5)
8 Bistro Bar Brygga
9 Cook's krog
10 Corsica
11 Hemma Gastronomi
12 O'Learys
13 Pastabacken
14 Still Café

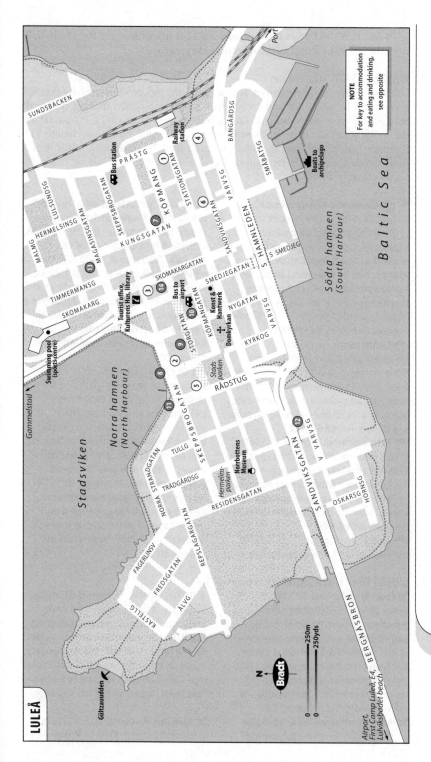

LULEÅ

NOTE
For key to accommodation and eating and drinking, see opposite

Baltic Sea

*Södra hamnen
(South Harbour)*

Boats to archipelago

BANGÅRDSG

SMÅBÅTSG

Port

S HAMNLEDEN

Railway station

④

⑥

STATIONSGATAN

VARVSG

Bus station

PRÄSTG

①

KÖPMANG

SKEPPSBROGATAN

KUNGSGATAN

⑦

SANDVIKSGATAN

S S SMEDJEG

SMEDJEGATAN

MALMG

HERMELINSG

LULSUNDSG

MAGASINSGATAN

⑬

TIMMERMANSG

SKOMAKARG

SKOMAKARGATAN

③

⑭

Tourist office, Kulturens Hus, library

Bus to airport

NYGATAN

VARVSG

Swimming pool (sports centre)

Gammelstad

Stadsviken

*Norra hamnen
(North Harbour)*

⑧

⑪

STORGATAN

②

⑨

⑩

KÖPMANGATAN

Konst & Hantwerk

Domkyrkan

KYRKOG

Stadsparken

⑤

RÅDSTUG

NORRA STRANDGATAN

TULLG

SKEPPSBROGATAN

TRÄDGÅRDSG

Hermelins-parken

Norrbottens Museum

RESIDENSGATAN

SANDVIKSGATAN

V VARVSG

⑫

OSKARSG

HORNSG

FAGERLINSV

FREDSGATAN

ÄLVG

KASTELLG

REPSLAGARGATAN

Gültzauudden

SUNDSBACKEN

N

0   250m
0   250yds

Bradt

Airport,
First Camp Luleå, E4,
Lulviksbadet beach

BERGNÄSBRON

16.00 Sat, 11.00–15.00 Sun) is in Kulturens Hus, a straightforward 10-minute walk from the bus station west all the way along Skeppsbrogatan.

🏠 WHERE TO STAY *Map, page 45*

Luleå has a large range of modern, central hotels, the pick of which we have detailed here. Prices at weekends and in summer drop significantly, making non-peak hotel rooms an absolute bargain. For such a relatively large city, it is unusual for the youth hostel not to be affiliated to the national youth hostel association, STF (Svenska Turistföreningen, the Swedish Youth Hostel Association), but it is of a good standard and relatively central. There's also the option of staying in nearby Gammelstad (page 48).

✳ 🏠 **Clarion Sense** Skeppsbrogatan 34; 📞0920 45 04 50; e cl.sense@choice.se; w clarionsense.se. Decked out in soft natural colours to reflect the changing seasons in the surrounding forests & unspoilt nature, this innovative hotel is a style-seeker's dream. There's a glorious pool & sauna suite on the top floor, too, offering great views over the city, as well an outdoor terrace which stretches virtually the whole way round the building. €€€€/€€€

🏠 **Comfort Arctic** Sandviksgatan 82; 📞0920 109 80; e co.arctic@choice.se; w arctichotel.se. An inviting hotel, close to the train station, with contemporary Nordic-style rooms. The attractive corner suites are spacious & bright. A good sauna & jacuzzi are on the 5th floor & a free evening buffet is served Mon–Thu. €€€€/€€€

🏠 **Elite Stadshotell** Storgatan 15; 📞0920 27 40 00; e info.lulea@elite.se; w elite.se. Built in the 1890s with a touch of French Renaissance style, this massive hotel is certainly a grand place to stay but rooms vary greatly in size & decoration. Ask to see the room first. The b/fast buffet, though, is Luleå's best. €€€€/€€€

🏠 **Amber** Stationsgatan 67; 📞0920 102 00; e info@amber-hotell.se; w amber-hotell.se. A pretty little family-run hotel close to the train station, offering a home-from-home experience in an old timber building dating from the early 1900s with individually decorated rooms. €€€

🏠 **Park** Kungsgatan 10; 📞0920 21 11 49; e hotellet@parkhotell.se; w www.parkhotell.se. A small family-run place in the centre of town with comfortable (if rather plain) rooms. Unusually for a hotel, there's access to a fully fitted kitchen which is ideal for self-catering. Their good-value summer & w/end prices are at the lower end of the price category. €€€

🏠 **City Sleep** (3 rooms/8 beds) Skeppsbrogatan 18; 📞0920 42 00 02; e info@ citysleep.se; w citysleep.se. Located in the basement, this modern youth hostel has windowless, rather small rooms which all share facilities. There's a decent kitchen & the communal areas are bright & comfortable. Free wireless internet access. No dorm beds. Dbl room €€

⅄ **First Camp Luleå** Arcusvägen 110; 📞0920 603 00; e lulea@firstcamp.se; w firstcamp.se/ lulea; ⏱ year-round. About 5km west of the centre in Karlsvik. A great riverside location with views of the city. A range of cabins of different sizes available. €€

✗ WHERE TO EAT AND DRINK *Map, page 45*

✗ **Cook's krog** Storgatan 17; 📞0920 20 10 00; w cookskrog.se; ⏱ 18.00 onwards Mon–Sat but generally closed during the summer holidays. Long-established, white tablecloth place serving an array of northern delicacies such as reindeer fillet & Arctic char. Menus change frequently but Cook's is renowned for its good quality meat & service with a smile. This is undoubtedly one of northern Sweden's best restaurants. €€€

✗ **Hemma Gastronomi** Norra Strandgatan 1; 📞0920 22 00 02; w hemmagastronomi.se; ⏱ 08.00–23.00 Mon–Fri, noon–23.00 Sat–Sun. This place is unique in Lapland – a top-quality deli & bistro all rolled into one serving a delicious variety of freshly produced Swedish home cooking dishes at lunchtime for just 110SEK & dishing up food all day long. In the evenings, it's substantial meat & fish dishes which hold sway, such as sirloin steak, grilled lobster & reindeer with salsa verde. €€€

✗ **Baan Thai** Kungsgatan 22; 📞0920 23 18 18; w baanthailulea.se; ⏱ 10.30–22.00 Mon–Fri,

11.00–22.00 Sat, 13.00–21.00 Sun. One of the most popular places for lunch in Luleå with a Thai buffet for 80SEK– eat here at lunchtime rather than in the evening since the quality of the food is not what it was when this place opened in 2000 & it's not really worth paying more for essentially the same dishes. However, it still makes a welcome change from traditional northern Swedish fare. €€

✳ ✗ **Bistro Bar Brygga** Skeppsbrogatan; ✆0920 22 00 00; w bistrobarbrygga.se; ⊕ mid-Jun–Sep 17.00 onwards daily. Also known as BBB, this ship & adjoining floating pontoons moored alongside Skeppsbrogatan is an inordinately popular place for a bite to eat & a drink during the summer months. Favourites such as smoked salmon, prawn salad & their ribs with chilli aioli & roast potatoes are always on the menu. €€

✗ **Corsica** Nygatan 14; ✆0920 158 40; w restaurangcorsica.com; ⊕ 11.00–23.00 Mon–Fri, noon–23.00 Sat & Sun. Mediterranean-style (though not overly authentic) meaty mains such as steak in Grand Marnier sauce or steak cordon bleu. Don't expect French cuisine at its finest – it's all a bit rough & ready – but it's a decent enough place to fill up if money is tight. Lunch featuring Swedish home cooking, pasta buffet or pizza is 95SEK. €€

✗ **Pastabacken** Magasinsgatan 5; ✆0920 22 70 85; w pastabacken.se; ⊕ 11.00–14.00 & 16.00–21.00 Mon–Thu, 11.00–22.00 Fri, noon–

22.00 Sat, 13.00–20.00 Sun. Owned by the same father & son team since 2007, this is actually one of Luleå's oldest eateries, & has been serving the masses since the 80s. In short, if you're looking for a cheap fill, this is it: seemingly endless varieties of pasta dishes are served from just 100SEK. There's also a good choice of pizzas from just 75SEK. €

✗ **Still Café** Storgatan 43; ✆0920 888 40; w stillcafe.se; ⊕ 11.00–21.00 Mon–Thu, 11.00–23.00 Fri & Sat. Actually more bistro than café, this new venture has become one of Luleå's most popular spots, with sunny outdoor seating in summer. The best coffee in town, plus a choice of bar meals such as fish & chips, burgers & tapas. €€

♀**Bishops Arms** Storgatan 15; ✆0920 27 40 30; w thebishopsarms.com/lulea; ⊕ 16.00–midnight Sun–Thu, 16.00–02.00 Fri, 13.00–02.00 Sat. Busy & central British-style pub attached to the Elite Stadshotell (see opposite) with a wide choice of beers & whiskies. Extremely popular watering hole also with bar meals such as burgers. €

♀**O'Learys** Västra Varvsgatan 25; ✆0920 22 85 80; w olearys.se; ⊕ 17.00–23.00 Tue–Thu, 17.00–03.00 Fri & Sat, 17.00–22.00 Sun. The Luleå branch of this ever-popular national chain of sports bars is a great place to catch a game while tucking into a juicy burger & it's one of the most popular places in town for a drink. €

SHOPPING If you're looking to pick up a genuine handicraft or two from northern Sweden, Luleå is home to an excellent store which sells nothing but: **Konst & Hantverk** is right in the centre of town at Smedjegatan 13G (⊕ 10.00–18.00 Mon–Fri, 10.00–15.00 Sat), and stocks a good selection of Sámi handicrafts as well as jewellery, gloves, hats and bags.

WHAT TO SEE AND DO

The city Central Luleå occupies a rectangular-shaped peninsula at the mouth of the Lule River. Running east–west across the promontory and right through the city centre, Storgatan is Luleå's main street, lined with shopping malls, restaurants and cafés. At the western end of the city centre, Rådhustorget square is dominated by the Neogothic red-brick **domkyrkan** (cathedral) (⊕ 10.00–15.00 Mon–Fri), which was built in 1893 to replace the previous church destroyed in the city fire six years previously; at 67m high, it is the tallest and most striking building in Luleå. The interior's plain white brick walls serve to accentuate the size and appearance of the enormous chandelier, which hangs above the aisle.

Norrbottens Museum (Storgatan 2; ✆0920 24 35 02; w norrbottensmuseum.se; ⊕ 10.00–16.00 Tue–Fri, 11.00–16.00 Sat & Sun, mid-Aug–late Jun until 20.00 Wed; free) The museum is a 10-minute walk west from the cathedral along Stationsgatan. It is informative and has a collection of exhibitions on regional history during the

1900s, and on local Sámi life and culture. Upstairs in a small cinema, Filmrummet, a wide collection of films is available for viewing; you choose the one you want to watch from the console by the entrance. The selection available changes frequently, though, if you're lucky, you'll be able to see *Herdswoman*, a film tracing the lives of three generations of Sámi women from near Umeå and their legal battle for grazing rights, which is particularly poignant.

Kulturens Hus (Skeppsbrogatan 17; ✆ 0920 45 40 80; w kulturenshus.com; ⏰ noon–16.00 Mon–Fri, 11.00–16.00 Sat; free) The arthall (*konsthall*) inside Kulturens Hus shows a changing collection of work from contemporary Swedish artists and sculptors.

Gültzauudden beach Occupying a windy location at the western extremity of the Luleå peninsula, Gültzauudden beach is a small sandy strand that's ideal for catching the rays or taking a quick dip. From the town centre you can walk here in about 20 minutes by taking Skeppsbrogatan west, then doing a dog-leg right into Residensgatan and then left on to Repslagargatan, then, finally, turn right into Fredsgatan, which leads all the way to the beach. Incidentally, the curious name for the promontory, or *udde(n)* in Swedish, is synonomous with that of Christian Gültzau (1796–1870), who was one of Luleå's wealthiest businessmen; he operated a shipyard here in the 1830s building sailing vessels.

Lulviksbadet beach In good weather, though, it's a much better idea to head for Lulviksbadet, a sweeping sandy bay, just 1.5km beyond the airport. Indeed, on sunny days, it seems virtually the entire population of the city is here enjoying the sunshine. Without your own transport, simply take bus #4 to the airport from Smedjegatan and then walk along the main road, from the airport junction (where there's a suspended military plane plonked on a plinth), for another 15 minutes or so until you come to a car park on the left-hand side. The sea here heats up quickly during the long days of summer as it's shallow for quite a long way out. Lulviksbadet is also where you'll find Luleå's popular **naturist beach**, which you can reach by heading through the furthest part of the car park from the airport, down to the sea, and then turning right, following the shoreline, continuing in the same direction you came, ie: away from the airport. See w scandinavianaturist.org for more details.

Gammelstad One of Lapland's top sights, Gammelstad, 11km northwest of Luleå, was added to the UNESCO World Heritage List in 1996. It is an outstanding example of what's known in Swedish as a *kyrkstad*, a 'church town' consisting of over 400 timber cottages, which were used on Sundays and during religious festivals by people attending services in the spectacular late medieval **stone church**, Nederluleå kyrka, around which they are grouped. The cottages provided overnight accommodation for parishioners who lived too far away to make the journey to the church and back in one day.

Of Sweden's 71 church towns, only 16 remain today, the largest and best preserved of which is Gammelstad, which consists of 408 gnarled **wooden cottages**. The combination of a strongly felt duty to attend church and the long distances involved in getting here, led to the construction of the church town in the mid 1500s. The ad hoc placing of the cottages suggests that the church town grew successively over the years, with cottages being added as and when they were needed. Miraculously, the *kyrkstad* has never been subject to fire. Traditions live on in Gammelstad and the cottages are used by parishioners three to four times every year when special 'church weekends' are held, or when confirmations take place shortly before midsummer.

Bus #9 runs roughly once an hour (timetable available at **w** llt.lulea.se) to Gammelstad from Smedjegatan in the centre of Luleå and takes about 35 minutes; alight at the stop called Kyrktorget.

Tourist information The tourist office in Gammelstad is located in the heart of things at Kyrktorget 1 (**↘**0920 45 70 10; **e** gammelstad@lulea.se; **w** visitgammelstad.se). In addition to a wealth of information about the church town, it also runs guided tours in English during the summer months (book online; 80SEK).

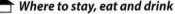
Where to stay, eat and drink

🏠 **Gammelstads Gästhem** Gamla Bodenvägen 11; **↘**0920 25 80 00; **e** info@gammelstadsgasthem.se; **w** gammelstadsgasthem.se. Offering both regular en-suite dbl rooms with b/fast & bedding included & more basic youth hostel rooms with bunk beds & sharing facilities (b/fast & bedding not inc), this option is perfectly located in Gammelstad. There's also a kitchen for self-caterers. **€€€/€€**

What to see and do

Hägnan Open-Air Museum (Friluftsmuséet Hägnan; ⊕ mid-Jun–mid-Aug 11.00–17.00 daily; free) Just down the hill from the cottages, Friluftsmuséet Hägnan is a rustic collection of old farmstead buildings spanning three centuries. They come from farms across Lapland and have been rebuilt in their original form to accurately portray country life from the 1700s onwards. Rural skills such as sheep shearing and flatbread making are also occasionally displayed.

Nederluleå Church (Nederluleå kyrka; ⊕ mid-Jun–mid-Aug 09.00–17.00 daily, rest of the year check with the tourist office; free) The city of Luleå originally grew up around Nederluleå kyrka, which was built during the 15th century and inaugurated in 1492. The opulence of the building is a clear sign of the economic prosperity of the town at the time, which was based on fur trading in the Lapland interior and salmon fishing on the coast. Originally intended as a cathedral, this is the largest church in Sweden north of Uppsala. Indeed, the lookout slit in the eastern gable suggests it was a useful fortification during periods of unrest, allowing boiling oil to be poured over unexpected visitors. The interior is ornate in the extreme. The altar screen with its finely carved wooden figures was made in Antwerp around 1520 at great cost to the local farmers who were presented with the bill. The ornate pulpit, replete with dashes of gilt, dates from 1712 and is the work of local carpenter, Nils Jacobsson Fluur.

Luleå Archipelago With over 1,300 islands, the archipelago off Luleå is unique: it is the only one in the world surrounded by brackish water. The archipelago is renowned for its rich birdlife and a profusion of wild berries, such as the delicious Arctic raspberry and the orange-coloured cloudberry, which ripen in late summer. Ideal for walking or lazing on the rocks, the islands can be reached by several boats from Luleå's southern harbour between June and August.

Information in English about the archipelago can be hard to locate online. Your best bet is to go to **w** lulea.se/skargard and then look for the English-language link about the archipelago where you'll also find boat schedules. A one-way ticket to any of the islands costs 150SEK (except Klubbviken; 75SEK one-way). The tourist office also has information about (limited) accommodation options in the archipelago which can also be booked online on the archipelago web pages referred to above.

The main islands to aim for are **Brandöskär**, remote and known for its hilly terrain; **Hindersön**, a pastoral farming island; **Kluntarna**, an island of small fishing hamlets and pine forest; or **Klubbviken** (actually a bay on the island of Sandön), which has the advantage of the best beaches and most frequent ferry connections.

MOVING ON FROM LULEÅ Train lines in Lapland are rare. However, Luleå is on the Swedish rail network and has daily **trains** north to Gällivare, Kiruna, Abisko and Narvik. Regional trains from Luleå to Kiruna are operated by Norrtåg; sleeper services to and from Narvik are run by the national railway company, SJ. Scheduled journey time (see box, above) to Kiruna is around 3½ hours; Narvik is around 7½ hours. Trains also run south from Luleå around 17.00 (for Stockholm and Gothenburg) and around 21.15 (Stockholm); full details at w sj.se.

Buses connect Luleå with Haparanda every few hours, as well as Arvidsjaur, Jokkmokk (via Harad for the Treehotel) and Pajala. Although there are also services to Gällivare and Kiruna, it is a much more enjoyable journey by train.

The **airport bus** leaves from bus stop 'B' on Smedjegatan (every 30mins Mon–Fri, hourly on Sat & every 30–60mins on Sun). All timetables are at w resrobot.se.

BODEN

From Luleå it's a short hop of around 35km, a mere stone's throw in these parts, northwest to Boden, a major junction on the Swedish rail network; from here trains run northwest to Gällivare, Kiruna and Narvik, southeast to Luleå and all points south. From the station, simply walk west for 10 minutes along Kungsgatan to get to the town centre.

Although first impressions of Boden are of a rather drab northern town, things get considerably more handsome around **Överluleå Church** (Överluleå kyrka; ⊕ 09.00–15.00 Mon–Fri) and its attendant church town, which were founded in 1826 and 1833 respectively. It's roughly a 20-minute walk from the train station, turning right into Strandplan once you've crossed Kungsbron bridge on

Kungsgatan. Pleasant enough in itself, the church's appeal benefits considerably from its location, perched on a hillock, surrounded by whispering birch trees and overlooking the water. Though much smaller in scale than Gammelstad, Boden's church town once spread down the hill to the lake, Bodträsket, with its 300 or so wooden cottages lining narrow little alleyways. Over the years, many of the buildings fell into disrepair; today around 30 cottages remain.

However, Boden's main focus is as Sweden's largest military town; seemingly everywhere you look you'll see young men in camouflage gear strutting purposefully (if somewhat ridiculously) up and down the streets. If you're interested in all things military, head for the **Defence Museum** (Försvarsmuseum; Granatvägen 2; 11.00–16.00 Tue–Sun; w boden.se/kommunen/kultur-och-fritid/forsvarsmuseum-boden; 60SEK), southwest of the town centre, which examines Sweden's defences from the 1800s onwards, concentrating on the strategic importance of Lapland, notably in defence against Russia.

HARADS AND TREEHOTEL

To be honest, Boden is not the sort of place you're likely to want to linger, and a much better idea is to press on northwest to the village of **Harads**, about 50km away along Route 97. True, it is barely more than a dot on the map, but it is surrounded by some glorious countryside, vast stretches of spruce forest and is home to one of Lapland's fastest-growing attractions: Treehotel.

 WHERE TO STAY, EAT AND DRINK

Arctic Bath Contact details as per Treehotel (see below). Opened in Jan 2020, Arctic Bath comprises 10 or so cabins, either elevated on poles by the lake's edge or actually floating on the water itself. They offer the last word in Nordic design, luxury & pampering. A stay here can be combined with a visit to the spa & wellness centre on site & is the perfect escape if you're in the money. *1-night stay starts at 9,600SEK.* €€€€

Treehotel `0928 103 00; e booking@treehotel.se; w treehotel.se. Harads is the location of the original Treehotel, found close to the banks of the Lule River at Edeforsväg 2A. Comprising a handful of stylish, ultramodern treetop cabins located on a south-facing ridge, the Treehotel is perfect for anyone looking for an unusual forest getaway – though, as you might expect, your back-to-nature experience in the tree canopy comes with a hefty price tag. Check out the website for the latest options since the cabins take various forms, including a giant bird's nest, a glass cube & even a UFO, suspended around 4–6m above the ground & accessed by ramp, bridge or electric stairs. Bathroom facilities & a restaurant are located in the nearby **guesthouse**, which also has regular dbl rooms for rent, decked out in vintage 1930–50s décor, both with (€€€€) & without (€€€) private facilities. *Prices at the Treehotel from 5,000SEK/night.* €€€€

WHAT TO SEE AND DO The Treehotel organises a whole host of summer and winter outdoor **activities**, ranging from yoga on ice (☼ winter only), elk safaris and meeting members of the local Sámi community. Full details and booking information is available on their website (see above).

For **dog-sledding** close to the Treehotel, look no further than Laplandhusky (m 070 563 64 40; e info@laplandhusky.com; w laplandhusky.com) who can be found in the hamlet of Krokfors, 23km northwest of Harads. Krokfors really is off-the-beaten-track remote, but don't let that put you off; this is the perfect opportunity to explore the vast expanses of empty countryside which dominate this part of Swedish Lapland. Run by expert guide Kim Jonsson, Laplandhusky offer a variety of different tours, including the rare opportunity to take part in a husky training week. Prices start from 1,790SEK for a 3-hour sled ride; if you're interested, full details can be found on their website.

STORFORSEN RAPIDS

Moving on from Harads, it's a straightforward journey of just under 90km along Route 97 northwest to Jokkmokk. Heading in the opposite direction (southwest from Harads) allows you to take in one of Swedish Lapland's greatest natural features. It's a drive of around 150km to Arvidsjaur, routing via the hamlet of Vidsel, from where it's a mere skip of 10km to the most impressive waterfall in the whole of northern Sweden: the magnificent Storforsen rapids.

Located on the Pite River, Storforsen is one of Europe's biggest white-water rapids, stretching over 5km and encompassing a drop of 82m, of which 60m is in one single fall. In times past, the river was used to transport timber to sawmills further downstream, though this practice has now died out throughout Sweden. Today the falls are part of a nature reserve which contains a number of marked hiking trails and picnic sites; large areas of the reserve are also accessible for people with disabilities. The rapids are surrounded by a fence to prevent accidents, but there are a number of viewing ramps which offer stupendous views of the thundering torrents of water which reach their peak around midsummer.

ARVIDSJAUR

Arvidsjaur (Árviesjávrrie in Sámi, meaning 'the lake of generous water' which refers to the good fishing in the eponymous local lake), 155km due west of Luleå, the same distance south of Jokkmokk and 100km to the southwest of the Storforsen rapids, lies in the heart of Sámi territory. Archaeological finds suggest that the Sámi lived in this area of northern Sweden long before the first settlers from the south arrived in the late 1500s. However, it was they who built the first chapel here in 1560 on the site of the original Sámi marketplace. In 1605, Karl IX declared Arvidsjaur a church town in order 'to Christianise the Lapp lands' and to make it easier for the Sámi to attend church. With the discovery of silver in the mountains to the northwest of the village in the 1620s, Arvidsjaur developed into a staging and supply town. The Sámi community existed in parallel to that of the silver pioneers, gathering on market days and for important religious festivals. In the 18th century, they built their own **church town**, a handsome collection of solid wooden huts known as **Lappstaden**, still standing today, which constitutes Arvidsjaur's main attraction.

Today, Arvidsjaur is best known as a leading winter test site for many of the world's top car manufacturers – the runway at the local airport is one of the longest in the north of Sweden which therefore enables international charter planes to land from across Europe. On the frozen lakes and various test tracks hereabouts, new car models and automobile equipment are put to the test in extreme weather conditions for several months each winter. Consequently, the test drivers are here in force each winter season and contribute greatly to the local economy.

GETTING THERE Appropriately enough, the **train station** is located on Järnvägsgatan, from where it is an easy 10-minute stroll up Stationsgatan to the tourist office on Storgatan. **Buses** arrive at the bus station on Västlundavägen, two blocks east of the tourist office. **Flights** from Stockholm arrive at the airport, 15km east of the centre; a taxi into Arvidsjaur costs around 350SEK. All public transport times can be found at w resrobot.se.

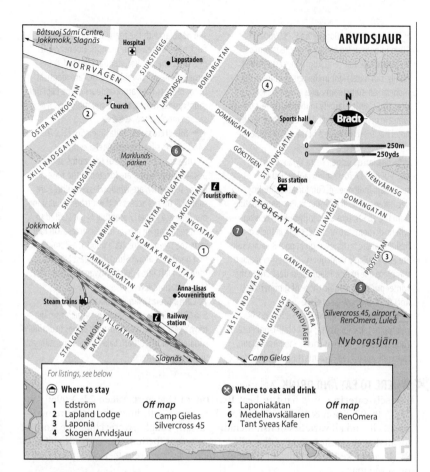

For listings, see below

Where to stay

1 Edström
2 Lapland Lodge
3 Laponia
4 Skogen Arvidsjaur

Off map

Camp Gielas
Silvercross 45

Where to eat and drink

5 Laponiakåtan
6 Medelhavskällaren
7 Tant Sveas Kafe

Off map

RenOmera

TOURIST INFORMATION The tourist office is right in the heart of things at Storgatan 13 (℡0960 175 00; e arvidsjaurlappland@arvidsjaur.se; w visitarvidsjaur. se; ⊕ mid-Jun–mid-Aug 09.00–17.00 Mon–Fri, 10.00–17.00 Sat, 11.00–17.00 Sun; rest of year 10.00–noon & 13.00–15.30 Mon–Fri), and can help with excursions and information about the Inlandsbanan. Alternatively, there's usually a second small tourist office at the train station (the wooden cabin just back from the platform near the station building) which is open in connection with train arrivals.

The variety of activities, both winter and summer, available from Arvidsjaur is in constant flux. While operators come and go, the tourist office always has the latest information about activities such as ice driving, elk safaris and dog-sledding in winter and kayaking and fishing in summer.

 WHERE TO STAY *Map, above*

☀ 🏠 **Skogen Arvidsjaur** Domängatan 9;
℡0960 28 10 00; e reception@skogenhotell.se;
w skogenhotell.se. Several of the town's oldest timber buildings, all beautifully surrounded by tall spruce trees, just a stone's throw from the main street, have been turned into hotel

accommodation. Interior design is a great mix of 50s styles with modern touches of wood & brass – the result is chic, smart &, frankly, rather desirable. Airy open veranda for summer dining, too. Free evening buffet for guests.
€€€€

🏠 **Edström** Stationsgatan 9; ☎0960 171 00; e info@hoteled.com; w hotelledstrom.se; ☺ closed late Jun–end Aug. Long-established family-run hotel right in the centre of town with modern, en-suite rooms, plus a gym & jacuzzi on site. Also catering largely to the winter test drivers who are in town for several weeks at a time, the hotel has tried to create a home-from-home atmosphere. €€€€

🏠 **Lapland Lodge** Östra Kyrkogatan 18; ☎0960 137 20; e info@laplandlodge. se; w laplandlodge.se. Comfortable, brightly decorated rooms in a former manor house dating from the 1850s, plus a recently built extension where all rooms are en suite; some in the old building share facilities. A great pool & sauna suite are also available to all guests altogether making this place one of Arvidsjaur's best deals. Note that winter prices are double those of summer. (Oct–Apr) €€€€/(May–Sep) €€€

🏠 **Laponia** Storgatan 45; ☎0960 555 00; e info@hotell-laponia.se; w hotell-laponia.se. Though not as smart as the Skogen Arvidsjaur, this well-appointed & comfortable place is still popular with the many test drivers who flock here in the winter months. Rooms come in 2 sizes: the smaller 'standard limited' & the larger 'premium' though facilities are identical. Décor reflects the natural colours of the Lapland countryside. There's a good swimming pool & sauna complex, too. €€€€

🏠 **Silvercross 45** Villavägen 56; m 070 644 2862; e silvercross45@telia.com; w silvercross45.se. Most of the rooms at this private youth hostel are located in the basement &, consequently, are windowless. Facilities are shared & there's access to the kitchen, a washing machine & a sauna. Reception is not staffed so be sure to ring on arrival to gain access. On foot, from the town centre, it's a good 15–20min walk; first head east along Storgatan, past Laponia, then turn left into Fjällströmsvägen, before the Statoil station. €€

⚠ **Camp Gielas** Järnvägsgatan 111; ☎0960 556 00; e gielas@arvidsjaur.se; w gielas.se. The town's year-round campsite with cabins beautifully situated beside Tvättjärn Lake, 1km or so southeast of the town centre. €

✘ WHERE TO EAT AND DRINK Map, page 53

For **self-catering**, it is hard to beat **RenOmera** (Larstorpsvägen 22; ☎0960 100 71; ☺ 09.00–noon & 13.00–17.00 Mon–Fri), which sells juicy chunks of reindeer meat, elk and all varieties of fish including locally caught Arctic char. The store is located at the eastern end of the village, just before the junction of routes 94 and 95. It is marked as 'Arvidsjaur Renslakt' or *renslakteri* (reindeer slaughterhouse) on some maps.

✘ **Medelhavskällaren** Storgatan 10; ☎0960 173 00; ☺ 10.30–21.00 Mon–Thu, 10.30–22.00 Fri, 11.00–22.00 Sat, 11.00–21.00 Sun. A large selection of pizzas from 80SEK & steaks, as well as a couple of Mediterranean-style dishes. €€

✘ **Laponiakåtan** Storgatan 45; ☎0960 555 00; ☺ Jun–Aug 11.00–14.00 & 17.00–22.00 Mon–Fri, noon–15.00 & 17.00–22.00 Sat & Sun. A cavernous building designed to resemble a Sámi *kåta* (tent) is the location of this summer-only restaurant across the main road from Laponia, which specialises in barbecued meats, including reindeer. Popular outdoor terrace at the rear overlooking the lake. €€

☕ **Tant Sveas Kafe** Stationsgatan 20; ☺ 09.00–16.00 Mon–Sat. The best café in town serving a range of speciality coffees & milkshakes as well as quiches, baked potatoes, salads & pancakes. They also have a range of homemade cakes using fresh berries. €

SHOPPING If you're looking for locally made handicrafts, **Anna-Lisas Souvenirbutik** (Stationsgatan 3; ☺ 09.30–17.30 Mon–Fri, 09.30–14.00 Sat; w presentbutiken.se) is a veritable treasure chest of goodies. With seemingly everything from hand-carved wooden spoons and woollen sweaters to leather rucksacks and jewellery, this is the place to come to browse to your heart's content. Quite simply, on your way to and from the train station, it's hard to walk by without succumbing to the urge to pop in and buy a knick-knack or two.

WHAT TO SEE AND DO

Lappstaden (☉ always open; free) From the tourist office, it is a walk of around 10 minutes northwest along the main street, Storgatan, and then right into Lappstadsgatan, to reach the fascinating Lappstaden, a tightly grouped cluster of square wooden huts, which make up the Sámi **church town**. The site is all the more remarkable since a couple of blocks of modern flats have been plonked unceremoniously next to the old buildings, making an awkward juxtaposition. Built in the 18th century as accommodation for people who couldn't make the journey to church and back in one day, 80 or so have survived today, thanks to the dogged preservation work of local schoolteacher, Karin Stenberg. Lappstaden is composed of 52 storage huts, raised off the ground on poles for added protection from the elements, and 29 *kåtor*, living-huts, about 4m² and with pyramid-shaped roofs. These dwellings are set on low wooden walls and built in traditional Forest Sámi style. They have a sloping trap door to allow the smoke from the fire to escape. Inside there was traditionally an earthen floor covered with birch twigs although now a concrete floor is more common. Today, the huts are still used during the **Storstämningshelgen Festival**, which takes place during the last weekend of August and is a great time to be in Arvidsjaur for the accompanying events such as reindeer lassoing competitions, musical concerts and all-round merriment.

Båtsuoj Sámi Centre (☎0960 65 10 26; e lotta@arctic-circle.se; w batsuoj.se) One of the most enjoyable things to do while staying in Arvidsjaur is to visit the centre in the village of **Gasa**, 70km west of the town along the E45 towards Slagnäs. This is not only one of the best places to see **reindeer** at close quarters, but it is also a chance to meet herders and learn more about their animals. Amazingly, there's a chance to see the dying art of milking a reindeer, a custom that was once commonplace when the Sámi lived a nomadic lifestyle and used everything their animals produced. A short visit to the centre of around an hour and a half, including coffee and a chance to taste dried reindeer meat while sitting around the fire in a *kåta*, costs 350SEK per person, or 550SEK with lunch included. A longer overnight visit, which also features information about the local flora and about the old shamanistic religion of the Sámi, is 1,300SEK and includes dinner and an overnight stay in sleeping bags on reindeer skins in a *kåta*. Breakfast is also included and there's free use of a boat and fishing equipment if desired.

Steam trains on the Inlandsbanan (☉ between mid-Jul & early Aug 17.45 Fri & Sat; w ångtågetarvidsjaur.se; 250SEK) Lapland is perhaps the last place you'd expect to find two ageing steam trains. Yet, Arvidsjaur is home to two graceful old ladies, built in 1912 and 1915, which were in service with SJ (Swedish national railways) until the late 1950s. Lovingly restored and maintained by local steam enthusiasts, the trains are still used every summer to pull vintage coaches from Arvidsjaur station west to Slagnäs, a journey of 53km along the Inlandsbanan. There's a licensed restaurant on board and on the return leg the train stops for around an hour at the southern shore of the sizeable (nearly 200km²) Storavan Lake for travellers to have a swim or a barbecue or just to relax on the sandy beach. Tickets can be bought on board the train and cost 250SEK, and the train gets back to Arvidsjaur for around 21.40.

The steam trains are kept behind the engine sheds at the corner of Tallgatan and Stallgatan, opposite the train station [map, page 53], should you want to see them up close.

Akkanålke Mountain and Auktsjaur spring For some truly spectacular views of the sweeping forest and mountainous terrain of this part of Lapland, head west along the E45 towards Slagnäs and take a left turn for Hedberg/Storberg (just before the hamlet of Kläppen). From opposite Järtajaure Lake, a car track leads off to the left for Akkanålke Mountain (750m). Translating from the Sámi as 'shoulder of the big mother', the peak is a sacred place to the local indigenous people and associated with a myth about the local Sámi woman, Rich Maja, born in 1661, who lived up here with her reindeer. Every morning she would don reindeer calfskins and, on her knees, play her magic drum so hauntingly that her reindeer would be enticed down from the fells and back to her farm.

Just beyond the turn that leads up to Akkanålke, there's a **sandy beach** in Storberg at the southern edge of **Järtajaure Lake**.

Heading in the opposite direction from Arvidsjaur, the E45 crosses the Inlandsbanan rail track after about 25km and passes through the hamlet of **Auktsjaur**. Just beyond the village there's a track leading off to the left, which leads to an enchanting **spring**, set deep in the forest, full of crystal-clear water around 6–7°C. The spring is just 150m from the gravel road and reached along a section of duckboarding.

ARJEPLOG

The 85km journey from Arvidsjaur northwest along Route 95 to Arjeplog (Árjepluovve in Sámi) passes through vast stretches of spectacular wilderness. Other than the odd isolated house, there are long stretches with no human habitation whatsoever. Indeed, this region is the most sparsely populated in the whole of Sweden; the municipality, which Arjeplog governs, is bigger than the whole of Northern Ireland (1.8 million inhabitants) yet has a falling population of less than 2,000 (in recent years Arjeplog has offered individuals 25,000SEK to relocate to the town). Understandably, Arjeplog is no megalopolis – there's really just one main street here, Storgatan, which branches off Route 95 and leads to what might, rather generously, be called the main square (essentially a car park), location for the **tourist office** inside the Silver Museum (Torget 1; ☏0961 145 00; e turist@ arjeplog.se; w arjeploglapland.se; ⊕ Jun–early Aug 09.00–17.00 daily; rest of the year 10.00–16.00 Mon–Fri, 10.00–14.00 Sat, Jan–Mar 14.00–18.00 Sun). Although wandering around little Arjeplog is pleasant enough, pausing by the water's edge and admiring Sweden's deepest lake, Hornavan (221m), there are two things you should see before you move on.

There are several daily **buses** between Arvidsjaur and Arjeplog; details available on w resrobot.se.

 WHERE TO STAY, EAT AND DRINK

🏠 **Hornavan Hotell** Skeppholmen 3; ☏0961 77 71 00; e info@hornavanhotell.se; w hornavanhotell.se. Offering wonderful views out over Hornavan, this comfortable, modern hotel is by far the best choice in Arjeplog. Rooms are bright & airy in modern Scandinavian style. €€€€/€€€

✗ **Frasses** Drottninggatan 2; ☏0961 101 01; ⊕ 11.00–20.00 Mon–Fri, 11.00–21.00 Sat & Sun. There's not exactly a lot of choice when it comes to eating in Arjeplog so chances are, sooner or later, you'll end up at this no-nonsense burger joint that rustles up something-&-chips for not very much. €

WHAT TO SEE AND DO

Silver Museum (Torget 1; ☏0961 145 00; w silvermuseet.se; ⊕ Jun–early Aug 09.00–17.00 daily; rest of the year 10.00–16.00 Mon–Fri, 10.00–14.00 Sat, Jan–Mar

14.00–18.00 Sun; 80SEK) Containing over 700 pieces of Sámi silver, the museum was founded by the former local doctor, Einar Wahlquist, who was posted to Arjeplog in the 1920s and promptly fell in love with it. He soon began collecting all manner of objects in an attempt to document the rich cultural history of the area in general and its Sámi population in particular. On display you'll see a number of highly ornate silver collars which were handed down from mother to daughter as well as other silver items such as belts, spoons and drinking cups. In the mid 1600s, silver was mined on Nasafjäll Mountain, northwest of Arjeplog close to the Norwegian border, and local Sámi were conscripted to transport the ore, using their reindeer, for smelting in Silbojokk, 60km away. Still today, Route 95, which links Arvidsjaur and Arjeplog with Norway, is known as Silvervägen.

Galtispuoda Mountain With your own transport, you're in for a treat: Galtispuoda is an 800m-high mountain just 15km north of Arjeplog which affords amazing views out over the surrounding wilderness. Get here by first heading back along the 95 towards Arvidsjaur and then by following the signs off to the left. On a clear day you can see all the way to Norway and easily pick out the numerous *eskers* (long gravel ridges) around Hornavan Lake which were left behind by retreating glaciers. Incidentally, Hornavan covers an impressive 260km² – the same size as the entire British city of Birmingham.

NORTHWEST TO JÄKKVIK AND VUOGGATJÅLME

From Arjeplog, Route 95 strikes out for the craggy chain of mountains which marks the border with Norway. The **views** on this stretch of the road are stunning – unlike in so many other parts of Swedish Lapland, the forest here is set back from the road, rising and falling over the surrounding hills, giving an awe-inspiring sense of the scale of the uninhabited territory you're passing through. Some 60km northwest of Arjeplog, the minuscule settlement of **Jäkkvik** is little more than a cluster of houses dependent on the tiny shop. From here, one of the least-walked sections of the **Kungsleden trail** (see box, page 58) heads across to **Adolfström**, a tiny village on Gautosjön Lake, 27km away, where the summer air is sweet with the smell of freshly scythed hay. The route makes an ideal day's hike through the beauty of the **Pieljekaise National Park**, just south of the Arctic Circle and contains the least disturbed flora and fauna in the entire Swedish mountains. There are simple hostel-style rooms and a **campsite** at Kyrkans Fjällgård (m 073 521 0369; e kyrkans. fjallgard@telia.com; w kyrkansfjallgardjakkvik.com; €).

Bus #104 operates between Arjeplog and Jäkkvik three times weekly (13.00 on Mon, Wed & Fri; 1hr); see w resrobot.se for details.

VUOGGATJÅLME Unpronounceable Vuoggatjålme (Sámi for 'fish hook channel'), 45km from Jäkkvik and just south of the Arctic Circle, is the ideal place to get away from it all. Only a handful of people live here, including the owners of the cabin accommodation in the hamlet (m 0961 107 15; e info@vuoggatjalme. se; w vuoggatjalme.se). The cabins couldn't be better situated, with views of Vuoggatjålmejaure Lake and the majestic snow-capped Tjidtjak Mountain (1,587m). From mid-June to mid-August they cost from 690SEK depending on size. If you're here in winter, bear in mind that Vuoggatjålme proudly boasts one of the coldest temperatures ever recorded in Sweden (–53°C, in 1966), although the minimum here is generally –40°C.

27km; 7hrs; moderate

One of the quieter sections of the Kungsleden trail begins in **Jäkkvik** to the northwest of Arjeplog and leads through the hauntingly beautiful **Pieljekaise National Park**. From the village shop walk back along the main road to the sign for Kungsleden car parking. The trail begins at the car park, climbing first through mountain birch forest before emerging on bare upland terrain dominated by **Mount Pieljekaise** (1,138m), which is said to look like a large ear (hence its name, which means just that in Sámi). From here, the views over the surrounding mountains are truly spectacular. The trail winds round the mountain and descends below the treeline into virgin birch woodland, carpeted with stately flowers like the northern wolfsbane, alpine sow-thistle and angelica. Pieljekaise National Park is also home to elk, bear, Arctic fox, wolverine, golden eagle and the gyrfalcon. It's a moderate 27km hike from Jäkkvik to **Adolfström** (all downhill after climbing out of Jäkkvik; allow 6–7 hours).

Cabin **accommodation** can be rented in Adolfström at Adolfströms Handelsbod och Stugby (❋ 0961 230 41; e info@adolfstrom.com; w adolfstrom.com; €) and Johanssons Fjällstugor (❋ 0961 230 40; e info@ fjallflygarna.se; w fjallflygarna.se; €); there's a village shop at the former.

Buses only leave Adolfström (the post box serves as the bus stop) three times weekly (17.00 on Mon, Wed & Fri; 1hr) for Arjeplog, so time your hike carefully and double-check the bus information at w ltnbd.se or w resrobot. se before setting out.

To hike on the Kungsleden trail from Abisko, see page 85.

The surrounding area offers superb **hiking** and a chance to enjoy nature. Björn operates a **helicopter service** which can take you right up into the mountains, allowing you to establish a base from which to strike out, thus avoiding the hassle of getting up there with heavy packs. An excellent trip takes you by helicopter (price on request) up to the **Pieskehaure cabins** (e fjallbokningen@stfturist.se; w swedishtouristassociation.com/facilities/ stf-pieskehaure-mountain-cabin; ◷ Mar–mid-May & Jul–early Aug; dorm beds €), stunningly located in the Arjeplogsfjällen Mountains, from where you can hike across to Kvikkjokk (64km; moderate – see page 63) and the Kungsleden in around three days. Before you leave, look carefully at the forest beside the main house – the eyes you might be lucky enough to see are likely to be those of elk, as there are dozens of them around the cottages.

JOKKMOKK

Winning the prize for Lapland's most unusual name, Jokkmokk (Jåhkåmåhkke in Lule Sámi; Dálvvadis in standard, northern Sámi) is the Swedish version of the original Sámi name, meaning 'bend in the river'. Squeezed into one particular *mokk* in the Lule River, the town of Jokkmokk, 160km north of Arvidsjaur, is one of Swedish Lapland's oldest settlements. In a royal reorganisation and categorisation of villages in Lapland in the 17th century, Karl IX decided that Jokkmokk, until then just a winter gathering place for the local Sámi, should have a church and a market. The winter market, known as **Jokkmokks marknad**, is still going strong over 400 years later. Held over the first weekend in February, the event draws around 30,000 people and is the best time to be in town, when the streets are full of stalls and any number of events.

Today Jokkmokk is a thriving, go-ahead sort of place that, together with the surrounding district, is home to around 2,800 people including a sizeable Sámi community. Indeed, there's not only a further education college teaching subjects such as reindeer husbandry and ecology entirely in Sámi, but also an interesting Sámi museum, Ájtte.

GETTING THERE Jokkmokk's **train** station is located on the northeastern edge of the town along Järnvägsgatan. However, Jokkmokk is not a big place and from here it is barely a 5-minute stroll up Stationsgatan to reach the town centre and the main street, Storgatan, which runs in an east–west direction. The **bus** station is centrally situated behind the Folkets hus building off Porjusvägen, which leads towards Storgatan.

TOURIST INFORMATION The **tourist office** (0971 222 50; e visit@jokkmokk.se; w destinationjokkmokk.se; ⊕ 09.00–noon & 13.00–16.00 Mon–Fri; during the winter market 09.00–18.00 Thu–Sat, noon–16.00 Sun) overlooks the main street from Stortorget 4.

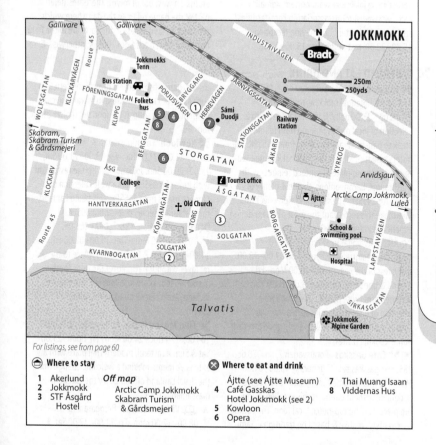

For listings, see from page 60

Where to stay

1 Akerlund
2 Jokkmokk
3 STF Åsgård Hostel

Off map
Arctic Camp Jokkmokk
Skabram Turism
& Gårdsmejeri

Where to eat and drink

Ájtte (see Ájtte Museum)
4 Café Gasskas
Hotel Jokkmokk (see 2)
5 Kowloon
6 Opera
7 Thai Muang Isaan
8 Viddernas Hus

🏠 WHERE TO STAY *Map, page 59*

🏠 **Akerlund** Herrevägen 1; ☎ 0971 100 12;
e info@hotelakerlund.se; w hotelakerlund.se.
Modern & stylish, the contemporary Scandinavian
design at this hotel is a treat to find in these parts.
With a more central location to boot, this newly
renovated hotel is altogether more pleasing than
its rival, the Jokkmokk, though its rooms tend to
be a little on the small side. On balance, though, a
sound choice. €€€€

🏠 **Jokkmokk** Solgatan 45; ☎ 0971 777 00;
e info@hoteljokkmokk.se; w hoteljokkmokk.
se. This lakeside hotel is a fine place to stay in
Jokkmokk, though you should go for a room
overlooking the lake (not the car park), if possible.
Huge restaurant in the shape of a *kåta* with Sámi
paintings & a stuffed reindeer for authenticity.
Fabulous sauna suite with attractive red & white
tiles in the basement. €€€€

🏠 **STF Åsgård Hostel** Åsgatan 20; m 070
366 4645; e jokkmokksvandrarhem@gmail.
com; w swedishtouristassociation.com/facilities/
stf-jokkmokk-hostel; ⏲ Jun–Aug reception
15.00–20.00; rest of the year 15.00–17.00.

Following a failed attempt to operate as a private
guesthouse, this old timber house from the 1920s
is now thankfully back under the watchful eye of
STF & open as the town's youth hostel. Rooms are
a bit on the cramped side & share facilities. Nice
location, though, set back in a pretty little garden
just off the main street. €

⛺ **Arctic Camp Jokkmokk** Notudden;
☎ 0971 123 70; e arcticcamp@jokkmokk.com;
w arcticcampjokkmokk.se. Beside the Lule River,
3km southeast of the town centre along Route
97. Tent pitch 195SEK. There are 2–6-berth cabins
here, too. €

⛺ **Skabram Turism & Gårdsmejeri** Skabram
206; ☎ 0971 107 52; e info@skabram.se;
w skabram.se. Friendly Richard & Patricia offer
comfortable, lakeside cottages & campsite
(complete with free-range chickens) in the village
of Skabram, 3km outside Jokkmokk (follow
Storgatan west out of town). The 'Gårdsmejeri'
part of the name refers to the dairy here which
produces its own cheese – the cows are in the field
next door. Tent pitch from 100SEK, otherwise €

✕ WHERE TO EAT AND DRINK *Map, page 59*

✕ **Hotel Jokkmokk** Solgatan 45; ☎ 0971
777 00; w hoteljokkmokk.se/restaurant-2;
⏲ 18.00– 23.00 daily. Hotel restaurant with a
selection of local dishes ranging from reindeer
steak to pan-fried rainbow trout from 255SEK. The
hotel's signature dish is the Jokkmokkspanna – a
mouth-watering plate of sautéed reindeer with
mushrooms, bacon, onions, thyme & plenty of
cream for 245SEK. The sweeping views over the
lake make this restaurant the most pleasant dining
experience in town. €€€

✕ **Ájtte** Kyrkgatan 3; ☎ 0971 170 70;
w restaurangajtte.se; ⏲ Jun–Aug 09.00–18.00
daily; rest of the year 09.00–16.00 Mon–Fri.
A good & popular choice for lunch (100SEK in
summer, otherwise 85SEK). Also good for a
selection of local specialities such as *renskav*,
souvas & Arctic char as well as some good Swedish
home-cooking dishes. €€

✳ ✕ **Café Gasskas** Porjusvägen 7; m 070 666
2853; w gasskas.se; ⏲ generally 16.00–01.00
Mon–Fri, though times are flexible. Don't leave
Jokkmokk without eating at this excellent Sámi-
run place, serving top-notch local food. The cuisine
is extremely creative & based on traditional Sámi

dishes (game, fish, berries) given a modern spin
such as Arctic char marinated in rowan leaves or
fermented birch soup. It's a good bet for live music,
too. €€

✕ **Kowloon** Föreningsgatan 3; ☎ 0971 100
56; ⏲ 11.00–21.00 Tue–Fri, 13.00–21.00 Sat,
13.00–20.00 Sun. Jokkmokk's Chinese restaurant
with lunch for 85SEK plus a wide selection of
Chinese mains from 115SEK. This being Lapland,
the restaurant serves pizzas from 80SEK. €

✕ **Opera** Storgatan 36; ☎ 0971 105 05;
⏲ 10.00–22.00 Mon–Thu, 10.00–01.00 Fri,
11.00–22.00 Sat & Sun. The best place to try
reindeer without paying over the odds (both
renskav & souvas are just 130SEK). Alternatives
include pizzas, Greek salad, *pytt i panna* or
schnitzel. €

✕ **Thai Muang Isaan** Porjusvägen 4; ☎ 0971
104 00; ⏲ 11.00–21.00 Mon–Fri, noon–21.00
Sat & Sun. A tasteful, modern Thai place with an
extensive menu, making a welcome change from
the usual Lapland offerings. Try the excellent
massaman curry. €

✳ ▭ **Viddernas Hus** Berggatan 10;
⏲ 08.00–17.00 Mon–Fri, 11.00–17.00 Sat. A

great café with plenty of Sámi influences on the menu & emphasis on homemade dishes using local produce including herbs & even angelica. Organic soups & quiches, too. €

SHOPPING Jokkmokk is a good place to pick up genuine Sámi handicrafts. At the small gallery and shop of **Sámi Duodji** (Porjusvägen 4; ⊕ 13.00–17.00 Mon–Fri, sometimes closed Tue), you will find a limited but tasteful collection of knives, jewellery and leatherware. The tourist office has a list of local handicraft producers who sell directly from their workshops.

Alternatively, **Jokkmokks Tenn** (Järnvägsgatan 19; w jokkmokkstenn.se; ⊕ 06.30–17.00 Mon–Thu, 06.30–15.00 Fri), one block north of the bus station, is a family-run business producing quality pewterware such as bowls, flower vases and ornate drinking spoons of Sámi design.

WHAT TO SEE AND DO
Ájtte Museum (Kyrkogatan 3; \0971 170 70; w ajtte.com; ⊕ mid-Jun–mid-Aug 09.00–18.00 daily; early May–mid-Jun & mid-Aug–mid-Sep 10.00–16.00 Tue–Fri, noon–16.00 Sat & Sun; rest of the year 10.00–16.00 Tue–Fri, noon–16.00 Sat; 90SEK) The best Sámi museum in Swedish Lapland, the appropriately named Ájtte (Sámi for 'storage hut') is the main sight in Jokkmokk and just a brief walk east along Storgatan from the town centre. Assembled around a circular apex known as the 'round room', the museum is composed of several exhibition halls detailing the life, culture and ecology of Lapland. Although labelling is in Sámi and Swedish only, it is easy to follow the displays, which begin with the pioneers who came to this part of Sweden in the 1600s, following on with a thorough section on traditional costumes and silver spoons. These gave the owner prestige and were an important status symbol in society. Next there is a display of taxidermy with a full-on display of the work of its resident taxidermist, Göran Sjöberg, whose stuffings have won several competitions: the collection of owls – including an eagle owl (*Bubo bubo*), Ural owl (*Strix uralensis*) and great grey owl (*Strix nebulosa*) – are truly impressive, and the massive golden eagle (*Aquila chrysaetos*) has to be seen to be believed. Ájtte rounds off with an animated virtual 3D helicopter flight over the Laponia World Heritage area, in the mountains northwest of Jokkmokk (see box, page 70), which is shown on nine vertical panels.

Jokkmokk Alpine Garden (Jokkmokks fjällträdgård; \0971 107 70; w ajtte.com/ jokkmokks-fjalltradgard; ⊕ mid-Jun–mid-Aug 11.00–17.00 daily; free) One block east of the museum, past the swimming pool and local school, a right turn from Storgatan into Lappstavägen will bring you to Jokkmokks fjällträdgård, a delightful alpine garden overflowing with local plant species. Even before the garden was established, the area along the banks of the Kvarnbäcken stream was particularly rich in alpine plants. Experts have now created areas within the garden that reflect the flora found in different habitats such as mountaintops, south-facing slopes, windy ridges and marshes. There's even a small section on edible plants that the Sámi have traditionally used.

Old Church (Gamla kyrkan; ⊕ not open to the public) Jokkmokk's first church was built in 1607 on the orders of Karl IX whose dream was to create an Arctic empire covering the whole of northern Scandinavia; churches were his way of nailing land for Sweden. A new church was built in 1753, but it burnt to the ground in 1972, leaving nothing but a pile of charred remains. Today, the church that stands on the same spot, between Köpmangatan and Västra Torggatan, is an exact replica of the original and is curiously still known by its politically incorrect name, Lappkyrkan. The church is surrounded by a double wooden wall that served as storage space for coffins (and bodies) during the winter months when the ground was frozen. Come the thaw, the coffins were then buried in the adjoining graveyard. The church's unusual octagonal design and oddly proportioned tower are of Sámi design, as are the colours of the interior – the blues, reds and yellows you will no doubt be familiar with from the Sámi flag.

The winter market With origins from 1602, when Karl IX decided there should be a market in Jokkmokk to generate tax revenue for his many wars, the great winter market is the event of the year in Swedish Lapland when Jokkmokk's population swells by ten times. Attracting over 30,000 visitors, this fun annual event is held on the first Thursday, Friday, Saturday and Sunday of February and it is a fantastic time to be in town, when the whole place takes on a Wild-West atmosphere. The streets are lined with stalls sagging under the weight of everything from bear skins to wooden knives – needless to say, much alcohol is consumed during the event and many people end up buying all sorts of unwanted knick-knacks. There are reindeer races held on the frozen lake, Talvatis, behind Hotel Jokkmokk, a fantastic spectacle as man and reindeer delight the crowds as they hurtle around the specially prepared track on the ice.

A smaller and less thrilling **historical market** is now held on the preceding Monday–Wednesday, when people dress in traditional costume and put on theatrical performances, speaking Swedish, naturally. It takes place at the eastern edge of the lake where Jokkmokk was first established.

Accommodation during the market is generally booked up two years in advance; if you fail to find anywhere to stay at the last minute, consider Arvidsjaur or Gällivare instead and take the bus into Jokkmokk.

Activities around Jokkmokk Between them, the local adventure companies, **Jokkmokkguiderna** (m 070 684 22 20; e jokkmokkguiderna@gmail.com; w jokkmokkguiderna.com) and **Laponia Adventures** (m 070 260 0537; e info@ laponiaadventures.com; w laponiaadventures.com) provide just about every kind of tour you can imagine. Both companies are based in Skabram (3km from Jokkmokk) and, in summer, specialise in kayaking, canoeing and hiking with little to choose between them, though Jokkmokkguiderna tends to be a little less expensive; a day's canoe rental, for example, booked with them, costs 400SEK. In winter Jokkmokkguiderna are into dog-sledding: between November and May they have any number of dog-sled safaris, starting with an hour's tour for 1,000SEK; while Laponia Adventures offer 3-hour snowmobile tours for 1,150SEK. There are full details of the myriad options available on the companies' websites.

MOVING ON FROM JOKKMOKK
Årrenjarka and Kvikkjokk Bus 47 runs to Kvikkjokk, passing Årrenjarka, from Jokkmokk once daily, terminating at Kvikkjokk church; timetables at w ltnbd.se.

Just 18km before Kvikkjokk, **Årrenjarka** (pronounced 'orr-uh-nyark-ah') is a truly idyllic little spot and a real find. Family-owned and operated since 1969, the cabin accommodation at this remote location in the mountains has a large following of devotees who come here for the wild, untamed landscapes (it's sandwiched between two mountains reaching over 900m) and the total stillness. Årrenjarka sits on a pretty, wooded promontory jutting out into Saggat Lake and faces west; all the cabins (some with their own saunas) are made of natural materials, furnished with wood-panelled interiors and have terraces looking out over the water. Plus, there's a campsite, restaurant and lounge bar here, too.

A classic Swedish mountain village, 127km northwest of Jokkmokk, **Kvikkjokk** (Huhtáan in Sámi) is surrounded by towering, snow-capped peaks reaching over 2,000m in height. The drive here along twisting Route 805 is one of the most stunning in Lapland, hugging the northern shore of the hauntingly beautiful ribbon-shaped Saggat Lake and offering jaw-dropping views of the unspoilt upland terrain that stretches north and west of here. Take a look at the map of this part of Sweden and you will soon see that man has made very few inroads in this remote corner of the country.

In the 17th century, tiny Kvikkjokk was at the centre of the silver-mining industry and even had its own smelting works. The famous botanist, Carl von Linné, visited in 1732 and was totally overwhelmed by the beauty of the mountains and their rich flora. Indeed, it was here as a schoolboy that the revivalist preacher Lars Levi Laestadius first developed an interest in botany, and also met the girl who was later to become his wife, Brita Cajsa Alstadius. The Laestadius family lived in Kvikkjokk from 1808 to 1816. Today, the main thing to see in the village is the pretty, **wooden church** which occupies the original site of the village's first church built in 1763. Although the present construction dates only from 1907, it remains one of the few examples of early 20th-century wooden church architecture in northern Scandinavia, since many other similar structures in Norway and Finland fell victim to the ravages of the Nazis' scorched earth policy. The interior is plainly decorated with white painted walls and simple pews.

 ### Where to stay, eat and drink

＊🏠 **ÅrreNjarka Fjällby** Årrenjarka 204; 📞0971 230 18; e info@arrenjarka.com; w arrenjarka.com. Cabins sleeping from 4 to 8 people. Those that sleep 4 share facilities in the service building, while the larger ones have an en-suite bathroom. The newest cabins also sleep 8 & have a private sauna. There are also 5 regular hotel rooms. 4-berth cabin €€€

🏠 **Kvikkjokk fjällstation mountain lodge** Storvägen 19; 📞0971 210 22; e info@kvikkjokkfjallstation.se;

w kvikkjokkmountainlodge.se; ⏱ late Feb–Apr & mid-Jun–Sep. Gorgeously situated beside the rushing torrents that form the upper reaches of the Lule River. Rooms have washbasins but otherwise share bathroom facilities, kitchen, & sauna. B/fast & evening meals. Dbl room/dorm bed €€/€

🔲 **Kvikkjokks Livs** Byavägen. A simple café at the entrance to Kvikkjokk beside the main road. Serves a range of fry-ups including reindeer burger & chips & meatballs, as well as coffee & cakes. There's also a small provisions store inside. €

Padjelanta National Park
Kvikkjokk is not only used as an access point to the **Kungsleden trail** (page 85), which passes through the settlement, but as a gateway for one of Sweden's most spectacular national parks: **Padjelanta**, whose Sámi name, Badjelánnda, translates as 'the higher country'. This is the biggest national park in the country and, as its original name suggests, the park is situated almost exclusively atop a reindeer-grazing mountain plateau, generally above the treeline. It's a popular destination with hikers in the know, since the **Padjelanta trail** which traverses the park on its 150km span from Kvikkjokk to Vaisaluokta (near Ritsem, page 70) not only sees less traffic than the better-known Kungsleden, but it's also relatively flat and easy going.

Whether you're walking the entire trail or simply flying in and out by helicopter for a short visit (page 65), one of the main places of interest in the park is **Staloluokta**, an ancient Sámi mountain camp named after the Sámi god or holy spirit, Stálo (the 'luokta' element of the name is the Sámi word for a 'bay'), tucked up close to

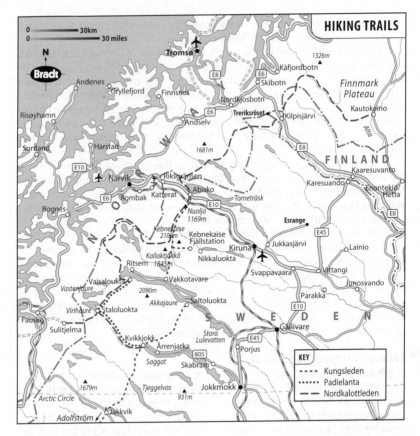

0 ——— 30km
0 ——— 30 miles

N

Bradt

Tromsø

Andenes
Gryllefjord
Finnsnes
Nordkjosbotn
Kåfjordbotn
1326m
Skibotn

Finnmark
Plateau

Risøyhamn
Andselv
Treriksröset
Kilpisjärvi
Kautokeino

Sortland
Harstad
1681m
FINLAND

Kaaresuvanto

Narvik
Riksgränsen
Karesuando
Enontekiö/
Hetta

Rombak
Katterat
Abisko
Torneträsk

Bognes
Nuolja
1169m

Kebnekaise
2106m
Kebnekaise
Fjällstation

Esrange

Kallaktjåkkå
Ritsem 1845m
Nikkaluokta
Kiruna
Jukkasjärvi
Lainio

Vaisaluokta
2090m
Vakkotavare
Svappavaara
Vittangi
Junosvando

Vastenjaure
Akkajaure
Saltoluokta
Parakka

Virihaure
Staloluokta
SWEDEN
Gällivare

Fauske
Sulitjelma
Kvikkjokk
Stora
Lulevatten
Porjus

Årrenjarka

Saggat
Skabram

KEY

1679m
Tjeggelvas
Jokkmokk
931m
- - - - Kungsleden
· · · · · Padielanta
— · — · Nordkalottleden

Arctic Circle
Jäkkvik
Adolfström

the Norwegian border and home to around 50 people during the summer months. What makes this place so special is its enchanting location atop two adjoining hillsides, one of which is forested, beside the shores of what are widely regarded to be the two most beautiful lakes in Sweden: **Virihaure** and **Vastenjaure**. Although technically two expansive mountain tarns, these serene, tooth-shaped bodies of water give the impression of being a single lake, perfectly located to catch the moody reflections of the surrounding, round-topped mountains. The camp has been used by generations of Sámi as a base for reindeer herding and as an important source of fresh fish from the two lakes. Today, in addition to the handful of modern cottages, which account for the mainstay of the dwellings here, there are also several wooden storehouses raised off the ground on stilts and traditional wooden *kåtor* bedecked with turf roofs. Indeed, one *kåta* is even the location for the village church – it's easy to spot; just look for the rickety wooden cross perched on the roof and the nearby diminutive bell tower.

Located beside the gurgling stream that tumbles down from the surrounding mountains providing the settlement with a vital supply of fresh water, you'll find the simple **cabin** which provides **accommodation** to passing hikers and visitors – there are also a couple of signposts dotted around the settlement giving directions to the cabin. Run by **Badjelánnda Laponia turism** (m 070 281 3003; e padjelanta@ padjelanta.com; w padjelanta.com; ⊕ late Jun–early Sep; €), the cabin has seven four-bed dorms and two double rooms (rather grandly known as VIP rooms). A model of green efficiency, its water is drawn from the neighbouring stream using a hand pump outside, while electricity is provided by solar panels. Naturally, as there's no running water, toilets are of the dry variety and are housed in a separate hut outside, while separate-sex bathrooms in the cabin itself are sluice-you-down affairs. There's a wood-burning sauna available for guest use, beside the stream down behind the cabin, perfect for soothing aching muscles after a long day on the trail; for the brave there's the option of an invigorating dip in the mountain stream, too.

Getting to Staloluokta and Padjelanta From Kvikkjokk, the Padjelanta trail leads northwest to Staloluokta passing through some spectacularly wild and lonely landscapes. This stretch of the trail also doubles up as part of the Nordkalottleden (see box, below); it's around 80km from Kvikkjokk to Staloluokta on foot, for which you should allow around four to five days. Much faster, and arguably more breathtaking, is the **helicopter** ride up to Staloluokta: **Fiskflyg** (✆ 0973 400 32; w fiskflyg.se) operate one daily flight in both directions between late June and August; book well in advance. True, the trip's not cheap (1,450SEK single; 30mins), but the views as you scud across some of Sweden's most remote and unsullied terrain are quite overwhelming. From late June to early August, Fiskflyg also fly once daily between Staloluokta and **Ritsem**, at the other end of the Padjelanta trail (1,450SEK single; 30mins), hence making it possible to fly all the way between Kvikkjokk and Ritsem via Staloluokta. In Staloluokta, there are two helipads located side-by-side

THE NORDKALOTTLEDEN TRAIL

Stretching a whopping 800km and traversing no fewer than three countries, the Nordkalottleden trail is one of Europe's least well-known hiking routes. In the south, the trail has two starting points: Kvikkjokk in Swedish Lapland and Sulitjelma in Norway (just across the border from Sweden's Staloluokta, page 63). Over its entire length, the trail is marked with stone cairns and signs, and it crosses the national borders of Finland, Norway and Sweden a total of ten times. At Staloluokta, the two starting trails join up and head northeast towards Vaisaluokta (near Ritsem, page 70), covering the same course as the Padjelantaleden, another of Swedish Lapland's long-distance hiking trails which runs through Padjelanta National Park between Kvikkjokk and Ritsem. After a detour that hugs the Norwegian–Swedish border, the trail then veers northwards and joins the Kungsleden for the section between Kebnekaise and Abisko. From here, the trail cuts across into Norway and strikes a course directly for the three-nation border post, Treriksröset (page 132) and Finnish border town of Kilpisjärvi. After another excursion into Norway and a change of direction, the route then finally heads southeast for its destination at Kautokeino in Norwegian Lapland. Naturally, nobody hikes the whole trail given the extreme distances involved, but sections of it are becoming increasingly popular with seasoned hikers looking for new challenges; the trail encompasses northern fell landscapes, lush birch forests, glaciers and steep-sided gorges, and stretches 380km in Norway, 350km in Sweden and 70km in Finland. It is open from July to mid-September. Unfortunately, very little material exists in English about the trail but an extremely detailed description is presented in Swedish at w karesuando.se/kdo/nordkalottleden.htm which Google does a passable job of translating.

3

below the settlement on the lakeshore; in Kvikkjokk the heliport is at the entrance to the village beside the main road and all buses in and out of the village go by; in Ritsem the heliport is also located towards the entrance to the village, beside the main road, and is served by all buses to and from Gällivare.

GÄLLIVARE

After the remote villages of the Swedish mountains, modern, go-ahead Gällivare (pronounced '*yelly-vaa-reh*'; Jiellevárre in Sámi), 90km north of Jokkmokk, comes as a welcome oasis. Although the indigenous Sámi had lived hereabouts for generations, it wasn't until the arrival of the railway line to Luleå in 1888 that the town began to grow. The newly opened mines, now one of the most important sources of iron ore in Europe, began to expand, and, indeed, Gällivare owes its very existence to mines located up the road in neighbouring Malmberget. Today, Gällivare is also an important railway junction as it's the terminus of the great Inlandsbanan railway (see box, page 69) that runs here in summer all the way from Mora in the province of Dalarna, over 1,000km away, as well as offering services on the Malmbanan between Narvik and Luleå. The town is home to around 8,500 people (including a sizeable Sámi community), many of whom are employed in iron-ore production. Incidentally, an unusually large number of local people have been found to suffer from the rare genetic disorder, CIPA, which stops the body from feeling pain or reacting to extremes of temperature; there are almost as many reported cases in the Gällivare district as in the entire United States.

GETTING THERE Trains run to Gällivare from Kiruna, Luleå and Narvik all year round, as well as from Arvidsjaur and Jokkmokk on the Inlandsbanan between June and mid-August, generally arriving around 21.30. The train station is at Centralplan 3; **buses** use the adjoining bus station. All public transport times are available online at w resrobot.se.

TOURIST INFORMATION Located at the train station, Gällivare's **tourist office** (Centralplan 4; ☏ 0970 102 20; e info@welcometogallivare.com; w welcometogallivare.com; ⊕ 08.00–18.30 Mon–Fri) also has bike rental (199SEK per day) and in winter even rents out kick-sledges (*spark* in Swedish).
Kayaks and canoes can be rented through Laponia Adventures (page 62) and Midnight Sun Adventure at Dahlsgatan 13 (m 070 577 1277; e hakan.ostlund65@ bredband.net).

Hiking and national park information Above the tourist office, the **Laponia Visitor Center** (Centralplan 4; ☏ 0973 410 10; e info@laponia.nu; w laponia.nu; ⊕ 08.00–18.30 daily) is the place to get the very latest information and advice if you're planning a trip into the national parks northwest of Gällivare. The knowledgeable staff here can help with trail suggestions, accommodation bookings and transport queries.

 WHERE TO STAY *Map, opposite*
🏠 **Scandic Gällivare** Klockljungsvägen 2; ☏ 0970 162 00; e gallivare@scandichotels. com; w scandichotels.com. Now part of the huge Scandic chain yet still with an emphasis on personal service, this rather expensive hotel offers rooms designed to create a home-from-home feeling with neutral colours, parquet floors & modern Scandinavian fittings. There's a swimming pool, 2 separate-sex saunas & jacuzzi here, too. €€€€

🏠 **Quality Lapland** Lasarettsgatan 1; ☎ 0970 77 22 90; e info@qhl.nu; w qhl.nu. Tastefully renovated & extended & now part of the Quality chain, this hotel is the smartest in town & now boasts a rooftop pool, sauna & open-air restaurant. Rooms are bright, airy & thoroughly Scandinavian in design with lots of subtle, natural colours. €€€€

🏠 **Pensionat Augustin** Tinghusgatan 3; ☎ 0970 550 40; e info@pensionataugustin.se; w pensionataugustin.se. Homely, good-value guesthouse in the centre of town with individually decorated dbls sharing facilities (sink in all rooms). Larger apts are also available in the building next door, sleeping up to 5 people (from €€€). €€€

🏠 **Bed & Breakfast Gällivare** Laestadiusvägen 18; ☎ 0970 156 56; e marita. johansson@telia.com; w bbgaellivare.se. A 15min walk from the centre to this cheery little B&B set in a quiet residential street. Charming owner, Marita, will do her utmost to make you feel at home & offers a free pickup for guests arriving on the Inlandsbanan. Rooms share facilities & there's a kitchen for self-catering. B/fast is an extra 80SEK. 4–6-berth cabins also available (€€). €€

🏠 **Stay in Gellivare** Lasarettsgatan 3; m 070 355 5430; e eltek1@hotmail. com; w inlandsbanan.se/res/stay-gellivare. Immediately opposite the train station, bright & airy youth hostel-standard shared dbl rooms with shared facilities that also have access to a sauna & kitchen. Excellent value for money. €€

🏠 **Gällivare Camping** Kvarnbacksvägen 2; ☎ 0970 100 10; e info@gellivarecamping.com; w gellivarecamping.se. A pleasant riverside campsite off the E45 towards Jokkmokk open all year which also functions as a youth hostel. Dorm beds in the YH section available for 270SEK pp. Dbl rooms €€ & cabins from €€

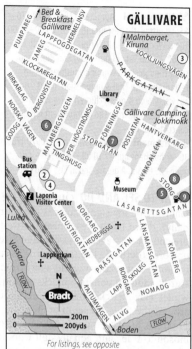

For listings, see opposite

🛏 **Where to stay**

1 Pensionat Augustin
2 Quality Lapland
3 Scandic Gällivare
4 Stay in Gellivare

Off map
Bed & Breakfast Gällivare
Gällivare Camping

✖ **Where to eat and drink**

5 Alla Tiders
6 Husmans
7 Manuella
8 Nittaya Thai
9 Nyfiket
Quality Lapland (see 2)

✖ WHERE TO EAT AND DRINK *Map, above*

✖ **Quality Lapland** Lasarettsgatan 1; ☎ 0970 77 22 90. The hotel's steakhouse is the place for well-prepared Lapland specialities, such as oven-baked Arctic char & succulent reindeer steak. €€€

✖ **Alla Tiders** Storgatan 18; ☎ 0970 102 54; ⏰ 10.30–18.00 Mon, Tue, Thu, 10.30–16.00 & 21.00–01.00 Wed, 10.30–16.00 & 21.00–02.00 Fri, 11.00–16.00 & 21.00–02.00 Sat. Fun, stylish bar & bistro (check out their multi-coloured chairs) which serves up quiches, salads & a variety of tasty

sandwiches daytime & then mutates into a bar with late opening 3 days a week. €

✖ **Manuella** Storgatan 9; ☎ 0970 123 80; w manuella.nu; ⏰ 14.00–21.00 Mon–Fri, 13.00–21.00 Sat, 13.00–20.00 Sun. The place in Gällivare for a range of pizzas, including deep pan (100SEK) &, unusually, genuine mozzarella pizzas, too. (Swedish pizzas generally bear but a passing resemblance to their Italian cousins.) Steaks & pasta dishes, too. €

✘ Nittaya Thai Storgatan 21B; ☏0970 176 85; w nittayathairestaurant.se; ⊕ 10.00–21.00 Tue & Wed, 13.00–21.00 Thu, 10.00–22.00 Fri, 13.00–22.00 Sat, 13.00–20.00 Sun. None too spicy though still a winning southeast Asian restaurant with Thai & Indonesian mains, such as *nasi goreng* & green chicken curry which makes a change from the omnipresent reindeer concoctions. €

⌷ Husmans Malmbergsvägen 1; ☏0970 170 30; w husmans.nu; ⊕ 10.00–20.00 Mon–Fri, noon–20.00 Sat. A greasy-spoon fast-food café

that serves the set lunch (100SEK) all day until it runs out. Also dishes up lasagne, schnitzel & meatballs with mashed potato. €

⌷ Nyfiket Lasarettsgatan 19; ☏0970 149 40; ⊕ 06.00–16.00 Mon–Fri. Gällivare's popular café & bakery serving fresh bread baked on the premises, open sandwiches, pastries & cakes. For the linguistically curious, the name is a play on words, combining the Swedish for 'curious', *nyfiken*, with 'new café', *nyfiket*. Leave feeling smug but sated. €

WHAT TO SEE AND DO Other than the mines described below, the only sight in Gällivare of any significance is the church, **Lappkyrkan** (⊕ Jun–Aug 10.00–16.00 daily), down by the river, near the western end of Prästgatan. Known as the 'one öre church' – as every household in Sweden had to contribute the princely sum of one öre (100th of a krona) towards its construction in 1747 – it is a delicate timber building that seems a world apart from the rest of the town centre, composed of sturdy, modern concrete blocks with quadruple-glazing against the biting Arctic winter. Having ticked off the church, you might want to have the briefest of glances around the town **museum** at Storgatan 16 (⊕ 11.00–15.30 Mon, Tue, Thu & Fri, 11.00–20.00 Wed, noon–14.00 Sat; free), though its collection of coffee cups, mosquito traps and equally dull wood carvings by local man, Martin Stenström, who spent all his life living alone in a cabin in the woods, is unlikely to excite.

Iron-ore mine Located up in Malmberget (effectively a suburb of Gällivare, a 10-minute drive away), mining giant LKAB's underground iron-ore mine (⊕ mid-Jun–mid-Aug 09.00–noon Mon–Fri; 300SEK; book at the tourist office) is well worth seeing. A bus takes visitors deep inside Malmberget Mountain, driving 40km or so to one of the points where iron ore is sliced out of the earth at a depth of 1,000m below ground. Here you will see LKAB's giant 90-tonne earth-moving trucks, which emit a truly deafening noise, and learn more about the hi-tech mining operations on which Gällivare is so dependent for survival.

Midnight sun tours Dundret hill up behind Gällivare is a favourite destination for midnight-sun spotters; special buses run from the train station to the end of the winding road up the hill (early Jun–early Aug 22.00 daily; 395SEK) and the trip includes a slideshow and history of Malmberget. Tickets are available at the tourist office and include coffee and cakes. Bear in mind that, on cloudy days, you won't actually see the sun, of course, though it will still be light.

Adventure activities In winter, snowmobiling and dog-sledding are popular activities from Gällivare – and, what's more, you'll pay much less here than at Icehotel up the road near Kiruna. For example, a full day out snowmobiling costs 2,495SEK when booked through **Sledrental** at Cellulosavägen (☏ 070 284 9994; e info@sledrental.se; w sledrental.se) – half of what Icehotel charges for the same activity. Laponia Adventures (page 62) is another local adventure company specialising in guided hiking tours into Stora Sjöfallet and, more adventurously, into Sarek National Park both in winter and in summer; prices vary but details are on the website.

SWEDEN'S GREAT INTERIOR RAILWAY: THE INLANDSBANAN

The idea of building a railway through the heart of Sweden was first mooted in the late 1800s, though it wasn't until 1937 that the entire stretch from Kristinehamn on Lake Vänern to Gällivare, a distance of 1,288km, was completed. Built in stages, and traversing some of Sweden's wildest and most remote terrain, the Inlandsbanan was conceived as a means of developing some of the country's most sparsely populated regions and of aiding the ongoing process of industrialisation. The Swedish parliament was also keen to build a new railway through the interior, away from the existing coastal rail line, which, it was deemed, could easily fall into enemy hands in the event of war. However, the 50s and 60s saw a dramatic increase in car ownership and passenger numbers on the line began to decline. Service reductions and partial line closures followed; passenger trains ceased in 1969 on large parts of the southern stretch of the line south of Mora and the axe finally fell in 1992 when SJ declared the entire operation financially unviable.

Keen to breathe new life into the Inlandsbanan, the 15 municipalities along the line clubbed together and created the private company which today administers it and runs tourist-oriented summer services between Gällivare and Mora, a two-day journey of 1,067km with an overnight stop in Östersund. Today, a trip on the Inlandsbanan is, of course, a means of getting from A to B, but it's much more about the experience of travelling through Sweden's remote, uninhabited interior – crossing the Arctic Circle on the way. Throughout the journey, the train conductor provides commentary in English and Swedish, picking out points of interest (perhaps, a beaver damming a stream; reindeer grazing in the forest; or quirky facts about the line itself) and the train pulls up now and then for a refreshment stop and a chance to stretch your legs; the tyranny of the timetable is not something the Inlandsbanan subscribes to. Full information, including ticket prices and details about the rail freedom pass (*Inlandsbanekort*) is at w inlandsbanan.se.

MOVING ON FROM GÄLLIVARE Between early June and mid-August the one-carriage diesel railcar that is the **Inlandsbanan** trundles daily down the single-line track bound for Östersund, 750km to the south, calling at Jokkmokk, the Arctic Circle, Arvidsjaur and all points south; departure is usually around 07.45. It is possible to reach Jokkmokk, Arvidsjaur (and Pajala) by **bus**; services operate daily and timetables are available at w ltnbd.se and w resrobot.se. All-year daily services run northwest to Kiruna and on towards Narvik as well as southeast to Luleå; connections are available at Boden for Stockholm and Gothenburg. Though do see the box on page 50.

RITSEM AND THE STORA SJÖFALLET NATIONAL PARK

Ritsem, a remote mountain village 185km northwest of Gällivare and 195km northwest of Jokkmokk, is located within the heart of the Stora Sjöfallet National Park, which preserves an area of alpine landscape, with imposing mountain ridges, boulder-strewn high plains and ancient pine forest. Before the construction of a hydro-electric power station in the early 1900s, the waterfalls, at the centre of the park, were some of the largest and visually striking in Europe; today, the falls area and the adjoining **Akkajaure Lake** no longer form part of the national park and effectively divide it

The Laponia World Heritage area is an inconceivably vast expanse of mountainous wilderness covering 9,400km² where the ancestral way of life of the Sámi, based on the seasonal movement of their reindeer, is still practised. Encompassing no fewer than four national parks (Muddus, Stora Sjöfallet, Sarek and Padjelanta) and two nature reserves (Stubba and Sjaunja), it stretches from just north of Jokkmokk all the way northwest, roughly in the shape of an arc, towards the Norwegian border. Laponia, the Latin term for Lapland, was established in 1996 by UNESCO, in order to preserve this unique area for future generations; traces of human remains up to 7,000 years old have been found. Despite the presence of three major hydro-electric power stations in Laponia, the region is still considered to be the largest area of transhumance in the world. Laponia is accessed most readily along the (unnumbered) 140km-long road from Porjus, which lies midway between Jokkmokk and Gällivare; the road ends at Ritsem.

in two. The lake is sandwiched between two of Lapland's highest mountains: to the south, **Áhkká**, known as the Queen of Lapland, which rises to a height of 2,015m with its glaciers; and to the north, **Kallaktjåkkå**, at 1,810m. There are only really two settlements of note in the park: tiny Ritsem, which perches on Akkajaure's northern shore, and even more diminutive **Vaisaluokta**, opposite on the southern shore; both are Sámi villages and are connected in summer by a boat service aimed at hikers. Indeed, Stora Sjöfallet is regularly visited by people walking both the **Kungsleden trail** (which cuts through on its way north to Abisko and south to Kvikkjokk; page 85) and the 140km long **Padjelanta trail**, which begins at Ritsem/Vaisaluokta. The **Nordkalottleden trail** also runs through the park; it heads west from Vaisaluokta on its way towards Kebnekaise via the Norwegian border. Naturally, hiking in any of the national parks is not something to undertake on a whim as the weather can often be challenging. (They are subject to heavy rain in summer.) There's more information about all Swedish Lapland's national parks at w fjällen.nu as well as from the tourist offices in Jokkmokk and Kiruna and the Laponia Visitor Center in Gällivare.

GETTING THERE By **road**, Ritsem and Stora Sjöfallet are accessed along the 140km route which heads northwest from Porjus, itself is located on the E45 route and the Inlandsbanan. **Bus** 93 covers this route once or twice daily on its 3-hour journey to and from Gällivare; timetables are at w ltnbd.se and w resrobot.se. From Ritsem, a **boat** sails over Akkajaure to Vaisaluokta in conjunction with the bus's arrival from Gällivare to give access to the Padjelanta and Nordkalottleden trails; details at w stfturist.se/ritsem. En route to Ritsem, the bus calls at Kebnats, where there's connecting **boat** access to and from the southbound Kungsleden and the Saltoluokta mountain lodge (not to be confused with Staloluokta) and at Vakkotavare, where the Kungsleden continues northwards; boat details for Kebnats are at w stfturist.se/saltoluokta. For details of the **helicopter** service to and from Ritsem, see page 65.

WHERE TO STAY, EAT AND DRINK For accommodation, there's an STF mountain cabin in **Ritsem** (☏010 190 2450; e ritsem@stfturist.se; w stfturist.se/ritsem; ⊕ Mar, Apr & late Jun–early Sep; dorm beds 500SEK; **€€**), with self-catering facilities, and a simpler STF hut at **Vaisaluokta** (⊕ late Jun–early Sep; w stfturist.se/vaisaluokta; dorm beds 450SEK; **€€**). Across from Kebnats, the well-appointed **Saltoluokta**

mountain lodge (✆ 010 190 2350; e fjallbokning@stfturist.se; w stfturist.se/saltoluokta; ☉ late Feb–late Apr & mid-Jun–late Sep; dorm bed 420SEK; €€€€) is a quite luxurious affair with its own restaurant.

KIRUNA

Swedish Lapland's best-known and most northerly town is Kiruna (pronounced with stress on the first syllable: KIR-oona, *not* kir-OON-a; Giron in Sámi), 127km north of Gällivare. Of course, its fame stems from nearby Icehotel which has been instrumental, over the years, in sending planeloads of tourists, and their kronor, Kiruna's way. Many arrive expecting a Swedish version of Florence or Paris – but with snow. They couldn't be more misguided. Kiruna is no tourist town; indeed, this hard-bitten, northern outpost owes its (mis)fortune to the ugly, brooding iron-ore mines that drive the local economy, yet they are also the cause of its current woes. Subsidence from the mines over a kilometre below the town is causing the ground to slip. Although it was decided in 2004 that the town would have to be relocated, it was only in 2012 that things really got going once Kiruna's new location had been finally decided – close to the airport in an area known as Tuolluvaara, around 7km east of the current town. In August 2013, the railway station was closed and a new station is now in operation 1.5km outside town, linked to the bus station by shuttle bus (page 73).

Swedish and Norwegian architects are now designing a new city centre a couple of kilometres away. It will be much more compact than the old one with a focus on sustainability, green architecture, pedestrians and public transport, rather than cars. However, new Kiruna won't be ready until around 2035 – expect disruption for the foreseeable future as the old town is torn down bit by bit and the E10 road is rerouted. Although most of the existing buildings will simply be demolished, the Stadshus and the church (both considered to be of architectural significance; page 74) will be dismantled and moved to the new Kiruna. Surprisingly, local people seem remarkably unperturbed by the prospect of their homes sinking beneath their feet, perhaps because the move is being funded by the state-owned mining company, LKAB, which is promising to build brand-new homes for everybody affected, and because without the mines Kiruna would cease to exist.

SOME HISTORY Although the Sámi had lived on the tundra around what is now Kiruna for countless generations, the first pioneers from the south came here in the early 1600s. They opened an iron-ore mine in 1647, yet it took a further two centuries for test drilling for ore to commence in Kiirunavaara Mountain, at whose foot the town was later to be founded. The decision by the Swedish parliament to build a railway line to transport the ore to Luleå (and later Narvik) for shipping abroad proved a significant turning point in the town's development and provided the basis of Sweden's economic prosperity in the 19th century. However, not all MPs were in favour of the new-fangled railway; one even declared 'it serves no purpose to build railways over mountains and rivers … to lead them in the opposite direction to cultivation, and all this to receive a few wagonloads of butter and ptarmigan'.

Despite misgivings in Stockholm, the line went ahead, reaching Kiruna at the turn of the 20th century; and just two years later the final section to Narvik was opened by King Oscar II in 1903. From 1900 onwards, people were beginning to spend the winter in Kiruna, the population snowballed and by 1910, Kiruna counted a respectable 7,500 inhabitants. Keen to avoid the mistakes of Malmberget

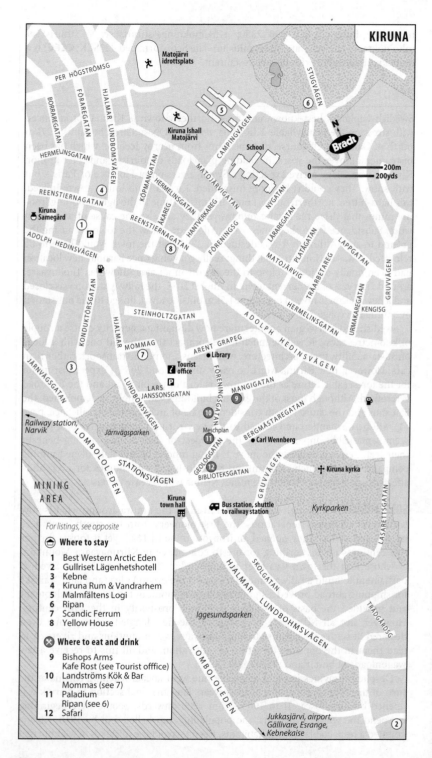

KIRUNA

Matojärvi idrottsplats

PER HÖGSTRÖMSG

BORRAREGATAN
FÖRAREGATAN
HJALMAR LUNDBOMSVÄGEN

HERMELINSGATAN

Kiruna Ishall Matojärvi

STUGVÄGEN

⑥

N

Bradt

0 ———————— 200m
0 ———————— 200yds

CAMPINGVÄGEN
MATOJÄRVIGATAN

⑤

School

NYGATAN

REENSTIERNAGATAN

④

Kiruna Samegård

① P

ADOLPH HEDINSVÄGEN

P

KÖPMANGATAN
HERMELINSGATAN
ÅKAREG
REENSTIERNAGATAN
HANTVERKAREG
FÖRENINGSG

⑧

LÄRAREGATAN
MATOJÄRVIG
PLATÅGATAN
TRÄARBETAREG
HERMELINSGATAN
URMAKAREGATAN
LAPPGATAN
GRUVVÄGEN
KENGISG

KONDUKTÖRSGATAN

STEINHOLTZGATAN

ADOLPH HEDINSVÄGEN

HJALMAR

MOMMAG

⑦

ARENT GRAPEG

● Library

JÄRNVÄGSGATAN

③

Tourist office

P

LARS JANSSONSGATAN

LUNDOMSVÄGEN

FÖRENINGSGATAN

MANGIGATAN

⑨

⑩

BERGMÄSTAREGATAN

Railway station, Narvik

LOMBOLOLEDEN

Järnvägsparken

STATIONSVÄGEN

Meschplan

⑪

● Carl Wennberg

GRUVVÄGEN

✝ Kiruna kyrka

GEOLOGGATAN

⑫

BIBLIOTEKSGATAN

MINING AREA

Kiruna town hall

🚌 Bus station, shuttle to railway station

Kyrkparken

LASARETTSGATAN

For listings, see opposite

⊖ **Where to stay**

1 Best Western Arctic Eden
2 Gullriset Lägenhetshotell
3 Kebne
4 Kiruna Rum & Vandrarhem
5 Malmfältens Logi
6 Ripan
7 Scandic Ferrum
8 Yellow House

⊗ **Where to eat and drink**

9 Bishops Arms
 Kafe Rost (see Tourist offfice)
10 Landströms Kök & Bar
 Mommas (see 7)
11 Paladium
 Ripan (see 6)
12 Safari

HJALMAR LUNDBOHMSVÄGEN

SKOLGATAN

Iggesundsparken

TRÄDGÅRDSG

LOMBOLOLEDEN

Jukkasjärvi, airport, Gällivare, Esrange, Kebnekaise

②

(Gällivare) where a shanty town had sprung up unchecked, the mine's first director, Hjalmar Lundbohm, wanted to make Kiruna a model community. He enlisted the help of one of the country's leading experts in architecture and social planning, and the new town began to take shape. Even the town plan was adapted to the climate; streets were built following the contour lines of the land in a highly irregular pattern to prevent the Arctic wind from howling through the centre. Sadly though, many of the original wooden buildings were ripped down in the 1960s as Sweden was swept by a wave of urban renewal.

GETTING THERE With flights from Stockholm by SAS and Norwegian, **Kiruna airport**, 10km east of the centre, is linked to the city by an airport bus, which runs in connection with flight arrival times (w horvalls.se; 110SEK). Norwegian-operated **bus 91** also runs between mid-June and late September (35SEK) and routes from Kiruna airport via Kiruna centre, Abisko and Riksgränsen en route to Narvik; the timetable is at w ltnbd.se. A **taxi** into town costs around 350SEK. **Trains** from Luleå, Gällivare and Narvik arrive at the new temporary train station, 1.5km west of the city centre. Free shuttle buses meet all arriving trains and run to the bus station. **Buses** pull in at the bus station opposite the Stadshuset, off Biblioteksgatan, a couple of blocks east of the main square.

TOURIST INFORMATION The **tourist office** is in the Folkets Hus building in the square (❧0980 188 80; e info@kirunalapland.se; w kirunalapland.se; ☺ late Jun–mid-Aug 08.30–18.00 Mon–Fri, 08.30–16.00 Sat & Sun; rest of the year 08.30–17.00 Mon–Fri, 08.30–15.00 Sat) at Lars Janssonsgatan 17.

🏠 WHERE TO STAY *Map, opposite*

🏠 **Best Western Arctic Eden** Föraregatan 18; ❧0980 611 86; e info@hotelarcticeden. se; w hotelarcticeden.se. Forget any notion of anonymous chain hotel, this place is a real find: Sámi art in a rustic setting sums up this stylish hotel venture in Kiruna. The mix of rough brick walls & wooden floors (actually a former school) set against Sámi designs & colours is most unusual – & appealing. State-of-the-art bathrooms, including massage shower cabins, to boot. €€€€

🏠 **Scandic Ferrum** Lars Janssonsgatan 15; ❧0980 39 86 00; e ferrum@scandichotels.com; w scandichotels.se/ferrum. It's hard to get more central than this smart, upmarket chain hotel with pleasantly decorated rooms, located in the town's main square. The superb top-floor sauna suite & pool makes a stay here worth considering. €€€€

🏠 **Kebne** Konduktörsgatan 7; ❧0980 681 80; e info@hotellkebne.com; w hotellkebne. com. Smart, modern hotel with Nordic-style décor throughout. Emphasis is placed on friendly, personal service & on providing quality accommodation at an affordable price. €€€€/€€€

☀ 🏠 **Ripan** Campingvägen 5; ❧0980 630 00; e info@ripan.se; w campripan.se. A 20min walk north of the centre, Kiruna's campsite is much more than a place to pitch a tent. It also has 90 hotel-standard cabins with wooden floors & bright & airy Nordic décor; half of them have their own kitchen. On site there's also a heated open-air swimming pool & jacuzzi, gym & even a stylishly designed spa section whose interior is a harmonious blend of natural stone & birch – there's even an ingenious water feature inspired by Lapland's mountain streams. Guests can watch the northern lights from the Aurora Theatre, an open-air viewing platform made of snow where you sit on the snowy benches, protected from the wind. Cabin €€€€/tent pitch €

🏠 **Gullriset Lägenhetshotell** Bromsgatan 12; ❧0980 147 00; e fabgullriset@kiruna.nu; w lkabfastigheter.se//lagenhetshotell/gullriset. Perfect for self-catering: 3 different sizes of en-suite apts (40 in all), each with fully fitted kitchen located a 20min walk from the centre. Access to sauna & laundry. Prices depend on size. €€–€€€

🏠 **Kiruna Rum & Vandrarhem** Hjalmar Lundbohmsvägen 53; ❧0980 666 66; e info@ kirunarum.se; w kirunarum.se. A popular choice right in the centre of town that fills fast – advance booking is essential. Rooms sleeping up to 4 people with a shared kitchen. Bed linen costs 50SEK pp. There's also a 2-person flat with kitchen & private facilities for 1500SEK. €€

🏠 **Malmfältens Logi** Campingvägen 3; 📞0980 675 00; e malmfaltens@kiruna.fhsk.se; w malmfaltensfolkhogskola.se. A sensibly priced budget hotel run by STF, barely a 10min walk from the town centre. Rooms are basic but all have a toilet, some also have showers; otherwise shared

facilities. Stunning views of Luossavaara mountain & access to a shared kitchen, too. €€

🏠 **Yellow House** Hantverkaregatan 25; 📞0980 137 50; e yellowhouse@mbox301.tele2.se; w yellowhouse.nu. A budget hotel-cum-youth hostel offering plain, simple dbls sharing facilities or dorm beds (from 170SEK). There's a fully fitted kitchen & a sauna. B/fast & sheet rental are extra. €

🍴 **WHERE TO EAT AND DRINK** *Map, page 72*

🍴 **Ripan** Campingvägen 5; 📞0980 630 00; ⊕ 11.00–14.00 Mon–Fri, noon–14.00 Sat & Sun & 17.00–22.00 daily; w ripan.se/restaurang. The place for top-notch Lapland cuisine (& open to non-residents, too): the grilled fillet of reindeer in red-wine sauce with horseradish butter & the baked Arctic char with crispy potatoes & spring onion sauce are both excellent. Also serves a set-price (225SEK) buffet 17.00–20.00. €€€

🍴 **Landströms Kök & Bar** Föreningsgatan 11; 📞0980 133 55; w landstroms.net; ⊕ 18.00–23.00 Mon–Thu, 18.00–01.00 Fri & Sat. Swedish home cooking with a Lapland twist is served up inside this bright & breezy bistro: try the elk soup with flatbread topped with Västerbotten cheese, grilled halibut with prawns & dill or smoked reindeer in cranberry sauce. €€

🍴 **Mommas** Lars Janssonsgatan 15; 📞0980 39 86 07; ⊕ 18.00–23.00 Mon–Sat. Inside the Scandic Ferrum, this steakhouse is a Kiruna institution & a good place for your meaty fix: juicy beef steak; classic burger with fries; grilled Arctic char; & several reindeer choices, too. The bar here is a popular place for a drink. €

🍴 **Paladium** Meschplan 5; 📞0980 632 00; ⊕ 16.00–20.00 Mon–Fri, noon–20.00 Sat &Sun. A surprisingly good pizzeria for Sweden where

pizzas tend to be less than authentic. The menu here asserts, reassuringly, that tomato sauce & cheese are included on all pizzas! The owner has also been awarded several international prizes for his pizzas. Order at the bar. €

☕ **Kafe Rost** Lars Janssonsgatan 17; w rost.nu; ⊕ 11.00–19.00 Mon–Fri,11.00–16.00 Sat. In the same building as the tourist office (page 73) with outdoor seating on the 1st-floor balcony. Good cakes & ciabatta sandwiches, as well as salads & quiches. €

☕ **Safari** Geologgatan 4; w cafesafari.se; ⊕ 08.00–18.00 Mon–Fri, 10.00–16.00 Sat. An attractive café made to resemble a favourite sitting room with elegant wallpaper, plus outdoor seating in summer in the little garden at the rear; serving homemade sandwiches, salads & pastries. The salmon lasagne is delicious, too. €

🍷 **Bishops Arms** Föreningsgatan 6; 📞0980 155 00; ⊕ 16.00–23.00 Sun & Mon, 16.00–midnight Tue–Thu, 16.00–01.00 Fri & Sat. Trying hard to be a British pub with seating in snug, little booths as well as around regular tables, this is classic Bishops Arms & a fine place for a drink or 2. Serves a range of pub grub, too, including elk burgers, pasta & salmon. €€

SHOPPING Carl Wennberg has been providing the good people of Kiruna with quality Sámi handicrafts since 1907. In the store at Bergmästaregatan 2 (📞0980 100 79; w wennberg.com; ⊕ 10.00–13.00 & 14.00–18.00 Mon–Fri, 10.00–13.00 Sat), you'll find any number of souvenirs to take home; there's seemingly everything here from handcrafted candlesticks to rucksacks made of reindeer hide. Naturally, this being Kiruna, the store is tourist-oriented and prices can be a little on the high side. Choose carefully, though, and you can still find something to please.

WHAT TO SEE AND DO Kiruna's sights are all linked to the town's mines in some way or other. The church, **Kiruna kyrka** (⊕ mid-Jun–mid-Aug 09.00–17.45 daily; rest of the year 10.00–15.30 daily), for example, on Kyrkogatan, was paid for by LKAB, owner and operator of the mine and the town's main employer. Although the church was voted Sweden's best-looking religious building in 2001, the exterior is a bizarre Neogothic interpretation of a Sámi tent, full of sharp points and angles. The building was purposely designed not to resemble a church, since Hjalmar Lundbohm, who ordered its construction in 1907, didn't want references to any specific religion. However, the local bishop objected on hearing there wasn't even to be a single cross in the church. The plain cross on the altar was the compromise decision. Many of the details inside the church are of wrought iron – as you would expect. Even the tower of the **Kiruna town hall** (Stadshus), at the junction of Hjalmar Lundbohmsvägen and Stationsvägen, is of wrought iron. The open design is topped by a series of iron spikes, a clock and 23 bells, which chime a couple of times a day; it was designed by Swedish sculptor, Bror Marklund, whose striking work can often be seen adorning Sweden's public buildings. Inside the town hall, there's a small art collection on display and occasional exhibitions of local Sámi handicrafts.

Lundbohmsgården (Lotten Erikssonsgata 34; ☏0980 701 10) In late September 2017, Lundbohmsgården, one of Kiruna's most historic buildings, was moved to its new home, Lotten Erikssonsgata 34, in Luossavaara, 3km to the northeast of the existing city. Ahead of the move, the construction of the building was carefully documented to allow an exact reconstruction of the original in the new town, which was taking shape at the time this guide went to print; however, it's expected to take several years for the building to be fully renovated and reopened.

Mr Kiruna himself, Hjalmar Lundbohm (1855–1926), the town's founding father, once lived at Lundbohmsgården, an elegant manor house whose construction began in 1895 at its original location in Igenjörsgatan.

Lundbohm travelled widely and actually spent more time living in Stockholm's chic Östermalm district than he did in Kiruna. His interest in art brought him into frequent contact with the great Swedish artists of the time, Anders Zorn and Carl Larsson, and he built up a considerable collection of paintings. He left his post as LKAB's managing director in 1920 and died six years later.

Kiruna Samegård (Brytaregatan 14; ☏0980 170 29; ⊕ 07.00–15.00 Mon–Fri; 50SEK) If all the talk of iron ore has dulled your senses, there's relief to be found at Kiruna Samegård, a considered **exhibition of Sámi culture** a 20-minute walk from the town centre north along Hjalmar Lundbohmsvägen and then left into Adolf Hedinsvägen. In the basement here, you'll find a fair display of Sámi traditional costumes together with a *kåta* to have a look at as well as a plethora of skilfully carved wooden cups and bowls.

The mine (⊕ only accessibly via a tour: times & frequency vary, depending on time of year & are given during the booking process; w kirunalapland.se/en/see-do/guided-tours-to-lkabs-visitor-centre; 380SEK; duration 2hrs 45mins; book at the tourist office or online) Although the iron-ore mine in Kiruna is the world's biggest, the tour is not a patch on what's available in Gällivare (page 68). If, however, you are still keen to go underground, you can visit what LKAB calls its Visitor Centre, a sanitised tourist attraction, admittedly based on the real thing, but a little tame. After departing by bus from the tourist office in Kiruna, visitors are taken 0.5km underground to the museum where exhibits, films and various multi-media presentations explain everything you ever wanted to know about iron-ore mining – without getting your hands dirty.

Dog-sled tours from Kiruna If the price of dog-sled tours from Icehotel in nearby Jukkasjärvi has left you panting, it may be good to know that there's a local company in Kiruna who offer an altogether more personal experience at a fraction of the price: **Husky Voice** (m 072 726 8807; e nfo@huskyvoice.com; w huskyvoice.com) based at Luossajokivägen 2. Run by multi-lingual French entrepreneur Stéphanie Peluchon (who left a career in subtitling in London to run husky tours in Swedish Lapland), Husky Voice specialises in dog-sled tours for a maximum of four people. Small groups like this offer a much more personal, hands-on experience than commercially orientated options. Tours operate from December to mid-April and include pickup from your accommodation in Kiruna: begin at 2000SEK per person for a 5-hour trip on a two-person sled where one person sits and one drives; there is a maximum of two sleds per tour. A number of summer activities such as a kennel visits and hiking tours are also on offer; full details can be found on the website.

AROUND KIRUNA: ESRANGE AND KEBNEKAISE Just 44km east of Kiruna, **Esrange** is Sweden's internationally renowned **space research station**. More than 500 rockets have been launched from this remote location in the Lapland hills since the start in 1966. The base is used to launch helium-filled high-altitude balloons that help with the study of the atmosphere and the monitoring of ozone depletion. Esrange is active in the reception and processing of satellite data. Owing to the base's northerly location, the earth's polar satellites pass within coverage range on virtually every orbit. The station is not open to the public.

It's from Esrange that Virgin Galactic hopes to operate private spaceships and fly the first space tourists into the dark beyond. As otherworldly as it sounds, a taster of what's in store can be found at w virgingalactic.com; it's estimated around 650 tickets have been sold for the first passenger-carrying flights into space: (w agent4stars.com/virgin-galactic-passenger-list/#.XS7V3uhKjIU). There'll be plenty of pre-flight training before what Virgin boss Richard Branson calls 'the most incredible experience of your life'. Space Port Sweden, based at Esrange, is aiming to become Europe's leading departure point for space travel.

For those who can't afford or indeed don't want to go up in space, the next best thing has to be an ascent of Sweden's highest mountain, **Kebnekaise** (Giebmegáisi in Sámi; 2,102m). The mountain is accessed from the village of Nikkaluokta, 66km west of Kiruna, from where a hiking trail covers the last 19km to the foot of the mountain and the **Kebnekaise mountain lodge** (📞010 190 2330; e fjallbokning@ stfturist.se; w stfkebnekaise.com; ☺ Mar & Apr & mid-Jun–late Sep; dbl room **€€€€**). The lodge has its own restaurant serving all meals, its own bakery as well as a sauna and a fully equipped kitchen for self-catering. There are two paths up the peak: the shorter one goes via the Björling glacier and is only recommended for expert climbers; the other, much longer, goes up the western face and is the one preferred by most visitors. Incidentally, the height of the mountain, whose peak is made up of glacial ice, has been recently reassessed and officially reduced (from the original 2,111m) as some of the ice has melted over the course of the past decade. Amaze your Swedish friends, as well, with the knowledge that Kebnekaise was first climbed, not by a Swede, but a Frenchman, Charles Robot, who made it to the summit in 1883.

There's a twice-daily **bus** (mid-Jun–late Sep), Nikkaluoktaexpressen, to Nikkaluokta from Kiruna bus and train stations routing via the airport (150SEK single; times are at w nikkaluoktaexpressen.se & w resrobot.se). A boat leaves from Nikkaluokta after the bus's arrival, which can shorten the 19km hike to the mountain by 6km. From Kebnekaise, it is a 14km hike to the **Kungsleden trail** at Singi.

If there's one thing that's put Lapland well and truly on the winter tourist trail, it is **Icehotel**. From Japan to Britain, the US to Italy, mention the name to any savvy traveller and everyone's heard about it, and, more often than not, wants to come here. Proof, if ever it was needed, that the man behind the project, Yngve Bergqvist, a southern Swede who moved to Swedish Lapland over 30 years ago, struck gold.

Back in 1989, he hit on the idea of building a simple igloo here in the village of **Jukkasjärvi** (Sámi for 'meeting place by the lake'), 20km east of Kiruna, as a showcase for local Sámi handicrafts and art. Some of those first visitors wanted to sleep in the igloo – something that wasn't commerically possible in any part of Lapland at the time. A veritable niche in the market, the concept was developed by Yngve and Icehotel was born, gradually transforming sleepy Jukkasjärvi, a remote Lapland backwater, into a tourist blockbuster that now pulls in 40,000 visitors every year. True, the project has not been without its local critics over the years, who have complained that the soul of their village has been destroyed by hordes of tourists, and, indeed, planning permission for various projects has been refused by the local authorities. Be that as it may, Yngve has been bestowed with countless tourism awards and is heralded as the man who breathed new life and vigour into the local economy, which had languished for years through lack of investment and interest from central government 1,300km away in Stockholm.

ICEHOTEL In late October each year work begins in earnest on the (re)construction of Icehotel. Using blocks of ice hewn from the Torne River, which flows through Jukkasjärvi, artists and sculptors from across the world slowly give shape to the new structure, which will consume around 1,000 tonnes of ice and 30,000 tonnes of 'snice', as Icehotel calls it, a combination of snow and ice which helps strengthen

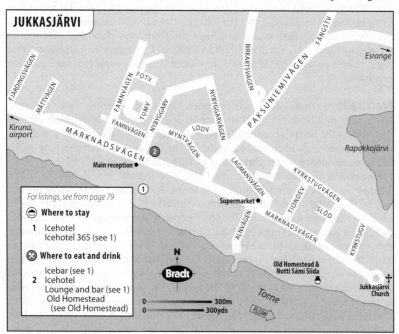

JUKKASJÄRVI

For listings, see from page 79

🏠 **Where to stay**
1   Icehotel
    Icehotel 365 (see 1)

❌ **Where to eat and drink**
    Icebar (see 1)
2   Icehotel
    Lounge and bar (see 1)
    Old Homestead
    (see Old Homestead)

Main reception ●

Supermarket ●

Old Homestead &
Nutti Sámi Siida

Jukkasjärvi
Church

Esrange

Rapakkojärvi

Kiruna,
airport

Torne

FLOW

0 ―――― 300m
0 ―――― 300yds

Bradt

N

the structure. When complete, Icehotel covers around 5,500m² of ground space and stands proud beside the banks of the river until May, when winter finally releases its grip on Lapland and the entire structure melts away back into the river. Whether you stay here or not, if you are in Lapland during the winter season, you should make every effort to get here because Icehotel really is an amazing sight. Although the actual details of the design and interior decoration vary from year to year, the overall shape of the hotel remains the same: one long arched corridor, naturally lit at either end by giant ice windows, forms the main walkway, from which other corridors then branch off to the left and right leading to the bedrooms and suites. Intricately carved ice sculptures adorn the interior seemingly at every turn and only add to the overall sense of amazement most visitors feel. Beside the main entrance, there's the Ice chapel, a smaller arched igloo, replete with ice pews and cross, which has become an inordinately popular place to tie the knot.

In 2016 **Icehotel 365** was launched; a permanent structure (run on solar power during the summer months) on the ever-expanding site, and featuring luxury ice suites with private facilities, crafted by selected artists, a bar and a gallery. This section is open to visitors all year round and allows you to stay in an ice suite even in summer.

Getting there Kiruna airport (airport code KRN), barely a few kilometres from Jukkasjärvi, is the perfect gateway to Icehotel. The **airport** is currently served by SAS and Norwegian, who fly here from Stockholm Arlanda (see page 73 for details of the airport bus). From Kiruna bus station, **bus** 501 runs to Jukkasjärvi (timetable at w ltnbd.se). If you are heading directly to Icehotel, which lies in the opposite direction to Kiruna, it makes sense to book a **taxi** transfer directly here (275SEK pp). Alternatively, Icehotel operates a pickup service from the train station for 275SEK per person; both transfers can be booked online via the Icehotel website. There's only one road into Jukkasjärvi, Marknadsvägen, and Icehotel is located on its right-hand side as you enter the village. Undoubtedly the most fantastic way to arrive is by **dog-sled**, which will meet you from your plane and pull you all the way to your bed – a trip of around 75 minutes. However, it is a pleasure that doesn't come cheap: 6,695SEK for a maximum of three people (advance booking necessary).

Practicalities There are two reception areas at Icehotel: one for cold accommodation (Icehotel itself) and one for warm accommodation; both are well signposted. The **warm accommodation** – a range of hotel rooms and chalets – is located immediately in front, and to the left, of the ice structure; checking-in for this accommodation is straightforward and just like in any other hotel.

However, if you are staying in the Icehotel or Icehotel 365, things are a little different. At check-in, you'll be issued with warm clothing and general advice on how to survive the night in sub-zero temperatures. Staff will also allocate you a locker in which to store your luggage since the hotel is open to **day visitors** (295SEK entrance including a guided tour) until 18.00 daily. In the warm area, there are also bathrooms and separate-sex saunas for use by overnight guests. When it is time to move into the room, the idea is you leave as many clothes as you dare in the locker and make a run for it – the temperature inside the Icehotel is pretty constant at around –5°C, whereas outside it can often be as low as –30°C. The sleeping bag you are provided with has been thermally tested and is designed to keep you warm in temperatures down to –35°C; it includes a special hood which you should draw over your head to avoid heat loss, leaving just your mouth and nose clear (this can be a little claustrophobic). In order to prevent sweating inside the sleeping bag, it is important to take all your clothes off and sleep naked; don't leave your clothes on the floor, though, because they'll freeze overnight; instead, stuff them right down inside the sleeping bag. Similarly, place your shoes on the bed beside you. You will be woken the next morning by cheery staff offering you a cup of warm lingonberry juice. Before breakfast it is a good idea to warm up with a morning sauna and a hot shower.

🏠 Where to stay *Map, page 77*

The **Icehotel** (Marknadsvägen 63; ☎0980 668 00; e info@icehotel.com; w icehotel. com; €€€€) is open from early December until late April. Like most other hotels, prices vary according to demand and date; stays at New Year and over Valentine's Day are separately priced. Moreover, the variety of different rooms and suites, both in the regular Icehotel and in the new Icehotel 365, is mind-boggling and varies from year to year – your best bet is to spend some time pouring over the website booking pages, working out what option best suits you and your pocket.

'**Cold accommodation**' inside the Icehotel comes in various forms and prices: a regular cold room costs from 4,300SEK in peak season, while suites generally cost upwards of 6,000SEK. **Beds** in all rooms are made of compacted snow and ice, raised off the ground and topped with a reindeer skin, on which you sleep in your sleeping bag.

For most people, the novelty of spending one night in the Icehotel is enough, and many people decide to stay on and book into the adjacent warm accommodation, which consists of regular double rooms and chalets. Known by the Sámi name *kaamos*, meaning 'blue light', the double rooms, located in four separate buildings to the left of the Icehotel, are stylish in the extreme: Nordic-style minimalism complete with wood panelling and soft lighting. The chalets divide up into what Icehotel calls Nordic chalets, altogether more stylish and comfortable, and the more cluttered Arctic chalets; although both have two separate bedrooms, the latter have a window in the roof allowing you to see the northern lights, weather permitting. Prices for both rooms and chalets are the roughly same (around 2,700SEK).

Another option is to stay in a cosy, candlelit log cabin deep in the forest. In winter, travel to the 'Rapid Lodge wilderness camp', as it's known, is by snowmobile, in summer by boat. There's no road here and no electricity either, though there is a wood-burning sauna. Dinner is provided on site by Icehotel staff. Accommodation prices vary depending on the times of year, how you get there and the level of exclusivity required – contact Icehotel for a quote, remembering that on Friday there is the option of a group tour to the camp with an overnight stay including dinner, breakfast and transport for a steep 5,995SEK per person.

✗ Where to eat and drink *Map, page 77*

The **Icehotel restaurant** ✳ (🕐 07.00–10.00, 11.00–15.00 & 18.00–midnight daily; €€€) on Marknadsvägen, opposite Icehotel, is the place to come for a warming breakfast; the extensive buffet is included in the price of all accommodation. An excellent buffet **lunch** is served daily for 135SEK. Reservations are a good idea if you intend to have dinner here, as demand for tables is high. Meals are a little pricey but the quality of the food is excellent: à la carte starters such as elk or reindeer carpaccio start at 145SEK; mains, such as tasty topside of reindeer in juniper-berry sauce or Arctic char served with a dill and mustard crème start at 235SEK; and desserts are around 165SEK. The set Ice Menu costing 995SEK for five courses merits a special occasion: it includes various kinds of roe, Lofoten salmon, elk tartare and fillet of reindeer and other Lapland delicacies; each cold course is served on an ice platter. Back on the other side of the road, there's a **lounge** and **bar** (☉ 10.30–18.00 daily), selling light snacks as well as wine and beer, located behind the warm accommodation reception area. Plus, there's the Icebar (noon–22.00 daily) inside the Icehotel 365, serving vodka in a glass made of ice.

Aimed at complementing the main Icehotel restaurant, the **Old Homestead restaurant** (☉ mid-Jun–mid-Aug 10.00–16.00 daily; Dec–Apr 17.30–21.30 daily; €€), at the eastern edge of the village within the Nutti Sámi Siida area (a 10-minute walk east along Marknadsvägen from Icehotel), is a more traditional place to dine. Housed in the former village school from 1768, the heavy wooden interior is typical of many buildings in Lapland and provides a more intimate dining experience. Main dishes such as smoked reindeer stew, halloumi burger and meatballs with lingonberry start at 195SEK; there's always a vegetarian option on the menu; once again, reservations are recommended.

For **self-catering** there's a small supermarket selling provisions just before the Homestead Museum on Marknadsvägen.

Activities There is no end to the activities you can take from the Icehotel. The exact range of tours varies from year to year, but the old favourites are always available: a 3-hour **snowmobile tour** out into the forest around Jukkasjärvi (1,395SEK pp with 2 people per machine); **northern lights tour** by snowmobile lasting 4 hours (2,095*SEK*) and a **dog-sled tour** of 90 minutes costing 1,495SEK per person including coffee and cakes by an open fire in the wilderness. Another interesting option is to spend a morning or afternoon with local Sámi people who'll give you an insight into their traditional way of life and let you try your hand at driving a reindeer sled (2,280SEK). You can also try your hand at ice sculpting – a 2½-hour course costs 725SEK.

JUKKASJÄRVI VILLAGE Other than Icehotel, the main attraction in Jukkasjärvi, a compact little village of barely 1,000 people, is the old Sámi **church**✳ (☉ 09.00–15.00 daily) hidden away, somewhat apologetically, at the eastern end of the main road, which ends here. A classic tall and narrow wooden structure built in 1608, and accordingly the oldest existing church in Swedish Lapland, the church is certainly attractive in its own right, but it is the startling **altarpiece** inside that really draws the eye, and offers an insight into the Sámi's often uneasy relationship with alcohol. Ablaze with colour, the triptych was carved by Swedish artist, Bror Hjorth, whose work is favoured as adornment to many of Sweden's civic squares and buildings. It was carved and donated to the church by the big name in iron ore around here, LKAB, which operates the mines in Kiruna.

The man in the nasty brown suit, featured in both main sections of the altarpiece, is the revivalist preacher Lars Levi Laestadius, who worked as the Sámi minister in Karesuando from 1825. Laestadius took it on himself to free Lapland from alcohol abuse and to show the Sámi the way to enlightenment through his teachings: hence the landlord stamping on a keg of beer; the return of a stolen reindeer; even confessions of sex by the couple with the long faces portrayed in the work. However, the Sámi really have the woman lit by a golden halo, Mary of Lapland (shown on the right of the altarpiece), to thank for their deliverance from evil. After meeting Mary, Laestadius found peace and conviction of his own beliefs and went on to found a religious movement that, to this day, still draws tens of thousands of followers across northern Scandinavia.

As you walk down Marknadsvägen to the church, you will see a collection of old wooden buildings on your right-hand side, just after the Icehotel complex. The

Nutti Sámi Siida (☉ w nutti.se; ☉ 10.00–17.00 daily; 180SEK), contains a worthy collection of how-we-used-to-live paraphernalia, such as spinning wheels and reindeer sledges, though it's unlikely to make the top line of your postcards home.

Summer in Jukkasjärvi Between June and August, Icehotel lets its double rooms and chalets at reduced, though still rather expensive, rates: doubles cost 1,615SEK while chalets go for 1,655SEK each and cold rooms in Icehotel 365 cost 2,500SEK. Both the main Icehotel restaurant (page 79) and the Old Homestead restaurant are open during summer (see opposite).

There's certainly no shortage of **activities** on offer, though perhaps the two most rewarding are **white-water rafting** on the Torne River (Tue & Fri; 1,565SEK) and a 3 hour trip into the wilderness to learn and test your survival skills (1,255SEK). **Canoes**, **mountain bikes and e-bikes, fishing equipment** and **stand-up paddleboards** are available for rent; prices start at 100SEK per hour. English-language **guided tours** of the Icehotel also operate in summer at noon and 16.00 daily between mid-June and late August (295SEK).

ABISKO AND AROUND

ABISKO Thanks to its envious position as the driest place in the whole of Sweden, Abisko, 94km northwest of Kiruna, is not only the place to work on your tan during the summer when the sun never seems to stop shining, but it is the place of choice in winter to see the northern lights when, similarly, the sky here is often free of cloud, a prerequisite for observing the phenomenon. Abisko is also one of the few places in Lapland that is properly geared up to seeing the northern lights, thanks to the designated viewing site, known as the **Aurora Sky Station** (page 82). Lying in a rain shadow, Abisko has mountains that divide it from neighbouring Riksgränsen (the wettest place in Sweden) to thank for its sunny disposition. Though the village itself comprises little more than a couple of housing blocks, a supermarket and a filling station, the setting couldn't be better; sandwiched between Nuolja Mountain and the 70km-long Torneträsk Lake, a vast ribbon-like expanse of water, Abisko really has got it made. However, should you choose to come here, you are more likely to spend your time a couple of kilometres further along the main E10 highway, which links Abisko with Kiruna, at the excellent **Abisko Turiststation**, a cross between a regular youth hostel and a mountain lodge. Incidentally, it is also possible to reach Abisko by **train** from Kiruna; though be sure to alight at the station named Abisko Turiststation, not Abisko Ö (train-speak for Abisko Östra, or east), which is the stop for the village and comes first when approaching from Kiruna.

🏠 **Where to stay, eat and drink** The **Abisko Turiststation** [map, page 85] (☎010 190 2400; **e** abisko@stfturist.se; **w** abisko.nu) is well signed from the main E10 highway and stands beside the road. It is open all year round though the main building (and therefore en-suite double rooms) is closed in May and October. Prices for accommodation vary very slightly between winter and summer. Rooms at the Turiststation are divided into two main types – there are more comfortable double rooms with private facilities (**€€€€** inc b/fast) in the main building, while in the separate Keron building behind there are cheaper, more basic dorm rooms with shared facilities (though there is a washbasin in the room), with access to a kitchen (450SEK pp; dbl room **€€€€**). There are also cabins (**€€€€**/night) for rent with a fully fitted kitchen, living room and two bedrooms sleeping either four or six. There are decent, separate-sex **saunas** with communal showers (⊕ 16.00–20.00) both in the main building and in the Keron section, as well as a **wood sauna** down by the lake. The Turiststation's **restaurant** serves a buffet-style breakfast, lunch and dinner, and in the basement you will find a **bar** with superb views out over the Torneträsk Lake, though it's only open in connection with special events. Provisions and a range of outdoor clothing and equipment from the likes of Norrøna and Fjällräven can be bought from the shop on the site; while the supermarket in the village stocks a larger range of food. In Abisko village itself you will find at the filling station Abisko's other eating option, the cheap-and-cheerful **Mack å Mat** (Kalle Jons väg 1; ✆0980 400 50; ⊕ 10.00–22.00 Mon–Fri, 11.00–22.00 Sat & Sun; €), a combined filling station, general store and restaurant which serves burgers, fries and pasta dishes for around 100–150SEK.

What to see and do
Nuolja Mountain and Aurora Sky Station
Bearing down on tiny Abisko from a height of 1,169m, **Nuolja Mountain** is easily accessible by **chairlift ✳** (*linbana* in Swedish; 150SEK single; ⊕ 09.30–16.00 daily, mid-Jun–mid-Jul 22.00–01.00 Tue, Thu & Sat, & in connection with evening tours – see opposite). To get to the base station for the chairlift from the Turiststation, first cross the E10 and follow the signs underneath the railway line, where you then turn right. At the summit you will find an agreeable **café** (which operates without electricity or running water; €) and one of the most breathtaking views in the whole of Lapland. As the chairlift whisks you to the top of the peak, you somehow forget that the view of Abisko and Torneträsk Lake is behind you. The spectacular panorama is all the more amazing, then, when you get off the chairlift and enter the café – the village, lake and entire valley are laid out before you through floor-to-ceiling windows. Nuolja offers the best views of **Lapporten**, the U-shaped valley edged by identical twin peaks that has, over the years, become Lapland's most enigmatic sight; Lapporten was traditionally used by reindeer-herding Sámi as an unmissable landmark during migration.

Tucked away in one corner at the rear of the café is a modest little room known rather grandly as the **Aurora Sky Station** (w auroraskystation.se; there's a live webcam feed streamed through the website), home to a scientific exhibition about the **northern lights** and containing all sorts of information about how to measure and even hear the lights, such as audio amplifiers to listen to electromagnetic oscillations in the atmosphere, which often sound like a series of whistles, hisses and clicks. The sky station, complete with a lookout tower, is open in connection with special tours to observe the aurora (⊕ late Nov–late Mar 21.00–01.00 daily; 745SEK, 1,925SEK inc dinner); tours include a return trip on the chairlift (20mins one-way) with warm clothing provided, a welcome drink and a short explanation about the aurora in layman's terms; advance bookings are essential as the number of tickets is limited. It's worth nothing, though, that tours are cancelled if it's too windy or if the temperature at the summit or the base station falls below -22°C, which makes operation of the chairlift too dangerous. In these cases, dinner is served at the Turiststation, instead, and there will be a walking tour to see the lights followed by an aurora film in the Naturum.

Other winter activities
The Turiststation (page 81) can organise a number of winter activities – all are bookable online in advance or once you arrive. Options include ice climbing, Nordic skiing, a visit to a local Sámi camp, a day trip to Narvik or a visit to Icehotel. Full details are available online at w abisko.nu. Alternatively,

w abikso.net, who are based in Abisko village, run dog-sledding tours – check out their website for further information.

Summer actitivies During the summer, the **chairlift** also operates in order to observe the midnight sun from Nuolja Mountain. Between mid-June and mid-August it runs from 09.30 to 16.00 daily and, during the period of midnight sun (mid-Jun–mid-Jul) it also makes the ascent every evening from 22.00 to 01.00.

From the top of the chairlift, there are a couple of enjoyable and easy, marked **hiking trails** back down towards Abisko. You head south through dwarf birch woodland down to an impressive canyon within Abisko National Park from where you can follow the Kungsleden trail (page 85) back to the Turiststation. Or, alternatively, you can head north on another trail that cuts down the hillside towards the village of Björkliden from where you can take the train the 7km back to Abisko.

Abisko Naturum (Adjacent to the Turiststation; **w** naturumabisko.se; ⊕ Dec–mid-Feb 14.00–17.00 Thu–Sat; mid-Feb–Apr 14.00–18.00 daily; mid-Jun–mid-Aug 09.00–18.00 daily; late Aug–Sep 09.00–18.00 Tue–Sat; free) For a quick canter through the flora and fauna of this part of Swedish Lapland, the Abisko Naturum is worth a quick look. Inside you will find examples of some of the vegetation and wildlife in the surrounding national parks.

STF (Svenska Turistföreningen, the Swedish Youth Hostel Association) maintains **overnight huts** and **hostels** between Abisko and Kvikkjokk (northwest of Jokkmokk) as well as between Ammarnäs and Hemavan at the southern end of the trail [map, page 85]; they are spaced at regular intervals, roughly every 15–20km, making it possible to hike between them comfortably in one day. There are no huts between Kvikkjokk and Ammarnäs, a distance of about 130km. Passing through several national parks along its route, the Kungsleden is an easy trail to tackle as it is well marked, streams are bridged and duckboarding has been placed over areas of marshy ground. At one or two points along the route, it is necessary to cross lakes; a rowing boat is provided on each shore for this purpose.

The Kungsleden is readily accessible by public transport. **Trains** will whisk you to the starting point in Abisko, whereas **buses** are available to collect you at the end of your hike at the following points: Nikkaluokta, Kvikkjokk, Jäkkvik, Adolfström, Ammarnäs and Hemavan. Other useful train stations (reached by buses coming down from the mountains) are Jokkmokk and Arvidsjaur on the Inlandsbanan (**w** inlandsbanan.se; see box, page 69); and Murjek and Luleå on the main line (**w** sj.se).

RIKSGRÄNSEN A small mountain village 34km from Abisko, tucked up tight against the border with Norway, Riksgränsen boasts that there's never any need for artificial snow. That's because the settlement is one of the wettest in the whole of Sweden, lying in the path of every low-pressure system that sweeps in from the Norwegian Sea, hence, when it is not snowing here, it is raining. That said, Riksgränsen is a popular winter sports destination, drawing holidaying Swedes from across the country to its 60-odd peaks over 1,350m; skiing is generally possible until mid-June. Riksgränsen is really about the surrounding countryside, since there's not much to the place itself; a couple of accommodation options, the train station and the E10 just about sums things up.

🏠 **Where to stay, eat and drink** Note that between July and September, only the café inside Meteorologen is open; there is no accommodation available anywhere on site during this time.

The top-of-the-range **Riksgränsen** (✆ 0981 641 00; e riksgransen@ laplandresorts.se; w riksgransen.se; €€€€), opposite the train station, has a whole array of **hotel** accommodation, including double rooms and self-catering apartments sleeping up to eight people. There's also a **youth hostel** here offering dorm beds (€) in rooms sleeping up to four people or double rooms (€€); all rooms have private facilities. There's also a well-appointed **spa centre**, boasting several massage rooms as well as outdoor hot tubs. For luxury, the swanky **Meteorologen Ski Lodge** (same contact details as the Riksgränsen hotel above; €€€€), has 14 individually decorated doubles in a century-old wooden building that what was once a far-flung outpost of the Swedish met office, once again opposite the train station. **Food** is available in the restaurant at Riksgränsen and Meteorologen where there's also a summer café serving sandwiches and cakes (⊕ late Jun–late Sep noon–16.00 Thu–Sun; €).

Moving on from Riksgränsen: the train to Narvik

Although there are daily **trains** southeast from Riksgränsen to Kiruna, Gällivare and Luleå, it's the train ride west through the mountains to Norway that really excites. This breathtaking railway line✳, an extension of Sweden's Malmbanan, officially known as the Ofotbanen in Norway, seems to slice through the craggy, frost-shattered mountains, which form the border between Sweden and Norway, as it connects Riksgränsen in Sweden with Narvik in Norway and offers some stunning fjord scenery to boot. The line may only be 42km long, but it packs in some extraordinary scenery, passing through 20 tunnels and descends around 500m on its way down to the sea. Barely 8km out of Riksgränsen, the train lurches into a lonely wayside halt known as Søsterbekk holdeplass, at the head of the Norddal Valley. Just beyond here, look out of the windows on the right-hand side of the train (when heading for Narvik) and you'll see the impressive, though now disused, Norddalsbrua Bridge. At 180m in length, this overlong bridge is totally unnecessary to transport the railway through Norddal and was built purely for strategic reasons since it could be blown up to prevent foreign invasion by rail. Embarrassingly, the Norwegians failed to dynamite their own bridge in April 1940, ahead of the impending German invasion, since they didn't have access to enough explosive. The Germans consequently repaired the limited damage caused to the bridge and invaded. The bridge was in use until 1988 when the rail line was moved to its current location and a new shorter bridge constructed instead.

However, it's beyond Norddal that things start to get really impressive as the train line balances precariously on narrow mountain ledges high above the southern shores of the Rombakfjord. Between the stations of Katterat and Rombak, the train affords some dazzling views of the upper reaches of the Rombakfjord: the combination of barren scree slopes soaring above the verdant shores of the fjord and the heart-stopping, sheer vertical drops from right outside the train window down to sea level over 300m below, make this one of the most scenically spectacular rail journeys in the whole of Scandinavia – and one not to be missed. West of Rombak, the visual delights continue as the train wiggles its circuitous way around countless rocky bluffs, dives in and out of tunnels and descends a further 250m to the warming waters of the Norwegian Sea. Departure times for the train trip between Riksgränsen and Narvik are posted up at both stations and can also be found at w sj.se.

Incidentally, between mid-June and late September there's also a bus, the #91, which calls in at Riksgränsen on its way between Kiruna airport and Narvik (timetables are at w ltnbd.se), though the bus ride can't compete with the train trip for impressive vistas.

HIKING FROM ABISKO: THE KUNGSLEDEN TRAIL Abisko marks the beginning of Sweden's best-known **hiking route**, the Kungsleden trail, which stretches around 430km south to Hemavan and passes through one of Europe's last remaining wilderness areas. The trail's popularity means that it can get pretty busy, particularly during the peak Swedish holiday season from mid-June to mid-August. It's significantly quieter in September when the weather is still good and the glorious reds, yellows and oranges of the Lapland autumn are starting to appear. Hiking this

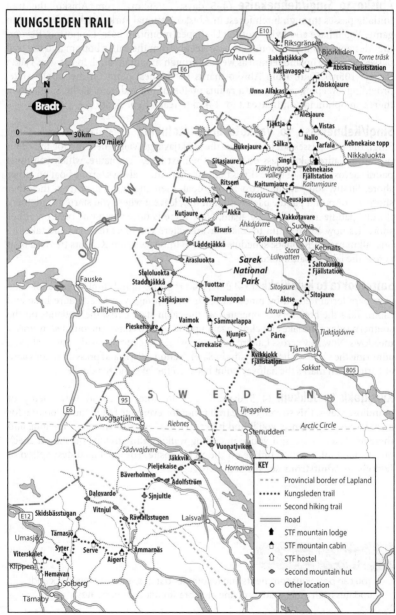

KUNGSLEDEN TRAIL

KEY
- ----- Provincial border of Lapland
- •••••• Kungsleden trail
- ·········· Second hiking trail
- —— Road
- ▲ STF mountain lodge
- ⌂ STF mountain cabin
- ⌂ STF hostel
- ◆ Second mountain hut
- ○ Other location

trail is an experience to cherish. Below is a brief outline of the 300km of the trail which fall within the geographical area of this guidebook, ie: Abisko to Adolfström. For more detailed information, check out w stfturist.se/kungsleden where you can also find opening times and the exact locations of the overnight cabins. In general, the whole trail is **moderately easy** to hike and doesn't require special stamina. To hike a more southerly leg of the route, see the box on page 58.

Abisko to Singi/Kebnekaise (4–5 days; 72/86km) From Abisko, the trail initially passes through birch forest in Abisko National Park which is abundant in game. You'll have good views of the U-shaped mountain pass, Lapporten. Beyond the Alesjaure cabin, the mountains rise steeply from the valley bottom and the trail passes over bare upland terrain as well as through mountain birch forest. The Tjäkta Pass (1,105m) 50km from Abisko marks the highest point on the whole route, providing sweeping views over a radius of 40km. Beyond here, at the Singi cabin, there's an option to continue east for 14km to reach Kebnekaise.

Singi/Kebnekaise to Vakkotavare/Saltoluokta (2–3 days; 37km) From Singi, the trail passes south through the Tjäktjavagge Valley heading for the cabin on Kaitumjaure Lake. Press on now to the next lake, Teusajaure, which you must paddle across a total of three times because there must always be one boat on either shore. Firstly, you paddle across in one boat, then attach the boat from the other shore to yours and paddle back with it in tow, leave it where you started, and, then, thirdly, paddle across the lake again. Now there is once again one boat on either shore. It's now 15km south to Vakkotavare where you meet the road and take the bus 30km east to Kebnats; schedules are at w ltnbd.se. From Kebnats there's a boat across the lake to Saltoluokta.

Saltoluokta to Kvikkjokk (3–4 days; 68km) A long uphill climb from Saltoluokta over bare terrain edged by pine and birch forest brings you to Sitojaure Lake and cabin. Take the boat service operated by the cabin staff. Cross the wetlands on the southern side of the lake and climb again up and over to Aktse, surrounded by grassy meadows. Now row across Litaure Lake (using the same procedure described above), admiring the views of the mountains in Sarek National Park, and press on to the cabin at Pårte which marks the halfway point between the lake and Kvikkjokk.

Kvikkjokk to Jäkkvik (4–5 days; 74km) Remote, wild and with plenty of grandiose views, this stretch of the trail is not for everyone but if you're looking for a wilderness experience, you'll find it here. Distances between cabins are long and there are lakes to cross; if you're intending walking this stretch you should check out detailed information online on the STF website. For a detailed description of **Jäkkvik to Adolfström**, see the box on page 58.

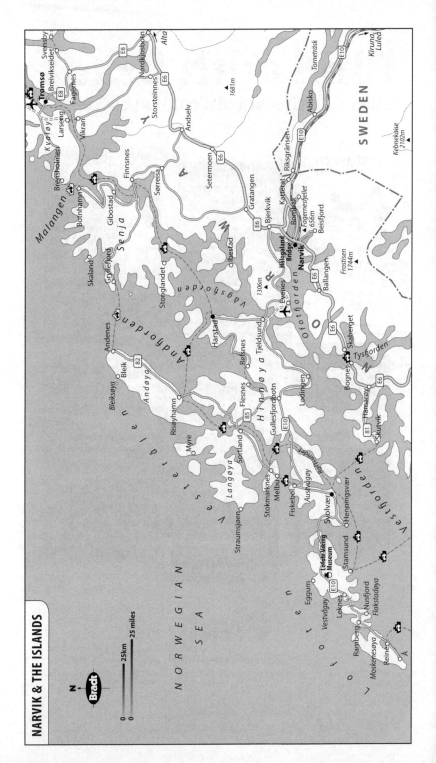

NARVIK & THE ISLANDS

NORWEGIAN SEA

SWEDEN

Kiruna,
Luleå

Kebnekaise
2102m

Frostisen
1744m

Tromsø
Svensby
Breivikseidet
Fagernes
Kvaløy
Larseng
Vikran
Brensholmen
Botnhamn
Malangen
Gibostad
Skaland
Gryllefjord
Senja
Skaland
Finnsnes
Sørreisa
Storsteinnes
Nordkjosbotn
Alta
Andselv
Setermoen
Gratangen
Bjerkvik
Rombak
Fagernesfjellet
656m
Beisfjord
Narvik
Hålogaland
Bridge
Kåfjord
Riksgränsen
Abisko
Torneträsk
1681m
Andenes
Bleiksøya
Bleik
Andøya
Risøyhamn
Myre
Stonglandet
Ibestad
Harstad
Revsnes
Tjeldsund
Evenes
Ofotfjorden
Ballangen
Skarberget
Tysfjorden
Bognes
Hamarøy
Skutvik
Straumsjøen
Langøya
Sortland
Melbu
Stokmarknes
Fiskebøl
Flesnes
Gullesfjordbotn
Lødingen
Hinnøya
Vågsfjorden
1306m
Vestvågøy
Andfjorden
Eggum
Leknes
Ramberg
Reine
Moskenesøya
Nusfjord
Flakstadøya
Stamsund
Lofotr Viking
Museum
Svolvær
Henningsvær
Austvågøy
Raftsundet
Vestfjorden

Bradt

N

0   25km
0   25 miles

E8
E6
E10

4

Narvik and the Islands

West of Narvik, the Norwegian coast curves gracefully into one of the most breathtakingly beautiful archipelagos of islands and skerries anywhere in Europe. The Vesterålen islands, and particularly their southern neighbours, Lofoten, offer jaw-dropping scenery quite unlike any other part of Lapland. The combination of sheer, granite peaks, which run spine-like through the entire chain, set against the narrowest of foreshores, gouged into countless rocky inlets and sandy bays, is of such elemental beauty that you will find it hard to leave. Dotted with pretty little fishing villages and traditional *rorbuer* cottages perched on wooden stilts by the shore, the islands are the best place in Lapland to go whale-watching. Travel by boat is very much part of a visit to Lofoten and Vesterålen; the coastal scenery, always stunning, is at its most spectacular around the impossibly narrow Trollfjord, hemmed in between the two island groups.

Although Narvik itself, destroyed during World War II, is not a handsome place, it is by far the best gateway to the islands; from here it is possible to reach Lofoten by both ferry and road. The highlight of any trip is end-of-the-road Å (pronounced '*oh*'), a gorgeous little village squeezed between craggy mountains on all sides – the mountain and coastal scenery at this very tip of the Vesterålen/Lofoten triangle is monumental. You also shouldn't miss the island capital, Svolvær, and charming Henningsvær on the way. At the opposite end of the archipelago, Andenes is the region's premier whale-watching centre and a good point from which to leave the islands in summer when there's a handy ferry route back to the mainland giving a head start on the journey north to Tromsø.

NARVIK

Narvik's never going to win any beauty contests. Its purpose in life is pure and simple: it provides an ice-free port for the export of iron ore from the mines at Kiruna and Gällivare, over the border in Sweden. The scene of fierce fighting in 1940 between German and British forces to gain control of the town's harbour and neutral Sweden's iron-ore exports (which ultimately provided the raw material to keep the German war machine in production throughout World War II), the town centre was totally destroyed during four air attacks by German warplanes. Following the Nazi occupation, rebuilding began apace but won few accolades for aesthetics – today's soulless concrete blocks, which dominate the town centre wherever you look, were born out of necessity rather than a desire to please the eye. However, there's a certain gritty charm to Narvik; its ugly, brooding dockyards slap bang in the centre of town and plain for all to see, give the place a pioneering edge. If you've tired of small, remote inland villages on your travels, you'd do well to spend a day or two here, recharging your batteries and enjoying the bustle and goings-on

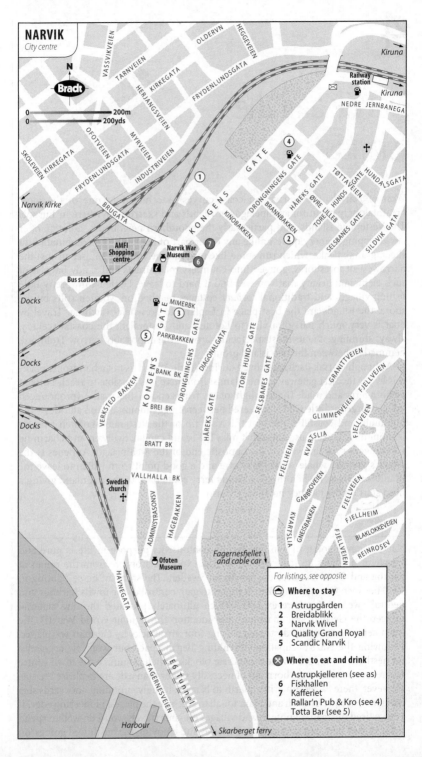

NARVIK
City centre

N

Bradt

0 ———————— 200m
0 ———————— 200yds

Kiruna

Railway station

Kiruna

NEDRE JERNBANEGA

VASSVIKVEIEN
OLDERVN
HEGEVEIEN
TARNVEIEN
KIRKEGATA
FRYDENLUNDSGATA
HERJANGSVEIEN
MYRVEIEN
OFOTVEIEN
SKOLEVEIEN
KIRKEGATA
FRYDENLUNDSGATA
INDUSTRIVEIEN

Narvik Kirke

BRUGATA

KONGENS GATE

DRONGNINGENS GATE
BRANNBAKKEN
KINOBAKKEN
HÅREKS GATE
HÅREKS ØVRE
TORE LILLEB
TORE HUNDS
SELSBANES GATE
TØTTAVEIEN
HUNDALSGATA
SILDVIK GATA

AMFI Shopping centre

Narvik War Museum

Bus station

Docks

MIMERBK

KONGENS GATE

PARKBAKKEN

BANK BK

DRONGNINGENS GATE

DIAGONALGATA

HÅREKS GATE

TORE HUNDS GATE

SELSBANES GATE

Docks

VERKSTED BAKKEN

BREI BK

BRATT BK

VALLHALLA BK

Docks

Swedish church

ADMINISTRASONSV

HAGEBAKKEN

HAVNEGATA

Ofoten Museum

Fagernesfjellet and cable car

Harbour

FAGERNESVEIEN

E6 Tunnel

Skarberget ferry

GRANITTVEIEN
FJELLVEIEN
GLIMMERVEIEN
FJELLVEIEN
FJELLHEIM
KVARTSLIA
GABBROVEIEN
GNEISBAKKEN
KVARTSLIA
FJELLHEIM
BLAKLOKKEVEIEN
REINROSEV
FJELLVEIEN

For listings, see opposite

Where to stay
1 Astrupgården
2 Breidablikk
3 Narvik Wivel
4 Quality Grand Royal
5 Scandic Narvik

Where to eat and drink
Astrupkjelleren (see as)
6 Fiskhallen
7 Kafferiet
Rallar'n Pub & Kro (see 4)
Tøtta Bar (see 5)

90

of the town and its harbour. In recent years a rash of companies offering outdoor adventure sports has sprung up providing visitors with plenty to keep them busy.

Incidentally, thanks to the Gulf Stream, spring comes much earlier here (and summer, mercifully, lasts that little bit longer) than on the other side of the mountains in Swedish Lapland. When it is −15°C in Kiruna, for example, with snow still thick on the ground, it can be above freezing in Narvik and the first spring flowers can be just starting to appear.

GETTING THERE Narvik is linked to Kiruna by both the E10 highway (later meeting the E6, which leads into town) and by **rail**. The train station is located on the northeastern edge of town, from where it is an easy 10-minute walk southwest along Kongens gate (actually the E6) into the town centre. The **bus** station is next to the AMFI shopping centre at the junction of Kongens gate and Brugata. Following the opening of the new Hålogaland Bridge across Rombaksfjorden in December 2018, it now only takes around 50 minutes to reach the town centre from Narvik/Harstad airport (flights from Oslo with SAS & Norwegian and regionally with Widerøe; code EVE) at Evenes, roughly 60km away. To do so, take the Flybuss from the airport, which runs in connection with flight arrivals and departures (w flybussen.no/narvik; 238NOK one-way; 357NOK return). Note that Narvik is not served by the Hurtigruten coastal ferry. Public transport times can be found at w 177nordland.no.

TOURIST INFORMATION The **tourist office** (℡76 96 56 00; e post@visitnarvik.com; w visitnarvik.com; ⊕ mid-Aug–mid-Jun 10.00–16.00 daily; mid-Jun–mid-Aug 10.00–19.00 daily) is located in the centre of town at Kongens gate 39.

WHERE TO STAY *Map, opposite*

Scandic Narvik Kongens gate 33; ℡76 96 14 00; e narvik@scandichotels.com; w scandichotels.com. A swanky hotel in the town centre whose sleek, oval design over 18 storeys has really won over the people of Narvik. Rooms are bright & airy & décor is inspired by the surrounding countryside. Fabulous views of the town & the Ofotfjorden from the rooftop bar. €€€€

Quality Grand Royal Kongens gate 64; ℡76 97 70 00; e q.royal@choice.no; w nordicchoicehotels.no. Decked out in a bright & breezy modern Scandinavian style in an attempt to compete with rival Scandic Narvik. Although it still plays second fiddle to the Scandic, it wins in terms of historical significance: the building served as the Gestapo's HQ & courtroom during the war. €€€€

Breidablikk Tore Hundsgate 41; ℡76 94 14 18; e post@breidablikk.no; w breidablikk.no. Does what it says on the tin: *breidablikk* literally means 'wide view', & that's what you get from this hilltop guesthouse which has been in business since 1950 & is located 2 blocks inland from the main street. All rooms have en-suite facilities & there's tasteful Nordic décor throughout. €€€

✳ **Narvik Wivel** Kongens gate 36; m 90 55 84 81 57; e hilde@narvikhotelwivel.no. One of Narvik's smaller & less fussy hotels, though still offering perfectly comfortable, good-quality rooms. What gives this place the edge over its bigger rivals is, of course, the price, but also the more homely feel. €€€

Astrupgården Kinobakken 1; m 99 49 99 40. Housed in an atmospheric old timber building (which also contains a bar on the ground floor), the youth-hostel-style rooms here are rather cramped, on the basic side & share facilities, but beggars can't be choosers at this price. Unbeatable value for Narvik. Also handy for the bus station. €€

WHERE TO EAT AND DRINK *Map, opposite*

✗ **Rallar'n Pub & Kro** Kongens gate 64; ℡76 97 70 00; ⊕ noon–midnight Mon–Sat, 15.00–midnight Sun. Inside the Quality Grand Royal hotel (see above), this eaterie offers a choice of local specialities: for example, fish soup; ribs; open sandwich with prawns & avocado. €€

✳ 🍽Fiskhallen Kongens gate 42; ⏱ 09.30–
16.30 Mon–Fri, 11.00–14.00 Sat. You can't beat
this simple little café (actually called Albert &
Sigbjørns Catering but known simply as Fiskhallen)
at the entrance to the fish hall for anything fishy:
fish burger; whale steak or a plateful of juicy fresh
prawns. Also does take-away. €
🍽Kafferiet Dronningens gate 47; w kafferiet.
com; ⏱ 10.30–02.00 Mon–Thu, 10.30–00.30 Fri
& Sat. The best of the town's cafés, set back from
Kongens gate up a flight of stone steps, dishing up
the likes of pasta, fish & salads. Of an evening this
place mutates into a bar, & a nightclub at w/ends. €

♀Astrupkjelleren Kinobakken 1; ☎76 94 49
00; ⏱ 21.00–03.00 Wed, Fri & Sat. This Narvik
institution, housed in a venerable old mustard-
coloured timber building (home to Astrupgården),
just off the main street, is really more bar than
restaurant these days, though it serves a small
selection of bar snacks. €
✳ ♀Tøtta Bar Kongens gate 33; ⏱ 18.00–00.30
daily. This chi-chi rooftop lounge bar on the 16th
floor of the Scandic Narvik hotel is a great place for a
drink or a bar snack, offering superb views to boot.
There's an outdoor terrace up here, too. €

WHAT TO SEE AND DO Look at any map of Narvik and you will quickly see how the
iron-ore **harbour**, owned and operated by LKAB of Kiruna, totally dominates the
town, engulfing about a third of it with loading quays, cranes, overhead walkways
and railway sidings. In recent years a tour has been available on Fridays giving a
potted history of the town and its harbour; ask at the tourist office for the latest
details. Whether you take the tour or not, the iron-ore trains – each one 750m long
and composed of a hundred or so wagons – which you're likely to glimpse during
your stay in Narvik make an oddly impressive sight as they trundle through town,
bound for the quayside and the end of their journey from Sweden.

Ofoten Museum (Administrasjonsveien 3; ☎ 76 96 96 50; w museumnord.
no/en/narvik; ⏱ 10.00–15.00 Mon, Wed & Fri; mid-Jun–mid-Aug 10.00–16.00
Mon–Fri, noon–15.00 Sat & Sun; 65NOK) Sandwiched between the Swedish
church and the quayside, the Ofoten Museum contains two main exhibitions of
note: the first is a history of the town, concentrating on the war years and German
occupation – be sure to see the atmospheric black-and-white film clips showing
life in Narvik in the 1920s and the pre-war buildings which were destroyed in
the ferocious fighting for control of the town. The second exhibition details
the construction by navvies (some of whom paid with their lives) of the Ofotbanen
railway across some of Lapland's harshest terrain to Riksgränsen just over the
border with Sweden (page 83). A film recounting the history of the line and its
construction is shown as part of the exhibition – take your seat in the mock-up
of a railway carriage. To mark the completion of the line in 1902, Norwegian
State Railways (NSB) moved part of their administration into the spacious and
rather elegant building that now houses the museum. The Germans also saw
the building's administrative potential and set up their own base in the building
during World War II.

Narvik War Museum (Narvik Krigsmuseum; cnr Brugata & Kongens gate;
☎76 94 44 26; w warmuseum.no; ⏱ 10.00–19.00 daily; 100NOK) Narvik's other
museum is devoted to the five years the town spent under Nazi occupation; the
Krigsmuseum is a joint venture run by two regional universities and the Red
Cross. The museum recounts the Battle of Narvik step by step which began on 9
April 1940, when ten German destroyers with 3,000 soldiers on board attacked
the town, sinking two iron-ore ships. The British responded by attacking the
German fleet and launching an air assault on the town a couple of days later. The
battle raged for two months before the British withdrew due to the worsening

situation in France; German occupation of Narvik began on 8 June 1940 and lasted until 8 May 1945. It is not widely known that the Germans established two concentration camps outside Narvik. The Beisfjord camp was the scene of a massacre that cost 300 prisoners, all Serbs, their lives (see box, page 94); the story is relayed in a moving video in English.

Fagernesfjellet and the cable car★ (☉ Jun & Jul 10.00–01.00 daily; Aug & Sep 10.00–20.00 daily; Oct 10.00–20.00 Sat & Sun; w narvikfjellet.no; 200NOK one-way, 295NOK return) One of the most rewarding things to do in Narvik is to take the breathtaking 7-minute ride on the town's cable car (*gondolbanen* in Norwegian) up Fagernesfjellet peak (656m) from where you can (weather permitting) see as far as the Lofoten islands; the view from up here really is quite unforgettable and the spot is justifiably known across northern Norway for its splendour. Indeed, it's a fine place to observe the midnight sun if you are here between late June and early August when the cable car runs until 01.00. A plethora of hiking trails criss-cross the mountain – the tourist office can help with details. During winter (roughly Nov–May) the cable car is a good way to access the ski slopes and cross-country trails available on the mountain. Skiing up here is pretty special since there are few other places in Lapland that offer such breathtaking views of the surrounding fjords and islands. For more information about ski rental call **Narvikfjellet** (m 90 54 00 88).

Wreck diving One of the most unusual activities available from Narvik is diving to the wrecks of planes and ships lost during World War II. Over 50 planes and 46 ships lie on the bottom of the surrounding fjords – 39 ships went down in Narvik harbour alone. Though you must be a qualified diver to attempt to reach the wrecks, the best way to get to them is on a tour organised by Swedish-run **Dive Narvik** (m + 46 70 563 3777; e info@divenarvik.com; w divenarvik. com), which arranges a variety of excursions and has full information about what you're likely to see.

Rallarveien: the navvy road During the construction of the Ofotbanen between Narvik and the Swedish border in the late 1800s, navvies accessed the remote terrain which would carry the new rail line via an access road, now known as *rallarveien* (Norwegian)/*rallarvägen* (Swedish). Today, the navvy road is a great place to hike or mountain bike and get up close to the spectacular mountain scenery on the border between Norway and Sweden.

MOVING ON FROM NARVIK From Narvik **buses** head north to Tromsø (443NOK) and west to the Vesterålen and Lofoten islands. It's a 4½-hour ride to Tromsø on board the number 100, while to Alta it's a 9-hour journey first on board the 100 to Nordkjosbotn, then the 160 to Storslett and finally the 150 into Alta; you'll need to buy separate tickets for each leg of the journey. If you are heading to the North Cape, you must first spend the night in Alta before continuing the next morning to Honningsvåg.

The Lofotekspressen runs via Narvik/Harstad Evenes airport (code EVE), Tjeldsund and Gullesfjordbotn to Svolvær (362NOK), Leknes and Å (443NOK from Narvik) in the Lofoten islands. To get from Narvik to Vesterålen, you must first take the Lofotekspressen to Gullesfjordbotn and then change for Sortland (334NOK from Narvik); for Harstad take the Lofotekspressen and change at Tjeldsund; times for all buses are at w 177nordland.no.

THE BEISFJORD MASSACRE

Located about 15km southeast of Narvik, Beisfjord was the location of one of the most brutal concentration camps in Norway during World War II. During the summer of 1942, the Germans began transporting 900 prisoners (over a third of them were under 25 years old) from Yugoslavia to northern Norway to work as slave labour, building defences against the Allies. On 15 July 1942, Beisfjord concentration camp was quarantined following an outbreak of typhus among the inmates. Two days later, around 600 men, regarded as healthy, were marched to Bjørnfell, 30km away, where another camp was established close to the Swedish border. On 18 July, the remaining 288 diseased prisoners were ordered to dig their own mass graves and then line up in front of them; in groups of 20, they were machine-gunned by the Norwegian and German guards. Any men who did not die instantly were buried alive. Around 100 men remained in the barracks, too weak to move. The buildings were doused in petrol and set alight; most prisoners perished in the conflagration. Those who tried to escape the flames by jumping out of the windows were shot dead. Of the original 900 prisoners who arrived at Beisfjord, a total of 748 men were either executed or burnt alive. For decades, the massacre and the atrocities that happened at Beisfjord were covered up because members of the Norwegian paramilitary group, Hirden, were involved. Norwegian collaboration during the war remains a painful and shameful topic and, even today, is not a subject that is readily discussed. For details of the Karasjok concentration camp, see page 173.

Finally, **trains** run southeast to Sweden calling at Riksgränsen, Abisko, Kiruna, Gällivare, Luleå and all points south to Stockholm (w sj.se). For coverage of the magnificent rail journey into Sweden at Riksgränsen, see page 84.

THE ISLANDS: VESTERÅLEN AND LOFOTEN

The scenic highlight of any trip to northern Norway, the Vesterålen (pronounced '*vester-oh-len*') and Lofoten ('*loo-fut-en*') islands are a rugged triangular-shaped archipelago off Narvik. Though totally void of Sámi culture, these green, mountainous islands make a perfect antidote to the remote villages of the forested heart of Lapland, and are readily accessible from Narvik, itself linked to Swedish Lapland by train and road.

The **Vesterålen islands** ('western isles'), predominantly Hinnøya, Langøya and Andøya, are the less dramatic of the two groups. Naturally, this being Norway, there are mountains wherever you look, but they are set back from the islands' towns and villages, often forming a backdrop to a view, rather than being the view themselves. From south to north the peaks become gradually less pronounced and craggy in nature – indeed, the north of Andøya is not mountainous at all but given over instead to enormous lowland peat bogs, cloudberry marshes and even coal deposits. Generally, there's a little more land available for farming in Vesterålen than Lofoten and as you travel around you will see tractors working narrow strips of precious flat land beside the coastline, although eking a living from agriculture so far north can never be more than borderline.

Settlements here tend to be nondescript, workaday affairs with few sights to set the pulse racing. The main centres to seek out are **Andenes**, a renowned base for

whale-watching safaris (page 101), and functional **Sortland** and **Stokmarknes**, from where the Hurtigruten ship begins its dramatic passage through one of the most spectacular stretches of the Norwegian coast, the narrow **Raftsundet** sound which separates Vesterålen from Lofoten. Branching off here, the impossibly tight 3km-long **Trollfjorden**, just 100m wide at its mouth, has to be seen to be believed; vertical rock walls towering to a height of 1,000m bear down on the huge ferries and inflatables which edge their way in here. Raftsundet notwithstanding, it is more the experience of travelling through the spectacular mountain and fjordland scenery, and the prospect of what lies ahead in Lofoten, rather than visiting villages for their own sake, that attracts people here.

The **Lofoten islands** (named 'lynx foot' by the Vikings after their supposed resemblance) really are something special. Overwhelmed by the 100km-long **Lofotveggen** (Lofoten Wall), a spine of sheer, snow-clad granite peaks and ravines that runs the length of the archipelago and quite simply takes your breath away, the extreme forces of nature have left their unforgiving mark on the geography of these islands. Smaller, narrower and infinitely more beautiful than their northern neighbours, their rearing mountains finally splinter into the Norwegian Sea beyond the beguiling village of Å in the south. Travel here is relaxed and enjoyable – the climate is generally mild and it is not uncommon for Lofoten to be bathed in warm sunshine while the mainland is depressed by heavy blankets of grey cloud. Spending the afternoon catching the rays on the rocks or the odd sandy beach or wandering through the winding backstreets of idyllic fishing villages is part of Lofoten's charm and it is hard to find anyone who doesn't succumb to this endearing side of island life.

The capital, **Svolvær**, is a good first place to head for; there's a fine selection of accommodation here to choose from, including plenty of traditional wooden fishermen's huts, *rorbuer* (see box, page 98), and some tasty fish suppers served up overlooking the harbour. However, it would be foolish to stop here and miss out on two of the islands' most endearing villages: picturesque **Henningsvær**, reached from the main road via a set of inter-connected islets; Nusfjord and Reine whose pretty painted houses huddle beneath dramatic mountain backdrops; and laid-back Å (pronounced '*oh*'), a gaggle of wooden shacks sitting snugly beneath the most impressive of peaks, seemingly at the end of the world.

GETTING THERE AND AROUND Travelling to and around both the Vesterålen and Lofoten islands takes time. If you have just a few days available, it is probably best to concentrate on just one group of islands, rather than to try to hurtle across the archipelago, wasting time waiting for bus and ferry connections. Distances are deceptively long and roads are often exasperatingly twisty, winding their way around deeply indented fjords and around obstinate mountains. Narvik is as good a place as any to begin a tour of the islands, either with or without your own car. To give an idea of bus fares: a single ticket from Svolvær to Å is 221NOK; Svolvær to Sortland costs 202NOK.

By car With three or four days in hand, and to avoid doubling back on yourself, it is better to start in the Lofoten islands, the more beautiful and scenically spectacular of the two island chains. From Narvik, first head southwest on the E6 towards Bodø then take Route 81 to Skutvik and the summer-only car ferry to Svolvær (m 90 62 07 00; e firmapost@torghatten-nord.no; w torghatten-nord.no; advance booking necessary).

Driving between the Lofoten and Vesterålen islands throws up two choices: either take the 25-minute **car ferry** (w torghatten-nord.no; roughly every 90mins) which operates between **Fiskebøl** (Lofoten) and **Melbu** (Vesterålen); or continue east from Fiskebøl on the E10 through a set of tunnels to Gullesfjordbotn, from where Route 85 heads north to Sortland.

Having reached Sortland in the Vesterålen islands, you then have another choice of routes: either east to busy Harstad via the **car ferry** between **Flesnes** and **Refsnes** (w torghatten-nord.no; hourly; 30mins); or north via Risöyhamn to Andenes, by far the better choice and a good place for whale- and birdwatching, from where there's a **car ferry** (w torghatten-nord.no; ⊕ late May–Aug, 2–3 daily; 1hr 40mins) to Gryllefjord and ultimately – via another ferry between Botnhamn and Brensholmen (w botnhamn.com/departuretimes.htm; late Apr–early Sep, 5–7 daily; 45mins) – north to Tromsø, a ravishingly beautiful drive through the Senja Mountains.

By bus Although more limiting, it is perfectly possible to see the best of the islands without your own car, travelling instead by **bus** and/or **ferry**. The general route outlined above for car drivers is equally feasible by public transport. First take the direct Lofotekspressen bus from Narvik to Svolvær (page 93). Then explore Lofoten by bus – services operate several times daily from Svolvær as far south as Å (228NOK one-way). Return to Svolvær and continue north by bus towards Sortland (221NOK one-way), the main transport interchange, from where you can pick up a connection for Andenes (182NOK one-way) or Harstad (257NOK one-way), should you want to explore more of the Vesterålen islands, or, alternatively, return to Narvik. Should you wish to miss out Andenes, there are also direct buses from Å and Svolvær to Harstad, as well as to Evenes airport; see w avinor.no/evenes for timetable details.

By air Widerøe operate to Leknes and Svolvær airports in Lofoten and to Stokmarknes, Andenes and Narvik/Harstad Evenes airports in Vesterålen. Hence, with some careful planning, it's possible to visit the islands by air. Services also serve Tromsø and Bodø airports on the mainland and full timetable details are available at w wideroe.no. In summer all these routes are included in the 'Explore Norway' air pass; see page 33 for details.

THE VESTERÅLEN ISLANDS

Harstad The largest town in Vesterålen with a population of around 21,000, Harstad's central position in the archipelago has always been its selling point. During the late 1800s, when plentiful catches of herring fuelled a boom in the local economy, the town became the perfect base for landing fish and transporting it to markets throughout the north, thanks to its good road connections. As herring stocks dwindled, Harstad turned to shipbuilding and maintenance; the production of shipping and fishing equipment; and even the import of coal from Svalbard, to make a living. In more recent years, oil exploration has played a significant role in the local economy and today the northern headquarters of Statoil are here, plus Norway's national producer of milk products, Tine, is also stationed here. If the number of heavy trucks that trundle in and out of town today is anything to go by, Harstad is still a key player in the distribution of goods throughout the north of the country.

Getting there

From Evenes airport An airport **bus** runs to Harstad from Evenes airport (44km) in connection with flight arrivals; journey time is around 50 minutes and tickets cost 230NOK single or 344NOK return. There's a schedule and full information online at w flybussen.no. Alternatively, a pre-booked **taxi** costs 395NOK per passenger (⟋77 04 10 00; w harstadtaxi.no). This price is only available when the taxi is booked in advance.

From Tromsø The fastest way between Harstad and Tromsø is by the Hurtigbåt **express boat** which operates two to three times daily to and from the designated quay in the harbour (opposite the bus station) and takes around 3 hours (640NOK one-way). Timetables are at w 177nordland.no. Alternatively, the Hurtigruten sails once daily between the two towns but takes more than twice as long.

Tourist information Harstad is unlikely to be the highlight of any trip to Vesterålen, but it's a pleasant enough town to wind up in if your travels bring you this way; plus it's a useful access point for the Hurtigruten. You'll find the **tourist office** (Sjøgata 1; ⟋77 01 89 89; e post@visitharstad.no; w visitharstad.com; ⏱ 10.00–16.00 Mon–Fri, 10.00–15.00 Sat, 11.00–15.00 Sun), close to the main square, where there's plentiful information to tempt you to stay longer.

🏠 Where to stay

🏠 **Clarion Collection Arcticus** Havnegata 3; ⟋77 04 08 00; e cc.arcticus@choice.no; w choice. no. The best hotel in town overlooking the harbour a short distance from the main square, Torvet, with stylish Scandinavian-style décor throughout & a top-notch sauna & gym. Free evening buffet included. Excellent w/end & summer rates. €€€€/€€€

🏠 **Scandic Harstad** Strandgata 9; ⟋77 00 30 00; e harstad@scandichotels.com; w scandichotels.com. Offers elegant rooms with typical chain hotel décor in the centre of town, most with views out over the harbour. One of the largest hotels in town whose w/end & summer prices are remarkably good value. €€€€/€€€

🏠 **Thon Hotel** Sjøgata 11; ⟋77 00 08 00; e harstad@olavthon.no; w thonhotels.no. The biggest hotel in town, located right by the water's edge, which is popular with summer tour groups.

Rooms here have been decorated with a maritime feel. Comfortable, modern & sensibly priced. €€€€/€€€

🏠 **Tjeldsundbrua Camping** Kvitnes 116, Evenskjer; ⟋99 41 19 00; e post@ tjeldsundbruacamping.no; w tjeldsundbruacamping.no. Halfway between Harstad (25km south) & Evenes airport (18km north), this attractive waterside campsite has great cabins of various sizes snuggling beside the heights of the Tjeldsundbrua bridge, as well as simple en-suite rooms in converted metal containers. Tents pitches 200NOK with access to showers & toilets. €€

🛖 **Harstad Camping** Nesseveien 55; ⟋77 07 36 62; e post@harstadcamping.no; w harstadcamping.no. A great waterside location for Harstad's campsite which is open all year round 5km south of the town centre. Tent pitch 200NOK; there are also cabins for rent from €€€

🍴 Where to eat and drink

🍴 **Brasseri Alo** Strandgata 9; w brasserialo.no; ⟋77 00 30 00; ⏱ 16.30–23.00 Mon–Sat. With a name like this, you may think French bistro. Wrong. Inside the Scandic hotel, this is a classy brasserie serving northern Norwegian dishes such as

seafood risotto, oven-baked halibut in a red-wine sauce or reindeer steak served with a port glaze. *Mains around 300–350NOK.* €€

🍴 **Egon Gründer** Sjøgata 11; ⟋77 00 08 50; ⏱ 10.00–23.30 Mon–Thu, 10.00–midnight Fri &

Sat, 11.00–23.00 Sun. Inside the Thon hotel, a not-too-adventurous menu of pad Thai & a few other stir fries, fajitas, spare ribs & steaks. Dependable & reasonably priced. €€

✳ ✗ **Bark** Rikard Kaarbøsgata 6; ☎40 55 55 50; w barkspiseriogbar.no; ⏰ 11.00–midnight Mon–Thu, 11.00–03.00 Fri & Sat. Urban chic with exposed heating pipes & shutters on the inside of the windows, this pleasing coffee house-cum-bistro is a real find. The best seller is the delicious fish gratin (199NOK), though the fish soup & pasta of the day are also worthy of closer investigation. €

✗ **Café De 4 Roser** Torvet 7B; ⒡; ⏰.11.00–23.00 Tue–Sat. A gloriously stylish continental-style café serving French, English, Italian & American b/fasts (all day) from 75NOK, homemade fish burgers, plus a range of salads & pasta dishes such as red pesto, tomato *concassé* & *ruccola*. Also, the best selection of coffees in town. Beer & smoothies available, too. €

♀**Milano** Strandgata 17; ☎77 07 94 10; w milano-harstad.no; ⏰ noon–midnight daily. Cavernous pizzeria whose generously sized pizzas go from 135NOK for a medium & really draw the crowds. There's seemingly every variety of pizza you can imagine – which come with a pouring of garlic sauce for extra zizz. €

What to see and do Having taken in the goings-on in the harbour and around the main square, there's little else to detain you in the town centre and it is a much better idea to either walk (30mins) or take bus 12 (w 177nordland.no; roughly hourly; 45NOK) to **Trondenes**, the original settlement of Harstad, located on the eponymous tapering peninsula to the east of town. On foot, from the tourist office, first follow Sjøgata, later becoming Strandgata and finally Skolegata as it snakes its way along the harbourside and then cuts up through town. Turn right into Hagebyveien (signed for Trondenes) and follow this road, passing an area of residential housing, until you reach Trondenes.

Trondenes Church (Trondenes kirke; ⏰ late Jun–early Aug 10.00–14.00 Mon–Fri) The main item of interest here, Trondenes kirke occupies a grassy knoll close to the water's edge. The church's setting is totally enchanting: surrounded by a well-kept graveyard and tall, swaying trees with snow-capped mountains in the background; there are good views from here back towards Harstad itself. Although the church's exact age is uncertain, it is thought it was completed on the orders of King Øystein Magnusson shortly after 1430, which makes it the northernmost medieval stone church in Europe; remarkably, the exterior is close to its original state. During the

STAYING IN RORBUER: TRADITIONAL FISHERMEN'S HUTS

While you are in Lofoten, try to stay in a *rorbu* (plural *rorbuer*), a wooden hut on stilts usually by the harbour. Traditionally painted red, they are easy to spot, as most towns and villages have signs up offering them for rent. They come in various shapes and sizes but are all based on the traditional hut used by fishermen for overnight accommodation before it became more practical to sleep on board their boats. Generally composed of one or two bedrooms (some with bunk beds), kitchen and bathroom with running water and electricity, some *rorbuer* are the genuine article and may be a hundred years old or so; others are more modern copies of the original, and though comfortable enough, lack the charm of the creaking old timbers. *Rorbuer* can be booked through tourist offices or directly where listed in the text. Prices vary according to standard and size, though you should expect to pay around 950NOK per night for a simple affair, or up to 3,000NOK for a luxury number with all mod cons.

late medieval period, the church served as the main place of worship for thousands of people across the entire north of Norway. It is likely that the current church was the third to stand here, replacing two other stave churches built in the 11th and 12th centuries. Inside, three ornate Gothic triptychs, fine examples of the medieval Church art of northern Germany, adorn the altar and date from the 1400s. Unusually, the Baroque pulpit is equipped with an hourglass to dissuade the priest from engaging in lengthy ecclesiastical ramblings.

Trondenes historical centre (Trondenes Historiske Senter; Trondenesveien 122; w stmu.no; ☉ mid-Jun–mid-Aug 10.00–16.00 daily; rest of the year 10.00–14.00 Mon–Fri, 11.00–16.00 Sun; 125NOK) Next door to the church the heritage centre is the place to get to grips with historical developments in this part of Norway through the imaginative use of multi-media exhibitions. Housed in a state-of-the-art building with a traditional turf roof, it not only contains examples of original Viking artefacts discovered in the area but also recreates the sounds and smells of the period with a multi-media show.

Adolf's gun (Adolfkanonen; w adolfkanonen.com; twice-daily guided tours mid-Jun–mid-Aug departing from Harstad by bus at 12.30 & 16.00; 195NOK) The other thing to see out at Trondenes is a massive World War II land-based gun, the only fortification from the war that has been restored, though its location inside a restricted military zone makes visits rather tricky. However, regulations stipulate that you must have your own transport to cover the kilometre between the entrance gate, about 1km up the hill from the church, and the gun itself. This is not provided by the guided tour.

The Arts Festival of North Norway (w festspillnn.no) Undoubtedly, the best time to be in Harstad is during the second half of June when the biggest cultural event in the whole of Lapland swings into action. A veritable orgy of music, theatre, dance, film and exhibitions featuring Norwegian and foreign performers, it generally takes place during the third or fourth week of June. Running in tandem with the main event, there are also special festivals aimed at children of different ages. Naturally, accommodation is at a premium during this period and must be booked well in advance.

Moving on from Harstad Harstad is a good place from which to reach other destinations in Vesterålen and Lofoten by ferry and bus. The Hurtigruten ship sails south at 08.30 to Sortland (4½hrs), Stokmarknes (6hrs 45mins) and Svolvær (10hrs), passing through the Raftsundet Sound and Trollfjorden. It sails north at 07.45 arriving in Tromsø at 14.15. By bus there are direct services from Harstad to Sortland, from where connections can be made to Andenes; for Svolvær, change at Tjeldsund. Car drivers might want to consider the car ferry that operates between Refsnes and Flesnes (w torghatten-nord.no; hourly; 30mins) as a way of shortening the journey between Harstad and Sortland. On leaving Sortland simply follow Route 83 signed for Sortland, which will take you to the ferry quay at Refsnes.

Sortland Try not to get stuck in Sortland, a dreary place utterly devoid of attractions (unless you consider the headquarters of the Norwegian Coastguard reason enough for your heart to flutter), just across the arching bridge which links the two islands of Langøya and Hinnøya. Given its strategic location on the E10, you have no choice but to pass through here en route to Lofoten, and, indeed, Sortland is a major traffic junction and bus interchange point for the islands. Backed by jagged peaks and fronting the narrow Sortlandsundet sound, you'd have hoped that Sortland could have made more of its geographically stunning location. Sadly, the mundane parallel streets of modern concrete blocks do little to raise the spirits and you are best using Sortland as a place to stock up on provisions, fuel or bus timetables.

Tourist information Admittedly, Sortland's **tourist office** (✆ 76 11 14 80; e turistinfo@vestreg.no; w visitvesteralen.com; ⊕ mid-Jun–mid-Aug 09.00–17.00 Mon–Fri, 10.00–15.00 Sat, noon–16.00 Sun; rest of the year 09.00–15.30 Mon–Fri) does its best to sell the town and is a good source of information on local bus routes. It is a 5–10-minute walk west of the bus station at Kjøpmannsgata 2.

🏠 *Where to stay, eat and drink* Should you find yourself in the unenviable position of having to spend the night in Sortland, perhaps waiting for the Hurtigruten ship, which sails southbound (for Svolvær and Raftsundet) at 13.00, or northbound at 03.00, there are a couple of places to stay and some decent places to eat.

🏠 **Sortland Hotell** Västerålsgata 59; ✆ 76 10 84 00; e post@sortlandhotell.no; w sortlandhotell.no. A comfortable hotel, 3 blocks back from the sound with newly renovated rooms – the best place to stay in town. Most of the superior rooms are now located in a newly built section of the hotel. €€€€

🏠 **Strand Hotell** Strandgata 34; ✆ 76 10 84 00; e post@sortlandhotell.no; w strandhotell. no. Another central option just a stone's throw from the town's main street. Check in is at the nearby Sortland Hotell (see above), which owns & operates this cheaper & less fancy option. €€€€

🏠 **Postmestergården** Nordlysvegen 35; ✆ 76 12 10 41; e asoelsne@online.no; ⊕ Jun–Aug. Simple B&B where b/fast costs an extra 75NOK. To get here from the town centre, take Vesterålsgata east to its junction with Kirkåsvegen; turn left into this street & you'll find the guesthouse a little further along at the junction with Nordlysvegen. €

✘ **Ekspedisjonen** Rådhusgata 26; ✆ 76 20 10 40; w ekspedisjonen.wordpress.com; ⊕ 10.00–18.00 Mon & Tue, 10.00–22.00 Wed & Thu, 10.00–23.00 Fri, 11.00–23.00 Sat. Down by Hurtigruten quay, the most tasteful & stylish option in the town centre. Serves up fishy mains, pasta dishes & salads, though there are some cheaper set lunch options, too. €

✘ **Hong Kong** Västerålsgata 70; ✆ 76 13 38 88; ⊕ 13.00–23.00 Sun–Thu & Sat, 13.00–midnight Fri. Predictable Chinese dishes. €

✘ **Milano** Torggata 17; ✆ 76 12 28 38; ⊕ 13.00–22.30 daily. In the main square, the most economical & reliable place to fill an empty stomach with pizzas, pasta & steaks. €

🍷 **Saabyes Bibliotek** Inside Sortland Hotell (see left); ✆ 76 10 84 00; ⊕ 18.00–22.00 Mon–Sat. Named after a local author who lived in Sortland for many years, this new hotel-restaurant serves local lamb & Arctic char among other locally sourced ingredients, & is certainly the most stylish place in town to dine. €€

Moving on from Sortland By **bus**, the most accessible destinations from Sortland are Andenes, Stokmarknes, Svolvær, Harstad and Narvik; timetables are at w 177nordland.no. When it comes to leaving Sortland, it's worth knowing some of the distances involved in reaching other towns in the region, which can be deceptively long: Andenes (101km); Harstad (80km); Narvik (200km); Stokmarknes (27km); Svolvær (79km); and Tromsø (411km). An airport bus runs from Sortland Hotell and the bus station to the **airport** in Stokmarknes (known as Skagen; 115NOK) in conjunction with Widerøe departures; another airport bus connects Sortland bus station with Evenes airport, 126km away (315NOK single; 472NOK return; buy online at w flybussen.no for these prices).

Andenes It is the chance to go **whale-watching** from Andenes, a small and rather attractive village, 100km north of Sortland, at the northernmost edge of Vesterålen, clinging to the very tip of Andøya Island, that brings most visitors to the islands. There's reputed to be a 95–99% chance of seeing whales on the safaris which leave daily from the harbour – sperm and minke whales are found in relatively large numbers in the waters off Vesterålen's northern tip, but amazingly **killer whales** are also present, which are the big attraction, and good enough reason to sign up for a whale safari here rather than elsewhere. Sperm whales are seen on most trips though it is hard to predict whether other species will put in an appearance. However, Andenes's secret is its proximity to the continental shelf and the nutrient-rich feeding grounds in the vicinity, which draw whales to the area. Incidentally, Andenes is the location of a research centre for marine biologists who are studying cetaceans in the waters of this part of the Norwegian Sea.

In summer and winter, gulls are also present here in large colonies, both the glaucous and Iceland varieties, and you'll see hundreds of them squawking raucously from the rooftops of the wooden buildings down by the harbourside – a favourite nesting location. Andenes is also the southernmost wintering area in Norway for Steller's eider ducks which migrate here from their breeding grounds along the Arctic coasts of eastern Siberia and Alaska; common and king eiders, purple sandpipers and long-tailed ducks can also be seen in Andenes at certain times of year. From around March onwards vast shoals of migrating Arctic cod congregate in the waters off Andenes to spawn; naturally, these easy pickings attract seabirds in great numbers. Other than freelance birdwatching at the harbour, Andenes is a good place to book **birdwatching trips**, in particular to see **puffins** (page 104) or **sea eagles**.

Getting there

By ferry from the mainland
Although it is possible to drive to Andenes along the E10 via Sortland, from whence Route 82 covers the last 100km or so north, a very useful ferry service operates between late May and August from tiny Gryllefjord (reached along Route 86 northwest of Finnsnes, off the main E6 from Narvik) across to Andenes, cutting out the tiring and extremely twisty drive across the Vesterålen islands. Operated by **Senja Fergene** (w torghatten-nord.no; passengers 180NOK, cars 482NOK), the ferry crossing takes roughly 1 hour 40 minutes and operates two or three times daily. For details of the ferry between Brensholmen and Botnhamn (which reduces the journey from Tromsø), see page 96.

By air
The fastest way to reach Andenes is by plane. The airport is barely 1km from the town centre and is readily accessible on foot – the walk into town takes around 10 minutes; simply follow Storgata in the direction of the lighthouse. Widerøe fly to Andenes from Tromsø (a flight of around 20mins), as well as from Stokmarknes.

Tourist information
Andenes's **tourist office** (℡ 41 60 58 52; e post@visitandoy. info; w visitandoy.info; ⊕ mid-Jun–mid-Aug 08.30–17.30 Mon–Fri, 10.00–17.30 Sat, noon–16.00 Sun; rest of the year 09.00–16.00 Mon–Fri) is located at Kong Hans gate 8. The friendly staff can help with accommodation bookings as well as the whale safaris and transport enquiries.

 ## Where to stay

Grønnbuene Rorbu Hotel Storgata 51; ℡ 76 14 90 90; e booking@andeneshotell.

no; w andeneshotell.no. The place to come for *rorbuer* in Andenes, though if you're looking for a traditional, old *rorbu*, you'll be disappointed. The place has expanded rapidly, building even more modern apts & suites, thinly disguised as *rorbuer*. A fine place to stay but no longer the real McCoy it once was. Check in is at the Thon Andrikken hotel next door (see right). €€€€

🏠 **Marena** Storgata 15; m 90 08 46 00; e info@hotellmarena.no; w hotellmarena. no. Around 30 bright & airy rooms, right on the main road & within easy walking distance of the harbour. The décor is plain & unfussy & this welcoming, privately owned hotel is an altogether sensible choice for a stay in Andenes. €€€€

🏠 **Fargeklatten Veita** Sjøgata 38A; m 97 76 00 20; e fargeklatten1@gmail.com; w fargeklatten.no. This creaking old wooden house from 1851 is a real find. Stuffed full of period furniture from the 1800s, it is one of the most atmospheric places to stay in the whole region. There are only 4 dbls here, which share facilities, so advance booking is essential (1 has a sea view for an additional 100NOK). €€€

🏠 **Thon Andrikken** Storgata 53; ☎76 14 90 90; e andrikken@olavthon.no; w thonhotels.com. The Thon chain has moved into Andenes & bought up seemingly everything. This hulk of a building on the town's main street features perfectly comfortable but rather run-of-the-mill modern, identikit rooms. €€€

🏠 **Andøy Natursenter** Hamnegata 1; ☎76 14 12 03; e post@hisnakul.no. Located next to the Whale Centre, the simple dbl rooms with shared facilities here are exceptionally good value, though other than free wireless internet access, they include no frills. A communal kitchen is available for self-catering. €€

✕ Where to eat and drink

✕ **Lysthuset Sørvesten** Storgata 51; ☎76 14 14 99; ⏱ 11.00–23.00 daily. Long-standing & well-respected restaurant serving quite exceptional fresh fish: 2 good choices are the baked salmon with cucumber & sour cream salad & the *boknafisk* (unsalted wind-dried fish) with creamed carrot & crisp bacon. €€

✕ **Riggen** Hamnegata 1C; ☎76 11 56 05; w riggen.no; ⏱ 11.00–21.00 Mon–Thu & Sun, 11.00–22.00 Fri & Sat. Inside the Whale Centre, you'll find the restaurant with the best views in town – looking right out over the sea. A mix of local dishes & international favourites aimed at tourists on the whale-watching tours. Pricewise, the best option is the eat-as-much-as-you-want buffet at 189NOK (250NOK on Sun). There's also a pub here that's open on Fri & Sat (21.00–02.30). €€

✕ **Arresten** Prinsens gate 6; ☎76 11 58 70; ⏱ 11.00–23.00 Mon–Thu, 11.00–02.00 Fri & Sat, noon–22.00 Sun. Located in the town's former jail (hence the name), this snug & intimate little Indian restaurant is a great place for the likes of chicken tikka massala, sweet & sour pork or cod fish curry. Also a popular choice for a beer. €

🍰 **Bårds Bakeri** Kong Hans gate 1; ⏱ 07.00–16.00 Mon–Fri, 07.00–15.00 Sat. The town's best café & cake shop with a small selection of light lunches available. There's also an agreeable outdoor terrace that catches the summer sun. €

🍺 **Mea Pub** Fridtjof Nansens gate 1; ⏱ 18.00–01.00 Wed & Thu, 15.00–02.30 Fri, 13.00–02.30 Sat, 15.00–01.00 Sun. With its collection of nautical knick-knacks & various banknotes behind the bar, this atmospheric fisherman's pub located by the harbour, opposite Grønnbua, is the best place in town for a beer. €

What to see and do
The Whale Centre (Hamnegata 1C; ⏱ late May–mid-Jun & mid-Aug–late Aug 08.30–16.00 daily; mid-Jun–mid-Aug 08.30–19.00 daily; early Sep–mid-Sep 10.30–15.00 daily; rest of the year 09.00–15.00 Mon–Fri; 130NOK) The aim of the Whale Centre's museum is to help visitors understand more about the life of the whales which can be found off Andenes through a series of exhibitions. The prime exhibit, is the complete skeleton of a 16m male sperm whale, which stranded on a nearby beach in September 1996 – the skeleton is truly massive and fills an entire room. The bones were labelled and placed in nets in the sea to be thoroughly cleaned before being reassembled and put on display.

The Northern Lights Centre (Hamnegata 1B; ◷ late Jun–mid-Aug 10.00–18.00 daily; 40NOK) Next door to the Whale Centre, this is a rather worthy attempt to explain the aurora borealis. Although the aurora can be seen, weather permitting, across the northern skies during winter, Andøya Island boasts greater activity thanks to its location under the auroral oval. Despite this, the centre fails to excite with its rather worthy displays about the science behind the phenomenon; the film showing displays of the northern lights is perhaps the centre's most engaging item.

Andenes lighthouse (Hamnegata; ◷ mid-Jun–Aug noon–15.00 daily; guided tours 11.00 & 16.00; contact the Andenes Museum; 90NOK) Built of cast iron and measuring 40m tall, the Andenes lighthouse can be seen right across town, resplendently painted in bright red. Its light has been shining bright ever since construction in 1859 and today there's even a webcam (w museumnord.no/en/andenes-museum) at the top of the 148 steep steps which lead up to the light, offering views of the town.

Andenes Museum (Andoymuseet; Richard Withs gate 9; w museumnord.no/en/andenes-museum; ◷ mid-Jun–mid-Aug 10.00–18.00 daily; early–mid-Jun & mid–late Aug noon–15.00 daily; Jan–mid-Mar 10.00–15.30 daily; 50NOK) The pretty white timber building with red window frames beside the lighthouse is home to Anodymuseet (known as Andenes Museum in English). Exhibitions focus on the Arctic regions with special attention given to local man, Hilmar Nøis (1891–1975), who spent no fewer than 38 winters in Svalbard hunting seals and polar bears; today several locations in Svalbard bear his name. In addition, there are displays on the ecology and geography of Andøya Island.

Trips by RIB inflatable Sea Safari Andenes (m 91 67 49 60; e post@seasafariandenes.no; w seasafariandenes.no) are the people to seek out should you fancy scudding over the sea in an RIB boat on the lookout for whales or birds. They operate daily

WHALE-WATCHING FROM ANDENES

Hvalsafari ✳ (☏ 76 11 56 00; w whalesafari.no) operates from late May to mid-September daily and has two vessels. There are several daily departures (detailed times are on the website) and booking at least a couple of days in advance is wise since the trips are often sold out weeks beforehand; bear in mind that bad weather or too few passengers can lead to cancellations. The boats take around an hour to reach the whales and the entire trip lasts from 1½ to 4 hours, costing 1095NOK, which includes entrance to the Whale Centre, a light meal on board and a certificate, which, frankly, you can live without. It is a good idea to have extremely warm clothes with you, including a hat and gloves, as it can get very cold out on deck waiting to see a glimpse of the whales. Expert guides are on hand to make sure you don't miss anything. From October to March, tours operate twice weekly on Wednesday and Saturday, generally at 10.00 or 11.00, to see the massive fin whales and killer whales which are present off Andenes; check the website for the latest information and remember that daylight at this time of year is in short supply. Smaller trips onboard RIB boats carrying a maximum of 12 people are available through Sea Safari Andenes (see above) during the summer months.

from the harbour between late May and September using inflatables which can accommodate up to 12 people. There are full details of all tours, including whale-watching and snorkelling with orcas, on their website. A 3-hour whale-watching trip in summer, for example, costs 1,100NOK.

Andøya Space Center (Bleiksveien 46; ℡76 14 46 00; w spaceshipaurora.no; ⏲ mid-Aug–mid-Jun 10.00–14.00 Mon–Fri; mid-Jun–mid-Aug 11.00–17.30 daily) On the road towards Bleik, the Andøya Space Center carries out research into the northern lights, firing rockets into the aurora in an attempt to learn more about the phenomenon. Inside, visitors can take a virtual trip into space on board the spaceship *Aurora* to experience the northern lights. There's also a film (*16 mins*) about the aurora which details some of the research work carried out on Andøya as well as exhibitions about Norway's contribution as a space nation. Visits cost 350NOK to ride the spaceship or 125NOK just to see the film and exhibitions. Tickets should be booked in advance online.

Puffin tours Andenes makes a good base from which to go **birdwatching** (w puffinsafari.no; ⏲ Jun–mid-Aug 13.00 & 15.00 daily; note that these times are approximate as the boat leaves once it's full, even if this is earlier than the times given; trips last 90mins; 500NOK). One of Norway's most spectacular seabird colonies is found on the island of Bleiksøya, a 20-minute boat ride from the village of Bleik, 10km southwest of Andenes. Home to 80,000 pairs of puffins and 6,000 pairs of kittiwakes, there's a chance to catch a glimpse of cormorants, razorbills and guillemots. Remarkably, the spectacular white-tailed sea eagle is also seen on every trip, generally circling high above the island searching for prey. Note that the 13.00 departure does not operate from early to mid-June and the puffins leave around 20 August. It's possible to reach Bleik by bus from Andenes (45NOK); timetables are at w 177nordland.no.

Stokmarknes From Sortland, the E10 hugs the shore of Sortlandsundet as it heads the 27km southwest to Stokmarknes, famous in Norway at least as the birthplace of Hurtigruten, the cruise specialists. As you cross the second of two bridges that lead into town you will catch sight of one of the line's former vessels, *Finnmarken*, standing high and dry beside the quayside currently used for Hurtigruten departures. Linked to the adjacent building, Hurtigrutens Hus, by a walkway over the road, the ship forms part of the main attraction in Stokmarknes: the **Hurtigruten Museum** (Hurtigrutemuseet; ⏲ Jun–Sep 10.00–16.00 daily; rest of the year 14.00–16.00 daily; w museumnord.no/en/hurtigruten-museum; 100NOK), an engaging collection of nautical paraphernalia that recounts the life and times of Norway's most famous shipping line.

The brainchild of local man Richard With, Hurtigruten (literally 'the fast line') first saw the light of day in 1893 when, with financial support from the Norwegian post office, who were keen to find a reliable way to get mail to outlying districts of the country, the first vessel, D/S *Vesteraalen*, entered service sailing between Trondheim and Hammerfest. Seemingly everything from an old upright piano that once helped entertain passengers to a video film of the engine room of the *Harald Jarl* is on display in the museum, from which a lift leads to the walkway across the MS *Finnmarken*. Built in 1956 in Hamburg, the vessel was in service until 1993, joining the museum six years later. Walking around this empty ship, exploring its deserted restaurant, lounges and corridors, is a curiously unsettling experience – strangely ghostlike.

Tourist information Like Sortland, Stokmarknes is another place you don't want to get stuck. The **tourist office** (↖76 15 00 00; w visitvesteralen.com; ⊕ mid-Jun–mid-Aug 10.00–15.30 Mon–Fri; rest of the year 10.00–16.00 Mon–Wed, 10.00–19.00 Thu) is located in the library inside Hurtigrutens Hus.

🏠 **Where to stay, eat and drink**

🏠 **Vesterålen Kysthotell** ↖76 15 29 99; e resepsjon@kystlandsbyen.no; w vesteralenkysthotell.no. A mere 7min walk from the town centre, across the bridge on the island of Børøya. Also has a number of *rorbuer* for rent for upwards of 3,500NOK/night. €€€€

✗ **Rødbrygga** Markedsgata 6A; ↖76 15 26 66; w rødbrygga.no; ⊕ 09.00–01.30 Mon–Thu, 09.00–03.00 Fri, 11.00–03.00 Sat, 16.00–01.30 Sun. Inordinately popular creaking old timber building (painted red) next to MS *Finnmarken*, which serves up a wide variety of pizzas & pasta dishes for around 149NOK, burgers from 104NOK as well as several steak dishes (around 234NOK) & fish main courses (from 149NOK). €

Raftsundet and Trollfjorden One of the most remarkable sights in the whole of Norwegian Lapland is now on the doorstep. The **Raftsundet** sound is a 20km-long strait, which separates the Vesterålen and Lofoten island groups – and it is through here that the Hurtigruten ship charts a careful course bound for Svolvær. From Stokmarknes the route first takes you under the arching bridge carrying the E10, past the airport, and seemingly straight towards a wall of sheer mountains. Roughly 45 minutes after departure, the ferries then make a sharp right turn to enter the strait: the scenery through the sound is spectacular: precipitous rock faces rising up from the sea, culminating in rows of craggy pinnacles and peaks which are dressed in snow even during the height of summer.

The highlight of the voyage through the sound comes when the superferries nudge their way into the narrowest of fjords, **Trollfjorden**, at roughly the halfway point. Barely 100m wide at its mouth, the fjord is edged by smooth, vertical walls of granite reaching up to 1,000m above sea level; it seems an impossible task to sail such a large vessel into such an impossibly tight inlet, but the ferries sail all the way to the head of the fjord, a distance of around 3km, before performing the most impressive of nautical pirouettes to turn round and inch their way out again. Needless to say, when the announcement is made that the ferry is about to enter Trollfjorden, there's one almighty scrum on board to get the best views. If you can't get up front to watch the boat enter the fjord, standing aft is equally as good as you can still appreciate the fjord in all its geological splendour. One note of caution, however: during the winter months, the Hurtigruten ship doesn't sail into Trollfjorden because of the extreme risk of avalanches and rock falls; check with the ship before departure for precise conditions and information. Once back into Raftsundet, it is another hour or so to Svolvær.

Incidentally, if taking one of the Hurtigrutens between Stokmarknes and Svolvær doesn't fit with your travel plans, you can still experience the Trollfjord – arguably even more breathtakingly – on a trip by **high-speed inflatable** from Svolvær itself (page 108).

THE LOFOTEN ISLANDS

Svolvær The charming, waterside town of Svolvær makes a great introduction to the Lofoten islands. True, it may not be as picture-postcard-perfect as the other small fishing villages to the south, but it is nonetheless an easy place to spend a couple of days simply chilling out in the harbour-front cafés and restaurants or heading out to the Trollfjord, if you missed it on your way here. In addition, Svolvær is one of the easiest places to reach in the entire island chain. Not only is the town served by Hurtigruten, direct buses from Narvik and a handy car ferry across the waters of Vestfjorden from Skutvik (a straightforward and much shorter drive from Narvik than heading here along the E10) but there's even an airport, 6km east of the town, with direct flights to the mainland.

Backed by a ring of stubborn mountains, Svolvær's development has been limited by difficult terrain. So instead, the town has spilled out seawards on to the islands which lie immediately offshore, all interlinked and connected to the town itself by a series of bridges and roads. Having said that, Svolvær is not a big place; the focus of life here is the main square towards the southern end of the town centre beside the harbour. Behind it you will find the two main streets, Vestfjordgata and Storgata, which run parallel to each other and are the location for most of the town's shops and other services.

Tourist information   Usefully located in the main square at Torget 18, the **tourist office** (✆76 07 05 75; e info@lofoten.info; w lofoten.info; ☺ late Aug–late May 09.00–15.30 Mon–Fri, 10.00–14.00 Sat; late May–late Jun 09.00–20.30 Mon–Fri, 10.00–15.00 Sat; late Jun–late Aug 09.00–20.30) has plentiful supplies of information about local accommodation, transport services and ideas on what to do with your day.

🏠 **Where to stay**   Svolvær is the capital of Lofoten and consequently the largest place on the islands, and there's no shortage of places to stay here, though you should consider booking ahead during the summer months since it is a popular destination for holidaying Norwegians.

🏠 **Fasthotel Lofoten** Sjøgata 4; m 94 89 48 06; e booking@fasthotels.no; w fasthotels. no. One of the Svolvær's cheaper hotels comprising a modern block on the edge of the town centre, though with perfectly respectable rooms; definitely worth a look if things seem full elsewhere. Since there is no reception, you can gain access using a door code emailed or texted to you on the day of arrival. Some rooms have balconies. €€€€

🏠 **Lofoten Rorbuer** Jektveien 10; m 91 59 54 50; e post@lofoten-rorbuer.no; w lofoten-rorbuer. no. Another great central quayside location. A total of 16 dbl rooms (some sharing facilities) & en-suite apts decked out with wooden floors, wood-panelling & chequered curtains. Some of the units have their own kitchen. €€€€

🏠 **Lofoten Suite Hotel** Havnepromenaden 2; ✆47 67 01 00; e post@lofoten-suitehotel. no; w lofoten-suitehotel.no. It doesn't get much more luxurious than this; brand new suites of varying sizes all featuring a bedroom, living room, kitchenette & balcony, overlooking the harbour. This towering wood-fronted structure of glass & chrome is perched above Bacalao (see opposite) & enjoys views to die for. €€€€

🏠 **Scandic Svolvær** Lamholmen; ✆76 07 22 22; e svolvaer@scandichotels.com; w scandichotels.no. Occupying the tiny island of Lamholmen in the middle of the harbour, accessed by the long Sjømannsgata causeway, the Scandic has accommodation in several attractive, maritime-style buildings located right on the water's edge. An excellent choice if Svinøya Rorbuer is full. €€€€

🏠 **Svinøya Rorbuer** Gunnar Bergs vei 2, Svinøya; ✆76 06 99 30; e post@svinoya.no; w svinoya.no. The accommodation of choice in Svolvær on the island of Svinøya, accessed via the Svinøybrua Bridge at the eastern end of Austnesfjordgata. 38 waterside rorbuer of different shapes, sizes & ages – some of which (number 18, for example) are original & over 100 years old. Others, including the larger Rorbu suites, are new-builds & contain more modern fittings. High season is Jun–Aug when prices are several hundred kroner higher than at other times of the year. There's a selection of comfortable, modern suites in the Vestfjordsuitene section. €€€€

🏠 **Thon Lofoten** Torget; ✆76 04 90 00; e lofoten@olavthon.no; w thonhotels.no. This towering glass & chrome structure looks totally out of keeping with the other diminutive buildings in Svolvær's main square, but it does enjoy an unbeatably central location. Rooms here are simply decorated in minimalist Nordic style & have great views out over the sea. €€€€

✕ Where to eat and drink

✱ 🏠 **Børsen Spiseri** Gunnar Bergs vei 2, Svinøya; 📞 76 06 99 30; w svinoya.no/en/restaurant; ⊕ 18.00–22.00 daily. Just to the right of the bridge as you cross on to Svinøya & the reception building for Svinøya Rorbuer (see opposite), this atmospheric restaurant housed in a former fish warehouse dating from 1828 is the place to come for a special occasion. With low ceilings, wooden beams & creaking floorboards, the candlelit ambience is the perfect place to enjoy top-of-the-range cuisine specialising in locally caught fish: the signature dish is traditional *boknafisk*, a cod dish with chopped boiled eggs & bacon chunks in a creamy sauce (330NOK). €€

✕ **Du Verden** Torget 15; 📞76 07 09 75; w duverden.no/svolvar; ⊕ 11.00–23.00 Sun–Thu, 11.00–03.00 Fri & Sat. Downstairs at this agreeable little restaurant they serve a wide choice of seafood dishes as well as pizzas (both with tomato sauce & crème fraîche bases), salads & pasta dishes. The good-value creamy fish soup (195NOK) is a particular favourite year-on-year & features both fish & seafood. €€/€

✕ **Bacalao** Havnepromenaden 2; 📞76 07 94 00; w bacalaobar.no; ⊕ 10.00–01.00 Mon–Thu, 10.00–02.30 Fri & Sat, noon–01.00 Sun. A stylish, airy brasserie with lots of glass & chrome that can more than hold its own against the best of any big city. Cheaper than its neighbour, Du Verden, there's fish soup, salads, pasta dishes, burgers & a choice of sandwiches from 139NOK. €

✕ **Fellini Svolvær** Vestfjordgata 8; 📞76 07 77 60; w fellinisvolvar.no; ⊕ 11.00–22.30 daily. A good & dependable family-run Italian restaurant in the centre of town, offering sensibly priced pasta dishes, pizzas & steaks as well as take-aways. €

What to see and do The reason to come to Svolvær is not to tick off a long list of blockbuster tourist sights – there really aren't any. Instead, the simple pleasure of wandering the streets in summer and sipping a coffee on the quayside is more than enough to keep most visitors happy for a few hours.

Magic Ice (Fiskergata 36; 📞76 07 40 11; w magicice.no; ⊕ Jun–Aug noon–23.00 daily; rest of the year 18.00–22.00; 225NOK) This is an impressive collection of ice sculptures stored at –5°C in a former fish-freezing plant. The sculptures are made from frozen tap water, which is then hewn into various fantastic shapes and figures. In the gallery area you'll also find a bar where you can sample vodka and schnapps – on the rocks, naturally. The exhibition is primarily aimed at tourists from the Hurtigruten ships who pour into the freezer to see what all the fuss is about when the ships are in port. If you can avoid the peak visiting times of 18.30–20.00 and 21.00–22.00 you'll have the place to yourself.

Northern Norwegian Art Centre (Nordnorsk Kunstnersenter; O J Kaarbøs gate; 📞76 06 67 70; w nnks.no; ⊕ 10.00–22.00 daily; free) Located right beside the Thon hotel in the centre of town, the Nordnorsk Kunstnersenter hosts alternating exhibitions of contemporary visual art, ceramics and handicrafts by Norwegian and international artists. There's also a permanent exhibition showcasing the work of local artist, Gunnar Berg (1863–93), who was known for his paintings of his native Lofoten. His most famous work is *Battle of Trollfjord* which was fought in 1890 between local fishermen and large steamship owners over fishing rights. He died at the age of 30 following the amputation of one of his legs after the discovery of cancer.

Lofoten War Museum (Lofoten Krigsminnemuseum; m 91 73 03 28; w lofotenkrigmus.no; ⊕ 10.00–16.00 Mon–Fri, 11.00–15.00 Sat, noon–15.00 Sun;

100NOK) The museum charts the British commando raids on the Lofoten islands in 1941 that were aimed at seizing herring oil to prevent the Germans from using it to manufacture explosives as well as displaying uniforms and countless other objects from World War II.

Boat trips to the Trollfjord ✳ Operated by **Lofoten Explorer** (**m** 97 15 22 48; **w** lofoten-explorer.no) from the harbour, trips by **high-speed inflatables** leave daily from June to August between 10.30 and 13.00 for an unforgettable excursion to the Trollfjord (895NOK) and the surrounding bays and islands. Bookings can be made at the company's office by the quayside and warm clothing is provided. If you missed the opportunity to travel by the Hurtigruten ferry through Raftsundet sound, calling in at Trollfjorden, this is an absolute must and one of the most memorable (and sensibly priced) excursions you can undertake while in Norwegian Lapland. Between September and May, excursions to the Trollfjord also include a **sea eagle safari** and operate at 11.30 from Wednesday to Saturday (895NOK).

Svolværgeita Mountain Svolvær is the place from which to begin a **hike** to the twin peaks you can clearly see in the distance to the northeast of the town, known as Svolværgeita, the Svolvær goat. Climbed for the first time in 1910, the mountain's summit is composed of two noticeable horns, a distance of 1.5m apart. Daring, some would say foolhardy, climbers leap precariously from one horn to the other to crown their achievement of climbing the peak. A path begins beside the E10, a short distance outside of the town itself (ask the tourist office for precise directions), though you should only consider hiking to the very top if you are an experienced mountaineer. The pinnacles are vertical rock faces that can only be ascended with specialist equipment – and a good deal of bravery.

Moving on from Svolvær From Svolvær, the quay is located in the centre of town a short distance south of the main square. The Hurtigruten sails south at 20.30 to Stamsund and north at 22.00 through Raftsundet to Stokmarknes, Sortland and Harstad (arrival 06.45). Ferries to Skutvik (for the short cut to Narvik) sail from a separate quay about a kilometre away on the other side of the town centre; take the road towards Å and it is signed off to the left once you've gone through the short tunnel which leads out of town. Bus timetables for all destinations from Svolvær are at **w** 177nordland.no. Regional departures (generally two or three daily) with Widerøe are from the airport 6km east of town beside the E10; all buses heading for the ferry at Fiskebøl call by though departures are infrequent.

From Svolvær, it is 26km to Henningsvær, 68km to Leknes, 134km to Å and 279km to Narvik.

South to Å The beguiling villages south of Svolvær conjure up the most exquisite combination of precipitous mountains and rugged coastal scenery Lofoten has to offer. In themselves, they make perfect day trips from Svolvær, or, in the case of Reine (page 110) and Å (page 111) in particular, wonderful off-the-beaten-track places to stay.

Henningsvær The drive out to tiny Henningsvær is simply gorgeous. The village is draped over the last island in a chain of skerries and islets that lie off the southwest corner of Austvågøy. Skipping from island to island, the minor road leading to the fishing village weaves its way around secluded sandy coves and rocky bluffs before it arches over a final narrow bridge and pulls into town. At the centre of the village is the harbour, a tight U-shaped inlet lined with handsome, brightly painted houses and boatsheds and backed by jagged peaks rising precipitously from the sea. It is a scene from a postcard and really is as beautiful as you might imagine. However, in season, it attracts coachloads of camera-snapping visitors who swamp the little place and steal its charm. Try to time your visit to early morning or late afternoon and you should have the maze of narrow lanes and passageways pretty much to yourself.

The quality of the light in the Lofoten islands has attracted many artists to the area over the years, transforming the little village into a northern Norwegian version of Cornwall's St Ives. As you wander around, sooner or later you will come across **Galleri Lofoten** in Dreyersgate (✆76 07 15 73; w galleri-lofoten.no; ⏰ 10.00–20.00 daily; 60NOK), which exhibits the work of northern Norwegian artists from the turn of the last century, widely regarded to be the golden age of Norwegian art. Over the gallery's three floors you will find paintings by the likes of Otto Sinding, Einar Berger, Gunnar Berg, Lars Lerin and even the Norwegian monarch, Queen Sonja, as well as a collection of photographs mostly of the Lofoten islands. Watercolourist Lars Lerin, who hails from neighbouring Sweden but lived for several years in Lofoten, is widely regarded as one of the Nordic countries' leading artists of this genre. More artwork plus a collection of glassware and ceramics is available for perusal (and purchase) at **Engelskmannsbrygga** (✆48 12 98 70; w engelskmannsbrygga.no; ⏰ Jun–mid-Aug 10.00–21.00 Wed–Sun; mid-Aug–Dec & Mar–May 11.00–16.00 Wed–Sun) at Dreyersgate 1 by the main square.

🏠 Where to stay, eat and drink

🏠 **Henningsvær Bryggehotell** Hjellskæret; ✆76 07 47 50; e post@henningsvaer.no; w henningsvaer.no. The most atmospheric place to stay in Henningsvær is this attractive, modern harbour-front hotel surrounded by fishing boats & built on wooden stilts over the water. €€€€

🏠 **Anne Gerd's Lofoten Guesthouse** Hagskarveien 330, Stamsund; m 99 52 99 45; e annegerd@online.no; w lofoten-guesthouse. com. A beautifully located, homely B&B overlooking the waters of Storfjordvatnet, roughly 55km west of Henningsvær between Stamsund & Leknes, with just 4 rooms, all sharing facilities. Friendly host Anne-Gerd also rents out a range of outdoor equipment such as bikes, kayaks & snow shoes. €€

🏠 **Den siste Viking** Misværveien 10; m 90 95 46 19; e post@nordnorskklatreskole.no; w nordnorskklatreskole.no. A more frugal choice located in the local mountaineering school & offering youth hostel-style accommodation in

dorms (300NOK/bed) & dbl – all sharing facilities. Access to the kitchen for self-catering. €

✗ **Fiskekrogen** Dreyersgate 19; ✆76 07 46 52; w fiskekrogen.no. Specialising in locally caught fish, in particular stockfish (dried cod), finer fare is available here than at Klatrekafé (see below). Starters such as the heavenly pan-fried cod tongues with cucumber salad, lemon & tartare sauce cost from 110NOK; mains go from 220NOK. €€

🍺 **Klatrekafé** Misværveien 10; m 90 95 46 19; ⏰ Feb–May & Oct–Dec 19.00–01.30 Wed, 19.00–02.30 Fri & Sat; Jun–Sep 16.00–01.00 Mon–Thu, 13.00–02.30 Fri & Sat, 13.00–01.00 Sun. This eclectic café has been variably described as half English pub & half Nepalese tea house, though neither description quite hits the spot. See for yourself while enjoying a decent selection of affordable Norwegian staples, as well as beer, & it's a good meeting place to boot. There's also live music here throughout the summer months. €

Leknes and the Lofotr Viking Museum
From Henningsvær it's a 60km drive to nondescript **Leknes**, the service centre for southern Lofoten and the location of the islands' second **airport** linked to the mainland by Widerøe. To be frank, there's no real reason to linger in Leknes, and it's a much better idea to break your journey around 14km before the town, just beyond the tiny village of Bøstad, at the engaging **Lofotr Viking Museum** (Vikingveien 530; ✆76 15 40 00; w lofotr.no;

⊕ Jun–mid-Aug 10.00–19.00 daily; May & mid-Aug–mid-Sep 10.00–17.00 daily; Nov–Jan noon–16.00 Wed, Sat & Sun; Feb–Apr noon–16.00 Mon–Sat; 200NOK). Here, you'll find a number of archaeological exhibits in a reconstructed longhouse, all offering a great opportunity to learn more about the Viking age. There's also the chance to taste Viking food and learn even more about the era from staff dressed in period costume. Additional activities range from axe-throwing and weaving to Viking arts and crafts and even gardening. All in all, this living museum makes a great stop on the long drive to Å.

Flakstadøya and Moskenesøya From Leknes, the E10 continues southwest towards the two final islands in the Lofoten chain, **Flakstadøya** and **Moskenesøya**, and you'll soon see that Lofoten saves the best till last. Rearing up from the sea for its last defiant stand before the maelstrom off Lofoten's southernmost point (page 112), Lofotenveggen offers a monumental backdrop to one of northern Norway's most dramatic seascapes.

Nusfjord A further 27km on from Leknes, and reached via a wiggly sideroad off the E10, handsome Nusfjord repays every effort to reach it and is widely regarded as Norway's best-kept fishing village. Indeed, the 50-odd *rorbuer* which huddle around the narrowest of harbours are the real thing – not modern replicas – and, naturally, add to the picture-postcard setting. Nusfjord is not a big place and its simple pleasures are to be found in wandering the narrow streets, perhaps peering into the smithy and the sawmill, and admiring the end-of-the-world location. True, Nusfjord's charms are no secret and the tiny place can feel swamped when a tour bus pulls in. Stay overnight, though, and you'll have the village virtually to yourself.

 Where to stay, eat and drink

⌂ Nusfjord Arctic Resort Harbour; ☏76 09 30 20; e booking@nusfjord.no; w nusfjordarcticresort.com; ⊕ all year. The *rorbuer* here come in all shapes & sizes (& prices) & some have even been granted protected status by the Norwegian Directorate of Cultural Heritage. There are full details, with photos, of all the options available on the website. During the summer, the attached Karoline restaurant serves up b/fast, lunch (⊕ 11.00–16.00) & fishy dinners (⊕ 17.00–22.00). €€€€

Reine ✳ If you thought Nusfjord was impossibly picturesque, wait until you get to Reine, a ravishing beauty of a village, 41km to the southwest. Reine perches atop a narrow promontory, linked to the mainland by a narrow causeway, just off the E10. From the viewpoint just off the main road, at a spot known as Reinehalsen, you will be treated to one of the most gorgeous views you can imagine: the timber houses of the village tumble across the small island, surrounded on all sides by bony islets, angular skerries and towering mountains. What's more, Reine is also the starting point for one of the **best hikes** (see opposite) in the whole of Lapland: from the top of Reinebringen (448m) you will be treated to panoramas of quite breathtaking beauty. Other than admiring the village and its picturesque surroundings, make sure you have a look at the **Eva Harr Gallery** (⊕ Jun–Sep 10.00–18.00 daily; Oct–May 10.00–17.00 Mon–Sat; free) inside the Kultursenter located on the main street where you'll find contemporary paintings and graphic art by the artist, interpreting the moody landscapes of northern Norway. A collection of paintings by Karl Erik Harr, one of Norway's most popular artists, has also been added to the gallery.

Where to stay, eat and drink

Reine Rorbuer Harbour; ☎76 09 22 22; e post@reinerorbuer.com; w reinerorbuer.com. You guessed it – 40 or so more *rorbuer* vying for your custom. These ones are in 2 locations – beside the marina & dotted around the northwestern tip of the promontory that is Reine. There are various types available &, once again, full details are on the website. The on-site restaurant is the place to enjoy local seafood delicacies from a terrace overlooking the harbour – weather permitting. €€€€

Hiking trips from Reine From the junction with the E10, follow the main road south a short way to the beginning of the Ramsviktunnelen where you'll see the old road (now a footpath) branching off on the left – follow this for another 400m and you'll come to the beginning of the hiking trail up **Reinebringen**. Here you'll see the path heading up the mountain (it's a big boggy in parts at the beginning); follow it all the way to a saddle of land at around 430m from where you have sterling views of Reine and the east Lofoten coast. From here, the trail continues off to the right to reach the peak (448m; about 1½hrs), where the panorama vistas become instantly visible.

An alternative hiking trail (90mins) leads from the hamlet of Vindstad, located on the western shores of Reinefjorden, across the mountains to Moskenesøya's west coast and the sandy cove at Bunesstranda. Get to Vindstad by (year-round) ferry from Reine (m 99 49 18 05; w reinefjorden.no; 2–3 daily; 50NOK one-way); the crossing takes 25 minutes and offers great views of the tooth-shaped Reinefjorden. The trail follows the narrow Bunesfjorden first of all until it reaches the settlement of Bunesfjord itself. It's up and over the mountain ridge that's in front of you now, in between the two peaks Skiva (848m) and Stamprevtind (759m), until you then drop down to the sands at Bunesstranda.

Boat trips from Reine Aqua Lofoten (m 99 01 90 42; w aqualofoten.no) operate a series of fun day trips by boat from Reine, including excursions to see the Mokstraumen maelstrom off Å (page 112). Full details of all the options are available online, including a couple of land-based hiking tours.

Å Don't be fooled by the name; there's more to Å than first meets the eye. A pure scenic delight at the very end of the E10, 10km southwest of Reine, this delightful village of old timber buildings enjoys one of Lofoten's most special locations. A narrow foreshore, squeezed up tight against the churning waters of Vestfjorden, fights for space against the unforgiving rock wall of the Lofotenveggen Mountains immediately behind. The resulting huddle of homes and fishing shacks, dating from the 19th century, makes Å one of the best choices to stay in the islands.

If Å has a speciality, it is fish museums; this tiny village has two of them on the harbourside. A dozen or so of Å's buildings have been turned into the **Norwegian Fishing Village Museum** (Norsk Fiskeværsmuseum; ☎76 09 14 88; w museumnord. no/en/norwegian-fishing-village-museum; ⊕ Jun–Aug 09.00–19.00 daily; rest of the year 10.00–17.00 Mon–Fri; 100NOK), which gives a detailed representation of life here in the late 1800s when the local fishermen were forced to pay rent for their homes in hard manual labour on the local merchant's farm. A couple of *rorbuer*, a boathouse and even a cod-liver oil plant have been preserved and offer a great insight into the hard – and dangerous – lives people lived in this part of Norway at the turn of the last century.

However, the bizarre **Stockfish Museum** (Tørrfiskmuseum; ☎ 76 09 12 11; w lofoten-info.no/backup-2015-02-17/stockfish.htm; ⊕ Jun–Aug 11.00–16.00 daily; 80NOK) is the real oddity. Proudly boasting to be the only stockfish museum in the world, the museum fishes out every last detail of the production of stockfish (dried fish), highlighting such oddball facts as 16 million kilograms of cod is hung out to dry every year in Lofoten and that during the drying process the fish loses 80% of its weight. Various forms of the fish are then sent for export to Portugal, Italy and Nigeria. Having perused the various gutting benches, rasps, forks and other exhibits, be sure to catch the film shown upstairs (which was shown on German television and extensively features the museum's dynamic curator) that is arguably the most illuminating element of the exhibition.

Neither museum has any real or meaningful address, simply wander around the tiny harbourside and you'll come across them.

An enjoyable **hiking trail** from Å leads across Moskenesøya's ever-narrowing width to the island's west coast. Begin by following the southern shore of Åvannet Lake, before climbing over the ridge of mountains that forms the island's spine. Beyond here, it is a straightforward hike to the spectacular lookout point on the southern side of Stokkvika Bay; allow around 4 hours for the return hike. Don't attempt the hike in bad weather as low cloud can obscure the mountains.

Where to stay, eat and drink There's a wide selection of *rorbuer* available in Å (**€€€€**) and hostel-style rooms in the Salteriet building in the village, all with a minimum two-night stay (though, to be honest, you'll pay over the odds for the end-of-the-road location; **€€€**). It all comes under the management of **Å Rorbuer** (📞 76 09 11 21; e post@arorbuer.no; w arorbuer.no) who also rent out boats from 650NOK per day.

There's a **youth hostel** (📞 76 09 12 11; e a@hihostels.no; w hihostels.no; dorm beds 250NOK, dbl room €) in Å, too, with rooms split between two different buildings, Hennumgården and the Stockfish Museum, where all rooms face the sea; both buildings are in the harbour area.

Eating options are pretty much limited to the **Brygga Restaurant** (📞 76 09 15 72; w bryggarestaurant.no; ⏱ noon–22.00 daily; €) in the harbour with light meals such as a tasty fish soup (165NOK) through the day and more substantial, though frankly overpriced, dishes in the evenings – fish is the speciality – and the nearby village **bakery**, Gammelgården, which serves excellent take-away cinnamon buns baked in the original oven from the late 1800s.

Boat trips to the Moskstraumen maelstrom In the channel between Lofotodden, the southernmost point of the Lofoten islands, and the island of Værøy, one of the world's strongest sea currents, the Moskstraumen maelstrom, is at work. This powerful system of tidal eddies and whirlpools is unusual in that it forms in the open sea (most maelstroms are found only in confined straits), owing to a combination of strong tides and a shallow ridge on the seabed which amplifies and swirls the current. Known during the Viking age and described in Iceland's *Poetic Eddas*, Moskstraumen has featured in various literary accounts over the centuries, most notably in Edgar Allan Poe's short story from 1841, *Descent into the maelström*, which was responsible for introducing the world 'maelstrom' into English. **Aqua Lofoten** (m 99 01 90 42; w aqualofoten.no; 895NOK) sail from Reine out to the maelstrom and round Lofotodden passing a couple of abandoned villages; they may be able to pick you up in Å on request, depending on booking numbers from Reine.

5

From the Gulf of Bothnia to the Arctic Ocean

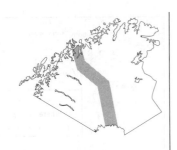

The trio of rivers that form the northern border between Sweden and Finland have created one of Lapland's most pastoral landscapes. Emptying into the Gulf of Bothnia, the Torne River flows lazily through flower meadows and undulating farmland dotted with haystacks drying during the long days of summer, passing sleepy villages where life takes on an enviably sedate pace. Gone are the pine forests and reindeer herds of the Lapland interior; here the whispers of the breeze through the birch trees and fields of grazing farm animals typify the southern stretches of the Torne Valley. However, north of Pajala, where the Torne River swings inland, the landscape becomes progressively less tamed. Now, the swiftly flowing Muonio River forms the border between the two countries, land given over to farming is rare and the rounded fells which predominate north of here begin to show their face.

Beyond Kaaresuvanto/Karesuando, the river changes course yet again, allowing the Könkämä River to run the final leg to the geographical point where Norway, Sweden and Finland all meet. Here the terrain is high, treeless tundra, the winters are long and hard and snow lies deep on the ground until well into May. Yet, as the land quickly falls away towards one of northern Norway's greatest expanses of open water, the Lyngen fjord on the Arctic Ocean, the warming influence of the Gulf Stream is clearly noticeable. Spring comes quickly here and temperatures are higher than those on the Gulf of Bothnia, where the chilling effect of the winter ice delays the onset of warmer weather.

The E8 highway runs the length of the valley from the Gulf of Bothnia to the Arctic Ocean and has two main uses. It provides a good access route to the North Cape (as far as Palojoensuu, from where Route 93 runs north to Alta via Enontekiö and Kautokeino) and it is the best way by far to reach Tromsø from central areas of Lapland. But it would be a shame simply to rush north without sampling some of the attractions en route. Tornio and Haparanda have the best choices of bars, restaurants and shopping for miles around. Kemi offers unique ice-breaker tours and a snow castle; whereas Muonio provides ready access to Finland's biggest and best centre for husky safaris, or, alternatively in summer, white-water rafting. The mark of the man who shaped northern Scandinavia more than any other, the revivalist preacher Lars Levi Laestadius, is felt throughout the area: a museum and his grave are in Pajala, and his rectory is open for viewing in Karesuando. For hiking fans, Kilpisjärvi in the far north has access to the three-country border post, Treriksröset, and some of Lapland's best high fell scenery.

THE GULF OF BOTHNIA
TO THE ARCTIC OCEAN

TORNIO, HAPARANDA AND AROUND

Occupying a strategically important site either side of the Torne River at the head of the Gulf of Bothnia, Finnish Tornio (Torneå in Swedish; Duortnus in Sámi) and Swedish Haparanda (Haaparanta in Finnish) are to all intents and purposes the same place. If you are travelling by public transport between Finnish and Swedish Lapland, you are likely to pass through, as the hub of roads which radiate from here have made the towns a key transport interchange for inter-Scandinavian connections (see box, page 118). Indeed, so commercially attractive is the towns' central location for the whole of northern Scandinavia, that the Swedish furniture giant, IKEA, opened its most northerly store in the world here in 2006, drawing customers from a radius of hundreds of miles: people travel to the Haparanda IKEA from as far afield as Tromsø and Murmansk. IKEA's strategic decision to open so far north has been a real boon for the local economy, since many other companies and stores have followed the retailer's lead and set up here, too, thus resulting in the development of the adjacent IKANO shopping centre, which opened just after IKEA came to town. Off the back of IKEA's success, yet another shopping centre, På Gränsen/Rajalla (literally 'On the Border', although it's actually in Finland) opened in 2008 and has proved immensely popular with local people.

Crossing from Tornio to Haparanda, or vice versa, couldn't be easier: passport controls are non-existent and locals simply walk or drive from one country to the other without even batting an eyelid. A road bridge carries the main E4 highway across a small island which links one town with the other. A second smaller road, Krannigatan, to the east of the IKEA store forms the second link; on this road there isn't even a border post, just a camera monitoring road traffic. Although there are no must-see sights in either Tornio or Haparanda, both places are agreeable enough to while away a day or so, and, by evening, there's a positive buzz in the bars of Tornio.

SOME HISTORY Until 1821, when Haparanda was founded, there was only one settlement here: Tornio, which still today is the more lively and interesting of the two. From 1105 until 1809, Finland was part of Sweden, and Tornio, founded in 1621 and the oldest town in the whole of Lapland, served the Swedish crown's interests in the north by functioning as a key market town. However, following Sweden's defeat against Russia in the Great Northern War of the 1700s, Finland was ceded to Russia and Sweden consequently lost its most important trading centre in the north. It was soon decreed that Tornio should be replaced, and in the early 1820s Haparanda began to take shape, but over the ensuing decades never really matched its bigger Finnish brother in terms of size or vibrancy. Today, the population of Haparanda is a mere 10,000, compared with Tornio's 22,500 and, accordingly, in most matters it is Tornio that dominates.

In the late 1990s, Haparanda and Tornio were declared a Eurocity – a European Union initiative that unites two adjoining towns or cities in two different countries. Although the label is no longer used, the spirit of co-operation and togetherness is very much alive. As you walk around, you will notice houses with television aerials pointing in different directions to pick up both Swedish and Finnish television and cash dispensers which issue notes in both Swedish kronor and euros; seemingly everything from central heating to the local fire brigade is centrally co-ordinated. The only thing that isn't is the time: there is still an hour's time difference between Tornio and Haparanda (Tornio is ahead).

TOURIST INFORMATION The **tourist office** (Finnish m 050 590 0562, Swedish ☎0922 262 00; e info@haparandatornio.com; w haparandatornio.com; ⊕ Swedish time: 08.00–17.00 Mon–Fri, 10.00–15.00 Sat) is located in the bus station (*resecentrum*; see box, page 118) at Krannigatan 5 in Haparanda. Inside there are two telephone lines, one handling calls from Finland, the other from Sweden; bilingual staff switch effortlessly from Swedish to Finnish depending on which phone is ringing.

WHERE TO STAY *Map, page 116*

🏠 **Cape East** Sundholmen 1, Haparanda; Swedish ☎0911 327 00; e info@capeeast. se; w capeeast.se. Now open again after a devastating fire, a stay at this ultra-swish & luxurious spa hotel on the banks of the Torne River, just 1.5km south of the town centre, is a special treat. There's a number of cold & hot tubs as well as a 25m-long swimming pool. €€€€

🏠 **Stadshotellet** Torget 7, Haparanda; Swedish ☎0922 614 90; e info@ haparandastadshotell.se; w haparandastadshotell. se. A grand old place dating from 1900 full of wood panelling, red velvet & opulent chandeliers. A stay here offers a taste of old-world elegance & it really is the hotel of choice for accommodation in Haparanda or Tornio. €€€€

🏠 **Park Hotel Tornio** Itäranta 4, Tornio; Finnish m 040 358 3300; e info@phtornio.fi; w parkhoteltornio.fi. Rambling place that has been in operation for around 75 years. Rooms can be rather boxy, though the whole place is now under new management & has benefited from a major refurbishment. Excellent sauna & pool complex in the basement. €€€€/€€€

🏠 **E-city Bed & Breakfast** Saarenpäänkatu 39, Tornio; Finnish m 044 5090 358; e bb@ecity.fi; w ecity.fi. A family-run homely place in the centre of Tornio with 8 rooms, 4 of which have private facilities (€15 extra). Fridge, kettle & microwave provided on each landing. B/fast inc. €€

🏠 **River Motell & Vandrarhem** Strandgatan 18, Haparanda; Swedish m 076 789 0559; e info@

5

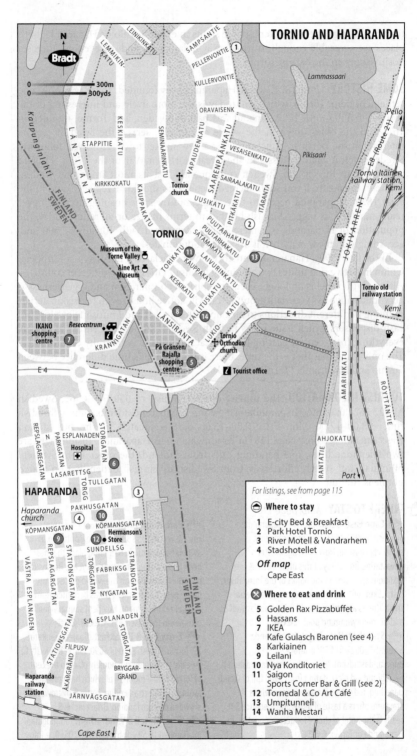

TORNIO AND HAPARANDA

Lammassaari

Pikisaari

Kaupunginlahti

FINLAND
SWEDEN

Pello

E8 (Route 21)

*Tornio Itäinen
railway station,
Kemi*

**Tornio old
railway station**

Kemi

Tornio church

TORNIO

**Museum of the
Torne Valley**

**Aine Art
Museum**

**IKANO
shopping
centre** 7

Resecentrum

**Tornio
Orthodox
church**

**På Gränsen/
Rajalla
shopping
centre** 5

ℹ️ **Tourist office**

Hospital

HAPARANDA

*Haparanda
church*

KÖPMANSGATAN

**Hermanson's
Store** 12

*Haparanda
railway
station*

Cape East ↓

For listings, see from page 115

🛏️ Where to stay
1 E-city Bed & Breakfast
2 Park Hotel Tornio
3 River Motell & Vandrarhem
4 Stadshotellet

Off map
  Cape East

✖️ Where to eat and drink
5 Golden Rax Pizzabuffet
6 Hassans
7 IKEA
  Kafe Gulasch Baronen (see 4)
8 Karkiainen
9 Leilani
10 Nya Konditoriet
11 Saigon
  Sports Corner Bar & Grill (see 2)
12 Tornedal & Co Art Café
13 Umpitunneli
14 Wanha Mestari

top Striking architecture and a stunning natural setting make Tromsø the perfect choice for a taste of urban Lapland (MVa/S) page 186

above left Wander around the relaxed streets of Honningsvåg at the very top of Europe – the gateway to the North Cape (SS) page 211

above right The largest church in the north of Sweden, Nederluleå church dates from the 15th century and is a clear sign Gammelstad's prosperity (P/S) page 49

below A *rorbu* (traditional fisherman's cottage) is a classic accommodation option in the Lofoten islands (c/S) page 98

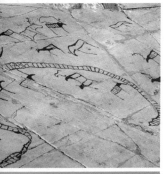

above You'll still see traditional Sámi dwellings, which provide effective protection from the driving wind and snow, pitched on the tundra right across Lapland (VB/S)

left Alta is home to the most extensive area of prehistoric rock carvings in northern Europe, dating from between 6,000 and 2,000 years ago (P/S) page 203

below left Sámi child in traditional dress; there are around 70,000 Sámi living across Lapland (JT/NNTB) page 16

below right One of the traditional wooden *kåtor* at Staloluokta is the village church (JP) page 64

above   Dried fish, known as stockfish, awaiting export from Lapland to Portugal, Italy and Nigeria, where it's a much-prized delicacy (EM/NNTB) page 111

right   The Sámi wear brightly coloured garlands and boots made of reindeer skin at traditional ceremonies (MV/S) page 20

below left   Sámi drum player, Ylläs, Finland; in Sámi mythology a shaman would use a *goavddis* or drum and would probably also perform a *joik*, a form of throat singing, to help him achieve a state of ecstasy and reach out to the spirits (LM) page 18

below right   Painting of revivalist preacher Lars Levi Laestadius in Jukkasjärvi church, Sweden: Laestadius founded a religious movement that, to this day, still draws tens of thousands of followers across northern Scandinavia (JP) page 80

bottom   Reindeer racing takes place at the Kautokeino Easter Festival (JT/NNTB) page 158

above Lapland's vast open spaces offer some of the most memorable wild camping you'll find anywhere in Europe (JO/S)

left White-water rafting on the Torne River offers a guaranteed adrenalin rush (HT) page 81

below Ride the chairlift up to the Aurora Sky Station high above Abisko for jaw-dropping views of the northern lights (DTW) page 82

above Cross-country skiing in the Lofoten islands in Norwegian Lapland takes in some of Europe's finest coastal panoramas (KFO/NNTB)

right Take a leaf out of Santa's book and hitch a ride with a reindeer (DTW)

below Snowmobile safaris are available across Lapland and are an exhilarating way to explore the countryside (HL)

above   Lapland's reindeer (*Rangifer tarandus*) are plentiful and hard to miss (SJ/S) page 7

below   The Arctic fox (*Alopex lagopus*) is well adapted to Lapland's harsh climate as it has small extremities, apart from a huge tail, which it can wrap around itself for extra warmth (NB/D) page 7

bottom left   Brown bears (*Ursus arctos arctos*) can weigh over 300kg (DT) page 7

bottom right   The lemming's (*Lemmus lemmus*) reputation for mindless self-destruction is undeserved — rather they potter about on the tundra, dig burrows and eat a lot (FF/S) page 7

above   Orcas (*Orcinus orca*) are one of the most common dolphins off the coast of Lapland and are very impressive to watch (BMJ/S) page 7

below left   If you're very lucky, you might spot the elusive lynx (*Lynx lynx*) (JP/S) page 7

below right Elk (*Alces alces*) are usually found close to pine forests and unlike reindeer they prefer to be alone (MC) page 7

Elk or moose ?

bottom right Surprisingly, it is wolverines (*Gulo gulo*) and not bears that pose the biggest threat to reindeer as predators (OP/S) page 7

As many as 175 species of birds (page 6) have been identified as breeding in Lapland, including:

top left   Pine grosbeak (*Pinicola enucleator*) (DT)

top right   Spotted redshanks (*Tringa erythropus*) (DT)

above   Snow bunting (*Plectrophenax nivalis*) (DT)

left   Ruff (*Philomachus pugnax*) male in breeding plumage (DT)

below   Hawk owl (*Surnia ulula*) (DT)

rivermotell.com; w rivermotell.com; ⏱ reception 16.00–21.00. The best choice for budget accommodation with comfortable dbl rooms, both

with & without private facilities (100SEK more; some with balcony or terrace facing the water), in a pretty location by the river. *50SEK for sheets.* €

✖ WHERE TO EAT AND DRINK *Map, opposite*

Although it is hard to generalise, eating is generally cheaper in Sweden, but drinking is less expensive in Finland: witness the one-way traffic over the bridge every evening when thirsty Swedes head off in search of a drink or three in Finland.

Tornio

✖ **Umpitunneli** Hallituskatu 15; ☎016 430 360; w umpitunneli.fi; ⏱ 13.00–midnight Mon, Tue & Thu, noon–04.00 Wed, 13.00–04.00 Fri, noon–04.00 Sat, noon–22.00 Sun. A cavernous restaurant, bar & club all rolled into one that draws the crowds like nowhere else. An extensive menu featuring excellent salmon & fried chicken among others. €€

✖ **Golden Rax Pizzabuffet** Länsiranta 10; ☎020 744 4923; w rax.fi; ⏱ 11.00–20.00 Mon–Fri, 11.00–19.00 Sat, noon–18.00 Sun. If money's tight, look no further than the Tornio outlet of this bargain-basement pizza chain. The eat-as-much-as-you-want buffet is just €11.95 & includes a soft drink. €

✖ **Saigon** Kauppakatu 13; ☎016 430 565; ⏱ 10.30–19.00 Mon, 10.30–22.00 Tue–Fri, noon–22.00 Sat & Sun. Not overly authentic (though good value) Vietnamese food. The eat-as-much-as-you-want buffet (⏱10.30–15.00 w/days & noon–17.00 Sat) is exceptionally good value, allowing you to fill an empty stomach for just €11.50. €

🖥 **Karkiainen** Länsiranta 9; w karkiainen. fi; ⏱ 08.00–18.00 Mon–Fri, 10.00–16.00 Sat, noon–16.00 Sun. The best of the cafés in Tornio, & one of the few that's open all w/end. Lights snacks & bar meals, too. €

🍷 **Sports Corner Bar & Grill** Itäranta 4; m 040 659 350; w parkhoteltornio.fi/en/restaurants/sports-corner-bargrill; ⏱ 17.00–23.00 Mon & Tue, 17.00–midnight Wed & Thu, 17.00–02.00 Fri & Sat. Serving up burgers & pizzas galore, this popular sports bar inside the Park Hotel (page 115) is a popular place for a drink & a bar snack with both locals & hotel guests. Several big screens showing the latest games & tournaments. €

🍷 **Wanha Mestari** Hallituskatu 5; w wanhamestari.fi/tornio-wanha-mestari; ⏱ noon–01.00 Mon, Wed, Thu & Sun, noon–02.00 Tue & Fri, 10.00–02.00 Sat. One of Tornio's

most popular bars, which is always full of locals & offers a rare chance in Lapland to play darts. Can get a little drunken. €

Haparanda

✖ **Hassans** Storgatan 88; ☎0922 104 40; ⏱10.30–20.00 Tue–Fri, noon–20.00 Sat & Sun. The cheapest pizzas in town (from 70SEK) including the much-loved kebab pizza, better value than Leilani, though the restaurant itself is rather basic. €

✖ **IKEA** Norrskensvägen 2; ⏱ 09.30–17.30 daily. Swedish classics such as meatballs & smoked salmon are always on the menu here. Excellent prices & a sensible option given the paucity of other choices in Haparanda. €

✖ **Leilani** Köpmansgatan 15; ☎0922 107 17; w restaurangleilani.com; ⏱ 10.30–20.00 Mon, 10.30–21.00 Tue–Thu, 10.30–22.00 Fri, noon–22.00 Sat, noon–21.00 Sun. A range of pizzas, Thai food & Chinese mains all from 89SEK. €

✖ **Tornedal & Co Art Café** Torggatan 46; w tornedalandcompany.com; ⏱ noon–18.00 Tue–Sun. A delightful new venture which is both an art gallery & a café, located in one of Haparanda's old timber structures, which once served as a shop. Exhibitions change roughly once every month. Handicrafts, delicatessen items & books are also for sale in the on-site store. €

🖥 **Nya Konditoriet** Storgatan 73; ⏱ 09.00–16.30 Mon–Fri, 10.00–14.00 Sat. An excellent café with good pastries – & a good range of chocolates, too. €

🍷 **Kafe Gulasch Baronen** Torget 7; ⏱ 18.00–late Mon–Sat. Known locally by its initials KGB, this atmospheric old pub attached to the Stadshotellet (page 115) is a popular place to start a pub crawl of Haparanda & Tornio. The unusual name harks back to the days when Haparanda was a frontier town on the new Russian border & traders made money selling supplies to Russia. €€

WHAT TO SEE AND DO
Tornio

Tornio Orthodox church ✳ (Tornion ortodoksinen kirkko; Lukiokatu 1; ⊕ Jun–Aug 10.00–18.00 Tue–Sat) Tornio's onion-domed Orthodox church is situated close to the Finnish customs post and provides an intriguing example of Finland's former position in the Russia of the Tsars. (Finland was an autonomous part of Russia between 1809 and 1917.) This ornate, narrow wooden structure, decorated in a warm mustard yellow and bedecked with two rooftop crosses, was commissioned by Tsar Alexander I and dates from 1884. Its classic Oriental design and appearance couldn't be more different from Sweden's altogether more conservative Lutheran churches.

Tornio church (Tornion kirkko; Seminaarinkatu 2; ⊕ Jun–Aug 09.00–17.00 Mon–Fri, 09.30–18.00 Sat & Sun) Dating from 1686, the wooden Tornio church remarkably survived the mauling of retreating German forces at the end of World War II and stands today as a masterpiece of 17th-century symmetrical design; it is also the oldest building in Finnish Lapland. It was designed by local peasant, Matti Härmä, who employed regular, rectangular shapes in its construction – the result works harmoniously on the eye and the church is considered one of the most beautiful in the north of Finland. The separate bell tower, which could be seen for miles in medieval times, was regularly used as a landmark by travellers.

Aine Art Museum (Aineen Taidemuseo; Torikatu 2; m 050 594 6868; w tornio. fi/en/culture-and-leisure/aine-art-museum; ⊕ 11.00–18.00 Tue–Thu, 11.00–15.00 Fri–Sun; €5) Tornio's Aine Art Museum was founded by local couple, Eila and Veli Aine, and traces its history, in one form or another, back to 1974. The aim of the museum is to show contemporary northern Finnish art, though there are often temporary exhibitions of modern European art, too. The museum's own collection contains a few classics: Elin Danielson-Gambogi's self-portrait, Werner Holmberg's *Midsummer Night in Tornio* and *Big Ida* by Unto Pusa.

Museum of the Torne Valley (Tornionlaakson maakuntamuseo; Keskikatu 22; m 050 597 1559; w tornio.fi/en/culture-and-leisure/museum-tornio-valley; ⊕ 11.00–18.00 Tue–Thu, 11.00–15.00 Fri–Sun; €5) This museum aims to present the cultural history of the people who live in the Torne Valley in both Sweden and Finland. Arguably, the most engaging and informative section is that dealing with World War II.

Tornio old train station Although the squat red-brick building beside Amarinkatu is nothing special to look at, it holds a significant place in Finland's history: Lenin returned to Finland and ultimately Russia after a period in exile through Tornio train station on 15 April 1917. His journey to Russia took him from Switzerland, through Germany by sealed train, then Sweden and finally Lapland. He had lived previously in the southern Finnish city of Tampere for two years after the failed revolution in Russia in 1905 and it was here that he first met Stalin. A plaque in Finnish and Russian on the side wall of the building commemorates his return to Finland *pakolaismatkaltaan*, 'as a refugee', bound for Helsinki and ultimately St Petersburg. Note that trains no longer use this station, departing instead from the unstaffed Tornio Itäinen station, a few blocks to the northeast.

Haparanda

Haparanda train station Haparanda's imposing train station, erected in 1918, is the most impressive building in town after the grand Stadshotellet. Constructed of red brick, replete with stone tower and lantern, it sits proudly atop a small hillock at Järnvägsgatan 21 at the southern end of Västra Esplanaden and Stationsgatan. It is still possible to discern the two different track gauges: the standard Swedish one (1,435mm) behind the station building and the broader (1,524mm) gauge of Finland in front of it, which provides Sweden's only rail connection to the east; the rail bridge over the Torne River to Finland carries both gauges. A metal plaque on the front wall of the station building commemorates the forced evacuation of people from northern Finland in the autumn of 1944, many of whom fled to Sweden through this station, as retreating German troops destroyed their homes.

Following a track upgrade and electrification of the line that connects Haparanda with Boden and Luleå, the resumption of passenger trains is still under consideration (and has been for years); the last service to Haparanda ran in 1992, though connecting services to Tornio and Kemi had already ceased four years earlier. Today, the line is used for freight; IKEA, for example, receives all its goods by rail.

Hermanson's Store (Hermansons Handelshus; Storgatan 74) This rambling timber construction on Haparanda's main street, complete with adjoining storehouses, dates from 1832 and has reopened as an atmospheric example of a general store from the early 1900s. Today, Hermansons, who originally began trading in 1905, sell gloves, belts, shirts, hats, wallets and other items of haberdashery, plus there's a **café** upstairs (€). Over the years, all manner of goods have been traded here – everything from cotton and thread to rare Russian furs. Opening times vary but if the flags are out beside the front door, they're open for business.

Haparanda church (☉ mid-Jun–mid-Aug 10.00–19.00 daily) Resembling a grain silo rather than a place of worship, Haparanda church on Östra Kyrkogatan has even won a prize for the ugliest building in Sweden. Completed in 1963 to replace the town's former wooden church, which burnt down, the new structure of copper plate is something the townspeople of Haparanda have come to endure rather than love.

MOVING ON FROM TORNIO AND HAPARANDA From the *resecentrum* in Haparanda (see box, opposite), **buses** run every 2 to 3 hours to Luleå from where you can pick up trains north to Kiruna and Narvik or south to Stockholm and Gothenburg. Timetables are available at w ltnbd.se. From the *resecentrum*, services also run south to Kemi (timetables at w matkahuolto.fi). Finnish **trains** call at Tornio Itäinen (Tornio east) station en route to Kemi and points south to Helsinki. Note

that Tornio Itäinen and (the disused) Tornio station (page 119) are two different stations. Check with the tourist office for the latest details on the possible (though unlikely) resumption of Swedish train services from Haparanda station.

SOUTHEAST OF HAPARANDA AND TORNIO: KEMI Just 25km southeast of Tornio and connected by regular buses (w matkahuolto.fi), the industrial town of Kemi (Giepma in Sámi) is not somewhere to head for per se; the town is quite unremarkable, renowned predominantly for its deepwater harbour, which handles 10% of Finland's exports. However, in winter, Kemi becomes an irresistible magnet for adventure travellers, drawn here by the unique opportunity to take a trip on the world's only private **icebreaker**. The *Sampo* was built in Helsinki in 1960 and ploughed its way up and down the frozen sea lanes of the Gulf of Bothnia for nearly 30 years until it was superseded by a breed of newer, wider icebreakers designed to meet the needs of the latest superfreighters. Although now officially in retirement from its icebreaking duties, the ship sails once daily between mid-December and mid-April for a tour of the icefields of the northern Gulf of Bothnia off Kemi; departures are at noon from Ajos harbour, 11km south of the town. While on board, don't miss the chance to don a bright-orange rubber survival suit and float in the icy water off the ship's stern – a quite unforgettable experience. Icebreaker trips can be booked through **Experience 365** (Lumilinnankatu 15A; ☎016 258 878; e sales@experience365.fi; w experience365.fi/icebreakersampo; from €240). It's also possible to travel out to the ship by snowmobile, scudding across the frozen icesheet to the starting point for the tour; from €399 per person, it's certainly not cheap (from €484 on your own snowmobile), but is a fantastic thing to do. Sadly, summer tours onboard the *Sampo* no longer operate.

Where to stay, eat and drink In addition to its icebreaker tours, Kemi offers the chance to stay in a snow castle (Limilinnankatu 15), a structure similar in design to Sweden's Icehotel (page 77), yet made out of frozen seawater rather than natural snow, which is too soft for construction purposes. Inside, there's generally a restaurant (dress warmly if you decide to eat here; inside temperature is −5°C), chapel, hotel rooms and a children's play area, though the exact layout changes from year to year. The castle is open from mid-January to mid-April (⊕ 10.00–18.00 daily; €29) for **day visitors** who are free to look around the entire structure, though should the urge take you, it's also possible to spend the night here: a double room replete with ice carvings costs a cool €430 and can be booked at w experience365.fi/snowhotel or on ☎016 258 878. For those daunted by spending a night in sub-zero temperatures, there are a few other options in town:

Seaside Glass Villas ☎016 258 878; w experience365.fi/seaside-glass-villas. The best of Kemi's other options & located in the snow castle area at Lumilinnankatu. These rectangular-shaped units featuring glass roofs & floor-to-ceiling windows are very stylish; they're located right on the shoreline, with unsurpassed views of the sea, which freezes over in winter. Note that the units are aligned in rows & only those at the very front enjoy uninterrupted views (for which you pay a premium: from €513 in winter & €150 in summer). €€€€

Merihovi Keskuspuistokatu 6–8; m 040 6853 500; e hotel@merihovi.fi; w merihovi.fi. A delightfully retro 1950s functionalist pile, right in the centre of town, whose restaurant is also worth a look (€€). €€€€/€€€

Puistopaviljonki ☎016 223 110; w puistopaviljonki.fi; ⊕ 10.30–21.00 Mon–Thu, 10.30–22.00 Fri, noon–22.00 Sat, noon–21.00 Sun. The town's airy former courthouse, which peers out over the harbour at Urheilukatu 1; traditional northern Finnish dishes & pizzas are the specialities. €

NORTHWEST OF HAPARANDA AND TORNIO: JOCKFALLET AND LINAFALLET

WATERFALLS Two of the most impressive waterfalls in the Torne Valley area are within striking distance of Haparanda and Tornio, and make an interesting detour on the way north towards Pajala. **Jockfallet**, the largest waterfall on the Kalix River, is located 150km northwest of Haparanda and Tornio (85km southwest of Pajala) and features the river's only salmon ladder, which around 8,000 fish climb every year to spawn. The waterfall spans a drop of 9m and is best observed from the road bridge virtually above the falls themselves. As the Kalix is one of Sweden's last unregulated rivers, its depth varies by up to 5m, depending on the time of year and the amount of snowmelt.

To reach the falls from Haparanda and Tornio, first make for Övertorneå and then head west on Route 391 towards Nybyn, from where you can swing north on to Route 392 towards the fabulously named Korpilombolo (a byword in southern Sweden for 'the middle of nowhere').

From Jockfallet, a series of minor forest roads lead around 45km northwest to the area's second mighty waterfall, **Linafallet**. These powerful falls have a drop of around 16m and are formed at the confluence of the Linaälven and Ängesån rivers. You can get fantastic views from the narrow footbridge which spans the Linaälven, about 1km upstream from the waterfall. To reach Linafallet from Jockfallet, first cross the bridge over the Kalix River and then head southwest towards Vallsjärv and ultimately the Ängesån River . At Ängesån, cross the Linaälven and head north.

Alternatively, Linafallet can also be directly accessed from Haparanda and Tornio by taking the E4 west, followed by the E10 northwest to Lansjärv, from where you turn right, and head for the Ängesån River. Upon reaching it turning left for the falls before crossing the Linaälven River. By this route, Linafallet is 165km from Haparanda/Tornio.

Once you're done with waterfalls, it's a drive of around 120km to Pajala (albeit along rather minor forest roads at first), heading initially northwest towards the hamlets of Satter and Ullatti. From here roads improve as you swing right on to the larger Route 394 and head in a northeasterly direction for Kompelusvaara and then Tärendö. Once beyond Tärendö, it's barely another 14km until you re-enter the Torne valley, turning right on to Route 395 for the final run into Pajala.

PAJALA AND AROUND

Heading north from Tornio or Haparanda, there's a choice of routes, which run parallel to each other either side of the Torne River: the E8 in Finland and Route 99 in Sweden. To reach Pajala, 180km north of Haparanda, it is easiest to take Route 99, but it is equally possible to drive the E8 as far as Pello, where you can cross the river into Sweden for the final leg of the journey. Alternatively, in order to see two of the most impressive waterfalls in the area, it's also possible to reach here via Jockfallet and Linafallet. For details of this route, see above.

PAJALA

Almost at the top of the map lay Pajala, surrounded by brownish tundra, and that was where we lived. If you turned back a few pages you saw that Skåne* was as big in area as the whole of northern Sweden, and green-coloured with farmland that was fertile as hell. It took many years for me to cotton on to the map scale and realise that Skåne would have fitted easily between Haparanda and Boden.

From Mikael Niemi's *Popular Music*, on growing up in Pajala in the 1960s and 1970s;
*Skåne is Sweden's southernmost province.

5

Obligatory reading for any visit to this part of Lapland, *Popular Music*, by Pajala's most famous son, Mikael Niemi, provides an illuminating insight into what life was like in this forgotten corner of Sweden just a few decades ago, following the growing pains of teenager Matti, who's obsessed with becoming a rock star. Remote and unknown to much of the rest of the country (at least if the prejudicial maps in the school atlas in the quote on page 121 are anything to go by), Pajala underwent a tremendous transformation thanks to the decision to exploit the iron-ore reserves in Kaunisvaara, a tiny village 25km to the north. Although mining began in 2011, with the ore being transported by road to the nearest Swedish railhead at Svappavaara near Kiruna, falling iron-ore market prices led to the mining company going bankrupt and the mine was closing in late 2014.

In addition to the *Popular Music* trail you can follow around town, Pajala has a few other sights, namely the largest sundial in the world and a small museum dedicated to the life and times of none other than Lars Levi Laestadius, who came here from Karesuando in 1849 and lived in the town until his death in 1861. His grave can be visited in Pajala cemetery.

Getting there Pajala is linked to Kiruna, Gällivare and Haparanda by direct bus, while connections to and from Karesuando can be made in Vittangi. All times are at w resrobot.se. Note that there are no services across the border into Finland. In order to reach Finnish Lapland by public transport either cross the border at Haparanda or at Karesuando.

Tourist information Pajala's **tourist office** (m 073 823 9398; e info@pajalaturism. bd.se; w pajalaturism.se; ⏰ 08.00–17.00 Mon–Fri) can be found in the town's bus station at Genvägen 55 (effectively Route 99), which runs through the centre of the town.

Where to stay *Map, opposite*

Smedjan Fridhemsvägen 1; ☎0978 108 15; e info@hotelsmedjan.se; ⓕ. Rooms at this centrally located establishment are rather unexceptional, & feel more suited to a youth hostel than a hotel. Be grateful it's still here & remember there's not much choice in Pajala. There's also a bar with an outdoor terrace on site, which has rather erratic opening times. €€€€

Å Pajala Camping & Pajala Stugby Rte 99, Tannavägen 65; m 073 364 5278; e hej@pajalacampingroute99.se; w pajalacampingroute99.se. Beautifully situated beside the graceful Torne River, the cabins here are surrounded by pine forest & make a great place to stay. Snug 2-berth ones with cold water & a hotplate; or larger 4-berth cottages with a kitchen & bathroom. Also budget rooms at 590SEK. €€–€€€

Where to eat and drink *Map, opposite*

Thai Dan Sai Medborgarvägen 3; m 072 731 3077; w thaidansai.se; ⏰ 11.00–21.00 Tue–Thu, 11.00–02.00 Fri, 16.00–02.00 Sat. The only Thai restaurant for miles around serving standards such as red chicken curry & other rice & noodle dishes, from 109SEK. Starters such as spring rolls with peanut sauce start at 45SEK. €

Tre Kronor Tornedalsvägen 11; ☎0978 107 70; ⏰ 10.30–20.00 Mon–Thu, 10.30–21.00 Fri, noon–21.00 Sat & Sun. This basic but good-value

pizzeria has pizzas from 85SEK as well as burgers & kebabs. €

Älvbodan Café & Home Tornedalsvägen 2; ⏰ 11.00–17.00 Mon–Wed & Fri, 11.00–20.00 Thu, 11.00–15.00 Sat. The latest reincarnation of a café in these premises. Pleasant enough though rather uninspiring, it also features a small shop selling the likes of candles & other home knick-knacks. €

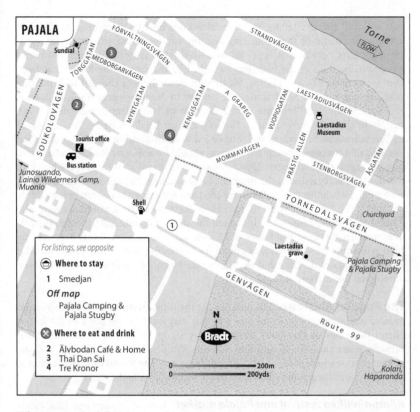

PAJALA

Sundial

FÖRVALTNINGSVÄGEN

STRANDVÄGEN

Torne

FLOW

TORGGATAN

MEDBORGARVÄGEN

SOUKOLOVÄGEN

MYNTGATAN

KENGISGATAN

A GRAPEG

LAESTADIUSVÄGEN

VUOPIOGATAN

Laestadius Museum

ÅSGATAN

Tourist office

Bus station

Junosuando, Lainio Wilderness Camp, Muonio

MOMMAVÄGEN

PRÄSTG ALLÉN

STENBORGSVÄGEN

Shell

TORNEDALSVÄGEN

Churchyard

For listings, see opposite

🛏 **Where to stay**

1 Smedjan

Off map

Pajala Camping & Pajala Stugby

Laestadius grave

Pajala Camping & Pajala Stugby

GENVÄGEN

N

Bradt

❌ **Where to eat and drink**

2 Älvbodan Café & Home
3 Thai Dan Sai
4 Tre Kronor

Route 99

0 _____ 200m
0 _____ 200yds

Kolari, Haparanda

What to see and do Undoubtedly the most dramatic event to befall Pajala was the air raid of February 1940, when Soviet planes, searching for Rovaniemi in Finland during the Winter War, dropped 134 bombs on little Pajala by mistake. A wide area of residential housing, along Strandvägen by the river, was laid to waste. Following a visit by Soviet officials to inspect the destruction, damages were duly paid to neutral Sweden and the rebuilding of modern Pajala began apace. Today, Pajala is a pleasant, leafy place to stroll around, attractively located on the southern bank of the Torne River, stretching for a couple of kilometres between three main roads: Laestadiusvägen, closest to the river and location of the town museum; Tornedalsvägen, the main shopping street; and Genvägen (Route 99), the main east–west thoroughfare.

Arriving at the bus station, you will be confronted by a massive wooden model of the **great grey owl** (*Strix nebulosa*) plonked on a plinth beside the bus stops, which in life sweeps through the neighbouring forests. With eyes of black and yellow and a white crescent of feathers on its head, it is one of Lapland's most impressive birds of prey. The only other sight to speak of in the town centre is the world's largest **sundial**, which is located at the junction of Medborgarvägen and Torggatan, a 2-minute walk up from the bus station. With a diameter of 38m, this oversized clock tells the real solar time, which is generally around 20 minutes different from the regular time.

Laestadius Museum (Laestadiuspörtet; Laestadiusvägen 36; ☎ 0978 120 55; ⏰ mid-Jun–mid-Aug 09.00–18.00 Mon–Sat; 50SEK) From the sundial, head north on Torggatan towards the river and then right into Laestadiusvägen, where you will find the Laestadius Museum, also known as Laestadiuspörtet, which is actually the name of the solid, single-storey timber house where the revivalist preacher Lars Levi Laestadius (1800–61) lived while rector here from 1849 until his death; he died in the bedroom, which, like the rest of the house, has been kept in its original state. During his time in Pajala he was charged with inciting rebellion among the Sámi across the border in Norway (page 156). Following the Kautokeino rebellion, the criminalisation of revivalism caused many local people to shun the movement in Norway and, in Pajala in particular, resistance to Laestadius's radical ethics and morale led to confrontation. In 1853, the bishop decided that two separate church services should be held, one for Laestadians and one for regular churchgoers. This marked the first real split from the Church of Sweden and is regarded as the moment Laestadianism became a movement in its own right. Laestadius died in February 1861 and his grave can be seen in the middle section of the old churchyard on Kyrkallén, further east off Laestadiusvägen. The guided tour of the museum helps to tell the story of Laestadius's life and his role as a preacher, botanist and father of 12 children. There's a small café here serving light refreshments – though no alcohol! It's interesting to note that Laestadius did indeed drink, despite his rabid rantings against alcohol – a little-known fact even among the population of Lapland.

The Popular Music trail In order to get the most from Pajala, you really need to have read *Popular Music*. Anyone who has may want to visit some of the scenes Niemi describes in the novel. Bright yellow signposts dotted around the town proudly point the way to locations such as Vittulajänkkä, Paskajänkkä and the sewage works, where Matti and his friends hung out. The tourist office has a map of the sights/sites for anyone who's keen to see more of *Pajala* the movie.

Römppäviikko festival and Pajala market Around 25 years ago, little Pajala made a big name for itself when it went public and declared that it needed women. There was quite simply a three-to-one gender imbalance in these parts and the gruff lumberjacks who lived and worked here had nobody to whisper sweet nothings to after a long day in the forest. The local authorities advertised in newspapers in the south of Sweden for single women to come to Pajala for a knees-up and possibly meet the man of their dreams. Sure enough, the story was picked up by journalists outside Sweden, the story appeared in newspapers across Europe, and before you could say 'timber!' busloads of women from across the continent were heading for Pajala for a drunken bash that the village has never forgotten. It was a great triumph: many of the amorous visitors decided to stay, and although several –30°C winters caused some to head south again, about 30 women have stayed the course and married local men. To mark the original event in 1987, the **Römppäviikko festival** (literally 'romp week') is held during the last week in September every year. A riot of drinking, dancing, music – and bizarre sauna endurance competitions – makes the cultural festival the best time to visit Pajala.

A close second, though, is the **Pajala market**, which is held the second weekend after midsummer and with around 45,000 visitors is one of the biggest in the north of Sweden. People pour into town from far and wide to pick up bargains from the street stalls or simply to enjoy the smell of popcorn, fresh fish or reindeer kebabs and perhaps take a ride on the funfair. It is a good-natured, fun event and is well worth attending if you are in the area at the right time.

Naturally, it is a good idea to book accommodation well in advance if you are planning to visit during either of the events.

NORTHWEST OF PAJALA
Junosuando and Camp Three Rivers Mention Junosuando to most Swedes and they'll look at you with a blank expression – barely anyone outside Lapland has ever heard of the place, and certainly couldn't locate it on a map with any confidence. Yet, that is precisely the charm of this remote village, tucked away 55km to the northwest of Pajala along Route 395 (and on the direct Pajala–Kiruna bus route). True, there may be precious few sights for visitors to tick off, but that's not the reason people come here. Instead, it is home to Junosuando Guesthouse, the best environmentally friendly accommodation in Swedish Lapland, offering the chance to experience rural village life first hand, and nearby Camp Three Rivers.

Where to stay, eat and drink Both the guesthouse and camp are operated by **Aurora Retreat** (m 070 675 5071; e info@auroraretreat.se; w auroraretreat.se), an altogether smaller venture than that at Lainio further north (see below), headed by Swedish–Canadian couple, Mikael and Maya.

Junosuando Guesthouse Kangasvägen 35; w auroraretreat.se/junosuandoguesthouse. This haven of stripped pine, potted plants & gloriously airy rooms & staircases can be found in the former vicarage, dating from 1928. The emphasis here is on minimal environmental impact & the food is organic where possible. Rooms both with & without private facilities are available. €€€

Camp Three Rivers ⊕ late Nov–early Apr & Jun–Sep. Located just a few km upstream from Junosuando, Camp Three Rivers offers you a chance to really get back to nature, by staying in a remote log cabin deep in the forest with no electricity & no running water. In addition to the main cabin with a kitchen, there is a sauna & 4 sleeping huts, each accommodating between 2 & 4 people & heated by a wood-burning stove. Various packages & options are available, including dog-sledding – full details are on the website, but a 3-night stay, for example, costs from 6,000SEK pp & includes transfer to & from Kiruna, accommodation, meals & the loan of snowshoes or skis. The camp is also open between Jun & Sep, when it's possible to stay as part of a 2-day guided canoe expedition, costing 2,000SEK pp, including overnight accommodation, dinner, b/fast & canoe rental. €€€€

Lainio wilderness camp ✳ [map, page 114] (✆0981 410 25; e info@lainio.com; w lainio.com) From Pajala it is a straightforward drive of around 90km northwest along Route 395 towards Vittangi to reach the right turn for Lainio, an isolated mountain village. Although the turn-off is an unnumbered minor road, the junction is signposted for Lainio. The road then twists and turns through extensive areas of bog for a further 30km, all the way to the village itself. Remarkably, about 80 people live in this remote outpost spread along the western bank of the mighty Lainio River. Indeed, the river is the village's *raison d'être*: it provides food, transportation and a source of tourism for the wilderness camp, **Lainio Vildmark** (⊕ closed during the winter), who've been drawing visitors to this forgotten part of Swedish Lapland for several decades. Accommodation is provided in a dozen or so self-catering rustic cabins (from €, plus 150SEK for bed linen), some with private sauna, of different sizes, all within a stone's throw of the river. Alternatively, you can camp for 150SEK per tent. Dinner is available if pre-booked and airport pickups are available from Kiruna airport (1,500SEK/car taking 4 people one-way).

The main reason to come here is to experience nature in the raw: surrounded by kilometre after kilometre of marshland and forest, Lainio really is a long way off the beaten track and it offers an opportunity to really get away from it all. Nature here is all around: there are bears in the forest, plentiful salmon in the river and reindeer up on the fells. During spring, summer and autumn, when the camp is open, the main activities are **salmon fishing** (equipment rental from 500SEK), **canoeing** (700SEK) and **drifting** (slowly riding the current in an inflatable dingy; 350SEK). The camp can also arrange **visits to the Sámi village** of Viikusjärvi, 30km to the north, to see reindeer (1,950SEK). Of the **hiking trails** available, the best one leads to a 7m-long canyon, edged by 20m-tall rock walls, just outside Lainio, where, incidentally, the fishing is reputed to be excellent.

MUONIO AND AROUND

From Pajala, Route 99 heads north to the hamlet of Muodoslompolo, from where Route 404 cuts east to the Finnish border and attractive Muonio. It's not possible to get to Muonio by bus directly from Sweden; coming from Haparanda/Tornio, first take a **bus** to Rovaniemi and then change there for Muonio. North of Muonio, buses run all the way to Kilpisjärvi; bus times in Finland are at w matkahuolto.fi.

Benefiting from its waterside location on the banks of the eponymous river, which forms the border with Sweden, Muonio is a delightful, peaceful little place. True, there's little to see here in terms of attractions; it is more the simple pleasure of being here and wandering around the streets that repays a visit – plus some superb and affordable **cabin accommodation** perched on a hill overlooking the town (see opposite). However, there's one good reason for coming here: if you are thinking of going on a **husky safari**, Muonio's proximity to the **Harriniva Holiday Centre**, just 3km south of town, makes it a less touristy alternative to the centre itself for somewhere to stay.

TOURIST INFORMATION Limited tourist information (⊕ 10.00–18.00 daily) is available inside the 'Kiela' building, Kilpisjärventie 15, beside the town's main road junction at the intersection of Route 79 from Kittilä and Route 21 from Tornio. Don't expect to glean masses here since knowledge of English is poor and sometimes the information desk is not even staffed.

WHERE TO STAY

Hotelli Jeris [map, page 134] Jerisjärventie 91; m 040 0177 600; e reception@hotellijeris. fi; w harriniva.fi/destinations/jeris. Some 20km southeast of Muonio beside Jerisjärvi Lake; from

Muonio take Route 79 back towards Kittilä for 12km & then swing left on Route 957 heading towards Pallastunturi & the hotel is on your right just after the bridge over the lake. A choice of smart dbl rooms in the main building & cabins in 2 separate locations: Jeriskylä, on the hill above the main hotel building, & Jerisranta, below the hotel & next to the lake. Although the lakeside cabins are smaller (sleeping up to 4 people), they are altogether more agreeable & cosier – & less expensive. All cabins have a fully equipped kitchen, TV & sauna. The hotel boasts a lakeside spa complex including a jacuzzi & 3 saunas (1 is a smoke sauna). During the summer, the hotel rents out canoes, rowing boats & mountain bikes. Lakeside cabin €€€€/night; dbl room €€€€

🏠 **Lomamaja Pekonen** Lahenrannantie 10; m 040 550 8436; e info@lomamajapekonen.fi; w lomamajapekonen.fi. For somewhere to stay look no further than this fantastically located year-round guesthouse & cabin accommodation on the main road that leads into the village from beside the filling station; this road is straight ahead of you when you come to the main junction when approaching from Kittilä. In addition to no-frills dbls, there is a range of well-equipped, comfortable cabins with & without private sauna. (The ones at the top of the hill enjoy the best view of the lake opposite & are also those with saunas.) There are canoes for rent. Dbl €€; cabins with/without sauna €€€

❌ **WHERE TO EAT AND DRINK** Two of Muonio's eating and drinking establishments are handily located close to each other near the filling station, while a third Thai restaurant is located inside the Kiela building.

❌ **Silk Coffee Shop** Kilpisjärventie 15 (inside the Kiela building); 📞040 187 2497; w thairavintolamuonio.fi; ⏰ 10.00–18.00 Mon–Fri, noon–18.00 Sat & Sun. This unexpected place thrills in pointing out that it is the northernmost Thai restaurant in the world. Be that as it may, it serves the usual run of sanitised southeast Asian mains for €14.90 each, as well as a w/day buffet served between 11.00 & 15.00 for €11.50. €

❌ **Uncle La Ban** Kosotuskeino 1; 📞016 533 111; ⏰ noon–21.00 daily. Run by a Palestinian family who somehow ended up in Muonio, this pizzeria serves up a wide range, including an excellent reindeer pizza, for around the €10–12 mark. €

✳ 🍴 **Swiss Café & Konditoria** Puthaanrannantie 5; ⏰ 10.00–18.00 daily; w swisscafemuonio.com. A real find – Swiss owned & run, this great little café serves up homemade cakes & sweet treats, including cheesecake & a heavenly Sachertorte, plus has lunch specials; owner, Agnes, moved here in 2012 after falling in love with Muonio. Everything is baked on site by genuine Swiss baker, Thomas, who also sells his photographs of the surrounding Finnish countryside inside. €

HARRINIVA

Harriniva Holiday Centre (m 040 0155 100; e sales@harriniva.fi; w harriniva.fi) The biggest and best husky centre (with around 400 dogs) in Finland, the Harriniva Holiday Centre, 3km south of Muonio along Route 21 towards Tornio, is the place to get your doggie fix. Established in 1973 by husband-and-wife team, Köpi and Maria Pietikäinen, Harriniva has developed a reputation over the years for well-organised, good-value husky safaris that are hard to beat. During the winter season, 95% of guests here are foreign, predominantly from Britain, France, Germany and Holland, which gives the entire place an enjoyable, cosmopolitan air.

All **accommodation** at Harriniva is clean, comfortable and warm. Prices vary according to time of year; high season is early December to early January and February to early April. Rates quoted here are all high-season prices. Accommodation in winter tends to be block-booked months in advance and it is unlikely you will find availability without booking an inclusive package. In summer, however, things are different and there is plenty of availability.

All double rooms have wooden floors and walls; some have their own sauna (**€€€€**). Apartments (**€€€€**) sleeping up to six people are of the same high standard as double rooms and include a television, fridge, microwave and airing cupboard. Breakfast is included in the double room and apartment rates. There's a choice of cabin accommodation sleeping up to four people, some with kitchenette, sauna, shower and toilet (**€€**).

Winter tours There are various lengths of husky safaris available at Harriniva. At the top end of the scale, for example, a **week-long tour** with your own dog-sled team, overnighting in log cabins with all food provided costs from €1,835. The cabins have wood-burning saunas but no running water or electricity. Although the pleasure of riding across frozen lakes and weaving your way deep through Lapland's snow-covered forests doesn't come cheap, it is not one you are likely to forget in a hurry.

Alternatively, Harriniva also operates **snowmobile** tours: a three-day safari covering up to 100km per day overnighting in log cabins, for example, costs €1,680 per person.

The full range of activities is detailed on the website w harriniva.fi.

Summer tours Between June and September, Harriniva specialises in trips on the Muonio River. There are **white-water raft tours** lasting 1½ hours for €45; or more sedate **canoeing tours** (min 4 people) of 2 to 3 hours at €50 per person. The Muonio River is considered one of the best salmon rivers in Finland and from the end of June to mid-August, **salmon fishing** is in season (€190 for a boat with an outboard motor and fishing equipment). Rowing boats are also available for rental at €35 per day. Since not all tours operate daily, it is best to check with Harriniva to find out exactly what will be available while you are there.

TORASSIEPPI ✳ Around 17km east of Muonio (take Route 79 towards Rovaniemi and then turn left on to the 907 towards Pallastunturi), the **reindeer and husky farm**, Torassieppi (Torassiepentie 212; m 040 170 1925; e torassieppi@harriniva.fi; w harriniva.fi/holiday-destination/torassieppi; ◷ closed May & Nov), is an altogether smaller and quieter resort than Harriniva itself. Dominating the minuscule village of the same name, the farm dates back to 1847 and has been run by the same family ever since, though there is no longer any meat production. Comprising just eight snug en-suite **cabins** (**€€€€**) and eight **twin rooms** (**€€€€**), this relaxing, lakeside retreat is great if you're looking for a personal and friendly place to stay. Alternatively, between mid-December and April you can also spend the night in a **snow igloo** for €100. The on-site **restaurant** serves lunch and dinner with an emphasis on locally sourced organic produce. The farm offers a guided visit plus a 15km **husky safari** for €160, as well as a number of **reindeer safaris**: a 1-hour night-time ride in search of the northern lights costs €130. It's also possible to visit the reindeer farm without doing a safari: €25 buys you a guided tour plus a visit to the original 19th-century manor house – one of the few timber buildings in Finnish Lapland which escaped the Germans's scorched-earth policy, and a visit to the modest museum which contains a few worthy tools, implements and other agricultural odds and ends originally used on the farm. Torassieppi also runs a couple of interesting courses which last around 3 hours: one teaches handicrafts (€50), while another offers participants the chance to learn to cook over an open fire (€60) and includes the price of dinner.

From Muonio, it is a mere 87km northwest to the twin settlements of drab Kaaresuvanto in Finland, and considerably more interesting Karesuando in Sweden, which face each other across the Muonio River; on the way you will pass through the hamlet of Palojoensuu, which is where Route 93 begins its journey north to Kautokeino and is a useful way of reaching the North Cape. Finnish **buses** run from Rovaniemi to Kaaresuvanto via Muonio; they continue from Kaaresuvanto to Kilpisjärvi; times are at w matkahuolto.fi. Swedish buses run from Karesuando south to Kiruna; see w resrobot.se for details. For details of the summer bus which runs from here over the border into Norway, see the box on page 131.

In Sámi, both places are known as Gárasavvon; you can walk between both countries here by simply crossing the bridge that spans the river, though remember the 1-hour time difference between Finland and Sweden. Given Kaaresuvanto's complete absence of attractions, you are far better off spending time in Karesuando exploring its connections with revivalist preacher Lars Levi Laestadius, who left his mark on the village after serving as the local minister for 23 years in the mid 1800s.

TOURIST INFORMATION Karesuando's **tourist office** (❦0981 202 05; e turistinfo@ karesuando.se; w karesuando.se; ⊕ 09.00–15.00 Mon–Fri) is a law unto itself: sometimes it's open, sometimes it's not; sometimes the staff reply to emails and queries, sometimes they don't. You'll find it in the customs building by the bridge across to Kaaresuvanto.

⌂ WHERE TO STAY

⌂ **Davvi Arctic Lodge** Käsivarrentie 3551, Kaaresuvanto;❦016 522 101; e info@davvihotel. com; w davvihotel.com; ⊕ usually Apr–Oct. Perched on a hillock on the Finnish side of the bridge, this smart hotel offers smart dbls in the main building & cabins located on the hill behind. Although open from Nov to Mar, it is only available as part of a pre-booked package tour with Transun. Summer opening varies from year to year. Dbl €€€; 2-person cabin €€€€

⌂ **Cabins in Keinovuopio** ❦0981 202 12. If you want to really get away from it all, the 4-berth cabins in nearby Keinovuopio, a tiny hamlet home to barely a dozen people, are perfect. Keinovuopio is not connected to Karesuando by road; in fact, it barely has a dirt track linking it to an even smaller hamlet, Kummavuopio. Instead,

get here by crossing over the bridge into Finland & continuing northwest towards Kilpisjärvi for about 80km where, just before the hamlet of Peera, there's a footbridge back over the river into Sweden & access to Keinovuopio. A daily bus leaves Kaaresuvanto at 14.35 for Peera arriving at 15.40 (Finnish time). €

Å **Karesuando Camping** Laestadiusvägen 185; m 070 605 1124; e karesuando.camping@ hotmail.com; w karesuandocamping.blogspot. com; ⊕ late May–early Aug. Located on the southern side of Karesuando (around 1.5km from the church on Route 99 towards Pajala, follow the signs), this riverside campsite has Sámi-style *kåtas* & regular cabins with & without running water & cooking facilities; showers are available in the service building & there's a smoke sauna. €

✗ WHERE TO EAT AND DRINK

✗ **Arctic Livs** Opposite end of Karesuando to the campsite on Route 45 out towards Kiruna by the filling stations; ⊕ 09.00–20.00 Mon–Fri, 10.00–20.00 Sat & Sun. Serving up burgers, steak & various reindeer concoctions for around 75–95SEK as well as a range of Asian dishes such as lemon chicken rice & spicy beef stew. Basic. €

✗ **Rajabaari** At the filling station in Kaaresuvanto; ⊕ 09.00–22.00 Mon–Fri, 10.00– 19.00 Sat, 11.00–21.00 Sun. Offers a good range of stomach-filling fry-ups, such as schnitzel with fries & tinned vegetables, for around €15. €

WHAT TO SEE AND DO Beyond the tourist office, you will see a simple log cabin, signed **Laestadius pörte** (⊕ always open; free), which served as the rectory of Karesuando's best-known resident, the preacher and botanist **Lars Levi Laestadius**, who lived here from 1826 to 1849. He raised 12 children in Karesuando with his Sámi wife, Brita Cajsa Alstadius. It was from this humble wooden shack, which Laestadius had built in 1828 and is now a listed building, that his revivalist teachings spread across Lapland attracting followers in three countries, prepared to lead a life of abstinence and repentance in accordance with his strict beliefs. Even today, there are many people in Karesuando who loyally adhere to his principles.

The cabin consists of one main room, decorated with pictures of the man and his followers doing their thing, together with a small hallway and larder. During his life, Laestadius did not only take it on himself to rid Lapland of the evils of alcohol abuse and lead its inhabitants on a path of righteousness and purity, but he was also a keen botanist. While a student at Uppsala University north of Stockholm, Laestadius undertook his first botanical research trip and, later, was dispatched by the Royal Swedish Academy of Sciences to carry out further studies at either end of the country in Skåne and Lapland. He became an internationally recognised botanist and was even a signed-up member of the Edinburgh Botanical Society. It seems fitting, therefore, that a **botanical garden** was opened in his memory in Karesuando in 1989. In front of the campsite, the modest garden contains many of the Arctic plants that grow across Lapland, including the rare poppy that carries his name, *Papaver laestadium*.

Vita Huset Museum (⊕ 08.00–11.00 & noon–15.00 Mon–Fri; 30SEK) The museum is along the Pajala road towards the youth hostel and the campsite. You will come across an elegant old white timber building dating from 1888, set back a little from the road, which once served as the residence of the provincial governor. Today it functions as Karesuando's museum, its name translating rather grandly as 'the White House'. Inside, ask the curator to point out the atmospheric black-and-white photographs from 1944 (they are hidden away in a side room) which show dozens of Finns fleeing the approaching German troops at the end of World War II. In particular look out for the dog-eared photograph of local woman, Olga Raattamaa (1881–1957), who earned herself the nickname, Empress Olga. Many Finns owe their lives to her bravery as she rowed them over the Könkämä River to safety in neutral Sweden and took care of them in her humble living quarters in Kummavuopio.

Kaarevaara Mountain For a breathtaking view of the surrounding tundra, head a couple of kilometres south out of Karesuando on Route 99 towards Pajala and take the right turn signed Kaarevaara. This road then leads to the top of the eponymous mountain (516m). On a clear day you can see all the way to Pältsa Mountain (733m) in the far northwest corner of Sweden, a point where Sweden, Norway and Finland all meet, known as Treriksröset (page 132). It is the best place for miles around to observe the midnight sun as it dips towards the horizon before circling overhead again. According to local Sámi, the nearby spring, *hilkkukaltio*, has special healing qualities and can even cure eye diseases. Ask at the tourist office for directions of how to get to the spring from the car park and the television mast at the top of the mountain.

KILPISJÄRVI AND TRERIKSRÖSET

From Kaaresuvanto, it is an uneventful drive of 110km along the E8, passing the footbridge from Peera to Keinovuopio (page 129), to Kilpisjärvi at the very end of the thumb-shaped chunk of land that forms Finland's far northwestern frontier. Unless you are heading on to Tromsø in Norway (a further 165km), the real reason to come to this remote location is to tackle some of Finland's highest peaks or to see Treriksröset, the three-nation cairn, which marks the geographical point where the Nordic nations of Sweden, Finland and Norway all rub shoulders. Incidentally, there's midnight sun in this part of Lapland, mainland Finland's most westerly point, from 22 May to 25 July, and, consequently, polar night from 25 November to 17 January.

KILPISJÄRVI Squeezed between the mountains of Saana (1,029m) and Salmivaara (598m), Kilpisjärvi is a modest little place that is popular with hikers lured here by the prospect of scaling Finland's highest fells – most of them over 1,000m high. There's no real village centre to speak of; instead, a handful of accommodation options, eateries and a supermarket are essentially all that's here, straddling the E8, which runs through the village. The quay for the boat, M/S *Malla*, which sails across Kilpisjärvi Lake towards Treriksröset (page 133), is 5km north of the main village, down below Kilpisjärven Retkeilykeskus and the fire station. Year-round **buses** run here from Rovaniemi via Muonio and Kaaresuvanto, while in summer there's an international service which continues over the border to Tromsø (see box, below); bus times are at w matkahuolto.fi.

Tourist information The Kilpisjärvi **visitor centre** (Kilpisjärven Luontotalo; ☏ 020 639 7990; e kilpisjarvi@metsa.fi; w kilpisjarvi.org; ⊕ Jun, Aug & Sep 10.00–17.00 Tue–Sat; Jul 10.00–17.00 daily) is located in the centre of the village beside the main road, Käsivarrentie, and is a handy place to stock up on maps and the latest hiking information. There's also information at w nationalparks.fi/kilpisjarvivisitorcentre.

 Where to stay, eat and drink For eating and drinking look no further than the **restaurant within the Tundrea complex** on Käsivarrentie (page 132; €), which dishes up a wide range of local specialities such as Arctic char and reindeer.

🏠 **Lapland Hotel Kilpis** Käsivarrentie; ☏016 3232; e kilpis@laplandhotels.com; w laplandhotels. com. In the shadow of Saana Mountain, this modern hotel has comfortable dbl rooms with fantastic views over the surrounding lake, as well as a range of self-catering apts. €€€€

🏠 **Kilpisjärven Retkeilykeskus** Käsivarrentie 14663; ☏016 537 771; e info@kilpisjarvicamping.

THE ARCTIC ROUTE: LINKING NORWAY AND FINLAND BY BUS

A hugely useful new bus service now links the northern parts of the Torne Valley with both Tromsø and Alta, making travel by public transport across large parts of Lapland possible for the first time. Norwegian company The Arctic Route runs a daily service in each direction between December and March, along the following route: Tromsø, Kilpisjärvi, Kaaresuvanto, Hetta, Kautokeino and Alta.

Schedules and fares can be found at w thearcticroute.com/book/#routes. Significantly, this is the first time in years that there has been a bus link between Hetta and Kautokeino, linking Finland with Norway via the remote Finnmarksvidda. Travelling via Karesuando and Kaaresuvanto rather than Narvik and/or Tromsø will also make significantly faster journeys from northern Sweden to Alta possible.

com; w kilpisjarvicamping.com. The tongue-twisting Kilpisjärven Retkeilykeskus, 5km north of the main village, has cosy en-suite dbl rooms & cabins with toilet & kitchen. Dbl & cabins both €€€

🏠 **Tundrea** m 040 039 6684; e info@tundrea.com; w tundrea.com. With a variety of well-appointed cabins (all with balconies & fireplaces) & 4-bed apts, this smart holiday complex is a dependable choice & has great views of Saana Mountain, to boot. Dbl €€€; cabins €€

Activities

Hiking and wilderness flights Some of the best views of the fells of this part of Lapland can be enjoyed from the top of Saana Mountain. Ask at the visitor centre for a map and information about the various **hiking trails** that lead up and around the peak. You're free to climb Saana's northern slope but access to the western slope is restricted from mid-May to August to protect an area of herb-rich forest, which has been the subject of a conservation order since 1988.

Helicopter flights are available from Kilpisjärvi. **Heliflite** (m 040 015 5111; e contact@heliflite.fi; w heliflite.fi) operates to various remote destinations in the surrounding wilderness. The flights are useful if you are planning some serious hiking or fancy fishing in some of the mountain tarns but don't want to hike there first. Trips, for example, start at €250 one-way; the price is per helicopter and for five passengers and luggage. The heliport is at the entrance to the village when arriving from Kaaresuvanto.

To Tromsø and the Hurtigruten coastal ferry Between June and mid-September a handy **bus** runs daily from Kilpisjärvi over the border to Tromsø in Norway, a beautiful, switchback ride all the way down to the Arctic Ocean. It leaves from Lapland Hotel Kilpis at 17.40 and Kilpisjärven Retkeilykeskus at 18.10 (Finnish time) routing via Skibotn (see box, opposite) and the Lyngenfjord and arriving into Tromsø at 19.25 (Norwegian time), providing a connection with the southbound (but not the northbound) Hurtigruten ferry, which sails at 01.30. Timetables and fares are at w eskelisen.fi.

TRERIKSRÖSET The cairn that marks the point where Norway, Sweden and Finland all meet has a somewhat chequered history. The first cairn was erected in 1897 by a team of Norwegians and Russians. (Finland was at that time a grand duchy within the Russian Empire.) The Swedes refused to take part in the ceremony due to an ongoing border dispute with Norway. The original idea of raising stone plaques bearing each country's national emblem was hurriedly ditched, and a simple cairn of stones was erected instead. In 1901, Norway and Sweden kissed and made up and it was decided to cover the cairn in concrete. However, the concrete ran out and there was only enough to cover the top part of the cairn, which, over time was destroyed by the extreme winter weather. A second cairn, still standing today and resembling a none-too-attractive concrete bunker, was built in 1926 and painted yellow. Perhaps a sign of Sweden's self-appointed role as the Nordic nations' big brother, there's much more interest in visiting the cairn among Swedes than Finns, and especially Norwegians, who would often rather forget that they share a border with a supercilious, patronising, puffed-up neighbour – at least, if their own prejudices are to be believed.

Getting there There are two options for getting to Treriksröset. Beginning at the car park beside the E8 just to the north of the Retkeilykeskus, a **hiking trail** of 11km (one-way; 3hrs; moderate), stony in parts, leads west through the alpine meadows and birch forest of **Malla National Park (Mallan luonnonpuisto)**,

It's said that today's map of Finland looks a bit like a one-armed person; the 'left arm' being the narrow corridor of land which stretches northwest of Muonio and Kaaresuvanto all the way to Kilpisjärvi. Between 1920 and 1944 a 'right arm' reached from Inarijärvi Lake as far as Petsamo on the Arctic Ocean (now in Russia), but was lost after World War II. The remaining 'left arm', though, stops short of the Arctic Ocean because all coastal territory bordering the Arctic Ocean is Norwegian not Finnish. However, during the 1920s and 30s, a movement for a Great Finland grew into a significant force in Finnish politics with a call for all areas outside Finland with a Finnish population (notably in Sweden's Torne Valley and Norway's Troms province) to be united with the Motherland. With the onset of World War II, the plans were dropped. Yet, it is against this very background of territorial expansionism that the Finns drew up carefully laid plans in June 1941 to annexe the Norwegian town of Skibotn, barely 48km away on the Lyngenfjord, to secure supply routes with Britain and America. Skibotn would become sovereign Finnish territory and a new harbour and airport would be built, linked, in turn, to the rest of Finland by a new road from Kilpisjärvi. The 'left arm' of the Finnish map would be finally outstretched to its full length.

The plans, however, were never put to the Norwegian authorities because just one week later Germany attacked the Soviet Union and the course of the war changed for good. The Finnish dream of accessing the Arctic Ocean lives on, though, even today as plans to build a new rail line north of Rovaniemi take shape (see box, page 145).

Finland's oldest, established in 1916, home to some of the country's rarest plants including Lapland rhododendron, glacier crowfoot and the gloriously named one-flowered fleabane.

Alternatively, the **boat** M/S *Malla* sails from Kilpisjärvi to the old Sámi settlement of Koltaluokta on the northwestern arm of Kilpisjärvi lake (w mallalaiva.com; ⊕ late Jun–late Sep 10.00, 14.00 & 18.00 Finnish time daily; 45mins; €30 return). From here there's a 3km path to the cairn itself, which is duckboarded in parts. The boat sails back to Kilpisjärvi at noon, 16.00 and 20.00. Be prepared for mosquitoes! A good combination is to take the boat there and then hike back, thus avoiding having to time your walk to coincide with the boat's sailing schedule.

LAPLAND ONLINE

For additional online content, articles, photos and more on Lapland, why not visit w bradtguides.com/lapland?

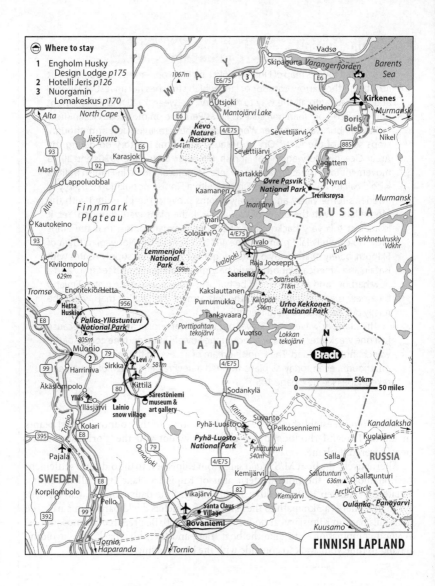

Where to stay

1 Engholm Husky
  Design Lodge *p175*
2 Hotelli Jeris *p126*
3 Nuorgamin
  Lomakeskus *p170*

Vadsø

Skipagurra *Varangerfjorden*

Barents Sea

1067m

E6/75 (3)

E6

Kirkenes

Utsjoki

Neiden

Murmansk

North Cape

Alta

E6

Mantojärvi Lake

Sevettijärvi

Boris Gleb

Jiešjavrre

Kevo Nature Reserve

4/E75

Sevettijärvi

Nikel

93

641m

E6

885

Karasjok (1)

Masi

92

Partakko

Vagattem

Lappluobbal

Kaamanen

Øvre Pasvik National Park

Nyrud

Murmansk

Finnmark Plateau

Inarijärvi

Treriksrøysa

Kautokeino

Inari

R U S S I A

93

Solojärvi

4/E75

Ivalo

Verkhnetulruskiy Vdkhr

Lemmenjoki National Park

599m

Ivalojoki

Lotta

Tromsø

Kivilompolo

629m

Raja Jooseppi

Enontekiö/Hetta

Saariselkä

Saariselkä 718m

Hetta Huskies

956

Kakslauttanen

Kiilopää 546m

Urho Kekkonen National Park

E8

Pallas-Yllästunturi National Park

Purnumukka

Tankavaara

805m

Muonio (2)

Porttipahtan tekojärvi

Vuotso

Lokkan tekojärvi

N

79

F I N L A N D

99

Harriniva

Sirkka

Levi

581m

4/E75

Bradt

Åkäslompolo

80

Kittilä

Sodankylä

0

50km

0

50 miles

Ylläs

Ylläsjärvi

Lainio snow village

Sarestöniemi museum & art gallery

Kitinen

Suvanto

Kandalaksha

Kolari

E8

Pelkosenniemi

Pyhä-Luosto

Kuolajärvi

395

79

Pyhä-Luosto National Park

Pyhätunturi 540m

Salla

RUSSIA

Pajala

Sallatunturi 636m

Sallatunturi

Kemijärvi

Arctic Circle

SWEDEN

E8

82

Kemijärvi

Oulanka Panajarvi

Korpilombolo

Vikajärvi

Santa Claus Village

392

99

Pello

Rovaniemi

Kuusamo

Tornio

Haparanda

Tornio

FINNISH LAPLAND

6

Finnish Lapland: Rovaniemi to the Finnmark Plateau

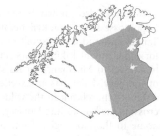

If you are looking for Santa Claus, you will find him, most readily, on the Arctic Circle in Finnish Lapland. Over the years, the Finns' well-executed campaign to convince the world that Father Christmas lives in Finnish Lapland appears to have paid off and, during the winter months, the airports here are full of charter flights bringing in children and their parents from all over Europe to see the fat man in the funny red suit. However, Finnish Lapland has much more to offer than just Santa – not least in terms of wildlife. If you haven't yet seen a reindeer, the chances are you will here. Birdlife is extremely rich and varied; many species, for example, are attracted to the largest expanse of open water in Lapland, Inarijärvi Lake, with its dozens of pine-clad islands and skerries.

A land of rounded hills and rolling forests rather than craggy mountains and deep valleys, the terrain of Finnish Lapland may be less mountainous than in neighbouring Sweden, but it is no less attractive. Tragically, the same cannot be said about the majority of towns and villages, which, as in Norway, were burnt to the ground at the end of World War II. Rebuilding was often uninspired and many settlements, with their graceless platoons of concrete blocks, fail to impress. Two of Lapland's largest and most vibrant Sámi villages, though not in Finland itself, are located just over the border on the vast barren expanses of the Finnmark Plateau and, when approaching from the south, more readily accessed from Finnish Lapland than from Norway. The plateau, with its countless mountain tarns and watercourses, is one of the last wilderness areas of northern Lapland: there are no roads, no villages, nor indeed any sign of human influence over an area of several hundred square kilometres.

The undisputed metropolis of Finnish Lapland is Rovaniemi and any visit to this part of the region is not complete without it. Quite unlike any other town in the area, Rovaniemi can not only boast a brash selection of bars and restaurants, but it also has a couple of respectable shopping centres, a cinema and an excellent museum covering all things Arctic. From Rovaniemi there are three main routes to choose from: northwest along Route 79 via Kittilä; northeast via Route 4/E75 via Sodankylä; and east on Route 82 via Kemijärvi.

From Rovaniemi, Route 79 leads northwest to the uneventful town of Kittilä, from where there's ready access to two of Finland's leading ski resorts: **Levi** and **Ylläs**. From Levi, the nippy Route 956 strikes off through some gloriously switchback terrain heading for Hetta, known for its husky centre and great hiking opportunities and ultimately Kautokeino over the border in Norway, the site of the great Sámi Easter festival, some quality jewellery and handicrafts and the historically significant Kautokeino rebellion (page 156).

Route 4 (also known as the E75) heads northeast from Rovaniemi towards unprepossessing Sodankylä before streaking north for the gold-panning centre of Tankavaara and the unspoilt terrain of the Urho Kekkonen National Park, ideal for independent hiking tours. Further north, Ivalo is the jumping-off point for bus travel to Murmansk in Russia, whereas enjoyable Inari, on the bony shores of Inarijärvi Lake, has an excellent Sámi museum and a glorious hiking trail to a remote church out in the wilderness. Beyond here, Route 92 swings northwest, crossing the border into Norway, and arriving in the Sámi stronghold of Karasjok, home to the Norwegian Sámi parliament, an informative museum and a dog-sledding centre. From either Karasjok or Kautokeino, you are well on your way to the North Cape, which is covered on page 214.

Heading east from Rovaniemi along Route 82 brings you first of all to lakeside Kemijärvi, which is also the terminus for train services routing up from Helsinki. Here, there's a choice of routes to take you further into this little-explored part of Finnish Lapland: Route 5/E63 and then Route 962 will take you north to the twin ski and outdoor centres of Pyhä-Luosto – key destinations for people travelling with leading British tour operator Canterbury Travel. Alternatively, Route 82 continues east towards the Russian border and the town of Salla from where it's a short drive to the associated skiing and hiking resort of Sallatunturi.

ROVANIEMI AND AROUND

If you believe the tourist office hype, Rovaniemi (Roavenjárga in Sámi) is the capital of Lapland. True, this is the capital of the Finnish province Lappi, and accordingly the centre of all activity and services in the area, but it is not the capital of the three-nation indigenous region, known to the outside world as Lapland and the subject of this guidebook. The Finns should be given credit, though, for promoting Lapland and heightening public awareness of its existence. Over the years, the Finnish tourist board has become exceptionally adept at linking Rovaniemi and its location on the Arctic Circle with Lapland and Santa Claus in the popular psyche, with the result that Rovaniemi receives the lion's share of winter tourists to the whole of Lapland and it is now possible to take a direct charter flight here from airports across Europe: the famous Santa Claus charters; no-frills airlines easyJet and Norwegian have also now joined the fray. Incidentally, Rovaniemi airport (Finland's third busiest) handles around 600,000 passengers every year – not bad for a place that is only Finland's 15th-largest city. Seemingly, the hordes of tourists who descend on the city in winter don't seem to mind a little artistic licence – it isn't actually on the Arctic Circle itself, although the magic line does slice through the airport to the north of the city.

Rovaniemi may well be the capital of Lappi province, but it couldn't be more different from the rest of Lapland if it tried. Home to the world's northernmost McDonald's, a H&M store selling the latest European fashions and a town centre square named after the local hard-rock group Lordi, who won the Eurovision Song Contest for Finland in 2006, Rovaniemi is certainly different. Forget any notion of jetting straight into the heart of Lapland and snapping photographs of Sámi in traditional dress leading their reindeer; instead, you are more likely to be snapped by the speed cameras that line the road out to the Arctic Circle.

SOME HISTORY Located at the confluence of two of Finland's major rivers, the Ounasjoki and the Kemi, the latter providing direct access to the sea, Rovaniemi traces its history back over 8,000 years, when it slowly emerged as a trading centre

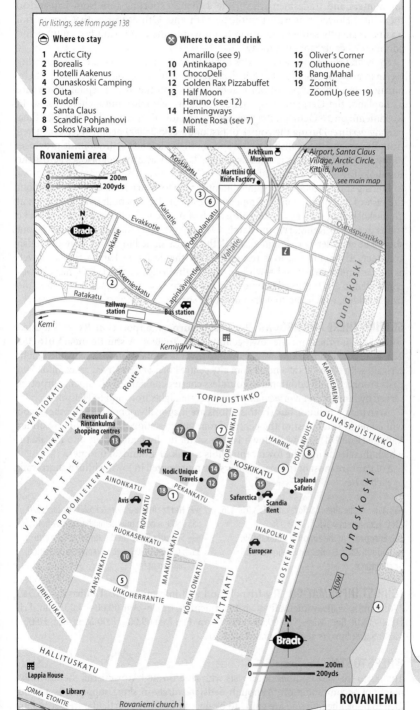

For listings, see from page 138

Where to stay

1 Arctic City
2 Borealis
3 Hotelli Aakenus
4 Ounaskoski Camping
5 Outa
6 Rudolf
7 Santa Claus
8 Scandic Pohjanhovi
9 Sokos Vaakuna

Where to eat and drink

Amarillo (see 9)
10 Antinkaapo
11 ChocoDeli
12 Golden Rax Pizzabuffet
13 Half Moon
Haruno (see 12)
14 Hemingways
Monte Rosa (see 7)
15 Nili

16 Oliver's Corner
17 Oluthuone
18 Rang Mahal
19 Zoomit
ZoomUp (see 19)

Rovaniemi area

0 ___ 200m
0 ___ 200yds

Koskikatu

Arktikum & Museum
↗ Airport, Santa Claus Village, Arctic Circle, Kittilä, Ivalo
see main map

Marttiini Old Knife Factory

Kairatie

Evakkotie

Bradt

N

Jokkatie

Pohjolankatu

Valtatie

Ounaspuistikko

Lapinkävijäntie

Ounaskoski

Asemieskatu

Ratakatu

Railway station

Bus station

Kemi ←

Kemijärvi →

VARTIOKATU

Route 4

TORIPUISTIKKO

KARINIEMENP

OUNASPUISTIKKO

LAPINKÄVIJÄNTIE

Revontuli & Rintankulma shopping centres

13

KORKALONKATU

HARRIK

POHJANPUIST

Hertz

17 11

7

19

KOSKIKATU

8

V A L T A T I E

POROMIEHENTIE

AINONKATU

Nodic Unique Travels

14

16

9

Lapland Safaris

ROVAKATU

18 1

PEKANKATU

12

15

Safarctica

Scandia Rent

Ounaskoski

Avis

RUOKASENKATU

MAAKUNTAKATU

INAPOLKU

KANSANKATU

KORKALONKATU

KOSKENRANTA

Europcar

10

5

UKKOHERRANTIE

VALTAKATU

FLOW

URHEILUKATU

N

4

Bradt

HALLITUSKATU

0 ___ 200m
0 ___ 200yds

Lappia House

JORMA ETONTIE

• Library

Rovaniemi church ↓

ROVANIEMI

for hunters and tradesmen who made a living exporting furs from Lapland to the south. However, it wasn't until the 11th and 12th centuries that Rovaniemi was permanently settled and began to grow into the administrative, cultural and commercial centre that it is today.

Sadly, the elegant wooden houses of old Rovaniemi are long gone; the retreating German army began its systematic destruction of the town on 10 October 1944 by burning down a number of old manor houses and the local hospital. Elsewhere in Lapland, the German troops tended to leave churches untouched. Not so in Rovaniemi: on 16 October, they set light to the town church and its belfry as their parting gesture. During the course of just one week, 25,000 people were evacuated from Rovaniemi to Swedish Lapland and south to Finland's Ostrobothnia province; in total, 90% of Rovaniemi's buildings were laid to waste and all bridges across the Kemijoki River were destroyed.

During spring 1945, the first inhabitants began to return from exile and set about the task of reconstruction. A temporary trestle bridge was built over the rapids at Ounaskoski and railway tracks were even laid on the ice of the frozen river to take trains across to Kemijärvi. In March 1945, it was decreed that the town's layout should be completely redesigned, a task that was assigned to the celebrated Finnish architect, Alvar Aalto, who is responsible for the design of Lappia House as well as Rovaniemi's library and town hall. The main bridge across the Ounasjoki was completed in 1951; it freed people from having to rely on ice roads, ferries and the trestle bridge, which had to be rebuilt every spring.

GETTING THERE AND AROUND Rovaniemi's **airport** (airport code RVN) is located about 7km northeast of the town centre along Route 4. A **shuttle bus** (✆ 016 362 222; w airportbus.fi; €7 one-way) runs into town in connection with scheduled flight arrivals, with drop-offs at a number of city centre hotels; alternatively a taxi into town costs around €25. In additional to countless charter companies, Rovaniemi airport is served by Finnair and Norwegian which operate flights from and to Helsinki.

Arriving by **train** or **bus** (both stations are diagonally opposite each other), you will come in southwest of the centre. From either station, take the subway under Valtatie (Route 4) and walk down Hallituskatu, finally taking a left into Rovakatu, which then leads into the town centre; it is a walk of around 30 minutes.

For **car hire** most of the main players are represented in town within a short walk of each other:

🚗 **Avis** At the airport & Rovakatu 21; ✆ 010 436 2360; e rovaniemi@avis.fi; w avis.fi
🚗 **Europcar** At the airport & Valtakatu 19; m 040 306 2870; e rovaniemi@europcar.fi; w europcar.fi

🚗 **Hertz** At the airport & Koskikatu 23; ✆ 020 555 2500; e hertz.rovaniemi@hertz.fi; w hertz.fi
🚗 **Scandia Rent** At the airport & Valtakatu 35; ✆ 016 342 0506; e rovaniemi@scandiarent.fi; w scandiarent.fi

TOURIST INFORMATION The friendly and well-informed **tourist office** (✆ 016 346 270; e info@visitrovaniemi.fi; w visitrovaniemi.fi; ☉ Jan–Apr 09.00–17.00 Mon–Fri, 10.00–15.00 Sat; May–Nov 09.00–17.00 Mon–Fri; Dec 09.00–18.00 Mon–Fri, 10.00–15.00 Sat & Sun) is at Maakuntakatu 29–31.

 WHERE TO STAY *Map, page 137*
Thanks to the vast number of tourists who pass through Rovaniemi, the town has plenty of accommodation. Although beds are rarely in short supply, it is a good idea to book ahead if you are going to be here in winter, in particular in December,

when entire hotels are often booked up by tour groups. Lower summer rates apply, generally, for stays from April to November; higher winter rates apply December to March, sometimes with a top rate applied over Christmas and New Year.

Hotels

🏠 **Arctic City** Pekankatu 9; 📞 016 330 0111; e hotel@cityhotel.fi; w cityhotel.fi. Popular with French tour groups, this family-run hotel has been welcoming guests for over 40 years. It's especially handy for the city centre. Rooms tend to be a little on the small side & less stylish than elsewhere in town, but rates are accordingly lower. The Monte Rosa Italian restaurant is handily located in the same building & doubles as the hotel's b/fast room. **€€€€**

🏠 **Santa Claus** Korkalonkatu 29; 📞 016 321 321; e rovaniemi@santashotels.fi; w santashotels. fi. With well-appointed Nordic-design rooms right in the heart of the town centre, this hotel is hard to beat for style & location, though it doesn't come cheap & prices double for the winter season. **€€€€**

🏠 **Sokos Vaakuna** Koskikatu 4; 📞 020 1234 695; e vaakuna.rovaniemi@sokoshotels. fi; w sokoshotels.fi. The swanky rooms are big on Nordic minimalist design, though try to avoid those that look directly on to Koskikatu & people's living rooms on the opposite side of the street. The sauna suite is disappointingly small. **€€€€**

🏠 **Scandic Pohjanhovi** Pohjanpuistikko 2; 📞 016 456 4014; e pohjanhovi@scandichotels. com; w scandichotels.com. This legendary place opened in 1936 & soon became renowned throughout Lapland as the place to eat, drink & make merry; Fri evenings saw loggers & lumberjacks from the surrounding forests pour into town to spend their hard-earned wages on booze. Today, things are a little more genteel & rooms, sadly, a little too staid for the money, though it's still a sound choice. **€€€€/€€€**

🏠 **Hotelli Aakenus** Koskikatu 47; 📞 016

342 2051; e hotelli.aakenus@co.inet.fi; w hotelliaakenus.net. Exceptionally good-value family-run hotel in town centre, which boasts 45 rooms with private facilities. Rooms are simply, though tastefully, decorated, but for superb value for money look no further than here. **€€€/€€**

Guesthouses, youth hostels and camping

🏠 **Borealis** Asemieskatu 1; m 044 3131 771; e info@guesthouseborealis.com; w guesthouseborealis.com. This family-run place is extremely handy for the bus & train station, though is a little way from the town centre. Friendly & cosy & the staff are a good source of local information. Rooms are en suite. **€€€€/€€**

🏠 **Outa** Ukkoherrantie 16; m 050 492 6991; e mika@guesthouseouta.com; w guesthouseouta. com. A Rovaniemi stalwart that's been providing simple but clean accommodation (with shared facilities) to travellers for years. No frills but excellent value. **€€€/€€**

🏠 **Rudolf** Koskikatu 41–43; 📞 016 321 3227; e rudolf@santashotels.fi; w rudolf.fi. Reception for Rovaniemi's youth hostel is at the Santa Claus hotel (see left). Although a youth hostel, this is not the cheapest place in town to look for a bed. Rooms here are on the large side, spotless but plain in the extreme. B/fast served at the Santa Claus for an additional €11.50. Dbls **€€€/€€**

⛺ **Ounaskoski Camping** Jäämerentie 1; 📞 016 345 304; e ounaskoski-camping@windowslive. com; w ounaskoski-camping-rovaniemi.com; 🕐 mid-May–late Sep. Beautifully situated on the banks of the Ounaskoski rapids across the bridge from the town centre; with sauna & small café. Tent pitch €16. **€**

✖ WHERE TO EAT AND DRINK   Map, page 137

There's no shortage of places to eat and drink. In addition to the rash of Tex-Mex places preferred by the locals (seemingly fed up with the likes of local reindeer and elk meat), you will find a couple of places serving up traditional Lapland delicacies.

Cafés and restaurants

✳ ✖ **Nili** Valtakatu 20; m 0400 369 669; w nili.fi; 🕐 17.00–23.00 Mon–Sat. The place to come if you want to sample northern Finnish

delicacies. With reindeer skin & antlers providing the interior décor, this Sámi-inspired restaurant is a real find – the only shame is that the owners are not Sámi themselves, but from Helsinki. Starters include salmon smoked over alder with ginger sour cream; mains feature braised loin of reindeer & pink topside served with rosemary potato rösti & raspberry sauce, smoked Arctic char with sage tzatziki & sautéed beef with a sauce made of young juniper shoots. €€€

✗ **Amarillo** Koskikatu 4; m 044 405 0211; w raflaamo.fi/en/rovaniemi/amarillo-rovaniemi; ⊕ 11.00–23.00 Mon–Thu, 11.00–02.00 Fri, noon–02.00 Sat, noon–23.00 Sun. Attached to the Sokos Vaakuna hotel & the best of Rovaniemi's Tex-Mex places, the interior here is much cosier than similar places & the food correspondingly better. All your Latin favourites including tortillas & fajitas, plus steaks & burgers. In addition to the attached bar, there's a pleasant summer terrace, which catches the evening sun & is a great place for a beer. €€

✗ **Monte Rosa** Pekankatu 9; 016 330 0111; w monterosa.fi; ⊕ 11.00–23.00 Mon–Fri, 15.00–23.00 Sat, 17.00–22.00 Sun. Inside the Arctic City (page 139), this is one of Rovaniemi's most popular restaurants, serving a range of Lapland delicacies, such as sautéed reindeer with pickled cucumber & cloudberry crème brûlée, as well as a few mainstream steaks & burgers. €€

✗ **Rang Mahal** Rovakatu 26; m 046 594 6887; w rangmahal.fi; ⊕ 11.00–21.00 Mon–Thu, 11.00–22.00 Fri & Sat, noon–21.00 Sun. This Indian place receives mixed reviews – the locals tend to think it's fine, whereas visitors sometimes are less satisfied. That said, Lapland is not awash with Indian restaurants & if you're longing for a chicken tikka masala at a reasonable price then definitely give it a whirl – & try to ignore the tacky décor. €€

✗ **ZoomUp** Koskikatu 10; 016 321 3243; w santashotels.fi/en/hotelsantaclaus/restaurants/zoomup; ⊕ 11.00–14.00 & 16.00–22.00 Mon–Thu, 11.00–14.00 & 16.00–23.00 Fri, 16.00–23.00 Sat, 16.00–22.00 Sun. A popular, trendy bistro located upstairs from the Zoomit bar in the Santa Claus (page 139). Serves salads & pasta dishes as well as a series of grilled dishes including burgers & steaks. €€

✗ **Golden Rax Pizzabuffet** Koskikatu 11; 016 348 3999; w rax.fi; ⊕ 11.00–19.00 Mon–Sat, noon–19.00 Sun. This upstairs restaurant is the place to come if you want to fill up on unlimited supplies of pizza, chicken wings, lasagne & salad. The quality of the pizzas, though, is poor but at €11.95 for as much as you can eat & drink (soft drinks), it is hard to beat. €

✗ **Haruno** Korkalonkatu 27; 016 342 4727; w haruno.fi; ⊕ 11.00–22.00 Mon–Sat, noon–22.00 Sun. A long-established & locally well-respected Italian whose inviting interior makes it the place to savour pasta dishes such as tagliatelle with meatballs & tomato sauce, *ragu de carne*, burgers & pizzas at very respectable prices. €

⊑ **Antinkaapo** Rovakatu 13; w antinkaapo. fi; ⊕ 07.30–17.00 Mon–Fri, 10.00–14.00 Sat. A reassuringly old-school café, perfect for a selection of gooey cakes & pastries, that's been around since 1984. €

⊑ **ChocoDeli** Koskikatu 18; ⊕ w chocodeli. fi/en; 11.00–18.00 Mon–Sat. For homemade bread, croissants, pastries & cakes, this chi-chi little bakery, chocolaterie & café is a real treat. There's not a whole load of space inside but if you're lucky enough to get a table don't leave without sampling the handcrafted chocolates. €

Bars and clubs

♀ **Hemingways** Koskikatu 11; w hemingways. fi; ⊕ 15.00–01.00 Mon–Thu, 14.00–02.00 Fri, noon–02.00 Sat, 14.00–midnight Sun. Attracting middle-aged tourists in droves, this snug English-style pub is a good choice for an early evening drink before dinner. €

♀ **Oliver's Corner** Koskikatu 9; w oliverscorner. fi; ⊕ 14.00–02.00 Sun–Tue, 14.00–03.00 Wed & Thu; 14.00–04.00 Fri, noon–04.00 Sat. The closest thing Rovaniemi has to a genuine Irish pub – though, of course, it's a little wide of the mark. Nonetheless, it's a popular place for a drink or two & also functions as a nightclub from Wed to Sat when it's open until 03.00 or 04.00. €

♀ **Oluthuone** Koskikatu 20; w rovaniemenoluthuone.fi; ⊕ 11.00–02.00 Mon–Thu, 10.00–03.00 Fri & Sat, noon–02.00 Sun. A locals' favourite serving the cheapest beer in town. The atmosphere can be correspondingly raucous. There's a big TV screen showing the latest matches. €

♀ **Zoomit** Koskikatu 10; w santashotels.fi/fi/hotelsantaclaus/ravintolat/zoomit; ⊕ noon–midnight Sun–Thu, noon–03.00 Fri & Sat. Facing Hemingways, & inside the Santa Claus (page 139) this brasserie-style watering hole couldn't be more different from its neighbour. Both café-bar & pub, it is justifiably popular with Rovaniemi's 20-somethings who come here to chat & pose in the large glass & chrome windows looking out on the town's main drag. €

☆ **Half Moon** Koskikatu 25; w halfmoon.fi; ⏱ 22.00–04.00 Wed, Fri & Sat. If you fancy a spot of karaoke, some 80s classics & the latest chart music while you're on the Arctic Circle, look no further than Half Moon which is buried away inside the Rinteenkulma shopping centre. Quite simply, the best & largest club in town with space for 1,500 revellers.

WHAT TO SEE AND DO Although Rovaniemi is today the main town in Finnish Lapland (and third largest in Lapland as a whole after Luleå and Tromsø), with a population of 60,000, it is not a big place. The town centre is based on a familiar grid pattern and within an hour or so you will have covered most streets of note on foot. In summer the combination of uniform white and grey buildings befuddles your view at every turn making every street look virtually identical, whereas in winter the buildings seemingly become less important and merge effortlessly into a cityscape that is dominated by streets of snow and ice. Owing largely to the rebuilding in the 1940s, though, Rovaniemi is not somewhere you are likely to want to linger and is best used as an entry point into Lapland before striking out further north for a more genuine taste of northern Finland. However, while here, make the most of Rovaniemi's attractions, which include the best museum in Lapland and the quintessential Lapland experience on the Arctic Circle featuring the ever-popular Mr S Claus.

Arktikum Museum (Pohjoisranta 4; ☎016 322 3260; w arktikum.fi; ⏱ Jun–Aug 10.00–18.00 daily; Sep–Nov & mid-Jan–May 10.00–18.00 Tue–Sun; Dec–mid-Jan 10.00–18.00 daily; €13) Just a 10-minute walk north of the town centre, Rovaniemi's Arktikum is an engaging combination of provincial museum and Arctic Centre that is totally absorbing and quite simply the best museum you will come across for miles around. The building itself is quite remarkable – entered through a giant arched glass atrium – it is built into the surrounding hillside, emerging here and there from beneath piles of stones and rocks.

Inside, you will find an array of considered and intelligently presented exhibitions and displays on various aspects of life in the Arctic. Downstairs, the Provincial Museum of Lapland section is the place to start. Here there's a fascinating exhibition dedicated to contemporary Rovaniemi; don't miss the evocative black-and-white video footage of the glory days, before World War II, when people from across the Arctic would flood into town, drawn by tales of the high life and good times. Compare that with the scenes of total devastation that followed, barely a couple of years later, with the retreat of the German forces from Lapland and the numbing effects of their scorched earth policy. The two scale models of pre-war and post-war Rovaniemi help to give an idea of just what happened here in 1944 – understandably, the mindless destruction of what was clearly an elegant and prosperous town is not something that is easily forgotten – or forgiven – in these parts. Elsewhere, in the rear far left-hand corner of the exhibition (behind the model of the man sitting on a sledge in a fur coat), you'll find some extremely rare black-and-white photographs of Petsamo on the Arctic Ocean, which belonged to Finland between 1920 and 1944; check out the amazing picture of a father and son in their rowing boat, towing a massive white Beluga whale. Next door, there's a collection of assorted stuffed this-and-thats including a snow bunting, lemming and golden plover; press the numbered buttons and you can listen to their calls. Look out, too, just to the right, for the stuffed wolverine – it's quite rare to see one of these in a museum and even rarer to come across one in the wild. Still downstairs, but across the main corridor, have a look inside the **Polarium Conference Hall**, where there's usually a film showing about the Arctic.

The **Arctic Centre** is the exhibition space which spans both floors of the museum where there's information on the various peoples who live in Arctic regions across the globe, plus a chance to learn more about how climate change is impacting life in the Arctic. Upstairs, opposite, you'll find a couple of rooms dedicated to Arktikum's **temporary exhibitions**. Incidentally, the truly enormous amethyst you'll see opposite the ticket desk in reception, weighing in at a whopping 650kg, comes from the mine in Luosto (page 178).

Marttiini Old Knife Factory (Vartiokatu 32; m 040 311 0600; w marttiini.fi;
⊕ 10.00–18.00 Mon–Fri, 10.00–14.00 Sat, also mid-Jun–Aug noon–16.00 Sun; free) While you are at Arktikum, consider a quick visit to the Marttiini Old Knife Factory housed inside a sturdy concrete building, opposite the museum, designed in functionalist style. The Finns make some of the best knives in the world, a skill that has naïvely earned them the misguided reputation in the other Nordic countries for always carrying a knife and being more than ready to use it. Check out the film, which is shown regularly, and you'll be left in no doubt that, when sharpness is everything, this is the place to come. There are countless varieties available from the factory shop on site and prices start at around €20 – you can even have the blade engraved with a slogan of your choice.

Rovaniemi church (⊕ mid-May–Aug & Christmas 09.00–21.00 daily) Back in the town centre, stroll along Rauhankatu where, at number 70, you will find Rovaniemi's parish church built in 1950 to replace the church destroyed by the Germans in 1944. Although the structure itself is nothing remarkable, take a step inside to see the massive altar fresco, *Fountain of Life*, created by Lennart Segerstråle. Measuring a whopping 14m in height, it draws on motifs from Lapland's nature and everyday life to portray the conflicting powers of good and evil in the human heart. Ask at the tourist office for details of occasional concerts that are held in the church.

Lappia House and the library (Library: ⊕ 09.00–19.00 Mon–Thu, 09.00–17.00 Fri, 10.00–15.00 Sat) An Alvar Aalto architectural classic at Hallituskatu 11, close to the bus station, Lappia House is one of Rovaniemi's most eye-catching buildings, completed in 1975. This mammoth structure of polished white stone with an arched roof of varying heights resembling a silhouette of Lapland's snow-covered fells, contains the town's theatre, concert hall and library. However, most interestingly for visitors, it is the Lapland section that is really worth exploring, particularly if you are curious to find out any aspect of the region – you will find it on the left of the main entrance. As the largest source of Sámi and other Lapland-related information in the world, you name it, they've got it covered – in several languages.

Snowmobile, husky and reindeer safaris Given the paucity of attractions in Rovaniemi itself, it makes perfect sense to escape from the town into the surrounding forests as soon as you've had enough of the town's sights, such as they are. Accordingly, there are a whole host of companies specialising in activities ranging from snowmobile safaris – which, incidentally, are much cheaper in Finland than in neighbouring Sweden, in part due to lower value added tax rates – to trips by reindeer or husky sled and cross-country skiing in winter, or, in summer, riverboat and fishing trips. The main operators are listed opposite with an idea of prices and length of each tour. There are full details on the companies' websites.

Lapland Safaris Koskikatu 1; ✆016 331 1200; e info@laplandsafaris.fi; w laplandsafaris. com. Tours include a visit to a husky farm & dog-sledding (€202), reindeer & husky safari (€186) & snowmobiling (€99).

Nordic Unique Travels Maakuntakatu 29–31; m 040 1453 300; e info@nordictravels. eu; w nordictravels.eu. Tours include an ice-fishing trip by snow-shoe hiking (€95), a sleigh ride by snowmobile to see the northern lights (with barbecue; €79) & a truly heart-stopping opportunity to take a sauna & go ice swimming (€99).

Safarctica Koskikatu 9; ✆016 311 485; e safartica@safartica.com; w safartica.com. Offering a huge variety of activities including a 2hr snowmobile trip (€99), a 2hr husky safari (€174) & a 3hr excursion to go ice floating in a frozen lake, complete with drysuit (€86).

The Arctic Circle and the Santa Claus Village [map, page 134] Think what you might about a tourist attraction based around the delights of meeting a child-loving old man with a long white beard dressed in a red suit, the **Santa Claus Village** (✆ 016 356 2096; w santaclausvillage.info; ◷ early Jan–May & Sep–Nov 10.00–17.00 daily; Jun–Aug 09.00–18.00 daily; Dec–early Jan 09.00–19.00 daily; free), one of Finland's top visitor sites 8km northeast of Rovaniemi, is quite within the realms of decency. Located smack bang on the **Arctic Circle**, an imaginary line drawn around the globe at latitude 66° 32' 35"N, it is easily accessible from Rovaniemi along Route 4 or by daily **bus** 8 (€3.50 one-way; 30mins; every 45mins), which leaves from the railway station and then calls at several stops in town, each emblazoned with an Arctic Circle/Santa Claus logo. The main attractions of the village are a small collection of gift stores, the Santa Claus Post Office and Office, where you can meet the great man, a reindeer enclosure and a handful of factory outlet stores including Iittala and Marimekko. It is also possible to fix up a short reindeer or husky sleigh ride here (page 144). For information on **accommodation** at the Santa Claus village, see page 144.

The first thing most people want to do when they arrive here is pose beside the **Arctic Circle sign**, which is located between the car park and the main entrance, and take lots of photographs. Give yourself over to this indulgence and snap away – it is one of the few signs marking The Circle, which is labelled in six different languages, though tellingly, not one of them is Sámi.

From here it is a short walk to the main building, Lahjatalo, which also goes by the name of the **Santa Claus Gift House**. Inside, on two floors, you will find a number of souvenir shops selling everything from T-shirts to reindeer skins in addition to a couple of cafés serving coffee, cakes and light snacks. It's also here that you will find an information desk with helpful staff who can help you out with any queries you might have.

The low building with a central tower immediately behind the gift house is where Father Christmas himself hangs out inside the **Santa Claus Office** (◷ early Jan–May & Sep–Nov 10.00–17.00 daily; Jun–Aug 09.00–18.00 daily; Dec–early Jan 09.00–19.00 daily; Santa fills his already ample stomach & takes a nap 11.00–noon & 15.00–16.00; free). Here, if you form an orderly queue, you can enter Santa's grotto and come face to face with the big guy with the beard. Whether you have children in tow or not, it is actually quite a fun thing to do – even if it is only to marvel at how the Finns have pulled off this masterpiece of self-promotion. Hidden among the trees behind the Santa Claus Office, you will find a reindeer enclosure where, if you've just jetted in, you are likely to get your first sighting of Lapland's best-known animal – though only between early December and early January.

Having placed your order for a new Ferrari next Christmas, head out the door of the **Santa Claus Office** (w my.posti.fi/en/santa-claus-main-post-office; ◷ Sep–May 10.00–17.00 daily; Christmas & Jun–Aug 09.00–18.00 daily) to your left and

6

cross the courtyard to the other building with a tower, the **Santa Claus Post Office**, where you can leave your name and address for the dubious pleasure of receiving a Christmas letter from Santa. If you still haven't had your fill of Santa, you can head off to the **Christmas Exhibition** in the building immediately behind the post office, where there's more information than you could ever hope to digest about Christmas traditions as well as centuries-old Christmas customs in Finland and elsewhere in the world – though, to be honest, you'll probably be suffering from Santa-fatigue by this stage. You can also have your photo taken with Santa here should the urge strike.

The inventive Finns, seemingly never content with the range of tourist attractions at the Arctic Circle, are forever dreaming up new temptations to delight and entertain (or relieve of cash, depending on your viewpoint) the planeloads of people who descend on Rovaniemi every winter; you're more than likely to come across some new venture or other – some stay the course, others go bankrupt after just a couple of seasons.

🏠 *Staying in and around the Santa Claus Village*

🏠 **Arctic Snowhotel** Lehtoahontie 27, Sinettä; ✆ 040 845 3774; e sales@arcticsnowhotel. fi; w arcticsnowhotel.fi; ⏰ early Dec–Mar. Located 30kms northwest of the Santa Claus village, this is another of Lapland's ice hotels (at least, a version thereof). If you're looking to be relatively close to the village but away from the madding crowd, this could be the place for you – indeed, the Snowhotel is in a rural location so it's a very different experience to staying in Rovaniemi itself. Between late Dec & late Mar it offers the chance to sleep in a thermal sleeping bag inside a room made entirely of snow – the beds are made of ice & topped with a regular mattress covered with reindeer hides. Prices start at €280 for 2 people in a dbl snow room. €€€€

🏠 **Arctic Treehouse Hotel** Tarvantie 3; m 050 5176 909; e info@arctictreehouse.fi; w arctictreehousehotel.com. Gorgeous square-shaped treehouses on stilts, full of Scandinavian design & style. The entire front of each treehouse is composed of a glass wall which looks out over the surrounding forest & Arctic sky. A tastefully small & low-impact venture that is, quite simply, lovely. Start saving up – the treehouses start at around €600/night. €€€€

🏠 **NOVA Skyland Hotel** Tähtikuja 6; m 040 560 3115; e sales@novaskyland.com; w novaskyland.com. Top-notch apts located in a series of semi-detached houses, each featuring an open fireplace, sauna, terrace & fully fitted kitchen. 1 wall is composed of an entire floor-to-ceiling window to blend effortlessly with the forest outside. Seemingly so exclusive you have to request a price quote rather than book online. €€€€

🏠 **Santa Claus Holiday Village** Tähtikuja 2; m 040 159 3811; e info@schv.fi; w schv.fi. Behind the Christmas Exhibition (see above) you'll find a tasteful holiday village of cabin apts. The apts sleep 2 adults & 2 children & include a sauna & kitchenette. Free airport transfers are included in the rates. Prices vary depending on the package you choose – there's even the option of a private visit from Santa himself. €€€€

🏠 **Santa Igloos Arctic Circle** Joulumaankuja 8; m 040 010 2170; e arcticcircle@santashotels.fi; w santashotels.fi/ en/hotels/igloos-arctic-circle. 70-odd luxuriously appointed glass-walled & -roofed igloos, perfect for watching the northern lights from the comfort of your bed. The igloos are fully heated & are available all year round. The regular bathroom is attached to the igloo, but not made of glass walls. €€€€

🏠 **Snowman World** Joulumaantie 5; m 040 5194 444; e info@snowmanworld.fi; w snowmanworld.fi. Another stylish glass igloo hotel at the Santa Claus Village, this one takes its cue from Sámi *kota* huts &, indeed, the igloos are roughly teepee shaped. Full of Scandinavian design & creature comforts, these igloos are often equally as exclusive & expensive as the neighbouring Arctic Treehouse Hotel (see left). Assume around €700/ night in Dec & Jan. €€€€

Reindeer and husky sleigh rides The **Arctic Circle Reindeer Farm** (m 040 0991 530; e napapiirin@porofarmi.fi; w porofarmi.fi; €18) just 1.5km from the

Santa Claus Village, Tamsintie 76 in the nearby village of Nivankylä, is the place to fix up a short ride on a sleigh pulled by reindeer. The trip covers about 500m and costs €30 per person, including a visit to the farm.

Alternatively, if you fancy dog power, husky-sled rides are available at the **Arctic Circle Husky Park** (m 040 824 7503; e office@huskypark.fi; w huskypark.fi; ⊕ Dec–Mar 11.00–15.00 daily; rest of the year 11.00–14.00 daily), close to the Santa Claus Village. Entrance to the husky park itself costs €10, whereas a sleigh ride of 500m is €30 per person; a longer trip of 2km is €40 per person.

Snowmobile safaris The **Arctic Circle Snowmobile Park** (Joulumaantie 5, Arctic Circle; m 050 4720 023; e info@snowmobilepark.com; w snowmobilepark. com) is located immediately opposite the Santa Claus Village and offers hour-long trips by snowmobile for €75. Full details can be found on the company's website. For more information on safaris from Rovaniemi itself, see page 142.

NORTH FROM ROVANIEMI: LAPLAND BUS ROUTES Look at a transport map of this part of Lapland and you will soon spot that rail lines pretty much expire at Rovaniemi. Northbound travel from here is now by **bus** along three main routes: **northeast**, following Route 4, towards Sodankylä, Ivalo, Inari and Utsjoki. At Utsjoki you can walk over the bridge into Norway to pick up services to and from Kirkenes; **northwest**, following Route 79, to Kittilä, Muonio, Karesuvanto (connections are possible here by, again, walking across the bridge into Swedish Karesuando), Kilpisjärvi and ultimately Tromsø in Norway. The only way to travel between these two main transport arteries is on an infrequent service that operates between Kittilä and Sodankylä, otherwise you have no choice but to backtrack to Rovaniemi and start out again. Timetables for all services from Rovaniemi can be found at w matkahuolto.fi.

see page 142.

ALL ABOARD! NEXT STOP, THE ARCTIC OCEAN

In 2007, the Northwest Passage (the sea route through the Arctic Ocean along the northern coast of North America), became open to shipping without the need for an icebreaker. The new route is expected to herald new transport opportunities for cargo ships operating between the Atlantic and Pacific oceans and, to that end, the Finnish government has declared that Finland should once again have access to the Arctic Ocean – between 1920 and 1944, the port of Petsamo (Pechenga in Russian) on the Arctic Ocean was Finnish territory and was the country's only port north of Kemi (600km to the south). In 2018, the Finnish government announced that a new Arctic rail route would be built from Rovaniemi to Kirkenes, routing via Sodankylä and Ivalo, but that further studies were needed before construction could begin, in order to assess the impact the new line would have on the local Sámi communities and their reindeer herds. In addition to moving passengers, the new route would ultimately allow goods to be transported by rail from central and southern Europe, via a proposed new tunnel between Tallinn and Helsinki, then north to Rovaniemi and Kirkenes for shipping along the north coast of Russia to markets in Asia. The Arctic railway would reduce cargo trips between Europe and Asia by 20 days.

For more information about the proposed railway, visit w arcticcorridor.fi.

Getting to the North Cape and Tromsø Rovaniemi is the starting point for the direct summer **bus** service (Jun–late Aug daily; 10hrs) to the North Cape running via Sodankylä, Ivalo, Inari, Karasjok, Lakselv and Honningsvåg (leaves bus station at 11.45 and arrives at North Cape at 22.15 in time to see the midnight sun, weather permitting; return journey departs from North Cape at 01.00, arriving back into Rovaniemi at 17.25; €132 one-way). It is a long and expensive journey by any measure, but the bus is comfortable and it is a direct service. It also calls at Rovaniemi's train station and airport on the way.

Between June and late September, another daily bus leaves Rovaniemi for Tromsø in Norway, routing via Kittilä, Muonio, Kaaresuvanto, Kilpisjärvi and Skibotn. Once again, tickets are not cheap (€102 one-way) but it is, by far and away, the easiest public transport option for getting to Norwegian Lapland's main town, which is useful for Hurtigruten passengers and for Widerøe's extensive regional flight network. The bus leaves Rovaniemi bus station at 11.40, departing from the train station 30 minutes later; arrival in Tromsø is 19.25. The return service leaves Tromsø at 07.25. Detailed timetable information for both services is available at w eskelisen.fi or ask at the tourist office for their Rovaniemi–North Cape and Rovaniemi–Tromsø handouts.

Getting to Sweden If you want to head to Sweden from Rovaniemi, be prepared for plenty of changes, since there is no direct service. The best idea is to first head for **Haparanda** and **Luleå**, from where you can decide whether you want to head north to **Kiruna** or south to Stockholm; there are **train** services from Luleå to both places. From Rovaniemi, first take a Finnish train south to Kemi (times available at w vr. fi), and then pick up a bus from immediately outside Kemi train station bound for Haparanda in Sweden (see the box page 118 for details of Haparanda's travel centre). From Haparanda there are then direct Swedish **buses** to Luleå. From Luleå onwards travel is by **train**, either northwest to Gällivare, Kiruna and ultimately Narvik in Norway; or all points south to Stockholm. Swedish train times can be found at w sj.se.

The tourist office in Rovaniemi, bombarded with requests for how to make this journey, have put together the best timings: ask for their 'Timetables from Rovaniemi to Sweden and Norway' handout.

NORTHWEST FROM ROVANIEMI: TOWARDS KAUTOKEINO

From Rovaniemi, Route 79 heads northwest following the course of one of Finnish Lapland's greatest rivers, Ounasjoki; a picturesque though uneventful 150km to reach the first town of any significance, Kittilä.

GETTING THERE – ARRIVING AT KITTILÄ AIRPORT Located beside Route 79 just 5km north of Kittilä and 13km south of Levi, Kittilä airport (airport code KTT) is a useful entry point for this part of Lapland and one of the main airports in the north of Finland. In winter there are direct flights to Kittilä Airport from several European cities, including from Helsinki with Finnair and Norwegian. **Taxis** run into Kittilä while **shuttle buses** link the airport with Levi, Ylläs, Muonio, Hetta and Kilpisjärvi though, at certain times of year, these must be booked in advance. Check w finavia.fi/en/airports/kittila for full details. Regular **buses** between Rovaniemi and Muonio also call at the airport; timetables are at w matkahuolto.fi.

KITTILÄ AND AROUND One of Lapland's dullest places, Kittilä has little to recommend it, but it is a useful entry point for this part of Lapland with charter flights operating in winter to the airport (see opposite). To be clear, nobody comes here to satisfy a burning desire to see Kittilä, a modern, charmless town that was totally destroyed by retreating German forces during World War II and whose reconstruction has been less than uninspired; they are here instead for two of Finland's best ski resorts: **Levi**, just 20km north, and **Ylläs**, 50km to the southwest. Kittilä is also a good jumping-off point from which to visit the Lainio snow village (page 148) and the excellent Särestöniemi museum and gallery (see below).

Where to stay, eat and drink Should you want to break the long journey north from Rovaniemi and need to stay in Kittilä, you'll find a couple of options:

Golden Goose Valtatie 42; 016 642 043; e info@goldengoose.fi; w goldengoose.fi. This friendly guesthouse has homely rooms with private facilities; some have their own balcony or kitchenette. €€€€/€€€

Hotelli Kittilä m 040 1812 499; e info@ hotellikittila.fi; w hotellikittilla.fi. Located beside the main road at Valtatie 49 & easily spotted thanks to an incongruous, life-size plane painted bright red outside (the owner is a plane buff). The newly renovated rooms now feature stylish Scandinavian-design features & rates include a buffet b/fast & use of the hotel's sauna & swimming pool. €€€€/€€€

Ounas Hovi Valtatie 49; m 040 1812 499; w ounashovi.fi; ⊕ 10.30–14.30 Mon–Fri. The restaurant inside Hotelli Kittilä offers a solid buffet lunch for around €9.50 & is your best bet in town. Also operates as a pub in the evenings (⊕ 17.00– 22.00 Mon–Thu, 17.00–02.00 Fri & Sat). €

Kahvila Herkkutupa Valtatie 37; ⊕ 09.00–17.00 Mon–Fri, 10.00–16.00 Sat. Café & bakery adjacent to the 'K' supermarket. €

What to see and do Kittilä won't hold your attention for long, though, but before you move on you should check out the only building that wasn't destroyed as the Germans withdrew northwards at the end of the war, burning everything in their path: **Kittilä church** (m 040 532 4624; ⊕ Jun–mid-Aug 11.00–15.00 daily; at other times on request), a handsome, cream-coloured wooden structure dating from 1831, can be found at Valtatie 93, roughly halfway between Hotelli Kittilä and Route 80 towards Kolari. The church was designed by architect Carl Ludwig Engel (1778–1840), who had a great impact on Finnish architecture during the first half of the 19th century. Engel is best known for his Empire style, a phase with Neoclassicism, and, in particular, the buildings surrounding Senate Square in Helsinki. Inside the church, look out for the Baroque pulpit which dates from 1687.

Around Kittilä
Särestöniemi museum and art gallery [map, page 134] (016 654 480; w sarestoniemimuseo.com; ⊕ noon–18.00 Tue–Sat; €12) Around 30km south of Kittilä, just east of the hamlet of Kaukonen on Route 79 towards Rovaniemi, you'll find a museum and gallery dedicated to the work of local artist, **Reidar Särestöniemi** (1925–81), who, with total justification, is considered one of Finnish Lapland's greatest painters. The Lapland landscape provided Särestöniemi not only with his motifs but also with the vivid colours which are prominent in much of his work. However, his paintings are also considered to have been influenced by other factors, too, notably some of the great names of European modernism, Russian art (he studied in Leningrad in the late 1950s), and even by cave paintings. The artist lived most of his life in Särestöniemi and today his gallery, studio and his home are open to visitors. The museum is 9km from the main highway at Kaukonen and accessed on a very small, country road.

Lainio snow village [map, page 134] (Lainotie 556; m 040 416 7227; e snowvillage@ laplandhotels.com; w snowvillage.fi; ☉ Dec–Apr; €18) Also 30km from Kittilä (and not to be confused with Lainio in Sweden; page 125), though west along Route 80 towards Kolari rather than south towards Rovaniemi, you'll come across what, to all intents and purposes, is a mini version of Sweden's Icehotel, officially known as 'Lapland Hotels SnowVillage'. Although it's billed as a snow village, the structure is in fact a giant igloo composed of interlinking corridors and rooms. Work begins on construction in November and although the exact size of the snow village varies from year to year it always has rooms to rent and an ice chapel. The Lainio snow village is open from December until April when the temperatures rise and the igloo melts back into the Lainio River. As at Icehotel in Sweden, beds in the rooms are made of snow and ice and overnight guests are provided with a thermal sleeping bag. A double room, complete with ice carvings, costs from €420. From the snow village, it's another 30km northwest to reach Ylläs.

Moving on from Kittilä: the bus to Sodankylä If you're planning to cross over to Sodankylä to access bus services operating north to Ivalo, you need to time your departure carefully. There's just one bus from Kittilä airport to Sodankylä – full details at w matkahuolto.fi. Timetables on this route vary between winter and summer, so always check the website for the latest times.

LEVI Just 18km north of Kittilä along Route 79 towards Muonio, Levi has been attracting Finns from across the country since the first ski lift opened here in 1964 and they're still waxing lyrical about the place today. Boasting over half a million visitors every year, this is arguably Lapland's main ski resort with 43 slopes and hundreds of kilometres of cross-country ski and snowmobile tracks – it has a reputation across Finland as a good-time party destination. Yet outside Finland, Levi remains little known – two out of three visitors here are Finnish. The skiing facilities are first class with over two dozen lifts, including a gondola and après-ski that compare favourably with better-known resorts in central Europe.

Unlike arch-rival Ylläs (page 150), Finnish Lapland's other principal ski centre, Levi is compact and the main ski lifts are within walking distance of all the central hotels. Indeed, the modest town centre is based on a handful of short streets, clustered around the main square, Levi tori. To be strictly accurate, Levi refers principally to the mountain here (530m), which is where all the ski slopes are to be found, whereas hotels, the tourist office and other facilities are actually located in the village of Sirkka beside Route 79, but this distinction is lost on most people and the whole place tends to go simply by the name Levi. During the quieter summer months, Levi can be a good place to hike the trails, which during the winter are busy with cross-country skiers. A good choice is the Levi Fell circle (upper route), which covers 18.5km and takes in some of the area's best scenery en route; ask at the tourist office for a map of the area.

Tourist information Levi straggles over a couple of kilometres alongside Route 79 and you will find the **tourist office** (☎ 016 639 3300; e levi@levi.fi; w levi.fi; ☉ 09.00–17.00 Mon–Fri, 10.00–16.00 Sat & Sun) at the northern edge of the village, beside the main road, at Myllyjoentie 2. **Buses** to and from Rovaniemi stop outside Hotelli Levintunturi beside the main road; find timetables online at w matkahuolto.fi.

Where to stay It is best to book your accommodation in Levi as part of a package tour which will include your flight, since booking somewhere to stay on arrival will work out much more expensive. However, if you are here for only a couple of nights, the tourist office can usually fix something up from its truly extensive list of overnight options, which include hotel rooms, apartments and log cabins. Reckon on paying around €140 per night for a double room during high season (mid-Feb–late Apr, Christmas & New Year); in low season (early May–late Aug & Oct) prices can fall, amazingly, by up to half. The main **hotels** have similar top-notch rooms and prices.

🏠 **Hullu Poro Penthouse** Rakkavaarantie 5; 016 651 0100; e sales@hulluporo.fi; w hulluporo.fi. One of Levi's largest hotels with a choice of opulent dbl rooms, some with their own sauna. Guests also have access to the excellent sauna area with jacuzzis, cold plunge pools & steam baths. €€€€/€€

🏠 **K5 Levi** Kätkärannantie 2; 016 639 1100; e k5@golevi.fi; w k5levi.fi. Generously sized, bright & airy dbl rooms, some with balconies, & all with their own sauna. €€€€/€€€

🏠 **Lapland Sirkantähti** Levintie 1630; 016 3232; e sirkantahti@laplandhotels.com; w laplandhotels.com. A mix of dbl rooms & well-appointed apts here, some with their own sauna & terrace. €€€€/€€

🏠 **Levi Igloos** Harjatie 4; m 045 1625 606; e sales@leviniglut.fi; w leviniglut.net. Located 10km southeast of Levi centre & at an altitude of 340m on the slopes of Utsuvaara Mountain, these glass igloos are a great way to see the northern lights & get in tune with Lapland's unspoilt surroundings. Naturally, there are curtains for privacy & a regular bathroom attached, too. Beware, though; they don't come cheap, starting at €625/night. €€€€

✳ 🏠 **Sokos Levi** Tähtitie 5; 016 321 5500; e sales.levi@sokoshotels.fi; w sokoshotels.fi. A luxurious hotel right in the heart of the village whose contemporary-design rooms are dressed in the varying seasonal colours of Lapland's landscapes. Superior rooms have their own private sauna. €€€€/€€€

🍴 **Where to eat and drink** In addition to the following listings, each of the hotels has a good quality restaurant serving local Lapland specialities as well as a range of cheaper burgers, salads and pizzas.

🍴 **Sapuška** Hiihtäjänkuja 10; 016 651 0100; w hulluporo.fi/en/restaurants/sapuska; ⏰ mid-Sep–Apr 18.00–23.00 daily. Despite the name, you'll be hard-pressed to find anything truly Russian or eastern European on the menu here, instead reckon on fondues, steaks & a few Mediterranean dishes such as escargots & coq au vin. €€€

🍴 **Pihvipirtti** Hissitie 10; m 040 714 8885; w hulluporo.fi/en/restaurants/pihvipirtti; ⏰ Sep–Apr 18.00–23.00 daily. Levi's long-established steakhouse serving up a selection of expensive beef, lamb & reindeer steaks accompanied by a sauce of your choice. €€€

✳ 🍴 **Ämmilä** Rakkavaarantie 5; 016 651 0500; w hulluporo.fi/en/restaurants/ammila; ⏰ 11.00–23.00 daily. The interior here is designed to look like an old country farmhouse; staff too often try to play the role of a farmhand. It's the best place for dependable Finnish home cooking with dishes such as reindeer with mash, lingonberries & pickled cucumbers, Wiener schnitzel & pan-fried rainbow trout with dill pickle. €€

🍴 **Wanha Hullu Poro** Rakkavaarantie 5; 016 651 0500; w hulluporo.fi/en/restaurants/wanha-hullu-poro. Adjacent to Ämmilä, this is the place for your burger fix. Choose from any number of unusual varieties on the burgerlicious menu including reindeer & Lapland cheese with lingonberries; 'aura burger' with blue cheese & figs; or a classic cheddar & bacon number. €€

🍴 **Renna** Hiihtäjänkuja 10; m 040 714 8889; w hulluporo.fi/en/restaurants/ristorante-renna; ⏰ mid-Sep–Apr noon–22.00 daily. The best place for pizzas & pasta in town. As well as the usual varieties of pizza, there's also a choice of more unusual variations such as roast reindeer with lingonberries or spicy reindeer meatballs with basil oil. €

🍷 **Vinkkari** Hissitie 6; w levi.ski/en/restaurantvinkkari; ⏰ mid-Sep–Apr noon–19.00 daily. Located at the bottom of the Levi North ski lift (it's the long red timber building), this is the bar in Levi & is known across Finland for its good-time après-ski scene, usually with DJs who expertly ramp up the singing & dancing. €

Activities During the winter months, downhill skiing is clearly the activity that draws most visitors to Levi. However, **cross-country skiing** is popular, too, with over 200km of trails to explore. **Snowmobile safaris** are also available, should you tire of the pistes; check out **PerheSafarit** (☍ 016 643 861; w perhesafarit.fi) who offer, among other options, a 2-hour trip around the mountain for €130 per person. Their office is located at Leviraitti 1, between the Sirkantähti Hotel and the Levi market food store. **Husky safaris** are provided by **Levi Husky Park** (m 040 5706 572; w levihuskypark.fi), based in nearby Köngäs, and are most easily arranged through the tourist office.

In summer, it's **hiking, canoeing** and **mountain biking** that are the main activities in Levi; canoes and mountain bikes are available for rent from PerheSafarit.

If you're not heading west of Kittilä to the Lainio snow village (page 148), then consider checking out Levi's own version: the **Levi ice gallery** (m 040 740 0925; e sales@luvattumaa.fi; w luvattumaa.fi; ⊕ mid-Dec–Apr 10.00–18.00 daily; €17) is built every year on the banks of the Ounasjoki River, at Akantie 180, 7km northeast of Levi centre, off Route 956 towards Köngäs, and like similar structures of snow and ice elsewhere in Lapland, it comprises a chapel, bar and overnight **accommodation** (from €340/dbl room/night). Inside there's also an ice gallery which showcases a variety of sculptures hewn from snow and ice, plus a regular **restaurant** (⊕ 10.00–18.00 daily).

YLLÄS Although not Finland's highest mountain (that accolade goes to Halti near Kilpisjärvi at 1,324m), Ylläs is the country's highest ski resort. Strictly speaking, Yl.lästunturi, to give its full name, refers only to the mountain here which rises to 718m while the villages at its foot are Äkäslompolo and Ylläsjärvi. However, in practice, the whole place tends to go by the name of Ylläs in much the same way that the name Levi is often used for its attendant village, Sirkka. Levi is a dirty word in Ylläs since the two resorts are locked in constant battle for the lucrative winter ski market. Ylläs may be smaller and less glitzy than its more easterly rival, but it still packs quite a punch and is a firm favourite with holidaying Finns, who come here for cross-country, rather than downhill skiing. Indeed, there are 330km of trails around Ylläs, in addition to the 61 slopes and 29 lifts. Although not shown on older maps, a road (the 9401) connects both Äkäslompolo and Ylläsjärvi, making it possible to drive directly between the two villages in around 15km rather than back-tracking around the mountain as used to be the case. Incidentally, one of the best times to be in Ylläs is during the **Ylläs Jazz Blues Festival** (w yllassoikoon. fi), which takes place during the last weekend in January when the town's bars and restaurants host live blues and jazz performances.

Äkäslompolo and Ylläsjärvi A long, elongated sort of a place, located by the shores of the eponymous lake, Äkäslompolo is much less compact than, say, Levi. That said, the village is not big, and most places are within walking distance although the ski lifts are best reached by the **ski bus** which operates from the main hotels. Unlike neighbouring Ylläsjärvi, which is really a tiny ski resort and nothing more, Äkäslompolo is a real village, if diminutive, and is home to around 350 people. Indeed, of the two, it's Äkäslompolo which makes the more agreeable base from its location on the edge of the **Pallas-Yllästunturi National Park** (w nationalparks.fi/ en/pallas-yllastunturinp).

In addition to the **airport shuttle** which comes here from Kittilä airport (page 146), Äkäslompolo is also connected by **bus** to Kittilä and Levi; timetables are at w matkahuolto.fi.

Where to stay

🏠 **Lapland Hotel** Äkäshotelli Äkäsentie 10, Äkäslompolo; ☎016 553 000; e akashotel@laplandhotels.com; w laplandhotels.com. With both regular hotel rooms, log cabins with sauna & larger self-catering apts both with & without saunas, this long-standing hotel is open during the ski season from Dec to Apr only. €€€€

🏠 **Lapland Hotel Saaga** Iso-Ylläksentie 42, Ylläsjärvi; ☎016 323 600; e saaga@laplandhotels.com; w laplandhotels.com; ⊕ closed May–mid-Jun, Oct & Nov. This hotel has an enviable location right at the foot of the slopes in Ylläsjärvi & offers a bewildering array of different types of chalets & apts as well as regular hotel rooms. There's also a beautifully appointed spa on site. €€€€/€€€

🏠 **Ylläs Humina** Tiurajärventie 27, Äkäslompolo; ☎020 719 9820; e yllashumina@yllashumina.com; w yllashumina.com; ⊕ year-round. The snug & comfortable hotel rooms here are located in log chalets behind the main restaurant. There are also several semi-detached self-catering lodges overlooking Äkäslompolojärvi Lake. €€€€

☀ 🏠 **Lodge 67° N** Äkäsentie 6, Äkäslompolo; m 040 671 1167; e lodge@yllaslodge.com; w yllaslodge.com; ⊕ all year. The accommodation of choice in Äkäslompolo. The spacious, wood-panelled rooms at this stylish & comfortable lodge boast balconies overlooking the national park, self-catering facilities & are decked out with inventive touches like real tree stumps as bedside tables. €€€/€€

Where to eat and drink

🍴 **Humina** Tiurajärventie 27, Äkäslompolo; ☎020 719 9820; w yllashumina.com/restaurant1.html; ⊕ 17.00–22.00 daily. Superb cuisine is on offer in the hotel restaurant where a 4-course set menu goes for €55. Alternatively, starters include a creamy mushroom soup or pike-perch in a rye crust, while the mains feature the likes of fried Arctic char with marinated beetroot or tenderloin of reindeer with barley & a garlic purée. €€€

🍴 **Poro** Sivalantie 22, Äkäslompolo; m 040 506 4020; w ravintolaporo.fi; ⊕ Dec–Apr 13.00–22.00 daily. A firm favourite for its tasty Lapland dishes such as elk tartare with gherkins & sour cream, willow grouse stew with chanterelle mushrooms & almond potatoes & oven-baked Arctic char with cep mushrooms – creative cuisines at reasonable prices. €€€

🍴 **Rouhe** Lompolontie 3, Äkäslompolo; m 040 506 4044; w ravintolarouhe.fi; ⊕ noon–22.00 daily. Serving up a good range of pizzas (from €13) as well as more substantial mains such as steak, lamb shank & chicken. €€

🍸 **Selvä Pyy** Sivulantie 1, Äkäslompolo; m 050 555 7709; w selvapyy.fi; ⊕ noon–midnight daily. An inordinately popular bar with foreign skiers who come here for a beer or 2 & 1 of the top-quality burgers on the menu. €

Activities Like many other winter resorts in Lapland, activities are not purely ski-oriented: husky-sledding, snowmobile safaris, reindeer sleigh rides and snow-shoeing are all available. One of the most enjoyable options, though, is a snowmobile tour up Yllästunturi Mountain – the trails are well maintained and relatively quiet and you'll get a real sense of exhilaration as you scud along at speeds of up to 40 or 50km/h. One of the main operators in Äkäslompolo is **Snow Fun Safaris** (Sivulantie 12; m 050 589 2223; e info@snowfunsafaris.com; w snowfunsafaris.com), who charge €60 per snowmobile for the first hour of rental (then less/hr for additional hrs) or €210 per day (8hr); snow shoes and walking sticks cost €15 per day; a half-day husky safari sharing a sled costs €210 per person (€300 for your own sled).

ENONTEKIÖ/HETTA AND AROUND From Levi, Route 956 strikes off north heading for Enontekiö/Hetta, a switchback ride through some wonderful fell-land scenery. However, heading for Enontekiö/Hetta is a confusing experience. Road signs reassuringly confirm that you are heading for **Enontekiö**, the name used on all maps of the region. On arrival in this pint-sized village, 37km south of the Norwegian border, you are welcomed into **Hetta**, which, even for the most linguistically challenged visitor, is clearly not at all the same name. The devil is in the detail: Hetta refers to the name of the village, whereas Enontekiö is the name of the surrounding district. Mention the name Hetta, though, to most Finns and they'll look at you blankly, since it is better known outside the immediate vicinity by its administrative title, Enontekiö. Don't say you haven't been warned.

To be fair, Hetta (as it's known locally) isn't really at the top of anyone's must-see list; it's an unassuming little place which runs for several kilometres, straddling Route 93 (which becomes Route 956), with no real focal point. However, what Hetta does have in plenitude is some of Lapland's most enchanting landscapes right on its doorstep and consequently makes a perfect base from which to strike out on a summer hiking or canoe trip (page 154), for example, or, in winter, on a husky safari through the enigmatic forests of northern Finland (see opposite). Hetta is the ideal gateway for the **Pallas-Yllästunturi National Park** – a glorious mountain plateau of primeval, boreal forest and bare fells which begins just south of the village and reaches down to Kittilä in the south; it's one of Finnish Lapland's most enjoyable expanses of unspoilt wilderness and draws nature-lovers from across the country.

As for the town itself, other than the **Fell Lapland Nature Centre** (see below), there's little to busy yourself with. Things come to life, though, during the annual **St Mary's Day** celebrations. Undoubtedly the best time to be in Hetta, this traditional Sámi festival is held over three days two weeks before Easter to mark the Feast of the Annunciation, when local people would traditionally gather to baptise their children, attend wedding ceremonies and bury their dead once the ground had begun to thaw somewhat. Today, the festivities include reindeer racing and lasso throwing on Ounasjärvi Lake in town as well as a number of art or cultural exhibitions and performances. There's more information from the tourist office (see below) and at w marianpaivat.fi. If you're planning to visit at this time, you should be sure to book somewhere to stay well in advance.

A **bus** runs here from Rovaniemi, Kittilä and Muonio, while another service links Hetta with Kaaresuvanto and Kilpisjärvi. Both services route via Palojoensuu (the junction of the E8 and Route 93) and terminate at Lapland Hotel Hetta (see opposite); timetables are at w matkahuolto.fi.

Tourist information
From the junction on the western edge of the village (where Route 93 heads north to Kautokeino), it is a further 2km east, along the main road (signed for Sirkka) to the **tourist office**, known as the **Fell Lapland Nature Centre** (Peuratie 15; ☏020 639 7950; e tunturi-lappi@metsa.fi; w nationalparks. fi/enfelllaplandvisitorcentre; ◷ Oct–Feb & May 09.00–16.00 Mon–Fri; Mar & Apr 09.00–17.00 daily; Jun–Sep 09.00–17.00 daily). The helpful staff here have maps and information about **hiking** in the Pallas-Yllästunturi National Park and can advise on hiking to Treriksröset, the point where Finland, Norway and Sweden all meet near Kilpisjärvi to the northwest. Inside the centre there's a small **exhibition** (◷ same hours as tourist office; free) of photographs and information panels, which tell the story of the Sámi migrations to the Arctic Ocean that endured for centuries, finally ceasing in the 1960s, when changing herding practices rendered the old ways obsolete. Special attention is paid to the difficulties that arose in 1889 when Norway closed its border with Finland, blocking traditional migration routes and ultimately forcing many families to abandon their homes to seek new grazing pastures across the border in Sweden.

Where to stay

Lapland Hotel Hetta Ounastie 281; 016 323 700; e hetta@laplandhotels.com; w laplandhotels.com. The best hotel in Hetta with smart, well-appointed rooms & also boasts a swimming pool, sauna, jacuzzi & a fitness room beside the main lake where there's an ice swimming hole in winter. There are apts too, in a separate building with small kitchenettes for self-catering. €€€€

Hetan Lomakylä Ounastie 23; m 040 0205 408; e info@hetanlomakyla.fi; w hetanlomakyla. fi. Cabins of varying standards occupying a pleasant location on the shores of Ounasjärvi Lake, plus a handful of tastefully decorated dbl rooms. €€

Hetan Majatalo Riekontie 8; 016 554 0400; e info@hetan-majatalo.fi; w hetan-majatalo.fi. Established in 1924, this well-respected hotel offers a good choice of comfortable, modern en-suite rooms with wood panelling (€€€). Simpler rooms with shared facilities in the attached guesthouse (known as the 'inn'). €€

Paavontalo Ounastie 350; 016 521 021; e paavontalo@co.inet.fi; w tosilappi.fi/ en. Located close to the main road at the eastern end of the village, beyond the turn for Fell Nature Centre, the simple cabins at this small holiday village sleep 2 to 4 people & have a fridge & kettle. Kitchen & bathroom facilities are shared. There are saunas & a hot tub for guests' use, too. €€

Galdotieva Fell Centre Ruijantie 2605, Palojärvi, 31km north of Hetta on Route 93; 016 528 630; e info@harriniva.fi; w harriniva.fi/ holiday-destinations/galdotieva/accommodation-galdotieva. A gloriously remote spot close to the Norwegian border with lakeside log cabins, all with electricity & fridge, though some without shower & toilet (facilities available on site). 4 cabins have their own sauna & those without shower & toilet are excellent value. With sauna €€; without shower & toilet €

Where to eat and drink
For **self-catering**, try the Galdotieva Fell Centre cabins (see above) – provisions can be bought at the tiny supermarket in Galdotieva, though the on-site restaurant (€€) also serves lunch and dinner (mains from around €15); breakfast is €9.

Alternatively, try the **café** inside the Fell Lapland Nature Centre (see opposite), which also serves lunch between 11.00 and 15.00 for €9.50 (€). **Hetan Majatalo** (€€) and **Lapland Hotel Hetta** (€€) have decent **restaurants**, which offer local specialities such as reindeer and charge around €25 for a main dish.

What to see and do

Hetta Huskies ✳ (016 641 590; Hetantie 211; w hettahuskies.com) Occupying over 20ha of forested land about 4km west of the village, this **husky farm** is worth a stop whether you're signed up for a sledding tour or not. The farm, which counts around 200 dogs, is run by an enterprising British–Finnish couple, Anna and Pasi, who have chosen to make their home in Finland's far north and are certainly no strangers to extreme conditions: both skied across Greenland in 2006 and Pasi reached the South Pole on skis two years later. At any time of year, the farm offers the chance to tour the kennels, meet the dogs and to learn about their training; a visit costs €10. There's a whole host of tours and activities available throughout the year and full details are given on the website. As an example, during the winter months, the farm offers a whole variety of sledding tours; while some of the shorter trips are aimed at visitors on the Santa Claus charters flying into Enontekiö airport, there are also other, longer excursions that are ideal for getting a taste of the surrounding wilderness landscapes of this part of Finnish Lapland; all tours include a visit to the husky farm itself. A 6km trip, for example, lasting about 90 minutes, costs €73, or €130 if you'd like to drive your own sled; a longer 6½-hour excursion goes for €285 on a shared sled.

In summer, the farm specialises in **kayaking** and **canoeing** tours on several nearby rivers including the Palojoki, which vary in price and length but a one-day trip, for example, costs €75; once again exhaustive details are on the Hetta Huskies website which also contains a tremendous amount of hard-to-find English-language information about the local area. If you're thinking of hiking, be sure to check out the 'Hidden Hetta Hikes' section on the website.

Pallas-Yllästunturi National Park Finland's third-largest national park covering over 1,000km², the Pallas-Yllästunturi National Park was established in 2005 to protect the fell chain in this part of central Lapland. A long, narrow, ribbon-shaped wedge of land stretching from Hetta in the north to roughly Kittilä in the south, the park contains a wide range of unique fell, forest and peatland habitats. Pallas-Yllästunturi is a veritable haven for naturalists: plants such as mountain bearberry, trailing azalea, alpine clubmoss and Lapland diapensia are all well represented. The fauna of the park is equally rich: in spring the snow bunting is among the first migratory birds to arrive and in summer around 150 species of bird can be seen in the park. Of the larger mammals, bear and elk are regular inhabitants of the park, whereas wolverine, lynx and wolf are less frequent visitors. For more information about the park, check out the informative English-language pages at w hettahuskies. com/en/location/national-park where there's also a map of the hiking trails.

Hiking trails Although there are several trails that wind their way through the park, the best and most easily accessible is the marked 55km-long **Hetta-Pallas trail** (55km; 3–4 days; moderate) for which you will need three to four days (summer only). From Hetta, first cross Ounasjärvi Lake by boat (ask at the tourist office for the exact starting point) and head south through the pine forest towards the Pyhäkero day shelter. **Wilderness huts** (all open and not requiring reservation) are situated at regular intervals along the trail at Sioskuru, Pahakuru, Hannukuru (where there's a sauna) and Nammalakuru. At the end of the trail, the **Pallastunturi visitor centre** (ᕆ 020 6397 930; e pallastunturi@metsa.fi; w nationalparks.fi/pallastunturivisitorcentre; ⊕ Oct–mid-Feb & May 09.00–16.00 Mon–Fri; mid-Feb–Apr & Jun–Sep 09.00–17.00 daily) at Pallastunturintie 557 can help with onward bus connections, or, alternatively check at w matkahuolto. fi. For **accommodation** at this end of the trail, there's the comfortable **Lapland Hotel Pallas** (ᕆ 016 323 355; e pallas@laplandhotels.com; w laplandhotels.com; ⊕ mid-Feb–Apr & mid-Jun–mid-Sep; €€€€) at Pallastunturintie 560, whose predecessor, incidentally, was used by holidaying German officers during World War II until they blew it up in 1944; or **Hotelli Jeris** (page 126), which can be reached on buses to Kittilä and Rovaniemi.

Getting to Norway from Hetta With your own car it's a straightforward drive of 37km from Hetta, north along Route 93, to the Norwegian border at the hamlet of Kivilompolo. Once across the border, a further 43km will see you in Kautokeino. A Norwegian-operated bus (#901) operates between Hetta and Kautokeino, terminating in Alta on its circuitous journey which began in Tromsø (see box, page 131). This is the first public transport along this route for years. Otherwise, limited Norwegian bus services serve Kautokeino from Alta and information can be found at w snelandia.no.

KAUTOKEINO

Occupying a lonely, isolated spot across the border on Norway's barren Finnmarksvidda Plateau, 80km north of Hetta, it is hard to see quite why

Kautokeino (Guovdageaidnu in Sámi, though known locally as plain 'Kauto') exists where it does. However, the translation of the village's Sámi name, 'halfway point', helps to throw some light on the matter, since the village is located midway between two traditional reindeer-grazing areas. Providing ready access to the Kautokeino River, on whose banks the settlement has grown, Kautokeino (the Norwegianised version of the Sámi name) slowly developed into a stopping point on the long migration.

Indeed, it is clear to see how important the village is to Norway's Sámi community: not only is Sámi virtually the only language you will hear on the streets and, therefore, a sign of cultural dominance, but it is the location for the Sámi high school and reindeer-herding college (the Sámi University offering a BA in reindeer herding and a PhD in the Sámi language among other courses), the Nordic Sámi Institute, the Norwegian Sámi parliament's language department and the National Sámi theatre – quite a feat for a place which counts a population of barely 3,000 people.

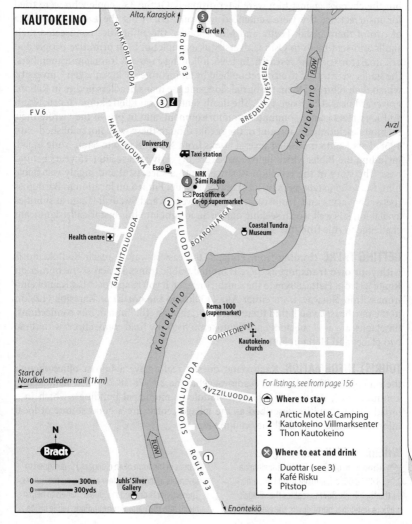

KAUTOKEINO

Alta, Karasjok

Circle K

GAHKKORLUODDA

Route 93

FLOW

Kautokeino

FV 6

BREDBUKTJUESVEIEN

Avzi

HANNULUOUKKA

University

Taxi station

Esso

NRK
Sámi Radio

Post office &
Co-op supermarket

Coastal Tundra
Museum

Health centre

GALANIITOLUODDA

ALTALUODDA

BOARONJARGA

Kautokeino

Rema 1000
(supermarket)

GOAHTEDIEVVA

Kautokeino
church

Start of
Nordkalottleden trail (1km)

SUOMMALUODDA

AVZZILUODDA

For listings, see from page 156

Where to stay

1 Arctic Motel & Camping
2 Kautokeino Villmarksenter
3 Thon Kautokeino

Where to eat and drink

   Duottar (see 3)
4 Kafé Risku
5 Pitstop

N

Bradt

0 ━━━ 300m
0 ━━━ 300yds

Juhls' Silver
Gallery

FLOW

Route 93

Enontekiö

SOME HISTORY: THE KAUTOKEINO REBELLION

The first ever Sámi uprising took place in Kautokeino in the autumn of 1852, sparked by long-lasting frustration about local living conditions. The Sámi felt a deep sense of exploitation when they considered their unequal relationship with Norwegian traders and their growing dependence on hard liquor (introduced by Norwegian merchants and pioneers from the south).

Following the closure of the land border between Norway and Finland in 1852, which deprived the local Sámi of traditional grazing pastures in Finland and thus threatened their traditional livelihood, a group of 35 Sámi Laestadians marched on the village, murdering a local shopkeeper whom they held responsible for the increasing alcoholism of the local inhabitants. They then burnt down his store and butchered the local policeman when he tried to intervene. The gang beat up the local priest when he tried to prevent the violence. The revivalist preacher Lars Levi Laestadius was charged in connection with the incident for whipping the local Sámi into a religious fervour and urging them to wage war on the unrepentant, but the charges against him were later dropped. Of the 33 people who were tried for insurrection, five were sentenced to death. Following the execution in Alta of two of them, Aslak Hætta and Mons Somby, the authorities confiscated their skulls and sent them to Oslo University as examples of both primitive people and criminals for scientific research. In 1996, following a request from family members, the skulls were traced to a collection held by an institute at Copenhagen University, which then returned them for burial alongside the men's headless bodies in Kåfjord graveyard near Alta (page 198). The death sentences on Ellen Skum, Henrik Skum and Lars Hætta were commuted to imprisonment, and in prison they wrote their memoirs including an account of the revolt, though these were not published until 1958. Lars Hætta translated several books from Norwegian into Sámi while in jail, including the Bible, which helped to secure his early release after 15 years behind bars. The story of the rebellion was made into a successful and highly watchable film, *Kautokeino Opprøret*, by local boy Nils Gaup. Filmed on location in Bardufoss (between Narvik and Tromsø) in Sámi, Norwegian and Swedish (English subtitles available), it is well worth seeking out for an insight into this historically significant challenge to rule from the south.

GETTING THERE

Coming from Finland, the easiest way to reach Kautokeino is **with your own transport** as there is limited public transport across the border on Route 93 from Hetta, 80km to the south.However, if you're approaching Kautokeino from within Norway, from either Alta (130km to the north) or Karasjok (128km to the northeast), you'll find there are better, though still limited, **bus** connections; timetables are at w snelandia.no. Kautokeino has only road connections with these two places and Hetta in Finland.

TOURIST INFORMATION

Kautokeino doesn't really have a tourist office though the staff at the **Thon hotel** at Biedjovággeluodda 2 (🛇 78 48 70 00; w kautokeino. kommune.no), up the hill from the huddle of municipal buildings, which in a broad sense could be described as the village centre, are a good source of local information and will do all they can to help.

 WHERE TO STAY *Map, page 155*

Thon Kautokeino Biedjovággeluodda 2; 🛇 78 48 70 00; e kautokeino@olavthon.no; w thonhotels.no. Built to replace the village's previous hotel that burnt down, the elegant Thon is built in the form of an elongated S, designed to resemble a herd of reindeer moving on the tundra. The exterior is dressed in wooden panels to help it blend into the natural surroundings, while inside the comfortable rooms are a haven of wooden floors, white walls & soft orange fabrics. €€€€

🏠 **Kautokeino Villmarksenter** Hannoluohka 2; \78 48 76 02. This rather austere establishment has extremely spartan rooms that take the prize for the smallest bathrooms in the whole of Lapland. When approaching from Alta, follow the signs on the main road marked 'Samisk høgskole/Sámi allaskuvla' & then turn immediately left. €€€

🏕 **Arctic Motel & Camping** Suomaluodda 16; m 48 04 09 97; e samicamp@me.com; w arcticmotel.com. Located at the southern end of the village, past the church & just over the bridge, this campsite also has a good selection of cabins, both with & without running water & kitchen facilities as well as a handful of regular dbl rooms, either sharing facilities or with private facilities (neither option has a kitchen; both €€). Cabins with no facilities €; with bathroom: €€

✕ WHERE TO EAT AND DRINK *Map, page 155*

As eating options are limited in Kautokeino, it may be a good idea to stock up on supplies at one of the two supermarkets in the village: Co-op (⏰ 08.00–23.00 Mon–Sat) and Rema 1000 (⏰ 07.00–23.00 Mon–Sat) are both located along the main road; note, though, that neither is open on Sunday.

✕ **Duottar** Biedjovággeluodda 2; ⏰ 17.00–22.00 Mon–Thu, 18.00–22.00 Fri–Sun. Located inside the Thon (see opposite), this is by far the best option in Kautokeino, offering a good selection of local specialities including a duo of smoked topside & grilled fillet of reindeer with all the trimmings & grilled Arctic char. There's a separate bar inside the hotel, too. €€

✕ **Pitstop** Fievroluodda 7; ⏰ 11.00–20.00 Mon–Fri, 13.00–20.00 Sat & Sun. Next to the Circle K filling station just up beyond the Thon hotel. You can order pizzas from 80NOK & kebabs from 160NOK. Cheap & cheerful. €

☕ **Kafé Risku** ⏰ 11.00–17.00 Mon–Sat. Hannoluohka (beside the main road, opposite Villmarksenter). Good for snacks, open sandwiches (40NOK), coffee & cakes. €

WHAT TO SEE AND DO In order to do Kautokeino justice, you really need to spend a couple of days here, meeting people and chatting, to try to get under the skin of the village. Like so many other Sámi settlements, it is not a visually appealing place, strung out rather aimlessly along Route 93, which forms the main street, and if you simply rush in and rush out again, you risk misunderstanding the Sámi community and may leave with the wrong impression. Since there are no sights here, appreciating what Kautokeino has to offer is more to be found in sharing a cup of coffee or a beer with one of the locals and discussing what life is like here, or heading out into the surrounding unsullied countryside and getting in touch with nature. The village is at its most animated during the Easter Festival (page 158) though it is relatively empty in summer when a third of the population is at the coast tending reindeer.

Juhls' Silver Gallery (Galaniittuluoda; \78 48 43 30; w juhls.no; ⏰ late Jun–early Aug 09.00–20.00 daily; rest of the year 09.00–18.00 daily) While in Kautokeino, make sure to visit the Juhls' Silver Gallery, a veritable treasure chest of locally produced top-quality jewellery, as well as other handicrafts of Scandinavian design. Established by man-and-wife team, Frank and Regine Juhl, back in 1959, the gallery has grown over the years and now offers an intriguing insight into their work and its influences over the decades they have lived in Kautokeino since moving here from Denmark and Germany, respectively. Quite remarkably, the couple met in Kautokeino and decided to settle here – at a time when there wasn't even a road to their house and the only access was by boat across the Kautokeino River. Both Regine and Frank developed a keen interest in nomadic cultures, carefully observing the style of dress and personal adornment of the local Sámi, which was to become a key element of their work and design. Although the Sámi had no tradition of silvermaking due to their nomadic lifestyle, they acquired silver chains and brooches through trade and these have now become a key part of their traditional dress on special occasions.

At their hilltop location overlooking Kautokeino, the workshop and showrooms have been extended over the years, and wandering through the complex from room to room is to explore the couple's work decade by decade – exquisitely beautiful silverwork, mosaics and lapidary are on display throughout the site which is made up of low-lying showrooms with pagoda-style sloping roofs designed to reflect the snowdrifts of the tundra. The gallery is an easy place to spend an hour or two simply strolling around and watching the craftspeople at work in the workshop. Free guided tours (15mins) operate throughout the day and help to explain the significance of the different rooms in the gallery and their connection with each other. There's a small café where you can get free coffee and biscuits. Juhl's Silver Gallery is 2.5km from the centre of Kautokeino, perched on a ridge by the west bank of the river. Follow the signs from the main road.

Coastal Tundra Museum (RiddoDuottarMuseat; Boaronjárga 23; m 48 11 72 66; w rdm.no/english/kautokeino_bygdetun; ⊕ Jun–Aug 09.00–18.00 Mon–Sat, noon–18.00 Sun; rest of the year on request; 50NOK) The small headland, by the bridge, that forces the Kautokeinoelva River into a sharp right-hand bend, is where you will find Kautokeino's diminutive museum, a collection of traditional Sámi timber store huts as well as a modest exhibition focusing on the cultural history of the Sámi people through a series of traditional costumes, tools and assorted other knick-knacks. The faded-black-and-white photograph (taken in 1932), just to the left of the museum reception, depicts the church which served the people of Kautokeino at the time of the rebellion; it stood in the village for nearly 250 years until it was destroyed in 1944 (see below). Other items of note include a silver chalice dating from around 1760 which was donated to the church by local priest, Johannes Hjorth, and the unusual dark blue 'horn hat', indeed, a hat with a horn on top of it. The hat was worn in church by local women until the rebellion in 1852 after which it was considered sinful to wear the hat as it was believed the devil lived in the horn; its appearance in public, consequently, fell out of favour.

Kautokeino church (⊕ Jun–mid-Aug 09.00–16.00 daily) Sitting squatly on a small hillock at the southern end of the village, just over the river, Kautokeino church is visible for miles around and, indeed, draws churchgoers from across the tundra – it is one of the best-attended churches in Norway, particularly at Easter. Although the first church to stand on this spot was constructed in 1701, it was tragically burnt to the ground by retreating German forces at the end of World War II. Today's church, completed in 1958, is unusually long in shape with a ridge turret above the entrance at its western end, which culminates in an onion-shaped steeple and spire. A roof-covered porch before the main door, supported by vertical and slanted wooden posts, is reminiscent of Sámi building design. The wood-panelled interior is decorated in the traditional Sámi colours – blue, green, red and yellow – and is lit by the original candelabra that was rescued from the village's first church.

Easter Festival Undoubtedly, the best time of year to be in Kautokeino is at Easter when the entire village is consumed by the week-long Easter Festival, a historically traditional event when the local Sámi community celebrate (albeit with snow still on the ground) the end of a long winter and look forward to the coming of spring. It is a time for religious festivals and wedding ceremonies. Although today's festival still is an important religious event, it is also the time for the **reindeer racing world cup**, a **film festival** focusing on the indigenous people of the Arctic, concerts, theatre performances and the **Sámi version of the Eurovision Song Contest** when, in addition to the selection of the best song, the best *joik* is chosen. There's more information at w samieasterfestival.com.

Hiking trails from Kautokeino Perfect for a short stroll through some of the local countryside, a signposted 4km-long **nature trail** (*natursti* in Norwegian; 1hr; easy) begins 8km south of the village, opposite the Fritidssenter campsite. At regular intervals along the path you'll find information boards with details of the local flora and fauna as well as Sámi culture. The trail also winds its way past an old Sámi worship place.

More challengingly, Kautokeino marks the start of the 800km-long **Nordkalottleden trail** (difficult), which weaves its way south to Sulitjelma and Kvikkjokk (see box, page 65). To get to the beginning of the trail, first take the road out to Juhls' Silver Gallery and then turn right for Bulet Eco Siida. Pass to the right of the buildings here and wind your way around the right-hand side of the lake, Buletjauri, where you'll find an information board marking the beginning of the trail.

MOVING ON FROM KAUTOKEINO Buses for Alta and Gievdneguoika (change here for Karasjok) arrive and depart from the Circle K filling station at the northern end of the village on the main road but also call at the Thon hotel (page 156). Plan your journey carefully since schedules are skeletal at best; timetables are at w snelandia.no.

NORTHEAST FROM ROVANIEMI: TOWARDS INARI AND KARASJOK

The other main road north from Rovaniemi, **Route 4/E75**, heads northeast for a grinding 128km before reaching uneventful **Sodankylä** (Soaðegilli in Sámi), the only place of any significance between Rovaniemi and Kakslauttanen (page 161).

SODANKYLÄ Sodankylä is not one of Lapland's most interesting or aesthetic towns, but it is worth a quick stop on the long road north from Rovaniemi. In addition to a decent Sámi art gallery, there are a few other diversions worthy of your time, notably one of the oldest wooden churches in the whole region. Sodankylä is reputed to be the coldest place in Finland; indeed, in January, although statistically the average temperature here is a chilling −14°C, it is commonly below −30°C.

Tourist information Sodankylä is effectively strung out along one long main road, Jäämerentie. The **tourist office** (m 040 746 9776; e info@sodankyla. fi; w visitsodankyla.fi; ⏰ 10.00–18.00 Mon–Fri, 10.00–16.00 Sat) is located with the art museum, beside the old church, at Jäämerentie 3, beside the junction with Kemijärventie. From the bus station, at the opposite end of Jäämerentie, the tourist office is a straightforward walk down the main road of around 10 minutes.

Where to stay The high season in Sodankylä runs from November to April, when test drivers from Peugeot are in town to put their latest models through their paces in Arctic conditions and during the Midnight Sun Festival in mid-June (page 161).

🏠 **Sodankylä** Unarintie 15; 📞 010 230 5000; e info@sodankylahotel.fi; w sodankylahotel.fi. Opened in 1968, this somewhat uninspiring hotel, just behind the bus station, is worth considering if everywhere else is full. Built of brick in late 60s/70s style & the biggest in town, it's comfortable enough but wins no prizes for design or charm. €€€€

🏠 **Karhu** Lapintie 7; m 040 122 8250; e info@hotel-bearinn.com; w hotel-bearinn.com. 2 blocks west of Jäämerentie, at the junction with Kasarmintie, this hotel, also known as Bear Inn in English, has modern & comfortable dbl rooms decorated in soft colours, all with private facilities. Rooms available with saunas & power showers. €€€€/€€€

🏠 **Majatalo Kolme Veljestä** Ivalontie 1; m 040 0539 075; e majatalo.kolmeveljesta@pp.inet.fi; w majatalokolmeveljesta.fi. Located just beyond the northern end of Jäämerentie, this plain & homely guesthouse with shared facilities has dbls with use of the kitchen & sauna. B/fast is included in the room rate. €€

⛺ **Nilimella** Kelukoskentie 5; 📞 016 612 181; e info@nilimella.fi; w nilimella.fi. Sodankylä's waterfront campsite (🕐 Jun–Sep) is across the river, diagonally opposite the old church, at the crossroads of Routes 4 & 5. Tent pitch €10. Also rents out cabins (€) & larger apts (€€); both sleep 2–4. There's also a pub, Piitsi, on site.

🍴 **Where to eat and drink** Make no mistake, Sodankylä is no gourmet's paradise.

🍴 **Päivin Kammari** Jäämerentie 11; 📞 016 319 633; w paivinkammari.fi; 🕐 10.00–21.00 Mon–Sat, noon–17.00 Sun. By far the best choice. A popular & elegant café, with outdoor seating in summer, which serves up an excellent smoked reindeer pasta dish in a creamy sauce for €15 as well as salmon, steaks & reindeer dishes from €19. €€

🍴 **Pizza-Paikka à la Riesto** Jäämerentie 25; m 040 722 2910; w pizzapaikkha.fi; 🕐 11.00–

21.00 Mon–Sat, noon–21.00 Sun. Opposite the bus station. This wins 2nd prize in the eating stakes. Pizzas cost around €10–12. €

🍴 **Revontuli** Jäämerentie 9; 📞 050 016 0573; 🕐 17.00–21.00 Mon–Thu, 17.00–03.00 Fri, 14.00–03.00 Sat. This dingy locals' drinking hangout comes at a distant 3rd, dishing up smoked salmon, sautéed reindeer & pepper steak all for around €15–20 as well as an array of pizzas. €

What to see and do Although Sodankylä can trace its history back to the late 17th century when local Sámi gathered here to celebrate key dates in the religious calendar, arriving by reindeer sled in winter and boat in summer, there's just one building still standing to remind today's visitor of times past. The town's fantastically preserved **wooden church** (🕐 Jun–mid-Aug 09.00–18.00 daily; entrance fee voluntary), dating from 1689 and known as *vanha kirkko*, was – unusually – spared the ravages of the retreating German forces during World War II, and today remains totally intact in its original position beautifully located beside the Kitinen River. Built of coarse timber and topped by a shingle roof, this compact church has an exceptionally narrow nave and a bulging pulpit that vies for what precious space there is with the pews. Beneath the floorboards, in the crypt, there's a collection of preserved mummies; if the churchwarden is around you may be able to coax them to let you down for a nose around. You will find the old church to the east of the tourist office, tucked away in the graveyard beside the town's more modern church, which is totally devoid of charm and interest.

Alariesto Art Museum & Gallery (m 040 746 9776; w visitsodankyla.fi/en/naejakoe-artikkeli/museo-galleria-alariesto-2; 🕐 10.00–18.00 Mon–Fri, 10.00–16.00 Sat; €5) Just beside the church, you will find one of Lapland's better Sámi art galleries, which contains the naivistic work of local artist Andreas Alariesto (1900–89) – plenty of brightly coloured, sometimes happy, sometimes sombre scenes of day-to-day Sámi life, with a fair smattering of reindeer and locals in traditional costume. Alariesto described his own work as an attempt to 'chronicle a world that had already passed, one that would fade into oblivion with my death', and his ultimate aim was to preserve the Sámi culture of which he was part.

Midnight Sun Film Festival (w msfilmfestival.fi) For one week each year during the middle of June, Sodankylä is overrun with film buffs, drawn here by the latest cinematic offerings of Finland's leading directors on show around the clock during the Midnight Sun Film Festival. The brainchild of local film producers, brothers Mika and Aki Kaurismäki, the festival aims to showcase the best of Finnish, European and world cinema, using the allure of the midnight sun to entice people to visit what is otherwise a singularly unattractive town. Appealing primarily to hardened film enthusiasts, the attraction of sitting for hours on end in a darkened cinema while there's 24-hour daylight outside remains a mystery to most other visitors. Naturally, accommodation is at a premium during the festival and if you are planning to visit at this time of year, you'd be wise to book somewhere to stay well in advance. There's more information about the event on the website and at the tourist office and it's wise to reserve tickets for the screenings in advance.

TANKAVAARA About 90km north of Sodankylä, just after the tiny hamlet of **Vuotso**, lies the **Tankavaara Gold Prospector Museum** (Tankavaarantie 11C; ✆016 626 171; w kultamuseo.fi; ⊕ Jun–Sep 10.00–18.00 daily; rest of the year 10.00–16.00 Mon–Fri; €12). This is the place to head for if you fancy trying your hand at prospecting for gold – every year, thousands of people come here to try their luck. The museum is interesting enough, tracing the history of the gold rushes in this part of Lapland, but it is getting your hands wet which is the real fun part of a visit here. Sadly, though, not everyone has the luck of the 11-year-old schoolboy who turned up a nugget weighing almost 40g. To pan for gold in the river here costs €8 per person, which then gets you some basic training and all the equipment you need. Naturally, you are allowed to keep any gold you might find. In early August each year, Tankavaara hosts the **Finnish National Goldpanning Championships** when hopefuls from across the country gather here to slosh piles of dirt and stones around.

🔼 **Where to stay, eat and drink** Should you want to stay here, there's comfortable accommodation available on site in well-appointed en-suite double rooms as well as rustic log cabins which share facilities (Tankavaarantie 31; ✆016 626 158; e info@ tankavaara.fi; w tankavaara.fi; rooms €€€; cabins €€). There's also a **campsite** here, charging €13 to pitch a tent. The **Wanha Waskoolimies** (old gold prospector) restaurant (⊕ 08.00–22.00 daily; €€) here serves up a tasty selection of Lapland delicacies including reindeer and locally caught salmon – an excellent choice for a starter course is the Lapland plate for €9 which includes cold smoked pike and warm smoked salmon with sour cream, pickles and flatbread.

KAKSLAUTTANEN ✳ The **hotel and igloo village** of Kakslauttanen Arctic Resort (✆016 667 100; e reservations@kakslauttanen.fi; w kakslauttanen.fi) is a real gem. A good 250km north of Rovaniemi, it has easily the best choice of **log cabin** accommodation in the whole of Finnish Lapland and makes for a great place to spend Christmas (page 163). If your heart is set on spending the night in an **igloo** but you resent paying the inflated prices charged by Sweden's Icehotel, you will be delighted to know that they are a little cheaper here.

Kakslauttanen isn't really a village; it is little more than an idyllic collection of log cabins and, during the winter season, a gaggle of igloos, beautifully located either side of a small river, directly beside Route 4, where a hole in the ice is kept open for those early morning dips. Kakslauttanen boasts the largest **smoke sauna** in the world with a capacity of around 100 people. Together with its smaller brother, the sauna is heated using woodsmoke and best entered once the smoke has died down somewhat, generally after an hour or so (€71 pp for min 8 people in the smaller smoke sauna; €60.50 for min 20 people in the larger; 2hr).

Airport transfers If you are flying directly to this part of Finnish Lapland and arriving at **Ivalo airport**, you can arrange a pickup for €29 per person each way, or, €432 each for pickup by snowmobile (min 4 passengers); all pickups must be arranged in advance.

Where to stay, eat and drink There is a great choice of accommodation at Kakslauttanen, located in both halves of the resort, the East Village and the West Village, and here we have detailed the most popular choices; prices are well into our top bracket for accommodation costs and are detailed on the website. Kakslauttanen's main **log cabins** are first class. Not only are they located a respectable distance from each other to allow a little privacy (something which can be hard to find in other similar establishments), but they are all built to the same high standards using the truly impressive dead standing pine. Imported from Russia, these rough-hewn tree trunks have a sizeable diameter of over 0.5m and conspire to give the whole village (they've been used to build the saunas and the main reception building, as well) a sturdy yet superbly cosy feel. Although the size of each cabin differs (they sleep from two to six people), every one comes equipped with a full kitchen, fireplace and sauna while outside there's a generously sized terrace, perfect for standing to cool off after a sauna. There is also a separate series of what Kakslauttanen terms its '**golddigger cabins**', located in the West Village on the banks of the river, which also have their own sauna and a kick sledge to help you get about the site.

Every winter between December and April, the hotel constructs its own more modest version of Sweden's Icehotel. The **igloo village** is generally composed of one main building of snow and ice housing several sleeping rooms, a restaurant, gallery and chapel – the temperature inside here only varies between –3°C and –6°C even if, outside, it's down to –30°C. Next door there are usually other smaller, **snow igloos**, which can sleep up to five people. If you choose to sleep in an igloo, you will be provided with a snug gown, sleeping bag, woollen socks and a hood to keep you warm.

Kakslauttanen also offers the chance to spend the night in a **glass igloo**, specially constructed of thermal glass in the shape of a regular igloo. The glass keeps the interior at normal room temperature and doesn't frost up and, naturally, offers clear views of the night sky, increasing your chances of seeing the aurora borealis (visible between late August and late April). Each glass igloo has a toilet, small shower and electrically operated reclining beds.

In addition to the possibility of preparing meals in the log cabins, room prices include half board. (Lunch can be purchased as an add-on if required.)

What to see and do You won't be short of things to do at Kakslauttanen: you can book seemingly any number of **reindeer**, **husky** and **snowmobile** safaris plus ice-fishing trips, horseriding and aurora-hunting tours; full details and prices are available on the website. A trip to the reindeer farm in the village of Purnumukka, 20km south of Kakslauttanen, for example, by shared snowmobile costs €142 per person for a 3-hour trip. Alternatively, a 2-hour husky-sled tour costs €152 per person and a snowmobile safari of the same duration is €110 per person; prices rise for your own sled/machine.

Santa's Home In an attempt to provide children at Kakslauttanen with a real Santa Claus experience, Santa's Home, a 5-minute drive away from the main resort, accessed by a long wooden bridge across the river, resort, has recently opened its doors. Here, kids can have a one-on-one meeting with the 'man in red' in an idyllic red cottage, where Santa's helpers are also on hand to provide that special touch of Christmas magic that no child can resist. Book your visiting slot via the website.

URHO KEKKONEN NATIONAL PARK From Kakslauttanen, a minor road leads east for around 7km to **Kiilopää** hill (546m), which marks the western extent of one of Finland's greatest national parks, Urho Kekkonen, named after the former president, and now one of Europe's last wilderness areas. Measuring a whopping 2,530km^2, the park is truly vast and it is therefore crucial that you plan any hiking trip here with extreme precision. Maps are essential, as the 190km of walking paths are poorly signed; there are cabins dotted throughout the park that can be booked in advance (see below). Don't worry, though, about having to carry water with you; the streams here are so pure you can drink water directly from them. You can find detailed information about the park at **w** nationalparks.fi/en/urhokekkonennp.

Tourist information and where to stay The best place to get the latest information about the state of the terrain – mostly upland hills, boggy in parts, and dense forest – is from **Tunturikeskus Kiilopää** (⊙016 670 0700; **e** kiilopaa@suomenlatu.fi; **w** kiilopaa. fi/en), a **hotel**, **youth hostel** and national park information centre, at the end of the road from Kakslauttanen, where staff can advise on booking cabins in the park itself. Open all year round (⊙ 08.00–22.00 daily) except May and October, the centre has dorm beds (**€**), private rooms (**€€€**) and log cabins (**€€€**); there's a **restaurant** and **smoke sauna** (⊙ 15.00–20.00 Tue, Wed & Fri; €10 for Kiilopää guests, otherwise €13) on site. Breakfast is not included in the room rates and costs an extra €12 per person. The evening buffet (⊙ 17.00–19.00) goes for €23.

SAARISELKÄ A further 12km north of Kakslauttanen along Route 4/E75, the pleasant, purpose-built holiday village of Saariselkä (**w** saariselka.fi) proudly bills itself as the most northerly ski resort in the world. It is a modest sort of place, consisting of just four hotels and two fells, Kaunispää (with chairlift) and Iisakkipää, for downhill skiing, and hence is unlikely to be the main reason for your travel to Lapland. Facilities at Levi near Kittilä, for example, Saariselkä's arch-rival, are more likely to appeal to those more used to the upmarket ski resorts of central Europe. However, if you are driving by, it is worth making the short detour to the top of **Kaunispää** hill (437m), signed off Route 4/E75 just to the north of Saariselkä, from where there are superb views of the surrounding fell land stretching for 70km or so on a clear day. The Panorama Café at the summit is a fine place to stop for a cup of coffee and a slice of cake to savour the view.

Where to stay, eat and drink

Santa's Hotel Tunturi Lutontie 3; ⊙016 681 501; **e** saariselka@santashotels.fi; **w** santashotels.fi/en/hoteltunturi. The best of the hotels offers a range of comfortable dbls, with free access to the hotel's saunas, & apts sleeping up to 13 people which feature their own sauna. The restaurant, Pirtti, in the main building serves up delicious salmon soup with rye bread for €9.50 as well as sautéed reindeer with mashed potato for €24. Dbls **€€€€**; apts **€€€€**/night

Activities Should you decide to stay in Saariselkä, the hotel can arrange a number of activities in addition to skiing, including **snowmobile** and **husky safaris**; prices available on request.

6

IVALO Just 23km north of Saariselkä, Ivalo (Avvil in Sámi) conspires to be the dullest place in the whole of Lapland. An ugly and soulless village, strung out aimlessly along the E75, there's only one real reason to be here: namely, to explore the unspoilt Ivalojoki River, which is widely regarded as the finest **canoeing** route in the whole of Finland. From Ivalo, it is 288km south to Rovaniemi and 39km north to Inari.

Tourist information Ivalo's **tourist office** (m 040 168 9668; e ivalo@metsa.fi; w inarisaariselka.fi/en/about-the-area/ivalo; ⊕ 09.00–16.00 Mon–Fri) is located at number 10 on the main road, Ivalontie. It can help with information about the Ivalojoki (see below) as well as hiking trails in the surrounding area.

Where to stay Should you find yourself in the unenviable position of having to spend the night in Ivalo, your best bet is the riverside **Hotel Ivalo** (016 688 111; e hotelivalo@hotelivalo.fi; w hotelivalo.fi; €€€€), Ivalontie 34, on the southern edge of town just past the Shell station.

Where to eat and drink When it comes to finding something to eat, look no further than the excellent and extensive lunch buffet served up at **Kultahippu** (Petsamontie 1; 016 3208 800; ⊕ 11.00–15.00 Mon–Fri; €) for just €11.50. Choices go downhill fast afterwards: the greasy spoon **Anjan Pizza** (016 661 909; ⊕ 11.00–22.00 Mon–Sat, noon–22.00 Sun; €) at Ivalontie 12, close to the Shell station, has a range of unappetising pizzas from €7, and the even less palatable **Lauran Grilli** (016 661 624; ⊕ 11.00–23.00 Sun–Fri, 11.00–01.00 Sat; €) opposite at number 10, which dishes up an identical range of pizzas at similar prices. The best place for a drink is the uninspiringly named **pubi.fi** (⊕ 13.00–22.00 daily), next door to Anjan Pizza. Beware, though: it is the local boozers' hangout and may not appeal to those of a nervous disposition.

Canoeing the Ivalojoki River From its source high in the hills east of Hetta, the river takes in an impressive range of canyons and rapids as well as some of Lapland's most pristine wilderness, as it flows northeast heading for Lake Inari. The 70km section between **Kuttura**, a small hamlet west of Saariselkä, and Ivalo is particularly suited to canoeing. Canoes and kayaks can be rented from **Luontoloma** (016 668 706; e luonto.loma@saariselka.fi; w luontoloma.fi; ⊕ 09.00–17.00 daily), who can be found opposite Santa's Hotel Saariselkä in Saariselkä itself, for €50 per day. Luontoloma also operate a variety of guided excursions on the Ivalojoki; full details are on the website.

Handicrafts and souvenirs Before you leave Ivalo, it is worth making a stop at **Lapland Shop** (⊕ 10.00–17.30 Mon–Fri, 10.00–16.00 Sat, noon–16.00 Sun), also known as Lahjatalo Ivalo in Finnish, on the main road, Ivalontie, just before the Lauran Grilli restaurant. Thanks to Ivalo's location well off the beaten tourist trail, it is a good place to pick up Sámi souvenirs, in particular reindeer skins, at considerably lower prices than in more touristy locations.

INARI AND AROUND

A short drive of 39km northwest from Ivalo, Inari is to Finland what Karasjok is to Norway. Home to Sámediggi, the Finnish Sámi parliament, Inari (Anár in Sámi) is the centre of Sámi culture in Finland. Although other Sámi groups and Finns have moved into the region for various reasons (people were resettled in Inari, for instance, when Finland lost the Petsamo region to the Soviet Union in 1944), the Sámi have historically always lived in the same place, around the rocky shores of Inarijärvi lake (Anárjávri in Sámi), and today constitute a distinct ethnic group within the Sámi community as a whole, with their own traditional costume and language. However, Inari Sámi is threatened with extinction since its speakers total barely 300, many of whom are elderly or middle aged, and few schoolchildren are learning the language.

Although Inari is a pretty enough place to wander around for an hour or so, there are several reasons that make it an ideal stop on the long haul between Rovaniemi and the North Cape: the best Sámi museum in the whole of Lapland is here; an enjoyable hiking route out to a wilderness church starts from here; and boat trips on the steely waters of the lake are available during the summer months.

TOURIST INFORMATION Clustered around the mouth of the Juutuanjoki River where it flows into Lake Inari, the village is little more than one elongated main road, Inarintie, which runs over a distance of a kilometre or so. The helpful **tourist office** (m 040 168 9668; e tourist.info@inari.fi; w inari.fi/en/tourism.html; ⊕ Jun–Aug 09.00–19.00 daily; Sep 09.00–18.00 daily; rest of the year 10.00–17.00 Tue–Sun), Inarintie 46, is handily located in the Siida Museum (page 167) and has masses of information about the surrounding area.

All **buses** use Hotel Inari as their main stop in the village. Between June and August, the direct bus to the North Cape leaves Inari at 17.00; for more details on getting to the North Cape, see page 214. Note that the service only runs as far as Karasjok during the rest of the year, arriving at 17.40 Norwegian time.

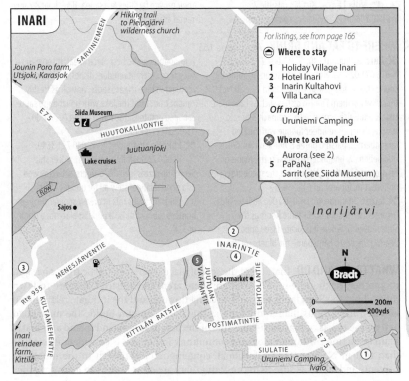

INARI

↑ Hiking trail
to Pielpajärvi
wilderness church

SARVINIEMEN

Jounin Poro farm,
Utsjoki, Karasjok

E75

Siida Museum

HUUTOKALLIONTIE

Juutuanjoki

Lake cruises

FLON

Sajos ●

Inarijärvi

For listings, see from page 166

🛏 **Where to stay**
1 Holiday Village Inari
2 Hotel Inari
3 Inarin Kultahovi
4 Villa Lanca

Off map
   Uruniemi Camping

✕ **Where to eat and drink**
   Aurora (see 2)
5 PaPaNa
   Sarrit (see Siida Museum)

MENESJÄRVENTIE

Rte 955

KULTAMIEHENTIE

Inari
reindeer
farm,
Kittilä

INARINTIE
(4)

(2)

JUUTUAN-
VAARANTIE

(5)

Supermarket ●

KITTILÄN RATSTIE

POSTIMATINTIE

LEHTOLANTIE

SIULATIE
Uruniemi Camping,
Ivalo ↓

E75

N

Bradt

0   200m
0   200yds

(3)

(1)

WHERE TO STAY *Map, page 165*
Hotels
🏠 **Hotel Inari** Inarintie 40; ✆016 671 026; e sales@visitinari.fi; w visitinari.fi/hotel-inari. This hotel has both plush en-suite dbls as well as rooms which incorporate a private sauna. If you want to meet local people, the restaurant here is the place to come; known as the 'living room of the village', it attracts diners & drinkers, though the former are greatly outnumbered by the latter, particularly on Fri & Sat nights, when things can get especially loud & drunken. €€€€

🏠 **Inarin Kultahovi** Saarikoskentie 2; ✆016 5117 100; e inarin.kultahovi@co.inet.fi; w hotelkultahovi.fi. Comfortable dbls overlooking the rapids on the Juutua River decorated in retro 1950s style with wood panels & bold Sámi colours. Those in the riverside wing have their own sauna & cost around €30 more. The hotel also has a great restaurant serving traditional Arctic dishes using meat from local reindeer herders & fish caught from the lake – all at reasonable prices. €€€

Cabins and camping
✳ 🏠 **Villa Lanca** Kittilän ratsutie 2; m 040 748 0984; e villalanca@villalanca.

com; w villalanca.com. Located next to the supermarket, this place has a handful of beautifully decorated dbl rooms & apts with kitchenette; furnishings & fittings have been carefully chosen & are stylish to a T. Plus, there's a trendy café & wine bar serving up cakes & fresh sandwiches as well as a selection of tapas. €€

🏠 **Holiday Village Inari** Inarintie 26; m 040 1706 069; e sales@visitinari.fi; w visitinari.fi/holiday-village-inari. Located 650m south of the centre, a range of cabins are available at this sedate holiday village (which is open all year), some with lake views & their own sauna & bathroom. It claims to have fewer mosquitos than elsewhere thanks to its location by the lake & surrounded by grassland. €

⛺ **Uruniemi Camping** Uruniementie 7; m 050 3718 826; e pentti.kangasniemi@ uruniemi.fi; w uruniemi.fi; ⏰ Jun–Sep. The village campsite is gorgeously located on the shores of Inari Lake about 2km south of Inari towards Ivalo & all buses to Inari stop outside. It also offers a choice of cabins; the larger ones have their private facilities & a sauna. Bike, boat & canoe rental available. €

WHERE TO EAT AND DRINK *Map, page 165*
✗ **Aurora** Inarintie 40; ⏰ 11.00–21.30 daily; ✆016 671 026; w visitinari.fi/restaurant-aurora. A sound choice, found inside Hotel Inari (see above), for classy northern Finnish dishes such as Lake Inari char & whitefish served with a spinach & potato terrine; delicious reindeer tongue with pickled lingonberries, parsnip purée & blackcurrant sauce; or blueberry & lingonberry panna cotta. Mains go for around €25, though there are cheaper burger options, too, for around €15. €€€

✗ **Sarrit** Inarintie 46; m 040 7006 485; w siida. fi/contents/restaurant; ⏰ same hours as the Siida museum, where it is located (see opposite). Bearing the north Sámi name for 'blueberry', Sarrit

is undoubtedly the best place to eat; it serves up a variety of different reindeer dishes, such as smoked reindeer in blue cheese sauce, as well as freshly caught trout from the lake with hollandaise sauce & boiled potatoes. The lunch buffet (⏰ 11.00– 15.00 daily) is €15. €€

✗ **PaPaNa** Inarintie 49; m 040 721 3650; ⏰ 10.00–22.00 daily. Sámi for 'reindeer shit'. Serves up pizzas, kebabs, burgers, salads as well as a good reindeer stew all for under €15. Its interior is a curious mix of greasy spoon café meets hunter's cabin. It's also a popular place for a drink or 3. €

WHAT TO SEE AND DO Inari is not the sort of place where you hurtle from one sight to another, ticking them off as you go; there aren't any. Instead, prepare to learn more about the Sámi lands you are travelling through and the intimate relationship between indigenous man and nature at the Siida Museum beside the main road and on the banks of Inarijärvi Lake, one of the best museums in Finland and Inari's main attraction. Although the Sámi community in Finland is considerably smaller than that in Norway, the professional, contemporary approach to the museum's contents and layout is sure to impress and there are clear lessons to learn for other museums elsewhere in the region. Other than the museum, a boat trip on Inarijärvi lake or a hike out to the Pielpajärvi wilderness church are the main reasons to linger.

Siida Museum ✳ (Inarintie 46; **m** 040 089 8212; **w** siida.fi; ⏰ Jun–Aug 09.00–19.00 daily, Sep 09.00–18.00 daily, rest of the year 10.00–17.00 Tue–Sun; €10).

From the entrance hall, a sloping walkway leads visitors to the main exhibition area on the first floor. Here, in a modest-sized room, an easy-to-understand timeline runs the circumference of the room recounting Sámi history from prehistoric times to the present day, placing events in Lapland alongside their chronological counterparts elsewhere in the world: for instance, while Che Guevara and Ayatollah Khomeini were at large, the Sámi were rejoicing at the completion of their new road to Sevettijärvi. The key theme of the museum, though, is nature and as you step into the main exhibition space it is as if you are suddenly immersed in the wilds of Lapland's fells. A series of floor-to-ceiling photographs measuring a whopping 10m wide by 5m high span the room, conjuring up resonant images of Lapland's landscapes and seasons. The sound of birdsong, the howl of the wind and the gentle trickle of mountain streams, played from surround speakers in the ceiling, add to the sensation of being out in nature and at the mercy of the elements. From displays on the variegated flowers that carpet the Lapland fells in spring to the fascinating life cycle of the brown bear, the exhibition is a real treat for the senses.

Although a number of smaller sections are worth a quick glance – namely those on religion, reindeer husbandry and the resettlement of the Skolt Sámi who fled from Petsamo to Inari after the end of World War II – you should continue your visit outside where during the summer months you can wander at leisure around a whole host of traditional wooden Sámi homes and outbuildings that survived the war years, only to fall into neglect and disrepair. Moved to the museum in the early 1960s, the dwellings form a key part of local Sámi culture, both from reindeer-herding Sámi and the fishing community of Inarijärvi, and cover a 7ha (17 acre) site behind the museum building.

Expect new exhibitions to be added until 2022 as the museum expands and renovates – a sure sign of the continued success of Siida.

Sajos (Inari Sámi for 'a semi-permanent place to camp'; Menesjärventie 2; **w** inarisaariselka.fi/en/company/the-sami-cultural-centre-sajos; ⏰ 09.00–17.00 Mon–Fri).

Diagonally opposite Siida on the southern bank of the Juutuanjoki River, Sajos is Inari's pride and joy: the Sámi cultural centre here houses the Finnish Sámi parliament, a library of Sámi-language books, auditorium and a small café (⏰ 09.00–16.00 Mon–Fri). Inspiration for the star-shaped building comes from Sámi handicrafts and the floorplan is said to resemble a reindeer skin or a Sámi man's headdress, depending on your point of view. The external walls are constructed from fire-resistant pine while inside spruce and birch are used extensively. Though as a visitor to Inari you're unlikely to have much call for the Sámi administrative services available, the inspirational building, funded by the European Union's regional development fund, is definitely worth a browse. Inside, you'll also find **Sámi Duodji** (⏰ 10.00–17.00 Mon–Fri), which has a wide range of tasteful souvenirs.

Inarijärvi Lake Covering an area of over 1,000km² and containing more than 3,000 islands, Inarijärvi is Finland's third-largest lake. To get an impression of the sheer scale of the lake, it is twice the size of Switzerland's Lake Geneva or Lake Constance on the borders of Germany, Austria and Switzerland and is consequently known locally as 'the Sámi sea'. For some truly spectacular views, head 7km south of

Inari along Route 4/E75 back towards Ivalo and take the right turn signed 'Digita Oy Inarin radio-ja tv-asema', which will lead you up a steep hill to the site of Inari's radio and television mast. From the car park at the foot of the mast, there are sweeping vistas out across the island-studded waters that reach all the way to the Norwegian and Russian borders. The lake empties northwards into the head of the Varangerfjord, part of the Barents Sea, via the Paatsjoki River. Of the 3,000 islands in the lake, the best known are Hautuumaasaari (graveyard island), which served as a cemetery for the Sámi people in ancient times, and Ukonkivi, a historical place of sacrifice.

The views of the lake will doubtless whet your appetite to take to the water, so head back into town and make for the bridge beside the Siida Museum where you'll find a small quay. This is the departure point for 2.5- to 3-hour **lake cruises** around Inarijärvi (m 040 0295 731; ⊕ mid-Jun–mid-Sep 1–2 daily, departures are generally at 13.00 &/or 17.00, details are at w visitinari.fi; €24), sometimes calling in at Pielpavuonio to pick up hikers from the Pielpajärvi wilderness church (see below).

Other activities from Inari In addition to lake cruises, a series of other activities is available in Inari – both water and land based – bookable through the tour operator Visit Inari at Inarintie 38 (m 040 1796 069; e sales@visitinari. fi; w visitinari.fi). In summer, for example, they offer 4- or 5-hour **fishing trips** on the lake at a cost of €110 and €140 respectively; **river rafting** on the Juutua River for €70 per person; and a **visit to a reindeer herder** to see reindeer and learn about handicrafts made from the animal (€90). Inarijärvi freezes every winter between November and early June, when exhilarating **snowmobile tours** across the lake can also be booked for €135 per person (€165 for your own snowmobile). Alternatively, husky safaris, reindeer sleigh rides and cross-country ski trips can be arranged with prices starting at €75. Full details and prices are on the website.

Pielpajärvi wilderness church Beginning from Sarviniementie, a short stroll of 2.5km will take you to a car park which marks the beginning of the worthwhile **hiking trail**✳ (4.5km one-way from the car park; allow about 1½ hours in each direction; moderate) north to the Pielpajärvi wilderness church (⊕ always open), built beside Inarijärvi in the 1750s and overlooking an undulating flower meadow. Though the church is now abandoned, visiting priests gave services in it until the early 1800s. Having stood empty for well over a century, it was taken back into use in 1940 after the church in Inari was bombed during World War II.

The path negotiates an area of old-growth pine forest on its way to the church and climbs to a modest height of 141m; although it is a straightforward hike to the church, take extra care if it is wet as the path (indicated by orange and red marker posts) can be extremely slippery – and be prepared to clamber over tree roots and small rocks. To return it is simply a question of retracing your steps, or continuing southeast from the church for a further 2.5km, to reach the inlet, Pielpavuono, and the landing stage for the boat that will call in here on demand during its tour of the lake. Check departure times before setting out at the tourist office (or call the telephone number listed on page 165) if you intend to return by boat. Before setting off, be sure to pack your insect repellent as the clearing in the forest where the church stands is renowned for horseflies and mosquitoes during the height of the summer.

Buying reindeer skins and meat Just 5km north of Inari on the road towards Kaamanen, you'll find **Jounin Poro**, run by local reindeer herder, Jouni Angeli, who sells reindeer skins and meat from his farm at Kaamasentie 490 (look out for the 'Jounin Poro' sign by the roadside). Though you'll need a phrasebook to hand as Jouni doesn't speak English, with a little sign language and basic Finnish you'll be able to pick up a reindeer skin for half the price of the souvenir shops and know, too, that the money is going directly to the herder himself. Jouni also sells fresh reindeer meat.

Inari reindeer farm From Inari, it's 13km southwest along Route 955 towards Kittilä to the hamlet of **Solojärvi**, the location for Inari reindeer farm (m 050 0666 444; e reindeerfarm@reindeerfarm.fi; w reindeerfarm.fi). The farm is a great place to learn first hand about Sámi traditions and culture and the importance of the reindeer to Scandinavia's indigenous population. Pre-booked group visits (price depends on the size of the group) to the farm last a couple of hours and include the opportunity to feed the herd of animals.

NORTH FROM INARI: KAAMANEN, UTSJOKI AND KARASJOK

KAAMANEN From Kaamanen, about 30km north of Inari, there's a choice of routes north: Route 92 cuts northwest for the Norwegian border at Karigasniemi and onwards to Karasjok in Norway (page 170), whereas Route 4/E75 continues north to Utsjoki. After the village of Kaamanen and just before the junction of the Utsjoki and Karigasniemi roads, keep an eye out for an evocative wayside **memorial to the Lapland War** of September 1944 to April 1945. Built of rusty red metal and shot through with circular bullet-like holes, the monument states starkly that 774 Finnish light infantry men were killed during the operations in Lapland, 262 went missing and 2,904 were wounded. During the Lapland War, these soldiers covered an exhausting 800km on foot and bicycle, roughly in line with Route 4, pursuing German troops who were retreating northwards across the remote and inhospitable terrain of Finnish Lapland.

UTSJOKI Utsjoki (Ohcejohka in Sámi) holds the title of the northernmost municipality in the European Union. Indeed, when Finland joined the EU in 1995, Utsjoki felt so neglected by Helsinki 1,300km to the south, let alone Brussels, that there were calls for the district to cede from Finland and join Norway across the Tana River and outside the Union. This is the only area in Finland where Sámi are in the majority and, hence, throughout the village you will hear various Sámi dialects in use, rather than Finnish, as the lingua franca. Although there's little to see in Utsjoki itself, the surrounding scenery more than compensates: the tiny settlement is dominated by the holy fell known as Áiligas (342m), a Sámi-fied Germanic loanword referring to the sacred, which was once a place of sacrifice to the reindeer spirits, *seiddi*.

Getting there Utsjoki lies at the confluence of the Utsjoki and Tana rivers. Route 4 runs south through the village towards Inari and doubles as the main street. You will find virtually all the services Utsjoki has to offer on this road. A bridge crosses the Tana River to provide access with Norway and the E6 highway; Kirkenes is 209km away, Karasjok 113km.

Where to stay

Holiday Village Valle Ellintie 25; m 040 0948 210; e info@holidayvillagevalle.fi; w holidayvillagevalle.fi. A much better choice & an altogether more customer-friendly experience than Pohjan Tuli. Located 2km from the centre of the village along Route 970 to Karigasniemi at

Ellintie 25, this place offers cabin accommodation with picture-perfect views of the Tana River, plus newly built comfortable dbl rooms, perfectly decked out in tasteful Scandinavian styles. Rooms & cabins €€€€

6

🏠 **Hotelli Pohjan Tuli** Hietaniementie 40;
m 040 416 9993; e hotellipohjantuli@gmail.com;
w pohjantuli.fi. About 7km south of the village
itself, this lakeside hotel has a choice of dbl rooms &
apts overlooking Mantojärvi Lake. €€€€/€€€

🏠 **Nuorgamin Lomakeskus** [map, page
134] m 040 0294 669; e info@visitnuorgam.
fi; w nuorgaminlomakeskus.fi. Some 43km east
of Utsjoki, in Finland's northernmost village,
Nuorgam, & overlooking the Tana River, cabins

(☉ summer only)& apts are available for rent
here. There is also a remote wilderness cabin,
Riekkola, available for rent all year round, with no
running water, electricity or internet connection
– the perfect place to get away from it all. Apts &
wilderness cabin €€€; summer cabins €€

🏕 **Camping Lapinkylä** m 040 0559 1542;
e niila.tapiola@luukku.com; w arctictravel.fi. In
Utsjoki on the main road. Cabins available between
Jun & Sep. Tent pitch costs €12. €€

✖ Where to eat and drink

In addition to the list below, there are two supermarkets selling provisions and two fuel stations, where, incidentally, both petrol and diesel are considerably cheaper than across the border in Norway.

✖ **Deatnu** Ellintie 25; m 040 0948 210;
w holidayvillagevalle.fi/en/restaurant; ☉ noon–
15.00 daily & 16.00–23.00 Mon–Sat, 16.00–22.00
Sun. The best place to eat around Utsjoki, located
in the Holiday Village Valle (page 169). Serves local
specialities such as freshly caught fish from the
Tana River as well a number of reindeer dishes.
Beautifully appointed, airy restaurant with lovely
views out over the river. €€€

🍽 **Giisá café** Utsjoentie 9; ☉ 09.00–17.00
Mon–Fri. Opposite the campsite – look out for
the Finnish sign Kahvila Käsitöitä, meaning 'café,
handicrafts'. Serves light snacks. €

🍽 **Rastigaisa** Utsjoentie 4; m 040 7008 154;
w rastigaisa.net; ☉ 08.00–21.00 Mon–Thu,
08.00–02.00 Fri, 14.00–02.00 Sat, 14.00–21.00
Sun. Opposite the supermarket. Bar & café, which
has pizzas & other light snacks. €

Hiking trails The main reason to come to Utsjoki is to go hiking. During the summer months, there's an enjoyable 10km return marked trail to **Mantojärvi Lake** (10km; 2–3hrs; moderate), 5km south of the village, where there's a church and a dozen old timber cabins which once served as overnight places to stay for people who'd travelled here to attend church. The path begins opposite the supermarket in Utsjoki before climbing up over Vuolleseavtetvárri fell (300m) in order to later descend towards the lake.

Another, more challenging marked trail (64km; 3 days; difficult) begins at Kenespahta, 20km south of Utsjoki, and leads through the Kevo canyon inside the **Kevo Nature Reserve** (Kevon luonnonpuisto), which is sandwiched between Routes 4 and 92 southwest of Utsjoki, terminating at Suttesjärvi, 10km east of Karigasniemi on Route 92. There's only one overnight cabin on the trail so you must have your own tent with you. Buses serve both the start and the end of the trail.

Moving on from Utsjoki: into Norway Since the late-2018 termination of direct bus services between Karasjok and Kirkenes via the E6 in Norway, it is no longer possible to pick up a Norwegian bus to either destination from across the Tana Bridge at Utsjoki. Instead, your best option is to continue by daily (except Sat) Finnish **bus** at 23.30 (w eskelisen.fi) to Tana Bru and then change for a Norwegian bus to Kirkenes; alternatively, take a Finnish bus to Nuorgam and then make your own way (via Route 895) along the remaining 23km to Skipagurra (on the E6) for Norwegian buses to Kirkenes. Check w matkahuolto.fi and w snelandia.no carefully before setting out.

KARASJOK Leaving Inari, Route 92 forges a lonely way northwest towards the border settlement of Karigasniemi before the pine and birch trees very slowly start to reappear and a lone television transmitter can be spotted in the distance – sure signs that civilisation is not far away. Nestling in a wooded river valley and better known to the local indigenous population as Kárášjohka, Karasjok is Norway's Sámi capital, home to 3,000 people, seat of the Sámi parliament, base for NRK's Sámi Radio and the true heartland of the Sámi language. Owing to easy road access (and bus links), Norwegian Karasjok is more readily accessed from neighbouring Finland than it is from many other destinations within Norway. For that reason, you'll find coverage of Karasjok in this chapter as opposed to the following one.

As you wander around the streets and pop in and out of the handful of shops here, you will quickly hear that Sámi is the dominant tongue (eight out of ten people speak it), recognisable even to the untrained ear by its soft guttural nature and total lack of sing-song tones so prevalent in Norwegian. To attend church on Sundays, in particular, and for other important occasions such as meetings or Sámi holidays, local people don their *gákti* or traditional costume, nowadays a sign of pride and belonging. Unlike many other villages further north, the Sámi here are in the majority and there's a real sense of a thriving community living comfortably within the Norwegian state rather than struggling to assert their identity against it.

Yet there's a much darker side to Karasjok which is little known to the English-speaking world; a harrowing and disturbing truth which has been kept quiet for decades and still today is not discussed. Hundreds of prisoners were tortured and murdered in the forests here by the Nazis who established a brutal **concentration camp**, aided and abetted by Norwegians, who chose to collaborate. During my last visit to Karasjok even the tourist office denied there had been a concentration camp here; for full details, see page 173.

Getting there
Karasjok sits around a kink in the river and is an important crossroads in this part of Norwegian Lapland; note that all roads are now named in Sámi rather than Norwegian. It comprises three main roads: the E6, Leavnnjageaidnu (formerly Porsangerveien), which enters the village from Lakselv (74km) to the north, transmuting into Ávjovárgeaidnu (formerly Kautokeinoveien; Route 92), beyond the main roundabout, and continuing west towards Kautokeino (130km); Deanugeaidnu (formerly Tanaveien, the continuation of the E6 northeast towards Tana Bru: 182km), which heads down the hill from the main roundabout towards the main shopping area and another roundabout; from where, Suomageaidnu (formerly Finlandsveien and built by slave labour during World War II), Route 92, crosses the river and heads southeast for the Finnish border at Karigasniemi (18km) and on to Inari (116km). Incidentally, Karasjok is the coldest place in Norway: during a particularly severe cold snap in January 1999, the mercury plummeted to a mind-boggling −51.2°C.

Tourist information
The **tourist office** (Leavnnjageaidnu 1; ☎ 78 46 88 00; e sapmi@sapmi.no; w sapmi.no; ⊕ Jun–mid-Aug 09.00–19.00 daily; mid-Aug–Dec 09.00–16.00 Mon–Fri, 10.00–16.00 Sat & Sun, rest of the year 10.00–14.00 Mon–Fri) is inside the Kafe Sapmi building, beside the gaggle of handicraft stores and workshops adjacent to the Scandic Karasjok (page 171).

🏠 Where to stay
Map, page 172, unless otherwise stated

For somewhere to stay, choices are limited to **Engholm Husky Design Lodge** [map, page 134] (page 175); the comfortable, modern pile **Scandic Karasjok** (Leavnnjageaidnu 49; ☎78 46 88 60; e karasjok@scandichotels.com; w scandichotels. no; €€€€), carpeted throughout in the Sámi colours of red, blue and yellow; the

6

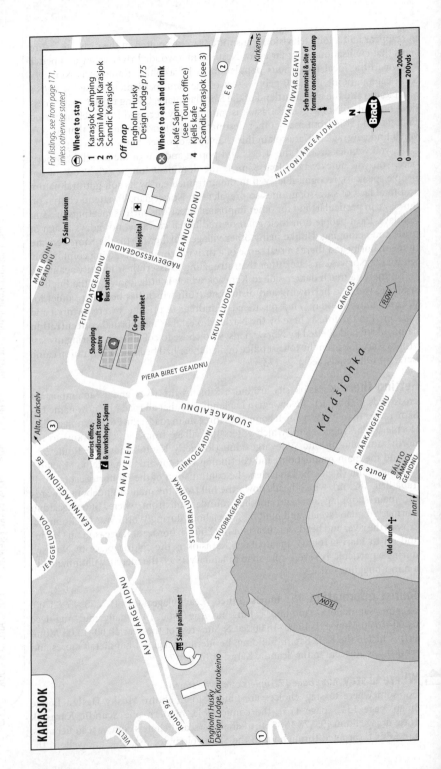

KARASJOK

For listings, see from page 171, unless otherwise stated

Where to stay
1 Karasjok Camping
2 Sápmi Motell Karasjok
3 Scandic Karasjok

Off map
Engholm Husky
Design Lodge p175

Where to eat and drink
Kafé Sápmi
  (see Tourist office)
Kjells kafe
4 Scandic Karasjok (see 3)

Kirkenes

IVVAR IVVAR GEAVLI

E 6

Serb memorial & site of
former concentration camp

NIITONJÁRGEAIDNU

0   200m
0   200yds

Bradt

Sámi Museum

MARI BOINE
GEAIDNU

Hospital

RÁDDEVIESSOGEAIDNU

DEANUGEAIDNU

FITNODATGEAIDNU
Bus station

Co-op
supermarket

Shopping
centre

PIERA BIRET GEAIDNU

SKUVLALUODDA

Alta, Lakselv

Tourist office,
handicraft stores
& workshops, Sápmi

SUOMAGEAIDNU

GARGOS

Kárášjohka

FLOW

E 6
LEAVNNJÁGEAIDNU

TANAVEIEN

GIRKOGEAIDNU

MARKANGEAIDNU

Route 92
BALTTO
SÁMMOL
GEAIDNU

Inari

JEAGGELUODDA

STUORRALUOHKKÁ

STUORRÁGEADGI

AVJOVÁRGEAIDNU

Route 92

Sámi parliament

Old church

FLOW

Engholm Husky
Design Lodge, Kautokeino

VIETTI

172

cheap and cheerful **Sápmi Motell Karasjok** (Deanugeaidnu 40; ✆ 78 46 64 32; e sapmimotell@gmail.com; €), heading out towards Kirkenes, whose rooms mostly share facilities; and all-year **Karasjok Camping** (m 97 07 22 25; e post@karacamp. no; w karacamp.no), which charges 100NOK to pitch a tent and also has cabins (€), youth-hostel-style rooms (€)and dorms (250NOK/bed), 1km or so after the Sámi parliament (page 175) and off the Kautokeino road, Ávjovárgeaidnu.

✗ Where to eat and drink *Map, page 172*

When it comes to eating, your best bet is the upmarket restaurant (w scandichotels. com/hotels/norway/karasjok/scandic-karasjok/restaurant-bar; ⊕ 17.00–22.00 Mon–Fri, 18.00–22.00 Sat & Sun) inside the **Scandic Karasjok** (€€€), which serves top-notch Arctic delicacies such as fillet of reindeer with lingonberries and oven-baked vegetables or pan-fried Arctic char with seasonal vegetables. For lighter meals, there are two choices: **Kafé Sápmi** (€) in the same building as the tourist office, which serves snacks and sandwiches, or **Kjells kafe** (⊕ 09.00–20.00 Mon–Thu, 09.00–03.00 Fri & Sat, 14.00–20.00 Sun; €) at Fitnodatgeaidnu 1 (down the hill from the roundabout outside the Sápmi theme park and inside the shopping centre beside the Co-op supermarket), which has burger and fries, salads and chicken and fries from 100NOK.

What to see and do Karasjok's attractions are subtle. While there's a certain pleasure to be gained in walking the streets and watching local people go about their daily lives, taking in one or both of the village's museums will give you a deeper understanding of Sámi life.

Sápmi (Leavnnjageaidnu 1; ✆ 78 46 88 00; w sapmi.no; ⊕ hrs as the tourist office; 130NOK). It is best to start with Sápmi, a sort of hi-tech Sámi theme park, which aims to provide visitors with an insight into local culture and history, predominantly through a creatively produced multi-media show. Visitors begin by watching a short video highlighting recent technological and global changes that have affected the Sámi way of life (the use of snowmobiles and helicopters, for example, in reindeer husbandry) before walking into the Stálubákti (Sámi for 'mountain spirit') **magic theatre**. Here, in a specially created cinema, complete with artificial northern lights in the ceiling, there's a fascinating insight into the ancient myths and beliefs that have shaped the Sámi community, as well as information about *joiks* and the ever-changing landscapes of Lapland. Immediately outside the cinema, you will find examples of traditional Sámi dwellings: the *siida* (Sámi camp or settlement) consisting of a summertime *lávvu* (tent) and the more substantial winter *goahti* (turf hut). During the summer months, there's usually a couple of reindeer grazing in the enclosure, too.

The Karasjok concentration camp Today, a modest memorial stone, completely hidden in a dense grove of birch trees, is all that bears witness to the horror which unfolded on the banks of the Kárášjohka River. It was here that the Nazis exterminated 350 Yugoslav prisoners, employing sadistic brutality which is numbing to comprehend. In July 1942, they transported the captives, who were mostly Serbs, over 5,000km from the Balkans to northern Norway, for one reason alone: to torture and then kill them. Karasjok was to be an extermination camp which would subject prisoners to prolonged periods of bitter cold and temperatures as low as −50˚C as part of their ordeal.

Dressed in rags and housed in unheated barracks, which gave no protection against the Lapland winter, the inmates toiled in the forests, chopping and cutting

MAMMA KARASJOK AND THE CONCENTRATION CAMP

Though most villagefolk in Karasjok obeyed the German order not to help the prisoners, one local Sámi woman risked her own life time after time. Known to the Serbs as 'Mamma Karasjok', Kirsten Svineng would take her sledge into the forest or out to the new road, wherever the prisoners were working, and secretly hide food parcels. Kirsten also helped several men escape by providing them with food, clothing and a map showing the route to neutral Sweden. The last inmate to come to her for help was just 17 years old, though, tragically, he was recaptured after being handed over to the Nazis by a Norwegian farmer who came across the boy about 50 miles from Karasjok. Harrowingly, the camp guards tied the boy to a tree and whipped him to death as they tried to establish the name of the person who had helped him flee. Neither he nor the 350 other prisoners, who were brutally tortured and murdered in Karasjok during the course of just five months, never once uttered Mamma Karasjok's name to the camp guards. After the war, Kirsten met a handful of the camp's survivors during a ceremony in Belgrade in 1957 where she was awarded Yugoslavia's highest honour and, several years later during a state visit to Oslo in 1965, Mamma Karasjok met President Tito, who personally praised her remarkable courage.

wood for the officers' stoves and were used to build a new road to the Finnish border – 'the road of blood' – as it became known. As the prisoners were systematically killed, their bodies were dumped as road-fill with the sand and gravel used in construction. On Sundays, the camp commander would personally supervise the prisoners' bathing and washing their clothes. Naked, they were driven by the camp guards, brandishing whips, into the icy waters of the river where they were forced to stand up to their necks for anything up to half an hour. When allowed out of the water, the commander would then select a dozen inmates who were sent back into the water while the others were forced to stand on the snowy riverbank, still naked and shivering in the freezing temperatures, to watch the grotesque spectacle; the river bathing claimed several men's lives each Sunday. Guards also routinely shot dead any prisoner who could not lift a log above shoulder height. By December 1942, work on the road to Finland was halted because the severe cold and 24-hour darkness were making it impossible for the surviving prisoners to continue with construction. Instead, one third were told they had been selected for forest duties; they were marched into the forest and unceremoniously machine gunned. Testimony from prisoners who survived indicates that the Norwegian guards were often more brutal in their dealings with the inmates, in an attempt to impress their German colleagues. The names of the 400 Norwegians who collaborated as camp guards are now known yet they will not be published.

Little information exists in English about the Karasjok concentration camp because, clearly, even after more than 70 years, there's still a profound sense of shame and embarrassment about what happened here; there is still no signpost indicating where the camp once stood. To get to the memorial and the site of the camp, first follow Deanugeaidnu east out of town and then take Niitonjárgeaidnu south towards the river. Look for the sign marked 'Idrettshall/Bibliotek' (sports hall/library) and turn left when you see it. Here, on the left-hand side of the road you've turned into, again unmarked, you'll see a footpath leading into the trees; it begins opposite the first brick building as you turn left. Follow this path to the memorial whose poignant inscription reads: 'To the memory of the Yugoslav prisoners of war who lost their lives in Karasjok during the war of 1940–1945 and who were buried here.'

Sámi Museum (Sámi Vuorká Dávvirat; also signed in Norwegian: De Samiske Samlinger; Mari Boine geaidnu 17; `\` 78 46 99 51; w rdm.no; ☉ Jun–Aug 09.00–18.00 daily, Sep noon–18.00 daily, Oct–Mar 09.00–15-00 Wed & Thu, noon–16.00 Sun, Apr & May 09.00–15.00 Tue–Fri, noon–16.00 Sat & Sun; 90NOK) Sadly, Karasjok's other museum, the Sámi Vuorká Dávvirat located on the other side of the Scandic Karasjok, is not a patch on Sápmi (or for that matter, the Siida Museum just over the border in Inari in Finland, page 167). However, if traditional costumes are your thing, you are in luck: the museum is stuffed full of them. From ornately decorated wedding costumes to red-and-blue Sunday best, they are all here, neatly hung in glass cabinets for your delight and delectation. The English-language labelling is at pains to point out that the *gákti* varies even within a particular region though, to be honest, the significance is likely to be lost on the uninitiated. More interestingly, the wearing of traditional costume was already becoming less common in the 1920s when men in Karasjok began donning Western-style hats in preference to more traditional Sámi headgear. Although the museum displays a series of old wooden tools, bowls and axes, there's little reason to linger. Immediately outside, you will find a collection of traditional Sámi wooden buildings as well as a series of pits in the ground used to hunt wild reindeer between 2900 and 800BC.

Sámi parliament (Sámediggi; *Sametinget* in Norwegian; ☉ 08.00–15.30 Mon–Fri) More engaging is the Sámediggi just beyond the roundabout on Kautokeinoveien, the world's first indigenous parliament opened in 1989, housed in a striking building in the form of a semicircle with wooden façades and triangular points in the form of a Sámi *lávvu*. In addition to gawping at the building's unusual construction, the main reason to venture here is to browse through the impressive number of English-language books held in the parliament's extensive library; seemingly everything from information on how to milk a reindeer to a children's school atlas in Sámi is on the shelves.

Old church (Gamle kirke; ☉ not open to the public) The only other sight to speak of in Karasjok is the Old church, on the south side of the river, about 100m over the bridge off Route 92 towards Finland. Located on a wide plain near the bend in the river, this evocative wooden structure with hipped roof, turret and steeple, dating from 1807, was the only building left standing in the village after World War II and is consequently the oldest church in Norwegian Lapland. The Gamle kirke soon proved too small, though, for the needs of an expanding village and in 1974 a modern church was built on the steep slope to the north of the river.

Engholm Husky Design Lodge [map, page 134] (m 91 58 66 25; e post@ engholm.no; w engholm.no) Karasjok makes a good base from which to explore the unspoilt nature in this corner of Norwegian Lapland. One of the best places to arrange activities in the vicinity is Engholm Husky Design Lodge, a husky farm and adventure centre 7km west of Karasjok, on the Kautokeino road (Route 92). Hand built, decorated and run by the enterprising Swede, Sven Engholm, who moved here from his native Malmö, 2,000km to the south, in the early 1980s, this riverside retreat offers just about any activity you'd care to mention. In winter Sven runs a

6

whole variety of **dog-sled tours** ranging from four to 11 days. Departure dates for the tours vary, as do prices (the 4-day trip, for example, costs 9,500NOK), but full details are available on the Engholm website. Other options include cross-country **skiing** or the exclusive opportunity to follow a Sámi family with their **reindeer** on their spring migration to the Arctic Ocean (51,000NOK) – once again, full details are available online. In summer, there's a wilderness tour with pack dogs who carry your pack. Pickups are available from Karasjok (300NOK) as well as from nearby airports.

Staying here is a real treat. Stay in snug two- to three-berth cabins (€€€€ pp); showers and toilets are in a separate building where breakfast and dinner are served (included in the room rate). In addition to a sauna and free wireless internet, the site includes a traditional Sámi turf hut, offering the chance to sit on reindeer skins around an open fire and enjoy an Arctic dinner (advance reservation required).

Moving on from Karasjok To continue from Karasjok **towards Kirkenes**, first take the weekday morning bus (⊕ currently 08.40) to Lakselv then change there for a service to Kirkenes, arriving around 16.45; times are liable to change on this route so double check **w** snelandia.no before you travel.

Direct services run a couple of times a day **to Hammerfest**. Change at Skaidi for connections to Alta. If you are hoping to take the bus to Kautokeino, it needs careful planning: there's just a handful of non-direct services per week; the best option is to take the 19.28 bus towards Alta and change for Kautokeino at unpronounceable Gievdneguoika. You'll find a useful list of bus routes at **w** snelandia.no/rutetabeller/2016buss.

The bus station is on Fitnodatgeaidnu, behind the Co-op supermarket off Deanugeaidnu and times can be found at **w** snelandia.no. Karasjok is connected **to Finland** by a daily bus that runs via Inari, Ivalo and Sodankylä to Rovaniemi; it leaves from the Scandic hotel. Between June and August this bus continues up to the North Cape, too; the timetable is online at **w** eskelisen.fi.

North of Karasjok, the Finnmark Plateau gradually falls away as you approach the Arctic Ocean; during the winter months, you'll note that temperatures generally rise as you descend towards the coast, while, conversely, in summer, it tends to get cooler as you leave the warming influence of the upland plateau behind you. In terms of distances, it's only around 75km along the E6 highway to the coast and the nondescript, straggly settlement of Lakselv, at the head of the Porsangenfjord; from Lakselv it's another 200km, following the E69 route up the western shore of the fjord to the North Cape.

EAST FROM ROVANIEMI

Around 30km east of Rovaniemi, in the hamlet of Vikajärvi, there is a parting of the ways: Route 4/E75 heads north towards Sodankylä while Route 82 continues east all the way to the Russian border. The outdoor activities centre and ski resort of Pyhä-Luostocan be reached both from Kemijärvi and from Route 4, south of Sodankylä, via the village of Torvinen, itself 77km north of Vikajärvi.

KEMIJÄRVI The first place of any significance, 100km east of Rovaniemi, Kemijärvi holds cult status among Finnish train spotters: it's the end of the line that stretches all the way up here from Helsinki, 900km or so to the south. Strictly speaking, the rail line actually continues to the Russian border (east of Salla the line is overgrown with trees and bushes and no longer used) but it's here, in Kemijärvi, that passenger services expire. Indeed, the railway reached the town in the 1930s and has driven the local economy ever since, transporting timber from the forests hereabouts down to the port at Kemi for export via the Baltic Sea. Timber has been Kemijärvi's lifeblood for years and still today the town hosts the annual **woodsculpting symposium** (w kemijarven-kuvanveistoviikot.fi), just after midsummer, which attracts woodcarvers from across the world who painstakingly craft their submissions alfresco.

Having admired one or two of the unusual wooden sculptures which are dotted around town following the previous symposia, there's little else to divert you in the town centre. Switch your attention, instead, to **Kemijärvi Lake**, which lies south of the town, straddles the Arctic Circle and is fringed by forested hillsides. Check with the **tourist office** at Kuumaniementie 2A (m 040 1892 050; e info. visit@kemijarvi.fi; w visitkemijarvi.fi; ⏰ 09.00–15.30 Mon–Fri;) to see whether **lake cruises** have restarted, as these once offered the rare chance to sail over the Arctic Circle.

🏠 **Where to stay, eat and drink** When it comes to finding somewhere central to stay in Kemijärvi, there's little to choose between the two main players: **Mestarin Kievari** (Kirkkokatu 9; ☎ 016 320 7700; e hotelli@mestarinkievari. fi; w mestarinkievari.fi; €€€), whose 20-odd modern rooms are comfortable enough, if unexceptional; while **Hotelli Kemijärvi** (Vapaudenkatu 4; m 046 5612 020; e info@hotellikemijarvi.fi; w hotellikemijarvi.fi; €€€) has accommodation of a similar standard, though feels a little more dated. A little out of town on the shores of Pöyliöjärvi Lake, **Lohen lomakeskus** (Lohelankatu 1; m 040 581 2007; e lohelanrantamokit@pp.inet.fi; w lohenlomakeskus.fi) is a holiday village offering both simple youth-hostel doubles (from €50) and cabins of various sizes (€€ for a 2-berth). For a bite to eat, your best bet is the **restaurant** inside the **Mestarin Kievari** (⏰ 07.00–22.00 Mon–Thu, 07.00–02.00 Fri, noon–02.00 Sat, noon–18.00 Sun; €), which serves up a diverse lunch buffet for just €11.90 (Sat €15) featuring lots of locally caught fish, but also dishes up some more unusual platters such as a meatloaf made of pike and, also, vendace from the lakes hereabouts – both for around €15. For a beer, there's a **pub** in the hotel or you could also try the popular drinking hole, **pubi.fi** (Jaakonkatu 6; ⏰ 11.00–18.00 Wed & Thu, noon–04.30 Fri & Sat, noon–18.00 Sun).

LUOSTO AND AROUND Titchy Luosto (w luosto.fi) is the perfect antidote to the full-on winter tourism that drives places like Rovaniemi. If you're looking for a modest, compact little village, where everything is within easy walking distance, it's hard to go wrong – Luosto consists of just two hotels, a couple of activities companies and very little else. In fact, most people here have come on a package holiday which promises just that. It's located at the foot of Ukko-Luosto fell (514m) where two main lifts will whisk you up to the summit for the handful of ski slopes. To be honest, though, people don't really come to Luosto to ski – it's more a destination to experience the winter activities which Finnish Lapland can offer; indeed, eight out of ten guests here have come from abroad for that very purpose. Thanks to its size, there is very little light pollution in Luosto which means the northern lights are more readily seen. Indeed, the hotels operate a texting service to your mobile phone if the aurora is spotted.

Most of the terrain hereabouts lies within the Pyhä-Luosto National Park, which spans around 150km² and is known for its steep fells, deep ravines, old-growth forest and wetlands. In summer, it's a favourite hiking area with a whole host of

different trails available: there are English-language details of the main routes at
w nationalparks.fi/en/pyha-luostonp/trails.

🏠 Where to stay

🏠 **Lapland Hotel Luostotunturi** Luostontie
1; ☎016 620 400; e luostotunturi@laplandhotels.
com; w laplandhotels.com; ⏲ closed May. Comes
complete with its own spa & is open all year
except May. There are comfortable, economy &
superior dbl rooms here as well as well-appointed
log cabins in the grounds of the hotel complex.
This hotel is used by Britain's long-established
tour operator, Canterbury Travel (page 25), for its
holidays to Luosto. €€€€

🏠 **Santa's Hotel Aurora** Luppokeino 1;
m 040 0102 200; e luosto@santashotels.fi;
w santashotels.fi; ⏲ Sep–Apr. Located a little
further down the main street. Here all rooms
have a private sauna & some also boast their
own fireplaces. In addition, the hotel has 10 glass
igloos, adjacent to the main building, which are
available in summer when the main hotel is closed,
since they have AC to combat the heating effect of
the sun on the glass. In summer, the hotel also lets
a number of rooms in log cabins, 400m from the
main building, known as Log Villa Borealis. €€€€

✗ Where to eat and drink
Most people come here on package deals and hence
eat in their hotel restaurant. The food at the **Aurora** hotel is especially tasty and
features locally sourced, often organic, ingredients. If you drop by here to eat, a
three-course set dinner (⏲ 16.00–22.00 daily; €€€) costs €42. In addition to the
two hotels, the main eating option is **Vaisko** (Hartsutie 1; m 044 7804 419; w luosto.
fi/en/business/restaurant-vaisko; ⏲ 14.00–22.00 Mon–Sat, 13.00–22.00 Sun; €€),
opposite the Luostotunturi hotel, where mains include a full range of reindeer
options, Arctic char, duck and a small selection of tapas.

What to see and do
Amethyst mine (w amethystmine.fi; ⏲ Dec–mid-Apr Mon–Sat in connection
with the snowcat departure from Luosto centre at 11.10, Jun–mid-Aug 11.00–17.00
daily; mid-Aug–Sep 11.00–16.00 daily; Oct 11.00–15.00 Tue–Sat; €19, €79 including
the snowcat) An unusual option is a trip to Luosto's amethyst mine, 5km southeast of
the village and the only one in Europe where the precious stones are mined by hand
using shovels and pickaxes; this method keeps the mine sustainable and also gets
around the fact that the mine is located within the national park. A visit to the mine,
at the top of Lampivaara hill, includes an explanation about the geology of the area as
well as a chance to dig for amethysts yourself – if you find one, and most people do,
you can take it away for free, providing that it will fit in the palm of your hand; any
larger and you must negotiate a price with the mine if you want to keep it.

In **winter**, the most fun way to reach the mine is by **snowcat and carriage**
(known, curiously, as a pendolino despite the fact that the carriage doesn't tilt
unlike trains of the same name on the Finnish rail network). Departures are from
opposite the Luostotunturi hotel, generally at 11.10, cost €79 per person and the
trip takes about 30 minutes to reach the mine. Note that in **winter** this is the only
transport available to the mine. In **summer**, it's not possible to drive all the way to
the mine since private vehicles are not allowed inside the national park; a 2.5km
walking trail begins at the Ukko-Luosto car park. Further details are on the website.

Activities In keeping with its size, Luosto has one main outfit offering activities:
Lapland Safaris (Luppokeino 2; ☎ 016 624 336; e luosto@laplandsafaris.fi;
w laplandsafaris.com), located between the two hotels. Details of the excursions on
offer are available online.

SUVANTO ✳ (w suvannonkyla.fi) Due east of Luosto and reached via Pyhä on Routes 962 and 9621 (a total distance of 44km), the ravishing village of Suvanto is immediately different. It is the only settlement in the whole of Finnish Lapland where all the buildings survived the destruction of the Germans as they retreated. It's not known why the Germans soldiers never reached Suvanto to set fire to the village as they did elsewhere in the province – but the result is breathtaking: houses, barns and storerooms of gnarled timber titillate the senses at every turn. In short, you should make every effort to get here to fully appreciate what Finnish Lapland used to look like and to comprehend the full horror that unfolded as entire villages and towns were systematically torched in the closing stages of World War II. Before you cross the bridge into the village itself, pause and turn left into the visitor car park and you'll see the old **cable-guided ferry** which once shuttled back and forth across the Kitinen River and provided the only access to the village – Suvanto's relative isolation is one theory, at least, as to why the Germans never got here. Today, all the buildings in Suvanto are protected by Finland's Board of Antiquities and Historical Monuments.

From June to mid-August a modest **museum** (free) is open in the village school which you'll see signposted 'Museokoulu' off to the right as you enter the village. Look out, too, for the small gallery and café, **Säpikäs** (◷ noon–18.00 daily; free), housed in a renovated barn where work by some of the artists, who come here to paint the old buildings, is on display.

The village houses Although Suvanto was first settled in the late 1700s, the current wooden buildings date, in general, from around a century later. Located on the northern shore of the river (and, hence, south-facing) in large open flower meadows, the buildings are designed according to the building techniques of the day – namely grouped around an **open courtyard**. Typically, the main dwelling house faces the cowshed across the courtyard, while on the third side a warehouse is usually found. Granaries, drying houses, smoke saunas and barns are then located outside the central courtyard. The buildings, all hewn of impressively sized logs, are just one storey in height and are usually heated by a stone oven. The colourful verandas, which you'll see adorning many of the dwelling houses, were added in the early 1900s, painted in lighter colours than the rich red ochre which decorates the outer walls of most of Suvanto's buildings.

SALLA Make no mistake, there's a lot in a name: Paris, city of light; Rome, the eternal city; Salla, in the middle of nowhere. Salla makes no bones about its remote location; in fact, the town positively thrills to the fact that it is, as its slogan proudly exclaims: 'in the middle of nowhere.' True, it takes time and effort to reach off-the-beaten-track Salla, a further 65km east of Kemijärvi and just 20km or so from the Russian border. However, outside Finland, Salla is still little known, which means that you'll not only get a very real sense of what backwoods Lapland is all about if you take the time and trouble to come here, but you'll also have some of northern Finland's wildest scenery and landscapes pretty much all to yourself. In summer, it's **canoeing**, **hiking** and **mountain biking** that are the main draws, while in winter, things are at their most lively. There's some superb **downhill skiing**, for example, to be had just south of town at Sallatunturi as well as an engaging **reindeer park** (page 183). However, it's the town's proximity to Russia which has moulded and scarred the Salla you see today – a visit here, consequently, offers a first-hand opportunity to get to grips with the terrible events that took place in this part of eastern Lapland during World War II. Salla found itself on the front line (page 180) and paid the ultimate price for its proximity to the Soviet Union. Salla lost half of its land area when Finland was ordered to cede territory larger than the whole of the Netherlands to Moscow in war reparations.

Some history Between November 1939 and February 1940, Finnish troops were engaged in the bloody **Battle of Salla** in an attempt to halt the advance of Soviet troops across Finnish territory. Soviet forces were under orders to annexe Finland; they were to march through Salla towards Kemijärvi, Sodankylä and Rovaniemi in order to reach Tornio, and, thus, effectively cut Finland in two. However, much to the amazement of the outside world, Finnish troops, with the help of Swedish and other Scandinavian volunteers, succeeded in halting the Soviet advance at the Kemijoki River. The Soviets withdrew to the village of Märkäjärvi (present-day Salla) and the Battle of Salla, which claimed between 500 and 700 lives, ended, two months after it had begun. Barely a fortnight later, at the signing of the **Peace Treaty of Moscow** in March 1940, Finland agreed to harsh war reparations which included ceding half of the Salla district to the Soviet Union, along with extensive areas further south, notably Karelia. The Finns were also obliged to build nearly 100km of **railway line, between Kemijärvi and Kelloselkä** (close to the present border between Finland and Russia) in order to connect up with the Soviet rail network and thus provide the Soviet Union with direct rail access to the Gulf of Bothnia from the White Sea – across sovereign Finnish territory. Following the end of World War II, war reparations saw Finland saddled with a debt to the Soviet Union totalling US$300 million, plus the loss of significant territory, including second city, Viipuri. Post-war paranoia led to the Soviet claim that the Finnish border came too close to the rail line between Leningrad and Murmansk, which had been of strategic military importance during the war. Accordingly, Moscow demanded that the border be moved westwards and Salla paid dearly: **50% of its municipal land area** was handed over to the Soviet Union and ten settlements, collectively known today as Old Salla (Vanha Salla in Finnish) including the former centre of the municipality, the village of Sallansuu, were unceremoniously erased from the map of Finland. Entire communities upped sticks and relocated on the Finnish side of the new border in and around the municipality's new centre-to-be, **Märkäjärvi**, which promptly changed its name to Salla and got on with the task of rebuilding; the Germans had destroyed 80% of Salla's buildings as they retreated northwards in the final stages of the war. Today, a sense of realism prevails in the municipality and though locals view the three highest peaks in the area (Rohmoiva 658m, Sallatunturi 636m and Välitunturi 604m – now all in Russia) with a melancholic nostalgia – they're clearly visible from the Finnish side of the border – there are no calls for Old Salla to be reunited with the new Salla. Instead, there is a tacit acceptance that Russia, 50 times the size of Finland, is best not provoked.

Getting there Buses from Rovaniemi and Kemijärvi arrive and depart from the filling station at Savukoskentie 13, while services for Sallatunturi pull up outside Spa Hotel Holiday Club Salla (page 182) on arrival there; timetables are available at w matkahuolto.fi.

Tourist information You'll find Salla's friendly **tourist office** (m 040 0269 838; e tourist.info@salla.fi; w salla.fi; ⊕ 09.00–16.00 Mon–Fri) at Myllytie 1, just east of Kuusamontie, right in the town centre.

⌂ **Where to stay, eat and drink** Modest, little Salla manages just one hotel and one eatery in the town centre.

🏠 **Hotelli Takka-Valkea** Savukoskentie 1; **m** 040 5858 285; **e** toivo.hakkanen@takka.inet. fi; **w** takkavalkea.com/en. Right at the heart of things, this has been run by a husband & wife team since the early 80s & has modern dbl rooms, some with private sauna. €€€

🍴 **Akkavaara** Myllytie 1; 📞016 832 477; **w** akkavaara.fi; ⏰ 10.00–15.00 Mon, 10.00–18.00 Tue–Thu, Sat & Sun, 10.00–19.00 Fri. Just off Kuusamontie, this café-cum-pizzeria has pizzas for around €9–10, salads from €7.50 & a number of burgers from €7. There's a set lunch here, too, on w/days for €9.80. €

What to see and do It's hard to get lost in Salla's pint-sized, anodyne centre and a short stroll along its main street, Kuusamontie (Route 950), is pleasant enough, glancing in the odd shop window here and there as you saunter. However, it's the railway station and its adjoining museum that constitute the only real attraction in town; you'll find both along Savukoskentie (Route 82), just east of the roundabout which marks the junction with Kuusamontie.

Salla train station From the roundabout, the train station is barely 100m down Savukoskentie, on your left-hand side; it's a low-set wooden building, painted mustard yellow, set back a little from the road. Behind it, there's no real platform to speak of – just a black-and-white sign announcing 'Salla' and three or four tracks, each heavily overgrown. Look to the east and Russia is barely 20km down the tracks. Although passenger services ceased to Salla in the 1960s, the line was in regular use until 2010 when the last freight train trundled down the tracks to Kemi laden with timber. The line west from here to Kemijärvi was officially closed in December 2012, pending any future decision about cross-border traffic to and from Russia (see box, below).

FROM RUSSIA WITH LOVE: THE RAIL LINE WITH A HOLE IN IT

The rail line between Kemijärvi and the Russian border via Salla has certainly had a chequered past. During World War II, it was deemed of strategic military importance since it allowed the easy transport of troops and equipment all the way to the Russian front. Consequently, it was destroyed and rebuilt several times though it was finally blown up by retreating German forces in the closing stages of the war. The Soviets clearly understood the line's potential and, as part of war reparations, demanded the Finns rebuild and maintain the line should it ever be required for Moscow's future (military) use. Incredibly, the Finns carried out regular engineering work on the line at the Kremlin's behest until the Soviet Union's collapse in 1991. Today, though track is still largely in place all the way from Salla to the Russian border, the line has now been mothballed following the demise of freight services. However, in order to accommodate a predicted increase in container traffic from China via Russia and Lapland up to the Norwegian coast for shipment to the United States, grand plans have surfaced to reopen the rail line on the Russian side of the border. There's just one snag: 75km of track is missing and nobody knows where it's gone. While the truth may never be known about who ordered the line to be ripped up, rumours naturally abound: some believe the valuable iron rails were simply stolen by the Russian Mafia, while others maintain Moscow may not welcome the presence of foreigners close to its burgeoning military base in the town of Alakurtti, 70km east of the Finnish border, should the line ever reopen.

Salla Museum of War and Reconstruction (Sallan Sota-ja jälleenrakennusajan museo; ☺ Oct–Jun 10.00–17.00 Tue–Sat; Jul–Sep 10.00–17.00 Tue–Sun; €5) Next door to the train station at Savukoskentie 12, Salla's museum of war and reconstruction is housed in another low-slung, mustard-yellow timber construction, which once provided a home to railway workers and their families. Its erection in 1948 was ordered as part of the extensive post-war rebuilding programme across the municipality, designed to replace the buildings which had been either lost to the Soviets or razed by the Germans. The key points of the reconstruction are recounted in exhibitions within the museum – by 1950, for example, over 400 new farms, several schools and even a new church had been built.

Sallatunturi Having seen Salla's museum, most people head south out of town, 10km along Route 950 (Kuusamontie), to Salla's *raison d'être*: the ski resort of Sallatunturi, located between the eponymous twin peaks (478m and 472m). With its modest 15 slopes and six ski lifts, true, this is not Val D'Isère but that's what makes Sallatunturi special. The skiing here is rarely overcrowded and there are plenty of pistes to go round. Presently, the resort is concentrated around the peak at 472m (west of Route 950), though plans are afoot to develop the opposite summit, too, on the eastern side of the highway. In winter or summer, this is really the place to stay and all manner of activities can be arranged through the Salla Reindeer Park, which is just 4km away (see opposite).

🏠 **Where to stay**

🏠 **Spa Hotel Holiday Club Salla**
Revontulentie 2; ☏ 030 0870989; e hotelsales.
salla@holidayclub.fi; w holidayclubresorts.com/
en/Resorts/Salla. Actually 2 hotels in 1, this
extensive site contains both a regular hotel (the
main building) with modern, comfortable dbls
& a spa & sauna suite (this is known as Hotel
Revontuli), while the cabins elsewhere in the
grounds (known as the Holiday Club) offer the
chance to self-cater. Reindeer tend to wander at

will through the grounds here. Revontuli €€€ &
Holiday Club €€

🏠 **Sallatunturin Tuvat** Hangasjärventie
1; ☏ 016 831 931; e tuvat@sallatunturi.fi;
w sallatunturi.fi. With around 70 cabins ranging
in size from cosy 1-roomers with a shower to larger
apt-style numbers sleeping up to 8 people, there's
bound to be a cottage here to suit your needs.
Styles & décor are a touch more modern than
across the road at the Holiday Club, too. €€

✕ **Where to eat and drink** For a bite to eat, your best bet is the **Kiela** (Hangasjärventie 1; ☏ 016 831 931; €€€€) restaurant, on the site of Sallatunturin Tuvat, serving accomplished (recognised by France's Chaîne des Rôtisseurs in 2008), if rather pricey, Nordic cuisine using locally sourced ingredients: a generous plate of sautéed reindeer with mash, lingonberries and pickled gherkins, for example, is €28. Another choice is the **Revontuli** à la carte restaurant inside the Holiday Club/Revontuli (☺ Dec–Apr 17.00–21.00 Tue–Sun), where they also rustle up a good line in Lapland specialities such as reindeer, venison and locally caught fish: a large bowl of creamy salmon soup, for example, goes for €13.50, while smoked reindeer with Lapland cheese is €26.

For a **drink**, there are bars inside both hotels.

Six Fells Hiking Trail (35km; 2 days; difficult) Actually part of the much longer UKK hiking route, the Six Fells Hiking Trail (Kuudentunturinkevelyreitti in Finnish) begins just 6km south of Salla at the Sallan Maja roadside café, on Route 950 towards Sallatunturi. Spanning 35km, the trail takes in some stiff ascents of spruce-covered fells and offers mesmerising views from their bare summits out over both Finland and Russia. The trail terminates at Varpulahti Lake, 4km south of Niemelä, which, in turn, is 25km south of Sallatunturi.

Salla Reindeer Park ✳ (Sallan Poropuisto; m 040 3525 248; w sallareindeerpark. fi; ⊕ 10.00–17.00 daily) Within easy striking distance of Sallatunturi, Salla Reindeer Park, just 4km south of the ski resort at Hautajärventie 111, is a great way to see **reindeer** at any time of year. The park always has around 40 or so animals which you can see up close on a short walking tour of the site. Alternatively, winter **sleigh rides** (⊕ Dec–Apr) can be arranged through the park: a 3-hour trip costs €93 per person, while a longer 5-hour safari goes for €183. It's a little-known fact that only male reindeer are used to pull sleighs during the winter months because the females are pregnant. Alternatively, **husky sleds** are also available: €112 for a 2-hour trip, €266 for 6 hours.

In summer (Jun–Sep), the reindeer park can also arrange **canoe trips** or even rowing boat tours to the Russian border under the midnight sun. Full details of all activities are available on the website.

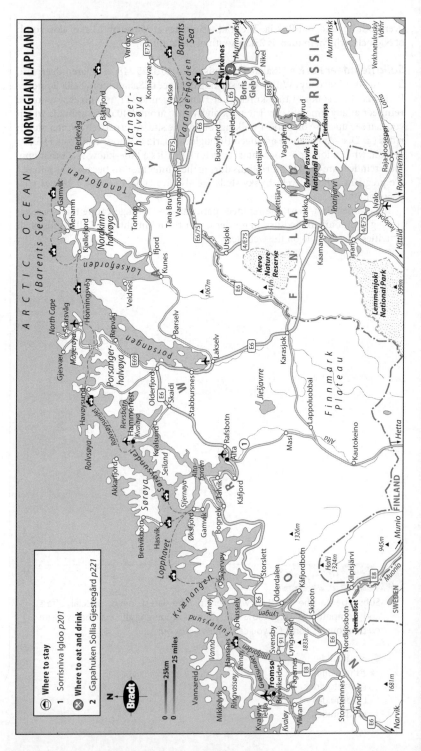

NORWEGIAN LAPLAND

Where to stay
① Sorrisniva Igloo p201

Where to eat and drink
② Gapahuken Sollia Gjestegård p221

0 ——— 25km
0 ——— 25 miles

ARCTIC OCEAN
(Barents Sea)

Barents Sea

RUSSIA

Murmansk

FINLAND

SWEDEN

North Cape

Hammerfest

Tromsø

Kirkenes

Øvre Pasvik National Park

Kevo Nature Reserve

Lemmenjoki National Park

Finnmark Plateau

Porsangerhalvøya

Nordkinnhalvøya

Varangerhalvøya

7

Norwegian Lapland: Tromsø to Kirkenes

A highly indented coastline of barren, tundra fells backed by monumental fjords, towering snow-capped mountains and rocky, windswept islands, makes Norwegian Lapland one of the most scenically rewarding places to travel in the whole of Europe. Quite unlike the densely forested heartlands of Swedish and Finnish Lapland where spruce and pine trees dominate the landscape, these coastal lands at the top of Europe, buffeted by the Arctic winds, are either completely devoid of trees or slavishly support a few dwarf species that have become specially adapted to the ferocious climate. It is a place where snow storms and blizzards sweeping in off the Arctic Ocean can persist for days during the long, dark winter, yet equally a land of exquisite beauty in spring and summer when the delicate flowers of the Arctic burst forth, profiting from the relentless 24-hour daylight of the midnight sun. The unforgiving geography of Norwegian Lapland is at its most awe-inspiring in the west, where the mountain chain reaches dizzying heights of 1,700m. Further east, the landscapes become less agitated, slowly falling away, to be replaced with plateaux of grey, weather-beaten rocks that slip effortlessly into the steely waters of the Arctic Ocean. Travel here is as rewarding as it is circuitous; often the quickest, shortest and most enjoyable way between two points is by boat, and it is with complete justification that the Hurtigruten coastal ferry, which plies the waters off the coast of Norwegian Lapland, is claimed to be the most beautiful sea voyage in the world.

Handsome Tromsø with its streets of old timber houses and 360° views of serrated peaks and mountaintops is well worth visiting. With good air and road links, it is an easy place to reach from elsewhere in the region. The town trades on its links with the Arctic and boasts a couple of excellent themed museums, in addition to an eclectic bar and restaurant scene – unusual for somewhere so far north. To the east, Alta's prehistoric rock carvings are exceptional, making the pint-sized town a worthwhile stop on the long journey to the North Cape, *the* destination in Norwegian Lapland. This remote, windswept headland at the very top of Europe has been big on the tourist trail for years. Souvenirs that bear that magic name and logo are much sought after and carry particular prestige – come here and be sure to buy the T-shirt to prove it.

From Europe's most northerly point, everywhere naturally lies south, albeit rather unsatisfyingly. However, take heart, one last place awaits: Kirkenes. A grubby former mining town hard on the border with Russia, Kirkenes is the end of the road. You're now as far east as Istanbul in Turkey and your nearest neighbour of any significance is Murmansk. Kirkenes's attraction is its proximity to Russia: there are daily buses across the border, a local market with *babushkas* selling their wares, as well as enjoyable boat trips down the river that forms the border between Russia and Norway. Should you be planning to cross the border into Russia, though, be sure to have arranged your visa in advance.

TROMSØ

The 'Gateway to the Arctic', as the city thrills in billing itself, Tromsø (Romsa in Sámi) is one of the undisputed highlights of Norwegian Lapland. Although geographically well out on a limb, it is worth making a special effort to get there to enjoy some rare urban sophistication, the like of which you won't find for miles around. Once known, quite ridiculously, as the Paris of the North, Tromsø can nevertheless boast a sophisticated café and restaurant culture, top hotels and several big-name stores; it has a couple of superb museums which will no doubt whet your appetite to learn more about the Arctic and maybe even to go there.

With a population of 73,000, Tromsø is the second-biggest town in Lapland, but if you talk to locals you will soon discover that they don't consider themselves to live in Lapland (despite the confusing fact that the town uses a reindeer as its emblem). For the record, Tromsø is the capital of Troms, a Norwegian province that is further north than both Sweden's Lappland and Finland's Lappi, two administrative regions, which, for people who live there, most definitely *are* part of Lapland. For most Norwegians living here, Norwegian Lapland doesn't begin until they cross the provincial border into Finnmark (the region which includes Alta, Karasjok, Kautokeino and all points east to Kirkenes). Most visitors seem happy to let the Norwegians argue among themselves, since as far as they are concerned everything above the Arctic Circle is Lapland – Swedish, Finnish or Norwegian.

SOME HISTORY Tromsø first enters the history books in 1252 when the northernmost church in the world was constructed here, in order to secure the surrounding coastal areas for Norway. Indeed, until the late 18th century, Tromsø consisted of little more than a church, its vicarage and several outlying farms and simple dwellings. In 1794, with a population of barely 80 souls, Tromsø was granted town status in an attempt to promote free trade across the north. Freed from restrictive trade practices previously imposed by Bergen and Trondheim, which until then had held a monopoly on trade with the north, the town began to prosper.

Despite suffering a naval attack by the British in 1812 during the Napoleonic Wars, the town continued to grow, largely due to the lucrative hunting of whales, seals and walrus off Svalbard that began in 1820. The harbour was often

TRØMSO
For listings, see from page 188

🛏 **Where to stay**

1	Clarion Collection With
2	Enter Tromsø City
3	Enter Tromsø Viking
4	Radisson Blu
5	Scandic Ishavshotel
6	Thon Polar

Off map
AMI
Tromsø Bed & Books
Tromsø Camping

✖ **Where to eat and drink**

7	Arctandria
8	Blå Rock
9	Du Verden
10	Emmas Drømmekjøkken
11	Fiskekompaniet Sjøsiden
12	Indie Kitchen
13	Kafe Globus
14	Kaffebønna
15	Kala
16	Ølhallen
17	Pastafabrikken
18	Presis
	Skarven Bar (see 7)
19	Smørtorget Kafe og Mat
20	Solid
21	Tromsø Tapas
22	Verdensteatret
	Vertshuset Skarven (see 7)

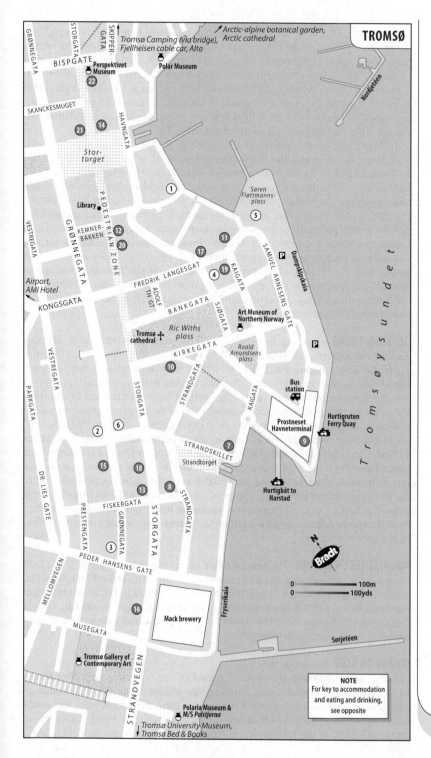

TROMSØ

GRØNNEGATA

STORGATA

SKIPPER-
GATA

BISPGATE

Tromsø Camping (via bridge),
Fjellheisen cable car, Alta

↗ Arctic-alpine botanical garden,
Arctic cathedral

Perspektivet
Museum
22

Polár Museum

Nordjetéen

SKANCKESMUGET

21 14

Stor-
torget

HAVNGATA

Library ●

1

Søren
Fløttmanns-
plass

5

GRØNNEGATA

KEMNER-
BAKKEN

12
20

PEDESTRIAN ZONE

17

11

VESTREGATA

FREDRIK LANGESGAT

4 19

KAIGATA

SAMUEL ARNESENS GATE

Dampskipskaia

P

Airport,
AMI Hotel

KONGSGATA

ADOLF TH GT

BANKGATA

SJØGATA

Art Museum of
Northern Norway

Tromsø
cathedral ✝

Ric Withs
plass

Roald
Amundsens
plass

P

VESTREGATA

STORGATA

KIRKEGATA

10

STRANDGATA

Bus
station

KAIGATA

PARKGATA

2 6

Prostneset
Havneterminal

Hurtigruten
Ferry Quay

DR LIES GATE

15

18

STRANDSKILLET

Strandtorget

7

9

13 8

STRANDGATA

Hurtigbåt to
Harstad

PRESTENGATA

FISKERGATA

GRØNNEGATA

STORGATA

3

PEDER HANSENS GATE

N
Bract

MELLOMVEGEN

16

Mack brewery

Fryserikaia

0   100m
0   100yds

MUSEGATA

Sørjetéen

Tromsø Gallery of
Contemporary Art

STRANDVEGEN

Polaria Museum &
M/S Palstjerna

Tromsø University Museum,
Tromsø Bed & Books

NOTE
For key to accommodation
and eating and drinking,
see opposite

full of British, Dutch, German and Russian ships drawn here by the rich pickings in the Arctic Ocean and by 1850, Tromsø had overtaken Hammerfest in the rush to harvest the waters of the north. Tromsø's links with the Arctic took a new turn in the early 20th century when expeditions to the north by Roald Amundsen, Fridtjof Nansen and Umberto Nobile departed from here. Indeed, it was from Tromsø that Amundsen set off by seaplane in search of his missing Italian competitor, Nobile, and other members of the Italia Expedition in 1928; Nobile returned, Amundsen did not. There is a statue in his memory erected in Tromsø harbour.

In May 1940, Tromsø served as the capital of free Norway for several weeks, welcoming the king and the Norwegian government, who fled here from Oslo as the resistance in the south showed signs of collapse. However, on 7 June 1940, they were forced to flee to England, continuing their fight against Germany in exile and urging the Norwegian people to resist the occupying forces in broadcasts on the BBC. Unlike many other places in the north of Norway, Tromsø escaped the scorched earth policy of the retreating German forces, which laid vast stretches of Lapland to waste. The post-war years were good to Tromsø: in 1964, the airport was opened, transforming communications with this part of the country in one stroke; and in 1972, the university was founded with specialist departments of Sámi studies and marine biology. Today the town is not only a service centre for the surrounding fishing and agricultural settlements but it is also the home of the Norwegian Polar Institute.

GETTING THERE Handling over half a million passengers every year, **Tromsø airport** (airport code TOS) is an excellent way of reaching this part of Lapland. There are direct **flights** from Oslo with SAS and Norwegian as well as from Stockholm in Sweden with SAS. The Norwegian airline Widerøe operates to Tromsø from various airports across the north of Norway; the flight to and from Kirkenes, for example, is well worth considering since it will save a one-way drive of 800km. Regular **shuttle buses** (w bussring.no/airport-express; 100NOK one-way/160NOK return) run into town from the airport terminal, while **local buses** 40 and 42 run into town (50NOK) from the bus stop in front of the airport car park. A **taxi** from the airport costs around 200NOK during the day on weekdays (prices increase at weekends and on weekday evenings). Coming from the south, the Hurtigruten **ferry** arrives at the quay in the town centre at 14.15; from the north it docks at 23.45. The Hurtigbåt **express passenger boat** from Harstad arrives 100m from the tourist office at an adjacent quay. All **buses** stop outside the tourist office, close to the ferry quay.

TOURIST INFORMATION The **tourist office** (Samuel Arnesens gate 5; ⤸77 61 00 00; e info@visittromso.no; w visittromso.no; ⏰ Jan–Mar 09.00–19.00 Mon–Fri, 10.00–18.00 Sat & Sun; Apr, May, Sep & Oct 09.00–16.00 Mon–Fri, 10.00–16.00 Sat; Jun & Jul 09.00–17.00 daily; Aug 09.00–17.00 Mon–Sat, 10.00–16.00 Sun; Nov & Dec 09.00–17.00 Mon–Fri, 10.00–16.00 Sat & Sun) is located within the new ferry terminal, Prostneset Havneterminal.

 WHERE TO STAY *Map, page 187*
Hotel accommodation in Norwegian Lapland can be expensive and rather bland. Particularly in the smaller towns, hotels are sometimes rather old 1960s buildings and consequently rather tired. Not so in Tromsø. Here, a cluster of great, top-notch hotels right on the harbourside means there's plenty of choice and standards are universally high. In short, if you are going to splurge and treat yourself, do it here.

🏠 **Clarion Collection With** Sjøgata 35–37; 📞 77 66 42 00; e cc.with@choice.no; w with. no. Pronounced 'vit' rather than the English 'with', this chi-chi harbourfront hotel is built on land reclaimed from the sea. Old-world charm meets modern Scandinavian design here in a perfect location right on the quayside. Be sure to choose one of the 40 rooms that have sea views. €€€€

🏠 **Enter Tromsø Viking** Grønnegata 18–20; 📞 77 64 77 30; e post@entertromso.no; w entertromso.no/en/hotels/viking-en. Part of a small chain of hotels & apts, each with their own character, Viking is a bright & airy little place with Nordic-style rooms & state-of-the-art bathrooms. Accommodation is a little on the cramped side, but prices are reasonable for the quality on offer. €€€€

✳ 🏠 **Radisson Blu** Sjøgata 7; 📞 77 60 00 00; e sales.tromso@radissonblu.com; w radissonblu. no. This waterfront hotel is one of the tallest buildings in town & definitely one of the most luxurious. Offering all the creature comforts associated with a leading chain – plush rooms & tasteful décor in neutral colours featuring a fresh mix of greys & whites. A truly amazing sauna suite, too, with fabulous views over the harbour from the saunas themselves. €€€€

🏠 **Scandic Ishavshotel** Fredrik Langesgate 2; 📞 77 66 64 00; e ishavshotel@scandichotels. com; w scandichotels.no/ishavshotel. A top-of-the-range hotel enjoying a wonderful harbourside location. Built to resemble the funnel & upper decks of a ship, this extravagant hotel is all chrome, glass & wood both inside & out. Rooms are generously proportioned, tastefully carpeted & contain nice touches of woodwork. Ask for one overlooking the harbour & it is hard to think of anywhere you'd rather be. The sumptuous b/fast buffet is one of the best you will find. €€€€

🏠 **Enter Tromsø City** Grønnegata 48; 📞 77 78 10 50; e post@entertromso.no; w entertromso. no/en/hotels/city-en. This place is a real find – great-value, contemporary-design dbls & apts in the city centre, all with self-catering facilities, including cooker, fridge & kettle. Dbls €€€ apts €€€€

🏠 **Thon Polar** Grønnegata 45; 📞 77 75 17 00; e polar@olavthon.no; w thonhotels.no. Smart budget rooms from this chain, which at its best (like here) offers good value for money. Located right in the heart of the centre, this is a sensible choice. €€€€/€€€

✳ 🏠 **Tromsø Bed & Books** Strandvegen 45 & 84; 📞 77 02 98 00; e booking@bedandbooks.no; w bedandbooks.no. Forget any notion of a hotel or even a regular B&B for that matter, here you'll find cosily decorated rooms in 2 typical Tromsø houses – in short, a home from home. Use of the bathroom & kitchen is shared – just like at home & you fix your own b/fast. Bed linen is an extra 50NOK. €€€

🏠 **AMI** Skolegata 24; 📞 77 62 10 00; e email@ amihotel.no; w amihotel.no. A pleasant mid-range hotel with comfortable though simply furnished rooms overlooking the town from a hilly location several blocks up behind the harbour; some rooms have private facilities & cost 100NOK more. €€

⚡ **Tromsø Camping** Arthur Arntzens veg 10, Tromsdalen; 📞 77 63 80 37; e post@ tromsocamping.no; w tromsocamping.no; 🕐 all year. Approx 50 cabins of varying sizes & standards plus camping. Get here by crossing the Tromsøbrua Bridge & heading southeast from the Ishavskatedralen; buses #20 & #24 come here – get off just after the cemetery at bus stop 'Båthavna' & then follow the river to the campsite. €€€

✖ **WHERE TO EAT AND DRINK** *Map, page 187*

Throughout Scandinavia, the distinction between cafés, bars and restaurants is rarely clear-cut. With a relatively small customer base, most places tend to offer a bit of everything in order to make enough money to survive and to pay their staff respectable wages. In Tromsø, things are a little different owing to the size of the town. However, most of the cafés and bars listed below also serve food.

Restaurants

✖ **Arctandria** Strandtorget 1; 📞 77 60 07 20; w skarven.no/restauranter/arctandria-sjomatrestaurant; 🕐 16.00–23.00 Mon–Sat.

High-class Arctic specialities in this elegant restaurant (upstairs from Vertshuset Skarven; page 190) which also has an extensive wine list. Expertly prepared mains include: pan-fried halibut with celery & mash, semi-dried stockfish (cod) with stewed carrot & bacon & whale steak with seasonal vegetables. €€

✕ **Du Verden** Samuel Arnesens gate 6; m 412 92 000; w duverden.no/tromso; ⏲ 11.00–23.00 Sun–Thu, 11.00–midnight Fri & Sat. A superb location right on the quayside overlooking the comings & goings in the harbour through floor-to-ceiling windows. The food here is as gorgeous as the setting: creamy soup of prawns & fish; smoked salmon salad & braised lamb shank with rosemary jus, as well as pizzas. *Mains start at 195NOK.* €€

✕ **Emmas Drømmekjøkken** Kirkegata 8; ☎ 77 63 77 30; w emmasdrommekjokken.no/en; ⏲ downstairs 11.00–22.00 Mon–Fri, noon–22.00 Sat; upstairs from 18.00 Mon–Sat. The exceptional cuisine here is among Tromsø's finest: downstairs (known as Emmas UNDER) is more café-style while upstairs is the formal restaurant. Up or down, the food is delicious: starters from 165NOK & mains from 255NOK. Menus change frequently but feature locally sourced produce prepared to international standards. The fish gratin, served at lunchtime in Emmas UNDER, is particularly delicious & good value at 185NOK. €€

✕ **Fiskekompaniet Sjøsiden** Killengrens gate; ☎ 77 68 76 00; w fiskekompani.no/en/eng; ⏲ 16.00–22.00 daily. Both traditional & modern seafood dishes on the accomplished menu at this pricey seafront (predominantly) fish restaurant which is widely regarded as the town's best: for example, a starter of salmon & scallop tartare with apple purée & rhubarb followed by pan-fried halibut in a creamy blue mussel sauce will make a delicious supper. A 3-course set menu costs 645NOK. €€

✕ **Indie Kitchen** Storgata 73; m 99 34 63 43; w restaurantindie.no; ⏲ 15.00–22.00 Mon–Thu, 15.00–23.00 Fri & Sat, 15.00–21.00 Sun. The chefs at this winning Indian restaurant grind their own spice mixes, which they claim gives their curries a truly authentic Indian flavour. A wide range of regional curries & Indian street-food snacks are served, including a mouth-watering butter chicken, lamb rogan josh & a zingy southern Indian prawn curry with cashews. *Mains around 230NOK.* €€

✕ **Kala** Grønnegata 36–46; ☎ 77 63 10 00 w kalarestaurant.no; ⏲ 15.00–21.00 Mon, 14.00–22.00 Tue–Thu, 14.00–23.00 Fri & Sat, 14.00–21.00 Sun. All your (expensive) southeast

Asian favourites, such as Thai sweet chilli chicken or Korean spicy pork. *Mains from 205NOK.* €€

✳ ✕ **Kafe Globus** Storgata 30; m 93 48 15 55; w globuskafe.no; ⏲ 10.00–20.00 Mon–Fri, 11.00–17.00 Sat. You should definitely eat at least once at this great little café serving a range of world cuisine. The signature dish is Eritrean *injera* (sourdough pancakes) served with spicy chopped lamb, spinach & cottage cheese as the 'Globus Plate' (205NOK). Alternatively, try the mouth-wateringly good chicken sandwich with Sri Lankan pineapple curry or the excellent Asian pumpkin soup with coconut milk & lime. There are always lots of vegetarian dishes on the menu & everything is cooked from scratch. €

✳ ✕ **Pastafabrikken** Sjøgata 17A; ☎ 77 67 27 82; w pastafabrikken.no/en; ⏲ 11.00–22.00 Mon–Sat, 14.00–22.00 Sun. Stylish to a T with its floor-to-ceiling windows & airy glass & wood interior, this great pasta & pizza restaurant really draws the crowds. There's seemingly every pasta concoction you could wish for from 155NOK; pizzas are from the same price. Order & collect your food at the bar. €

✕ **Tromsø Tapas** Stortorget 5; ☎ 77 68 27 27; w tromsotapas.no; 15.00–23.00 Mon–Sat. An extensive range of hot & cold tapas; all hot dishes are cooked over charcoal. Choose from hot dishes such as gratinated scallops, glazed pork ribs, or duck breast in blueberry sauce; cold options include dates wrapped in bacon & stuffed with manchego cheese, chorizo sausage with potatoes & red onion or smoked reindeer with flatbread. *Reckon on around 100–150NOK/dish.* €

✕ **Vertshuset Skarven** Strandtorget 1; ☎ 77 60 07 20; ⏲ 15.30–22.00 daily. Downstairs from Arctandria (page 189), this modern brasserie offers a range of good-value open sandwiches as well as a generous plateful of fresh prawns & a delicious fish stew. The prices are exceptionally good, the food excellent. €

Cafés and bars

⛾ **Kaffebønna** Stortorget 3; ☎ 77 63 94 00; w kaffebonna.no; ⏲ 07.30–18.00 Mon–Fri, 09.00–18.00 Sat, 10.00–18.00 Sun. Located in the main square at the eastern end of Storgata, this specialist coffee shop is where you will find Tromsø's best coffee & a mouth-watering selection of cakes & pastries, which are also available to take away from their bakery next door. €

Smørtorget Kafe og Mat Sjøgata 11; 08.00–17.00 Mon–Fri, 10.00–17.00 Sat, 11.00–17.00 Sun. An agreeably shabby-chic little place, renowned across town for its 2nd-hand furniture. It serves freshly baked bread & cakes, as well as a number of lunch specials &, all in all, is a great place to watch the world go by through the floor-to-ceiling windows. €

Solid Storgata 73; 10.00–02.00 Mon–Thu, 10.00–03.30 Fri & Sat, noon–02.00 Sun. Perfectly located on Tromsø's main pedestrian street, this place is a café by day serving a daily lunch special, though by evening it mutates into a popular bar with a great vibe & a good selection of cocktails & shorts. €

Verdensteatret Storgata 93B; 11.00–02.00 Mon–Thu, 11.00–03.30 Fri & Sat, 13.00–02.00 Sun. An artsy & airy café with orange walls & bar stools plus regular tables, attached to a cinema which first opened its doors in 1916. Popular with the city's gay community, too. €

Blå Rock Strandgata 14–16; 11.30–02.00 Mon–Thu, 11.30–03.30 Fri & Sat, 13.00–02.00 Sun. The place for rock 'n' roll. Signed pictures (& guitars) on the walls from greats like Elvis, the Rolling Stones & even REM. The largest selection of different beers in town. Also serves burgers. €

Presis Storgata 36; 77 68 10 20; w presistapas.no; 16.00–22.00 Tue–Sat. A chilled tapas bar with a dark interior that's a good place for a drink if you fancy a nibble or 2 at the same time. It's been around since 2004 & is a locals' favourite, so it's worth booking a table. €

Ølhallen Storgata 4; w mack.no/en/olhallen; 11.00–00.30 Mon–Thu, 11.00–01.30 Fri, 10.00–01.30 Sat. This noisy beer hall complete with stuffed polar bear is a Tromsø institution, attracting the city's hardened drinkers from early in the morning. It may not be the most genteel place for a drink but it certainly shows a darker side to Tromsø's (& northern Scandinavia's) character. €

Skarven Bar Strandtorget 1; 18.00 to late Tue–Thu, 15.00 to late Fri & Sat. One of the best watering holes in town, especially when the sun's shining, when people drape themselves over the extensive outdoor terrace taking the rays. Soft music & an altogether agreeable place for a quiet drink & chat. €

WHAT TO SEE AND DO It is a pleasure to wander around the streets and harbour area in Tromsø. Since the city was relatively untouched by World War II, there are plenty of old timber buildings, painted a mêlée of reds, greens and yellows, to please the eye – and, quite unusually for a town in Lapland, there's life on the streets in the evening. Although the city has a sizeable population, the centre is not big and is easily negotiated on foot. In fact, you can walk from one side of the central shopping area to the other in just over a quarter of an hour. It is a good idea to start your wandering down by the harbour, which is where most of the main hotels are located; from here you can head inland to take in the main pedestrian street before continuing west to one of the town's most enjoyable museums, Polaria.

Tromsø cathedral (Domkirke; Sjøgata 2; generally 13.00–15.00 Mon–Fri) In the town centre, the main sight is the *domkirke*, built in 1861 in Gothic Revival style, which dominates the surrounding streets from its imposing position in Stortorget off Kirkegata; for what it's worth, this is the northernmost Protestant cathedral in the world and the only one in Norway made of wood. The construction of the handsome timber building was part funded by the town's merchants who had grown rich on the trapping trade in the Arctic. Sadly, due to a lack of volunteers, the cathedral is usually closed. However, you can see the interior every afternoon and evening when **classical music concerts** are held here during the summer months (Jun & Jul 14.00 daily; Jun–mid Aug 23.00 daily; afternoon 80NOK & evening 190NOK).

Polar Museum * (Polarmuseet; Søndre Tollbudgata 11; 77 62 33 60; w en.uit.no/tmu/polarmuseet; Jun–Aug 09.00–18.00 daily; Sep–May 11.00–17.00 daily; 60NOK) Enjoying a prime location on the harbour front, Tromsø's Polarmuseet is housed in a former customs warehouse dating from 1830 and contains some of the most fascinating exhibits you will find in Lapland. It is fitting that Tromsø has an entire museum dedicated to its links with the Arctic, since the town owes much of its prosperity today to the hunters and trappers who based themselves here during the first half of the 19th century.

Ground floor The museum kicks off on the ground floor with an exhibition about trapping in the Arctic; beside the rather unsavoury mock display of a stuffed reindeer being slaughtered, there's information about the early Svalbard expeditions whose main target over a 25-year period was walruses. The hunts were ended when walrus numbers in Svalbard began to plummet. In the 20th century, the focus turned to polar bears and Arctic foxes; the latter were trapped on the inhospitable Norwegian island of Jan Mayen, the former on Svalbard. Sealing from ships was a common practice and began in Norway in the mid 1800s (it continued for around a hundred years) when seal skins were used to make shoes and rope and their blubber was boiled down to produce lighting and heating oil. Incidentally, a similar practice using pilot whale blubber was once commonplace in the Faroe Islands. Room 2 on the ground floor is given over to the life of trappers and hunters who lived on Svalbard in the 17th and 18th centuries. Although **Svalbard** was known during medieval times and appears in the Icelandic sagas by its understated Norse name, Svalbard (literally 'cold coast'), the islands were discovered in 1596 by Dutch explorer Willem Barentz (c1550–97; often Anglicised as William Barents), who sailed here in search of the Northeast Passage to China. His crew gave the islands their more common name, Spitsbergen, meaning 'pointed mountains'. Finds from Barentz's camp from the time, such as knives, gunpowder measures and an oil lamp, are on display. More remarkable, however, are the artefacts from a Russian trapping station in the west-coast settlement of Russekeila, probably dating from the 1700s, including boatbuilding tools, a frame for drying socks and even a clay pipe.

First floor Upstairs, one of the greatest explorers the world has ever known, **Roald Amundsen** (1872–1928), is given pride of place. After dropping out of university where he was studying medicine, Amundsen did everything possible to improve his qualifications as a polar explorer, first joining a sealing trip in the Arctic and then participating in an expedition to map the magnetic South Pole. It was during this voyage that he decided to lead an expedition to the **North Pole** through the Northwest Passage. Indeed, after buying the former sealing ship, *Gjøa*, in Tromsø in 1901, he sailed from Oslo (then called Christiania) to the North Pole where he spent two years collecting data. On arrival in Nome in Alaska in 1906, the *Gjøa* became the first vessel to sail through the Northwest Passage. However, it is Amundsen's race against Britain's Captain Robert Scott to reach the **South Pole** that really earned him international fame. He and four of his men reached the pole on 14 December 1911, over a month ahead of Scott's expedition, who died on their way back to base camp. Among a glorious selection of Amundsen's thermal underwear and other polar necessities, a series of evocative black-and-white photographs of the men and their expedition really bring the exhibition to life; the expressions on their faces clearly show the hardship they endured.

Amundsen's next goal was to reach the North Pole by air. In May 1926, he flew the airship, *Norge*, with an international crew of 16 members from Ny Ålesund in Svalbard across the Arctic Ocean and the North Pole, dropping the Norwegian, American and Italian flags at the pole as they crossed to Alaska. Amundsen had now planted the Norwegian flag on both poles and sailed both the Northwest and

Northeast passages. Just two years later when news reached Amundsen that one of his former crew members, Italian Umberto Nobile, had crashed while returning from the North Pole in the airship, *Italia*, Amundsen set out from Tromsø in the flying boat, *Latham*, to search for the missing explorer. Tragically, although Nobile and eight of his men returned to safety, radio contact with Amundsen was soon lost and he and his crew were never seen again.

Another Norwegian legend, at least in Tromsø, is also honoured on the first floor: Henry Rudi, known to his friends as 'the polar bear king'. Henry spent his first winter on Svalbard in 1908, when he managed to kill no fewer than 90 polar bears. That was just the start of his dubious career, and over a 40-year period he was responsible for the deaths of 713 polar bears in Svalbard, Greenland and the Norwegian Arctic island of Bjørnøya. Admired across the country for his bravery, Rudi was awarded the king's medal of honour for his work in the Arctic. He died in 1970.

Second floor The top floor is dedicated to another of Norway's polar greats, Fridtjof Nansen (1861–1930). Together with his colleague, Hjalmar Johansen, he set off in search of the North Pole by dog sled in March 1895 after his ship, *Fram*, had become locked in pack ice. Nansen's diary, various letters and atmospheric black-and-white photographs from the expedition, are on display here. However, it's the truly enormous polar bear skin, slung from the museum roof, which Nansen gave to Johansen once they had safely returned months later, that's the real eye-catcher.

Perspektivet Museum (Storgata 95; ✆77 60 19 10; w perspektivet.no; ⊕ 10.00–16.00 Tue–Fri, 11.00–17.00 Sat & Sun; free) From the Polarmuseet it's a short stroll west along Bispegata to reach one of Tromsø's best, but often overlooked, museums: Perspektivet. Predominantly a **photographic museum**, Perspektivet aims to recount the contemporary history of Tromsø and has a collection of 400,000 images to draw on. Exhibitions change frequently, though there is usually a section devoted to what's known as the 'Pomor trade' – commercial dealings between Russian fishermen and businessmen in the north of Norway which gave rise to a pidgin language '*russenorsk*' (see box, page 220). The building the museum occupies is also of interest as it was the teenage home of local writer, Sara Fabricius (1880–1974). After moving here from Oslo at the age of 13, Sara lived in Tromsø for five years – a period which left clear marks on her literary work; her breakthrough came under the pseudonym of Cora Sandel with the publication of her debut novel, *Alberte and Jacob*, in 1926. A modest exhibition in the museum recounts key moments in Fabricius's life – today she's regarded as one of Norway's most significant authors.

TROMSØ INTERNATIONAL FILM FESTIVAL

For the best part of 30 years, the Tromsø International Film Festival has been drawing film buffs to this part of Norwegian Lapland every January. In addition to the mainstream programme, where films are shown either in English or with English subtitles, there are generally also productions from filmmakers across the Arctic rim – northwest Russia, Canada and Alaska. Films are shown both inside the Verdensteater cinema (Storgata 93) and at a handful of locations around the town, as well as on an outdoor snow screen erected in the town centre. More information is available at w tiff.no.

Art Museum of Northern Norway✳ (Nordnorsk kunstmuseum; Sjøgata 1; ☎77 64 70 20; w nnkm.no; ⊕ 10.00–17.00 daily; 80NOK) A 10-minute walk back along Storgata, turning south into Kirkegata, will bring you to Tromsø's worthwhile Nordnorsk kunstmuseum. With northern Norway as the dominant theme, the museum hosts permanent and temporary exhibits of paintings and sculptures from the early 19th century to the present day. Though the museum's permanent collection is not especially large, it is buoyed up by frequent loans from other museums. All the big names in the world of northern Norwegian art are here though: Axel Revold, Willi Midelfart and Kjeld Gabriel Langfeld, to name but a few. Particularly pleasing is *Morgen* by Revold (1927), which portrays a naked youth lying by the fjord, dreamily gazing out over the awe-inspiring nature of his homeland. Look out, too, for *Laestadius Teaching the Laplanders* by François-Auguste Biard (1798–1882) for an artistic impression of the fur-clad revivalist preacher, Lars Levi Laestadius, and his work in Lapland, which is enough to put the fear of God into anyone. Exhibitions change frequently but the museum always displays both its paintings by Edvard Munch (1863–1944) *Portrait of Mrs Schwarz* and *Parisian model*; *Winter, Reine in Lofoten* by Otto Sinding (1842–1909); and *Trissa at work* by Christian Krohg (1852–1925).

Tromsø Gallery of Contemporary Art (Tromsø Kunstforening; Muségata 2; w tromsokunstforening.no; ⊕ noon–17.00 Wed–Sun; free) There's more contemporary art for your perusal at Tromsø Kunstforening, which displays changing exhibitions of modern art by Norwegian and international artists. The gallery is housed in a handsome Neoclassical building dating from the late 1890s, opposite the Polaria Museum.

Polaria Museum (Hjalmar Johansgata 12; ☎77 75 01 00; w polaria.no; ⊕ mid-May–Aug 10.00–19.00 daily; Sep–mid-May 10.00–18.00 daily; 145NOK) At the opposite end of town, the Polaria Museum is an easy stroll of 10 minutes or so from the town centre; simply follow Storgata west past the Mack brewery (see below). Dedicated to the pristine nature of the Arctic, the museum's key exhibit is the absorbing 15-minute panoramic film of the flora and fauna of Svalbard. The film was mostly shot from the air by helicopter and when viewed on the five giant 180° surround-screens in the specially constructed cinema inside the museum, you get a dizzying sense that you are there, skimming across the tundra, banking hard round every mountaintop. But it is the seals in the museum's aquarium that really steal the show. You can get up close to them by walking through a glass tunnel that slices through their watery habitat. The seals are fed at 12.30 and then again at 15.30. Several smaller tanks contain examples of much of the marine life of the Arctic – everything from cod to starfish. Immediately outside, **M/S Polstjerna** (w en.uit.no/tmu/polstjerna; ⊕ mid-Jun–mid-Aug 10.00–17.00 daily; 40NOK), makes an incongruous addition to the museum. After admiring the living seals inside, it seems strange then to be proudly presented with a former sealing ship for inspection and onboard perusal; between 1949 and 1981, the Norwegians used the *Polstjerna* on expeditions that killed a total of 100,000 seals.

Mack Brewery (Macks ølbryggeri; w mack.no/en/visit; ⊕ tours 14.00 & 15.30 Mon–Fri, 14.30 Sat; 180NOK) You guessed it, yet another 'northernmost in the world' boast. This time the title goes to Macks ølbryggeri, the Mack brewery, established by local bigwig Ludvig Mack in 1877, and which still today operates as a family-run concern. The beer of choice across the whole of Norwegian Lapland,

Mack really has established itself as a market leader over the years and, in an attempt to maintain its position, is constantly reinventing labels and slogans, championing its spurious links to the Arctic and the polar bear. It seems to work. Enjoyable hour-long tours of the brewery include a valuable half-litre of the golden nectar and a less than gorgeous badge; tours start and end at the Ølhallen pub, Storgata 4.

Out of the town centre Though most of Tromsø's attractions are all located within the confines of the town centre and are easily reached on foot, there are a couple of other sights, a little further afield, which are worthy of your attention and easily reached on the bus.

Arctic-alpine Botanical Garden (Arktisk-alpin botanisk hage; w uit.no/tmu/ botanisk; ⊕ dawn to dusk; free) Lovers of all things bright and beautiful won't want to miss the world's most northerly botanical gardens – the Arktisk-alpin botanisk hage is situated 4km north of the town centre, adjacent to Tromsø University's Breivika campus, and easily accessed by bus #20. You'll find plants from each of the world's continents in the gardens, in bloom between May and October. A good idea is to take bus #20 to the gardens, visit the Plantarium, follow the Geology Walk through the birch forest to the gardens proper, and then return to town on bus #42.

Arctic cathedral (Ishavskatedralen; Hans Nilsens veg 41; w ishavskatedralen. no; ⊕ Jun–mid-Aug 09.00–19.00 daily; mid-Aug–Dec 14.00–18.00 daily, Jan–Mar 13.00–18.00, Apr & May 14.00-18.00 daily; 50NOK) The most audacious structure by far in Tromsø is the startlingly white, concertina-like Ishavskatedralen, located on the southern side of the cantilevered Tromsøbrua Bridge (take buses #20 and #24 from the town centre or walk over the bridge). Built in 1965 and inspired by the angular shapes of the Arctic winter ice, the cathedral is composed of 11 immense triangles of white concrete, representing the remaining 11 apostles after

WINTER ACTIVITIES IN TROMSØ

Owing to changes in the course of the Gulf Stream and, consequently, the herring shoals, **humpback** and **killer whales** can now be seen in the fjords off Tromsø between November and late January/early February. Several companies offer **whale-watching tours**, either by regular boat or by RIB inflatable, with prices starting at 1,550NOK per person; all tours can be booked at w visittromso.no. Remember, though, that there's full polar night in Tromsø between 27 November and 15 January so daylight (actually a sort of golden twilight) is limited to just a few hours around midday since the sun doesn't rise above the horizon. As elsewhere in Lapland, **dog-sledding** and **reindeer-sleigh** trips can be fixed up too, with prices starting at 1,750NOK and 1,450NOK respectively. Full details are on the tourist office website. Keen to win its share of the lucrative **northern lights** tourism market, Tromsø also offers a bewildering array of tours which essentially come in two forms: either, the chance to go off **hunting for the aurora** (by bus, minibus or boat) or, alternatively, the option of settling into one place and simply **waiting for the light show to begin**. A northern lights chase by bus, for example, costs 1150NOK, while a trip to Buvik Beach, where you wait for the lights sitting around a camp fire, costs 1,550NOK. Full details are on the tourist office website.

the betrayal. The entire east wall is formed by a huge stained-glass window, one of the largest in Europe, portraying the Return of Christ. Have a glance, too, at the organ which is designed to resemble a ship when viewed from below. Free organ recitals are held daily in June and July at 14.00. Nightly midnight sun concerts also take place every evening between June and the middle of August at 23.00.

Tromsø University Museum (Norges arktiske universitetsmuseum; Arctic University of Norway; Lars Thørings veg 10; w uit.no/tmu; ⊕ Jun–Aug 09.00–18.00 daily; Sep–May 10.00–16.30 Mon–Fri, noon–15.00 Sat, 11.00–16.00 Sun; 70NOK) Located about 3km south of the town centre, Tromsø University Museum is the place to come for your first encounter with Norwegian Lapland's Sámi culture. The museum hosts a decent and thoughtful exhibition about the region's original inhabitants with displays of traditional costumes, tools and other quintessentially Sámi knick-knacks. However, it's the collection of **medieval church art** which really catches the eye. Collected from churches across the north of Norway, the carvings date from the time of the Reformation. There's also a chance to learn more about the northern lights – an exhibition on the aurora explains how and when the phenomenon occurs. Bus #37 comes here from the town centre, or, alternatively, you can walk here in around 30–40 minutes.

The Fjellheisen cable car (w fjellheisen.no; ⊕ Jun & Jul 10.00–01.00 daily; Aug–May 10.00–23.00 daily; 150NOK one-way; 210NOK return) Before leaving Tromsø, it's worth making every effort to get over to the cable car, across the Tromsøbrua Bridge, for an unforgettable trip to the summit of Storsteinen peak (421m), where there's also a café. From the base at Solliveien 12, the cable car runs every half-hour up the mountain that has views out over the whole of the town. To get here from the town centre, take bus #26 but note that the cable car doesn't run in poor weather.

Seakayaking and boat trips Tromsø's island location makes it an ideal base from which to explore the coastal waters of this part of northern Norway. Between mid-May and August, a whole host of kayaking tours are available, all of them bookable at w visittromso.no/booking. Options range from a seakayaking day trip past remote fishing villages (1,200NOK) to an overnight tour in search of the midnight sun (9,875NOK inc overnight camping in yurts). Experienced guides accompany each tour. Alternatively, and somewhat less energetically, Tromsø also offers a wide choice of boat trips: a fishing trip off Tromsø (from 1,450NOK); an Arctic fjord cruise with the chance of seeing white-tailed eagles, seals and porpoises (1,550NOK); and a variety of sightseeing tours by RIB inflatable (from 750NOK) – and these are just some of the options. Generally, the boat trips operate a slighter longer season than the seakayaking – usually April/May to September.

MOVING ON FROM TROMSØ The Hurtigruten **ferry** leaves from the quay beside the Scandic Ishavshotel. Departure times are 18.30 northbound for Hammerfest (arrival 05.15), Honningsvåg (arrival 11.15) for the North Cape, and Kirkenes, a total journey of 40 hours or so; southbound the Hurtigruten leaves at the unsociable hour of 01.30 for Harstad (arrival 08.00) and the Vesterålen and Lofoten islands. Incidentally, the hotel has unofficially agreed to store luggage during the day free of charge for passengers leaving on the 01.30 departure. If you have a drink in the hotel while waiting for the boat, you will see it arrive outside and can make a last-minute dash without waiting outside in the cold. The Hurtigbåt **express passenger boats** leave for Harstad between two and four times daily (Mon–Fri) and twice daily at the weekend. The quay is adjacent to the Hurtigruten; timetables are at w 177troms.no.

Daily buses leave the bus station outside the tourist office for **Narvik**, a 4-hour journey, and **Alta**, a ride of around 2½ hours; timetables are at w tromskortet.no.

Between June and mid-September there is a daily bus to **Finland** departing at 07.25 (Norwegian time) and running via Kilpisjärvi (11.00 Finnish time), Muonio (13.50), Kittilä (15.30) and Rovaniemi train and bus stations (around 17.30); detailed

THE TWELFTH MAN – EXCEPTIONAL BRAVERY IN WARTIME LAPLAND

Wartime resistance fighter Jan Baalsrud (pronounced bowls-rood; b1917) is one of northern Norway's greatest heroes. In the face of quite extraordinary odds and ultimate personal sacrifice, which involved amputating his own toes without anaesthetic, Baalsrud fled across the province of Troms, pursued relentlessly by occupying Nazi forces for over two months, before finally reaching neighbouring neutral Sweden, with the help of local Sámi and their reindeer.

Baalsrud and 11 other Norwegian resistance fighters had originally been trained by the British to blow up a German aircraft control tower in northern Norway. However, their operation, which took place in spring 1943, became compromised – he was the only one of the 12 to survive a German attack on their boat as it approached the Norwegian shore. Fleeing for his life, Baalsrud dived into the icy waters of the Norwegian Sea, losing one of his shoes in the process – a seemingly inconsequential event that would have terrible consequences.

From late March to early June Baalsrud was on the run, his physical condition worsening. Severe frostbite, gangrene and snow blindness rendered him totally dependent on the kindness of local people, who risked their own lives in helping the commando on his journey to Sweden. While sheltering in a hut north of Skibotn, Baalsrud was forced to cut off one of his big toes and part of another toe to stop the spread of gangrene. Later, close to death and in a cave in the mountains high above Skibotn (where he had been hiding from the Germans for almost a month), he amputated his remaining nine toes to save his feet from gangrene.

Having successfully evaded German patrols, Baalsrud was finally rescued from the cave by locals and handed into the care of local Sámi, whose reindeer pulled him across Finland and ultimately into Sweden, where he was flown by seaplane to hospital in Boden.

After the war, Jan Baalsrud was awarded the British MBE and Norway's St Olav's Medal, together with Oak Branch, in recognition of his outstanding bravery. He lived for over 25 years in Tenerife before returning to Norway shortly before his death in 1988, aged 71. His ashes are buried in the churchyard in Manndalen (just off the E6 around 30km northeast of Skibotn), in a grave close to the entrance. The grave is shared with one of the local men who helped him escape to Sweden, and the simple yet poignant inscription on the headstone reads 'Thank you to everyone who helped me to freedom in 1943'.

In late July an eight-day annual remembrance walk retraces Baalsrud's escape route across Troms, covering a remarkable 200km.

timetable information is available at w eskelisen.fi. From December to March, daily scheduled buses run from Tromsø to Alta via Kilpisjärvi, Kaaresuvanto, Hetta and Kautokeino until March (see box, page 131).

Flights to Svalbard and all points east
Other than Oslo, Tromsø is the only place in Norway with direct flights to Svalbard. SAS operate regular services to the main settlement, Longyearbyen (airport code LYR); full details about the islands and how to get there are contained in *Svalbard: The Bradt Travel Guide*, which is the definitive source of information on the Norwegian Arctic. Even if you are not detouring to Svalbard, it is well worth considering flying to destinations east of Tromsø since distances are comparable to similar journeys you might undertake to cross entire countries in central Europe; for example, Tromsø to Alta alone is 405km. The plucky Norwegian airline Widerøe (w wideroe.no) operates to some extremely remote airstrips across the north of the country and has some attractively competitive fares if booked in advance.

Heading east by road and ferry
Take one look at a road map of this part of Norway, and you will soon realise how difficult road transport can be. If you are heading east from Tromsø by car for Alta and destinations beyond you will save yourself a drive of around 120km by using two car ferries to help you cross the fjords of Ullsfjorden and Lyngen, which inconveniently get in the way of all road journeys east, forcing the main highway, the E8, into a lengthy detour. Although it is no faster to take the ferries, and works out more expensive, it is more than worth it because the ferries not only break up a very long journey, but they also afford views of some of the most dramatic mountains in northern Norway. First, head out of Tromsø on the **E8** (synonomous with the E6 at this point) and then turn left at Fagernes on to **Route 91** heading for the first ferry from **Breivikeidet** to **Svensby**; departures are roughly hourly and take 20 minutes. Once in Svensby continue on Route 91 heading east for the next ferry from **Lyngseidet** to **Olderdalen**; once again this ferry sails roughly hourly and is timed to connect with the arrival of the previous ferry into Svensby, giving you enough time to drive between the two; the crossing is 35 minutes. From Olderdalen, continue by the E6 northeast to Alta, a distance of around 230km. Timetables for both ferries are at w tromskortet.no.

ALTA AND AROUND

KÅFJORD Just 20km before Alta, you'll reach the tiny village of Kåfjord, at the head of the fjord of the same name. A mere dot on the map maybe, yet this little settlement has two compelling stories to tell. Not only was Kåfjord the scene of a daring **Allied raid** on the **battleship** *Tirpitz*, which the Germans had hidden away in the well-concealed fjord, but, it's also the resting place of two **Sámi men** who were **beheaded** following the Kautokeino rebellion of 1852 (page 156). Their sorry graves in the churchyard mark the final chapter in a little-known scandal which the Sámi, at least, have not forgotten – nor forgiven.

What to see and do
Kåfjord church and graveyard Signed from the E6 highway, Kåfjord's handsome timber church, completed in 1837, was built in Neogothic style by the English, who had begun copper mining in this part of Lapland ten years previously. For over 50 years, the church served the small English community that lived here;

behind the church, even today, you'll find several of their graves. The British soldiers, who died in the attack on the *Tirpitz* in 1943 (see opposite), are also remembered close to the graveyard entrance.

However, the churchyard is better known among the Sámi for two other graves, namely, those of **Aslak Hætta** and **Mons Somby** who were beheaded in Alta on 14 October 1854, for their part in the **Kautokeino rebellion** two years earlier. A small hill on Torsvei, in the Midtbakken district of Alta, is where the **executions** took place, though, tellingly, no memorial denotes the event or the location. The probable resting place of the bodies is marked by two headstones, which are totally isolated from the main graveyard and the church, down a steep slope off to the left of the entrance. At the time of their interment, Norwegian law stated that anyone condemned to death may only be buried 'on the dark side of the church', ie: the north side, in the shadow of the church. In 1996, members of the men's families managed to locate Hætta and Somby's heads in a collection of skulls held by Copenhagen University. Duly returned, the families requested that the heads be reunited with the men's bodies and they are now buried where the gravestones stand today. A conciliatory offer by the local priest to erect a memorial stone in the main part of the graveyard was unceremoniously rejected by the men's families. Though the boundary of the original graveyard is, in theory at least, marked by the posts which stand just behind the two graves, their location at the foot of the slope (the level of the main graveyard has since been raised) only adds to the poignancy of how scandalously these two men were treated in both life and death. Here is perhaps the most tangible evidence of the marginalisation of the Sámi.

You'll find the grave of Carl Johan Ruth, the Swedish-born merchant and shopkeeper of Kautokeino, who died following the rebellion, located to the rear and to the right of the church.

Tirpitz museum (m 92 09 23 70; w tirpitz-museum.no; ⊕ mid-Jun–Aug 10.00–17.00 daily; 100NOK) Just beyond the churchyard and, once again, well signposted, you'll come across the informative *Tirpitz* museum, which is essentially the private collection of local man, Even Blomkvist. The Germans used Kåfjord as an Arctic hideaway for the *Tirpitz* and other battleships during World War II, in order to attack the Allied convoys which sailed off the northern Norwegian coast laden with supplies to be landed in Murmansk. It was while the *Tirpitz* was sheltering in Kåfjord between March 1943 and November 1944 that the British attempted a daring submarine raid on the ship on 22 September 1943. Though the attack failed to sink the *Tirpitz*, she was badly damaged; she finally sank during another raid, this time in Tromsø, on 12 November, 1944. The complete story of the *Tirpitz* is told in a 25-minute English-language documentary, shown in the museum, narrated by respected British journalist, Ludovic Kennedy. Elsewhere in the museum, you'll find a scale model of the battleship, personal effects of the crew on board including shaving brushes, toothpaste and Reichsmark banknotes – as well as splinters from the British bombs used against the ship.

ALTA Despite its dramatic setting at the head of the eponymous fjord, Alta is not one of Norwegian Lapland's most attractive towns. Post-war reconstruction has done the place few aesthetic favours and today Alta consists of a rash of ugly concrete blocks that loom either side of the main E6 as it weaves through the settlement over a distance of 2–3km. If there is a town centre it is the gaggle of ten or so streets that lie south of the E6 called **Alta Sentrum**. Here you will find Alta's pedestrianised shopping street, Markedsgata, lined with shops, restaurants, a couple of hotels and the main shopping centre, AMFI. It's here, too, you'll find Alta's new pride and joy, the Northern Lights Cathedral. From Alta Sentrum it is roughly 1.5km southwest along the main road, known as Altaveien, to the town's only other area of note, **Bossekop**. Equally architecturally challenged, this diminutive area of suburban streets was once home to Dutch whalers who settled here in the 17th century; indeed, the place name is derived from a Sámi word meaning 'whale bay'. Today, it

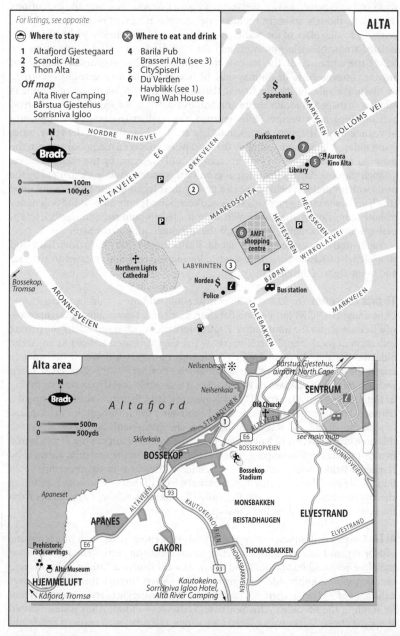

is the location of Alta church, which dates from 1858 (sadly, badly damaged during the war), a handy supermarket and a couple more hotels.

As drab as Alta itself may be, it does have a couple of saving graces. Indeed, one attraction is of world-class: the most extensive area of **prehistoric rock carvings** in northern Europe dating from between 6,000 and 2,000 years ago are to be found just outside the town centre. Now added to the UNESCO World Heritage List, the 5,000 carvings known as petroglyphs were carved into the coastal rocks at the head of Altafjorden by the area's first settlers and depict, among other things, the hunting of reindeer, elk and bear during the Stone Age. Alta is the location for another of Lapland's icehotels, the **Sorrisniva Igloo Hotel**, a smaller and altogether more agreeable version of the more commercialised Jukkasjärvi original in Sweden, which makes a highly unusual overnight accommodation choice in winter (see below).

Getting there Alta is 240km from the North Cape, 571km from Kirkenes and 405km from Tromsø; it is a major transport hub for this part of western Finnmark and sooner or later you are likely to wind up here. Direct **buses** run to Alta from Tromsø to the west, from Gievdneguoika (for Kautokeino) to the south and from Karasjok to the east. There are buses to and from Honningsvåg (change here for the North Cape) and Hammerfest to the north; timetables can be found w snelandia. no. All services call at the bus station between Markveien and Dalebakken in Alta Sentrum and buses to the east make a stop at the airport. Alta **airport** (code ALF) is useful for flights to and from Oslo with SAS and Norwegian as well as regional services to Tromsø, Kirkenes and a good few other smaller airstrips with Widerøe.

Although it is possible to **walk** from the airport into town (a distance of around 4km) by simply following the main E6 up the hill, there are several buses that run into town: the **town bus**, known as Bybussen, runs roughly once an hour along the main road outside the airport (62NOK into town; 33NOK if bought via the Snelandia app); there is also a dedicated **airport bus**, Flybussen (same prices); plus intermittent **long-distance buses** also call in at the airport; departure times are posted up inside the terminal building and are online at w snelandia.no.

Tourist information Alta's **tourist office** can be found in the town centre at Labyrinten 3 (m 99 10 00 22; e post@visitalta.no; w visitalta.no; ⏰ Jun–mid-Aug 09.00–20.00 daily; mid-Aug–mid-Feb & Apr–mid-Jun 08.30–16.00 Mon–Fri; mid-Feb–Mar 09.00–18.00 daily).

🏠 **Where to stay** *Map, opposite, unless otherwise stated*
Alta has a choice of several central hotels as well as a number of campsites; it is worth booking ahead in summer when the town fills up with coach parties breaking the long journey up to the North Cape.

🏠 **Altafjord Gjestegaard** Bossekopveien 19; ☎78 43 19 60; e email@altafjordgs.no; w altafjordgs.no. Comfortable dbl rooms with private facilities (some with sea views) at this small guesthouse down in Bossekop. It's worth asking about special deals as it's a little off the beaten track. €€€€
🏠 **Sorrisniva Igloo Hotel** [map, page 184] Sorrisniva, 20km south of Alta; ☎78 43 33 78; e info@sorrisniva.no; w sorrisniva.no; ⏰ late

Dec–early Apr. Located on the banks of the Alta River & made entirely of snow & ice; there's a shuttle bus for overnight guests from Alta. Each room contains a block of snow & ice, topped with reindeer hides, where you bed down for the night inside a snug sleeping bag. Come here for the experience, not a good night's sleep. €€€€
🏠 **Thon Alta** Labyrinten 6; ☎78 48 49 00; e alta.resepsjon@olavthon.no; w thonhotels. no/alta. Located above the main AMFI shopping

centre in the pedestrian centre, this new hotel is right in the thick of things & makes a good choice if you want to stay centrally. The modern rooms are brightly decorated in warm oranges & greens. €€€€

🏠 **Scandic Alta** Løkkeveien 61; 📞78 48 27 00; e alta@scandichotels.com; w scandichotels.no. A vast, white hulk of a building in the heart of town offering everything you'd expect from a top-notch hotel. Rooms here are decorated in modern style with wooden floors & Nordic décor; rooms on the upper levels have great views of the town & fjord. The hotel is popular with coach parties in summer

so be sure to book well in advance. €€€€/€€€

🏠 **Bårstua Gjestehus** Kongleveien 2A; m 99 33 88 89; e post@baarstua.no; w baarstua.no. A 10min walk north of the town centre, this cosy little guesthouse has just 8 decent-sized rooms, all with a kitchenette & private bathroom. €€€

⛺ **Alta River Camping** Steinfossen 5; 📞78 43 43 53; e post@alta-river-camping.no; w alta-river-camping.no; ⏰ all year. The best of the town's campsites located 4km south of town beside the river on Route 93 towards Kautokeino & in operation since 1968. Cabins & dbl rooms with shared facilities also available. €

✖ Where to eat and drink *Map, page 200*

✖ **Brasseri Alta** Labyrinten 6; 📞78 49 40 00; ⏰ 11.00–23.00 Mon–Thu, 11.00–01.00 Fri, noon–01.00 Sat, 16.00–23.00 Sun. Beggars can't be choosers when it comes to finding somewhere to eat in Alta. This is the restaurant inside the Thon &, to be honest, it does a decent, if rather expensive, job of staving off the hunger pangs: starters of mussel bisque or reindeer heart are both excellent, as are mains of fish of the day or beef tenderloin. €€€

✖ **Du Verden** Markedsgata 21; m 45 90 82 13; w duverden.no/alta; ⏰ 10.00–midnight Mon–Sat, noon–22.30 Sun. A stylish brasserie-cum-lounge bar with both sofa seating & regular tables. On the menu you'll find blue mussels, king crab, fish stew, reindeer steak & a creamy pasta dish with chicken & bacon among other things. €€

✖ **Havblikk** Bossekopveien 19; m 90 13 33 8; ⏰ 11.00–20.00 Mon, 11.00–22.00 Tue–Fri, 15.00–23.00 Sat, 14.00–20.00 Sun. A snug little restaurant inside the Altafjord Gjestegaard down in Bossekop which lives up to its name 'sea view'.

Serves a good range of fish & reindeer dishes & is worth looking up if you find yourself in this part of Alta. €€

✖ **CitySpiseri** Markedsgata 3; m 99 11 24 46; ⏰ 11.00–01.00 Mon–Thu, 11.00–03.00 Fri & Sat. A modern & airy bistro, attached to the cinema, serving the likes of stir-fried beef satay, omelettes, fish & chips, chicken salad & smoked reindeer burgers. There's outdoor seating, too, on the main street in summer. €

✖ **Wing Wah House** Markedsgata 4; 📞78 43 37 00; w wingwahhouse.com; ⏰ 15.00–22.00 Mon–Thu, 11.00–23.00 Fri & Sat. Stylish Chinese restaurant that also does take-away, serving all your favourites, such as spring rolls, satay beef & chicken with peanuts at reasonable prices. €

♀ **Barila Pub** Markveien 10; ⏰ 11.00–01.00 Sun–Thu, 11.00–03.00 Fri & Sat, 18.00–01.00 Sun. More bar rather than cosy pub, the interior here is rather plain & simple but it's a fair enough place for a drink & has outdoor seating on the main street in summer. €

What to see and do Aware of the vast potential that exists around northern lights tourism, Alta has ramped up its game, eager to steal the lucrative tourist krone, away from places like Tromsø. Rather grandly, the town now bills itself as 'The City of Northern Lights', and has even built the **Northern Lights Cathedral** (Nordlyskatedralen; w nordlyskatedral.no; ⏰ mid-Aug–mid-Jun 11.00–15.00 Mon–Fri, mid-Jun–mid-Aug 09.00–19.00 Mon–Sat, 13.00–19.00 Sun;50NOK) to stake its claim – now, the main sight in town. The Nordlyskatedralen is located at the western end of the main pedestrian street, Markedsgata, and its sleek and shimmering titanium exterior is visible from across town. The spire twists and turns in the form of a spiral above the main structure of the cathedral and has been designed to resemble the shifting movement of the aurora in the night sky. Inside, the interior is stark: bare concrete walls and a floor of Norwegian oak shaped into tiny rectangles. It is dominated by a massive bronze statue of Christ, nearly 4.5m tall, head reclined and arms outstretched, staring up to heaven. As you enter the cathedral you walk through a circular pillar, which rises into the spiralling tower. Inside the pillar you'll see a suspended golden ladder (designed to resemble Jacob's Ladder), while the pillar's outer walls are adorned with ornate, golden mosaics of the 12 apostles. Inside the Nordlyskatedralen, a new exhibition, **BorealisAlta** (w borealisalta.no; ⊕ mid-Aug–mid-Jun 11.00–15.00 Mon–Fri, mid-Jun–mid-Aug 09.00–19.00 Mon–Sat, 13.00–19.00 Sun; 150NOK) aims to explain the science behind the northern lights as well as recounting some of the stories and myths surrounding the phenomenon in Sámi culture through a series of interactive displays.

Having seen the Nordlyskatedralen and BorealisAlta, Alta town centre is not going to hold your attention for long, but while you are here it is worth strolling up and down the pedestrianised centre and having a look around the two **shopping centres** in Alta Sentrum: Parksenteret and AMFI. Inside both, you will find an impressively large array of shops for a town with a population of barely 15,000 people, including an outlet of Vinmonopolet and a bookshop selling local maps inside the larger AMFI. If you are here in winter, keep an eye out for the well-executed ice sculptures that adorn the central shopping area; anything from pop stars to snowmen can make an appearance.

Boat trips from Alta Alta itself is not overburdened with sights and attractions, so, while you're here, why not consider getting out of town and taking a boat trip to see some of the unspoilt coastline hereabouts. Boat rental is available from several outlets, both with and without a skipper. There are various options available ranging from sea-fishing tours to a trip by boat up to the North Cape. Prices are on request and all companies are open to suggestions as to where you'd like to go and what you'd like to do.

Alta Havfiske m 97 12 03 08; e post@
altahavfiske.no; w altahavfiske.no
Storekorsnes Ferie & Fritid Øvreveien
62; m 90 57 03 38; e post@storekorsnes.no;
w storekorsnes.no

Tappeluft Opplevelser m 97 59 80 94;
e vibeke@tappeluft.no; ◼

Alta Museum (m 41 75 63 30; w alta.museum.no; ⊕ mid-May–mid-Jun & mid-Aug–mid-Sep 08.00–17.00 daily; mid-Jun–mid-Aug 08.00–20.00 daily; mid-Sep–mid-May 09.00–15.00 Mon–Fri, 11.00–16.00 Sat & Sun; Oct–Apr 80NOK, May–Sep 120NOK) Alta Museum is located right beside the main E6, 5km west of the town centre, in an area known as Hjemmeluft (Jiepmaluokta in Sámi, meaning 'seal bay'), about 1.5km west of the junction with Route 93 to Kautokeino. The Bybussen runs here from the town centre. After paying your entrance fee, forsake the museum's more mundane interior exhibitions and head immediately outside to see the star attractions, the **prehistoric rock carvings** ✳, which are located in two main areas immediately behind the museum building. Wooden walkways have been constructed to save the carvings from the rigours of thousands of pounding feet and it is imperative you do not stray from the path; allow 45 minutes or so to see the main area (to the left of the museum when looking out over the fjord). When combined with the second area of carvings to the right, you will need about 90 minutes in total; the walking paths run for a total length of around 3km.

Amazingly the petroglyphs were not discovered until the early 1970s; they'd simply lain hidden under layers of mud since their creation up to 6,000 years ago.

Painstaking restoration work was carried out on some of the carvings and today around 20% have been repainted using the same red colour as the originals to give an impression of how they were intended to be seen. Hammers and chisels made of rock or horn were used to make the carvings, which portray any number of different Stone-Age subjects: the hunting of wild animals such as elk and reindeer, catching birds, fishing, skin boats, weapons, people in procession, dancing and magical symbols to name but a few.

The 5,000 carvings are found in five different locations around Altafjorden (the museum area is just one of the five). It is thought they had more than one purpose: some were clearly made to worship gods or to relate ancient myths whereas others were aimed at placating the spirit of totem animals or ensuring fertility and prosperity. Today experts regard the carvings as an attempt by our ancient ancestors to immortalise their surroundings and express their ritualistic view of the world in what we now regard as art. The rock carvings are visible only between May and late September or early October (depending on the weather), since once the first snows of winter have fallen the carvings remain covered until the spring thaw.

Inside the museum It's best to concentrate on the entrance level of the museum where a series of exhibitions tells the history of Alta and the surrounding region of Finnmark. It is safe to forego the rather tedious displays on hunting and fishing, and home in instead on a fascinating story hidden away in the museum's far left-hand corner: a black-and-white photograph of protestors holding a banner reading 'La elva leve' ('Let the river live') is a poignant reminder of the bitter conflict that was fought out here in the early 1980s over the future of the **Alta River**.

Take a look, too, at the remarkable display of **medieval altarpiece sculptures** on display around the corner: the figure of Norway's patron saint, St Olav, was carved around 1490 in northern Germany and is a sign of the prosperity of Finnmark during the late medieval period when exports of dried fish to the rest of Europe brought much revenue to this part of Lapland.

INDIGENOUS RIGHTS: THE ALTA DISPUTE

The Alta Dispute is the moving story of local Sámi activists who took on the might of the Norwegian state over plans to dam the Alta River and produce hydro-electric power. Their efforts attracted international attention and marked a turning point in Sámi–state relations. Demonstrations were held at the dam construction site in nearby Stilla as well as in Oslo where five young Sámi staged a hunger strike outside parliament, bringing work on the dam to a standstill. Matters came to a head in 1981, when 600 Norwegian police forcefully removed 1,100 peaceful protestors from the construction site. During the course of the Alta Dispute the Sámi learned how to work with the media and influence public opinion, which, certainly in the north of Norway, was strongly against the dam. However, construction work continued unabated and the Alta River was finally dammed in 1987. The Norwegian government set up two committees to investigate the issue of Sámi rights in the light of the protests whose findings paved the pay for the setting up of the Norwegian Sámi parliament, Sámediggi, in Karasjok and the recognition of the Sámi as an indigenous people in the Norwegian constitution in 1988.

You'll also find on this floor an exhibition about the research into the aurora borealis carried out in Alta. The first permanent northern lights observatory in the world was established at the summit of nearby Haldde Mountain in 1899. Through this, and continuing research, we now know that strong displays of the aurora can adversely affect people's heart rates, cause a greater risk of heart problems and can even damage electrical appliances.

There's little of interest downstairs – a jumble of ski medals and fishing equipment – so head instead for the small **café** by the entrance which serves simple snacks and sandwiches.

Sorrisniva Igloo Hotel (↘78 43 33 78; e info@sorrisniva.no; w sorrisniva.no; ⊕ for visits noon–20.00 Mon–Sat; €€€€) Even if you don't want to spend the night in sub-zero temperatures tucked up inside an igloo, it is worth making the 20km trip south from Alta to see the Sorrisniva Igloo Hotel. To get here take Route 93 towards Kautokeino and follow signs for Sorrisniva. Built every year between Christmas and New Year, the igloo hotel stands proudly beside the banks of the Alta River until it melts in late April. It is considerably smaller and more intimate than its world-famous bigger brother, Icehotel, in Jukkasjärvi in Sweden (page 77), though you'd be forgiven if you thought the Norwegians had simply copied the Swedish model. Like the Icehotel, the Sorrisniva Igloo Hotel has a chapel, an ice bar and plenty of ice sculptures to adorn the interior. The theme of the sculptures and interior décor changes from year to year but there is always a vast ice swan in the entrance hall (the Old Norse meaning of *alta* is 'swan') to welcome visitors, who pay 200NOK for the pleasure of setting foot inside the igloo.

Should you decide you want to stay here in one of the 30 rooms (or one of the two suites, which are slightly larger and contain ice sculptures), you will be provided with a thermal sleeping bag and plenty of blankets. There's a cosy lounge in the adjacent service building with television, where you can relax in the warmth or, alternatively, enjoy an outdoor jacuzzi under the stars before repairing to your own freeze-box for the night; the average temperature inside the igloo is –4°C to –7°C. A night here costs 4,720NOK per person and includes transfer to and from Alta, sauna and breakfast the next morning. The sauna, showers, toilets and lounge are in the more conventional service building next door, which is fully heated. The hotel can arrange a variety of excursions including a 2-hour **snowmobile tours** (whether you are staying here or not) including transport from Alta and a tour of the igloo hotel at a cost of 1,900NOK per person per snowmobile; full details of all the options available are on the website.

TOWARDS HAMMERFEST: SKAIDI From Alta, the E6 continues its relentless journey north, first threading its way around the head of Altafjorden before climbing and clipping across a barren upland plateau. Bear in mind that sections of this stretch of the E6 can be ferociously windy and are prone to snowdrifts in winter, which can close the road. The red-and-white barriers along the road are lowered if driving conditions become too hazardous. If this happens, you have no choice but to wait for a snow plough and then drive in convoy behind the plough as it reopens the route for vehicles. Once up on the plateau (385m) and now a full 86km out of Alta, you will finally come to the first settlement of any significance: Skaidi. However, this diminutive hamlet is little more than a crossroads and is more strategic to bus travellers than car drivers since it is sometimes necessary, depending on schedules, to change buses here when travelling to and from Hammerfest, 57km to the northwest.

If you tired of northernmost superlatives in Tromsø, it is time to brace yourself because there are more to come in Hammerfest, a surprisingly likeable little place that is overtly proud of its self-declared role in life: the northernmost town in the world. Hammerfest, at a latitude of 70.7°N, was locked in fierce battle for years with nearby Honningsvåg (latitude 71°N) for this prestigious and lucrative title. In the end, Hammerfest won the right to call itself a town since its population is three times the size Honningsvåg's, a mere village in comparison. However, the title is also disputed by Longyearbyen in Svalbard and the Alaskan town of Barrow who also consider themselves towns. And, while the debate continues, on the ground the title means very little. Whatever the truth, Hammerfest makes a good staging post on the long journey up to the North Cape.

SOME HISTORY Named after its superb anchorage (*hamran* was the name of a group of rocks, now lost to landfill, which boats were once fastened to, hence the place-name element *fest*), throughout its history, Hammerfest has always been an important ice-free base for trapping and fishing in the waters of the Arctic. The hunting of whales, seals, walruses and polar bears was the mainstay of the local economy for several centuries. Hunters and trappers rarely settled here permanently and by 1699 there were only three married couples, a priest and a merchant eking out a living here. In 1809, during the Napoleonic Wars, Britain attacked the settlement from two warships offshore, causing the inhabitants to flee with their possessions. The British ships spent eight days in port, giving the sailors plenty of time to loot the church's donation box and silver. In 1890, Hammerfest fell victim to another disaster: a fire, which began in the bakery and ripped through the tiny town, destroying half the houses. Germany's Kaiser Wilhelm II was the biggest single donor of aid to help with the reconstruction; incongruously, he was a keen sailor and often called in at Hammerfest on board his yacht.

One of Hammerfest's other boasts is that it was the first town to install electric street lighting after two local merchants had been thrilled by a demonstration of the new-fangled invention at a trade fair in Paris.

As the German army retreated in 1944, they burnt Hammerfest to the ground. With the help of the Marshall Plan, reconstruction began and today there is no building in Hammerfest that is more than 65 years old except the church, which remained standing. The recent artificial enlargement of the island of Melkøya, just outside the harbour, and the construction of a gas terminal there has brought new prosperity to the town. Creating new jobs to replace those lost from the fish-processing sector, the plant will handle exports from Norway's gas fields in the Arctic Ocean. Indeed, urban regeneration northern-Norwegian-style has continued apace in recent years and the town's former Findus fish factory has now been transformed into a stylish arts centre, theatre and cinema, the AKS or **Arktisk Kultursenter**; you'll see this new hulking structure of steel and wood down on the harbourside. Its gleaming glass walls are intended to symbolise the ice that holds Hammerfest in its wintry grip for several months each year.

GETTING THERE Steaming into Hammerfest on a Hurtigruten **ship** with the horn blaring is infinitely the best way to arrive, seeing the town as generations of sailors have, banking steeply up the hillsides behind the harbour. However, arriving from the south, it is a pleasure that unfolds rather blearily at 05.15 as the ship puts in from Tromsø. Southbound departures are more sensibly timed at 12.45. The quay is located on the southern side of the harbour. Hammerfest's **bus** station can be found close to the tourist office on Hamnegata, also down by the harbour. The **airport** (code HFT) is just over 3km to the north of the town; there's no bus connection but you can walk into town in around 40 minutes by simply descending the hill from the airstrip and then following the main round around the harbour; a taxi costs around 130NOK (☎ 78 41 12 34).

TOURIST INFORMATION The **tourist office** (Hamnegata 3; ☎78 41 21 85; e post@ hammerfest-turist.no; w visithammerfest.net; ⏱ Jun–mid-Aug 08.00–19.00 Mon–Fri, 09.00–16.00 Sat & Sun; mid-Aug–Sep 09.00–16.00 Mon–Fri, 10.00–14.00 Sat & Sun; Oct–May 09.00–16.00 Mon–Fri, 10.00–13.00 Sat & Sun) is by the harbour.

WHERE TO STAY *Map, below*

🏠 **Thon Hammerfest** Strandgata 2–4; ☎78 42 96 00; e hammerfest@olavthon.no; w thonhotels.no/hammerfest. Enjoying a great location on the waterfront, this comfortable & well-appointed hotel is one of the best places to stay in Hammerfest with modern, Nordic-style rooms. €€€€

🏠 **Scandic Hammerfest** Sørøygata 15; ☎78 42 57 00; e hammerfest@scandichotels.com; w scandichotels.no. An attractive waterfront setting for this red-brick hotel just south of the tourist office – the location is perfect for easy access on foot to the centre. The rooms are smart & comfortable & many

have great views of the harbour with all its comings-&-goings. €€€€/€€€

🏠 **Hammerfest Motell** Storsvingen 11; ☎78 41 11 26; w hammerfestmotell.no. Just 1.5km south of the town centre, this motel is ideal for anyone looking to self-cater & who also wants a little more room than is available in a regular hotel dbl. All rooms come with a kitchenette & are en suite. There's a couple of supermarkets within easy walking distance, making this a sensible money-saving option. €€€

🏠 **Smarthotel** Strandgata 32; m 41 53 65 00; e post.hammerfest@smarthotel.no;

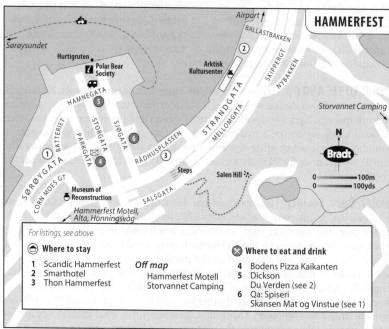

For listings, see above			
🖤 Where to stay			
1	Scandic Hammerfest	*Off map*	
2	Smarthotel	Hammerfest Motell	
3	Thon Hammerfest	Storvannet Camping	
🟢 Where to eat and drink			
4	Bodens Pizza Kaikanten		
5	Dickson		
	Du Verden (see 2)		
6	Qa: Spiseri		
	Skansen Mat og Vinstue (see 1)		

w smarthotel.no. A welcome addition to the town, this budget hotel is right next door to the cultural centre. It has great sea views from most of the rooms as the building rises over 9 floors & is located right on the waterfront. €€€

⚑ Storvannet Camping (7 cabins) Storvannsveien 103; \78 41 10 10; e storvannet@ yahoo.no; w nafcamp.no/campingplasser/3281-Storvannet-NAF-Camping; ⊕ late May–Sep. Cabins & camping. You can get here on foot by following Skolebakken, or by taxi from town for around 130NOK. Cabins €€

✕ WHERE TO EAT AND DRINK *Map, page 207*

✕ Skansen Mat og Vinstue Sørøygata 15; \78 42 57 00; w scandichotels.no/hotell/norge/hammerfest/scandic-hammerfest/restaurant-bar/restaurant; ⊕ 17.00–22.00 Mon–Sat. Inside the Scandic hotel, this is Hammerfest's most upmarket restaurant; an intimate little place with gorgeous sea views. The imaginative menu is a treat for seafood lovers: semi-dried cod (*boknatorsk*) with bacon & mustard; duck breast in cherry sauce; or reindeer fillet in a game sauce with lingonberries are all delicious. €€€

✕ Dickson Sjøgata 3; \78 41 38 78; w dicksonrestaurant.org; ⊕ 15.00–23.00 Tue–Sat, 15.00–22.00 Sun. Hammerfest's long-standing Chinese restaurant, known for its large portions, serving classics such as spring rolls, beef in sweet & sour sauce & Chinese chicken curry. Thrill to the fact that this is the most northerly Chinese restaurant in the world. €€

✕ Du Verden Strandgata 32; m 45 25 07 00; w duverden.no/hammerfest. Located in the same building as the Smarthotel, the Hammerfest version of this small chain is a winner, not only in

terms of its ideal waterfront location, but also its menu choices: a starter of lobster soup with fennel baked with oranges followed by a main cause comprising a shoulder of lamb with Jerusalem artichoke & mushrooms. A dessert of orange layer cake with mascarpone makes a special treat. €€

✕ Bodens Pizza Kaikanten Storgata 27; \78 41 49 00; w kaikanten.no; ⊕ 15.00–23.00 daily. Decorated in the style of an old-fashioned American tavern, this is the place for pizza in Hammerfest (a medium costs 175NOK) with a wide range of different toppings available. Doubles up as a bar open until 01.00 Sun–Thu, 03.00 Fri & Sat. €

☀ ✕ Qa: Spiseri Sjøgata 8; \78 41 26 12; ⊕ 10.00–midnight Mon–Fri, 11.00–01.00 Sat, 13.00–20.00 Sun. Trendy waterfront bistro serving freshly prepared dishes at value-for-money prices which really draw the crowds. There tends to be a Middle Eastern edge to the menu, with options such as tabbouleh, chargrilled meats & pittas featuring heavily. €

WHAT TO SEE AND DO Hammerfest is little more than one main street, Strandgata, running parallel to the sea, with two or three side roads branching off perpendicular. Within this small grid, you will find virtually everything Hammerfest has to offer: a small shopping centre, a market where you can pick up Sámi knick-knacks in summer and one or two other souvenir shops aimed at Hurtigruten passengers who hurtle around town for 90 minutes, seemingly visiting every store in sight, while the ferry is docked.

Polar Bear Society (Isbjørnklubben; Hamnegata 3; w isbjornklubben.no; ⊕ same hrs as the tourist office, page 207; free) The town's main attraction is this diminutive museum-cum-society, which is located in the same building as the tourist office, down by the Hurtigruten quay. Established in 1963 to provide brave visitors who had ventured to the northernmost town in the world with a certificate of their achievement, the society today doles out the said diploma, dutifully signed by the Mayor of Hammerfest, membership cards, a polar bear badge made of silver and assorted other bits and bobs of questionable worth; life membership costs 180NOK. Thankfully, membership of what must surely be one of the most peculiar societies on the planet is not obligatory and it is a much better idea simply to wander around the museum taking in the exhibits. The history of Hammerfest is told in a series of annotated black-and-white photographs, which clearly show just how significant the hunting of polar bears, in particular, has been in Hammerfest over the centuries. Should you have a predilection for animals of the Arctic, stuffed, then you are in luck: you name it, everything from a polar bear to an Arctic fox is on display here.

Museum of Reconstruction (Gjenreisningsmuseet; Kirkegata 21; ✆78 40 29 30; w gjenreisningsmuseet.no; ⊕ Jun–mid-Aug 10.00–16.00 daily; rest of the year 09.00–15.00 Mon-Fri, 11.00–14.00 Sat & Sun; 80NOK) Much more engaging, albeit a bit of a mouthful, Gjenreisningsmuseet offers a gripping account of the dramatic events of World War II in this part of Europe and the forced evacuation of 50,000 people from Hammerfest and other towns in the east of Norwegian Lapland. As Nazi troops fled the advancing Russian forces, the German commander in Lapland, General Lothar Rendulic, implemented a scorched earth policy, under which virtually every building in Norwegian (and Finnish) Lapland was burnt to the ground.

In the immediate post-war period, the Norwegian government tried and failed to control the return of people to the north; locals ignored the authorities and returned to begin the reconstruction of their homes. Counting more than 11,000 photographs as part of its collection, the museum has a small auditorium where a moving film about the war and its effects is available for viewing; the archive footage of German soldiers throwing snowballs and playing with local Sámi children

---

THE MAN WHO BURNT LAPLAND: GENERAL LOTHAR RENDULIC

All houses will be burned to the ground or destroyed… only in this way may it be avoided that the Russians with their strong forces, backed by the buildings and a local population well acquainted with the local area, follow our troops… Sympathising with the local population is not appropriate.

Although Adolf Hitler himself issued the uncompromising order for Lapland to be set alight, the dictat was actioned by **General Lothar Rendulic**, who commanded all German forces in Finland and Norway. Born in Austria in 1887, Rendulic was called to the German army in 1938 following the annexation of Austria to Germany. A close confidante of Hitler, the Führer ordered Rendulic in 1944 to draw up a plan to capture the Yugoslav partisan leader, Josip Tito. Following his posting to Lapland, during which half of all buildings in Finnish Lapland and large tracts of northern Norway were razed to the ground, Rendulic led several commands throughout Europe and finally surrendered during the Prague Offensive in May 1945. After the war, Rendulic was interned and convicted of war crimes at Nuremberg and sentenced to 20 years' imprisonment though he was **cleared of charges concerning the scorching of Lapland**. His sentence was later reduced to ten years – something the local populations of Norway and Finland, many of whom were forced to spend the Arctic winter of 1944–45 in the open countryside after losing their homes and livelihoods as a direct result of his action – were at a loss to comprehend. He was released from prison in 1951 and later worked as an author and in local Austrian politics. Rendulic died in Austria in 1971. Lapland has not forgotten him.

followed by the total devastation of the town and the evacuation of the population makes a poignant juxtaposition. One of the thorny questions the museum also addresses concerns the future of the dozens of buildings that were constructed in Hammerfest between the end of the war and 1960. Many of these structures now need entirely renovating and local worthies are currently agonising over whether to keep the buildings, seen as a symbol of post-war courage and resilience, or to knock them down and start again.

Salen hill Panoramic views of Hammerfest and the barren coastline and islands hereabouts are just a short walk away from the centre of town. Salen hill is the place to head for – the path begins at the stone steps across from the NRK (Norwegian broadcasting) building on Salsgata. A footpath then zigzags up the hillside to a viewpoint at 86m above sea level. As you climb you'll see Hammerfest's avalanche protections – wooden fences placed parallel to the hillside aimed at preventing snow from drifting and falling on to the houses below. The walk to the top only takes around 10 minutes.

Boat trips from Hammerfest Although there are no designated boat tours out of Hammerfest, you can still explore the islands and fjords off the town on board the **regular ferry**, SørøysundXpressen, which shuttles back and forth across the **Sørøysundet sound**. Boats sail from the quay off Sjøgata and stop at various islands (sailing schedules vary). Trips take anything from 1 to 2 hours depending on the number of stops the ferry makes – you simply buy a round-trip ticket (172NOK) and stay on the boat, returning to Hammerfest at the end of the circuit. There are two or three sailings daily (except Sat – 1 only) and times can be found at w snelandia.no. Buy your ticket on board the boat, which also accepts credit cards.

MOVING ON FROM HAMMERFEST The Hurtigruten **ferry** sails northbound from Hammerfest at 06.00 arriving in Honningsvåg 5 hours later in readiness for excursions to the North Cape (page 214). Southbound departures are at 12.45 with arrival in Tromsø 11 hours later. From Hammerfest there are **bus** services to Karasjok as well as to Kirkenes via Lakselv and also to Honningsvåg and Alta; for timetables see w snelandia.no.
    From Hammerfest, it is 142km to Alta; 180km to Honningsvåg; 208km to the North Cape; and 541km to Kirkenes.

TOWARDS THE NORTH CAPE

Back on the E6 at Skaidi, the next section of the road towards the North Cape leads first to **Olderfjord**, which occupies a glorious position on the west bank of the mighty **Porsangen fjord**, an inlet of the Arctic Ocean edged by bare, rounded hills. This section of the road can be hard going – the wind up here can be alarmingly fierce at the summit (437m). Some 23km east of Skaidi, things get markedly easier once you drop down into Olderfjord and embark on Europe's northernmost road, the E69, which leads all the way to the North Cape via an impressive array of tunnels. Clinging precariously to the shores of the fjord the road veers around gnarled headlands of shattered rock where it can, and where it can't it plunges into the hillside through a tunnel; the first of these is Skarvbergtunnelen (length 2,980m). If the automatic door at the entrance is closed, drive up to the blue sign and wait for the door to rise.

REPVÅG The next tunnel, Sortviktunnelen (length 496m), is a mere babe in comparison, and you are now well on the way to the turning on the right for **Repvåg**, a pretty little fishing station, huddled around a wharf, which teeters on stilts on a narrow neck of land that juts out defiantly into Porsangen fjord. The handful of wooden buildings here, all painted in traditional red and sporting white window frames, were spared the ravages of the departing German troops after World War II and remained standing, in contrast to nearby Honningsvåg, for example, which was burnt to the ground. Inside, much of the decoration and furnishing is made of driftwood or features bits and bobs from the fishing industry. Consequently, this is one of the premier places to stay around Honningsvåg and offers a chance to experience life on the coast of northern Norway a little off the beaten track. Incidentally, although Repvåg is now linked to the E69 by a 2km by-road, in the 1970s it was once a busy harbour with ferries shuttling back and forth carrying all road traffic bound for Honningsvåg and the North Cape. This before the days of the North Cape tunnel, which now links the mainland with Norway's northernmost island, Magerøya, doing away with the need for a ferry connection.

🏠 **Where to stay, eat and drink** Between May and September accommodation at the **Repvåg Fjordhotell og Rorbusenter** (↖78 47 54 40; e post@repvag-fjordhotell. no; w repvag-fjordhotell.no) is available in a number of traditional fishermen's cottages, *rorbuer* (**€€€**), right on the wharf. Rooms are simple but snug and a night spent here is sure to please; the view of the fjord and the surrounding islands is unusual. The hotel **restaurant** specialises in locally caught fresh fish; during the summer months the fjord is brimming with coalfish, whereas in autumn and winter cod and haddock are attracted into its sheltered waters. It is possible to make your own way out on to the fjord by renting one of the three small **boats** the hotel has available. Alternatively, there's a nature **trail** that begins right outside the hotel's front door and leads through an area of reindeer pasture.

HONNINGSVÅG A marvel of modern engineering now stands ahead of you: **Nordkapptunnelen**. Opened in June 1999, the tunnel replaced the stomach-churning ferry, which once bobbed across the sound from Kåfjord to Honningsvåg and, in officialese at least, goes by the bizarre name of *Fatima: fastlandsforbindelsen til Magerøya* (the mainland connection to Magerøya). This 6.8km-long submarine tunnel reaches a depth below water of 212m as it traverses the sound.

Blinking in the daylight as you emerge from the tunnel, it is not long before you are plunged into yet another two tunnels: Sarnestunnelen (length 190m) and then Honningvågstunnelen (length 4.44km). Finally, at the T-junction on the approach to Honningsvåg, take a right (left goes towards the airport and ultimately the North Cape) and drive into the northernmost village in the world: the 71st parallel of latitude slices ignominiously through the Shell filling station on your right-hand side.

Getting there The first stop for **buses** is outside the waterside tourist office on Fiskeriveien, below the Scandic Honningsvåg hotel on the main road, from where they continue around the harbour and terminate at Rådhuset, above Honningsvåg's other two hotels. Arriving by the Hurtigruten coastal **ferry**, you will dock 100m to the east at the dedicated Hurtigrutekai. The ship arrives daily here from the south at 11.15 and departs again for all points north at 14.45, allowing passengers time to make a trip by bus to the North Cape; it departs daily southbound at 05.45. Widerøe serves the tiny **airport** (airport code HVG), 5km north of the village; there are only sporadic bus connections between the airport and Honningsvåg itself but the 45-minute walk into town is straightforward and feasible if you're stuck. Alternatively, try for a **taxi** (✆78 47 22 34; 120NOK) though bear in mind there are only a handful vehicles on the island and you may have to wait your turn. Flying in and out of Honningsvåg's tiny airstrip is not only dramatic but it also affords great views of the North Cape.

Tourist information The **tourist office** (✆78 47 70 30; e info@northcape.no; w northcape.no; ⏰ mid-Jun–mid-Aug 09.00–17.00 Mon–Fri, 11.00–16.00 Sat & Sun; rest of the year 11.00–14.00 Mon–Fri) is at Fiskeriveien 4, below the Scandic hotel on the main road. Tourist office staff here are friendly and knowledgeable and can help with accommodation, tours to the North Cape and making sense of northern Norway's complicated bus routes and times. For details of **car rental**, see page 221.

🏠 Where to stay

🏠 **Árran Nordkapp** Kamøyvær; ✆75 40 20 85; e aina@arran.as; w arran.as. Located in the fishing village of Kamøyvær, 9km north of Honningsvåg on the North Cape road, this Sámi-run family hotel offers no-nonsense modern rooms with just a hint of Sámi design. €€€€

🏠 **Scandic Bryggen** Vågen 1, Honningsvåg; ✆78 47 72 50; e bryggen@scandichotels.com; w scandichotels.no. Without doubt the most charming hotel in the village. The Scandic Bryggen occupies 2 buildings: 1 is a group of former wooden warehouses that has been tastefully converted & occupies a prime location on a couple of jetties at the head of the harbour. Rooms here are a little on the small side, but worth it for the location. The building next door is less charming with concrete walls rather than timber, though its modern rooms are decent enough. It has superb views from its wharf location out over the harbour, too. €€€€

🏠 **View North Cape** Utsikten 12; m 48 06 87 35; e reception@theviewhotel.no; w theviewhotel.no. Perched on a hill overlooking Honningsvåg, the 50 rooms at this new hotel are a treat to behold. Fresh, contemporary design (rain showers in the bathrooms), not to mention the views, gives them the edge over some of the more tired accommodation in town, if you don't mind the walk up here. €€€€

🏠 **North Cape Cabins** Skipsfjorden; m 95 13 88 91/91 71 19 64; e post@ northcapecabins. no; w northcapecabins.no. These 3 little wooden cabins in Skipsfjorden, 7.5km north of Honningsvåg on the way to the North Cape, are idyllic. Each sleeping 2, they are located right beside the fjord with sweeping views. They are right beside the road too & vehicle noise can disturb the peace. Bed linen & final cleaning costs are extra. €€

🏠 **North Cape Youth Hostel** Kobbhullveien 10; m 91 82 41 56; e nordkapp@hihostels.no; w hihostels.no. Located close to the junction of the main E69 & the main road into town, this handy youth hostel, 2km from the centre, is open all year round & offers excellent-value dbls as well as dorm beds. There's also a kitchen for self-catering. Dbls €€ & dorm beds €

⚠ **Nordkapp Camping NAF** Skipsfjorden; ✆78 47 33 77; e post@nordkappcamping.no; w nordkappcamping.no; ⏰ May–Sep. The closest campsite to Honningsvåg (a tent pitch costs 170NOK), located 8km north in Skipsfjorden. Dbls €€ cabins with kitchenette €€ bungalows with fitted kitchen €€€€ & camping €

🍴 Where to eat and drink

🍴 **Corner Spiseri** Fiskerveien 2A; ✆78 47 63 40; w utelivinordkapp.no/corner; ⏰ 10.00–23.00 Mon–Thu, 10.00–02.00 Fri & Sat, noon–23.00 Sun. Hidden away down by the harbour & behind the tourist office, this cosy bistro overlooking the water has a wide menu ranging from deep-fried cod tongues to whale stew as well as more usual offerings such as pizza, pasta & burgers. €€

🍴 **King Crab House** Sjøgata 6; m 91 33 08 45; ⏰ 11.00–23.00 Mon–Thu, 11.00–02.00 Fri & Sat, noon–23.00 Sun. Overlooking the harbour, this stylish restaurant is the place to come for your fish-fix, though it doesn't come cheap: locally caught king crab is on the menu as well as a range of other seafood such as fried halibut, steak blue mussels & creamy fish soup. €€

🍴 **Arctic Sans** Storgata 22; m 95 22 88 21; ⏰ 10.00–21.00 Mon–Fri, 11.00–21.00 Sat, 13.00–20.00 Sun. A new café on the main road, serving fish, Chinese & other southeast Asian dishes as well as fish & chips & burgers. The food is

OK though the painted breeze-block walls inside are rather less palatable. €

🍷 **Nøden** Larsjoda 1B; ⏰ 20.00–02.00 Thu & Fri, 13.00–22.00 Sat. Close to the tourist office & a little up the hill to the left. This is Honningsvåg's only pub – decked out in traditional British style with darts & billiards, too. Often shows football games & arranges pub quizzes. €

What to see and do Honningsvåg, 240km from Alta, is a strangely likeable sort of place. There's a pluckiness about the village that appeals – not least because its exposed location on the edge of one of Norway's most inhospitable islands, Magerøya, actually suggests that it really ought not to be here. Indeed, nearby Hammerfest has robbed Honningsvåg of the title of northernmost town in the world despite various attempts by local worthies to have their village upgraded and reclassified; having said that, Honningsvåg is no metropolis. The heart of the village is its **harbour**, a U-shaped affair, around which a couple of parallel roads fit neatly. It is here, by the water's edge, that you will find the **Arctico Ice Bar** (w arcticoicebar.com; ⏰ generally Apr–Oct 10.00–21.00 daily, though times change daily, exact details online; Apr, May & Sep in connection with the Hurtigruten ferry arrival from the south; 149NOK), housed in a former fish storage plant. Inside the building, which is kept at –5°C, you'll find a circular bar made of ice, a video screen made of snow and a few ice chairs dressed with reindeer skins. Run by two Spaniards, José and Gloria, who have fallen in love with all things Arctic, the ice bar is certainly quite an oddity and definitely worth a visit; visitors are provided with warm overalls and the entrance fee includes a couple of drinks. Incidentally, all the ice used is cut every year from a nearby lake.

The harbour is also the location for most other things you're likely to need: **hotels**, **restaurants** and **shops**. Honningsvåg is undoubtedly at its most picturesque at the head of the harbour where one of the hotels appear to perch somewhat precariously on three stilted wharves.

North Cape Museum (Nordkappmuseet; Fiskeriveien 4; ✆ 78 47 72 00; w nordkappmuseet.no; ⏰ Jun–mid-Aug 10.00–18.00 daily, Sep 11.00–15.00 daily, Oct–Mar 11.00–15.00 Mon–Fri, Apr & May 11.00–16.00 Mon–Fri; 60NOK) Once you've made a circuit of the harbour and peered at the various comings and goings down by the Hurtigruten quay, there's really little else to occupy your time and you should head for the Nordkappmuseet museum in the same building as the tourist office which holds an evocative exhibition about the reconstruction of the village immediately after World War II. As the German forces retreated during the winter of 1944 they burnt the whole of Honningsvåg to the ground. Black-and-white photographs show only the church left standing; it became a focal point for the reconstruction effort and was even used as a bakery at one time. Barracks were hurriedly erected to house former inhabitants as they returned after the forced evacuation.

The museum has a mini display about local birdlife, including the Gjesværstappan islands off Magerøya's northwest coast, which are home to one of Norway's largest puffin colonies – and an event that has left leading wildlife experts baffled. Quite inexplicably the birds return to the islands, after spending the winter out at sea, on the same day every year, 14 April, and at the same time during the late afternoon. In total the islands are home to around three million nesting birds including gannets, Arctic skuas, cormorants and white-tailed eagles. Upstairs, on a small mezzanine floor, staff have mounted a display about the North Cape and its magnetic attraction to countless visitors from across the world over the years. Long though the journey to Europe's most northerly point may be, it was even more arduous before the road opened to the cape in 1956. Then visitors, including the Norwegian king, Oscar II, came ashore in Hornvika Bay, just to the east, and faced a steep climb up the cliff to reach the North Cape Plateau (307m). This royal visit did much to finally put the North Cape on the tourist map.

Northwest to Gjesvær: bird safaris The tiny village of **Gjesvær**, 35km northwest of Honningsvåg, is the location for boat trips out to the Gjesværstappan maritime nature reserve, which comprises three islands which lie immediately off Gjesvær, 15km west of the North Cape itself. The reserve contains the biggest colony of puffins in Finnmark, as well as large numbers of gannets, fulmars, kittiwakes, guillemots and razorbills. There are even Arctic skuas and white-tailed eagles here, too. Tours are operated by **BirdSafari.com** (m 41 61 39 83; e olat@ birdsafari.com; w birdsafari.com) at Nygårdsveien 38 in Gjesvær. Departure times vary depending on the time of year but full details can be found on the website; a safari costs 720NOK per person.

Kamøyvær Head north out of Honningsvåg, past the airport, and pretty soon the road starts to climb up over the barren rock that makes up much of Magerøya. Drive past the Scandic Nordkapp, with its conspicuous tepees, and turn right just afterwards off the E69 on to the narrow road that leads down into the pretty little fishing village of Kamøyvær, squeezed between the hills and the sea. Here, at Duksfjordveien 4, you'll find the **East of the Sun Gallery** (✆ 78 47 51 37; e evart@ evart.no; w evart.no; ⊕ generally open in connection with the Hurtigruten northbound ship's arrival & departure times; free), run by German artist Eva Schmutterer, whose paintings and handicrafts are inspired by the wild natural landscapes of the far north. Should the urge for something colourful strike, samples of Eva's work are available for purchase in the gallery.

Other activities from Honningsvåg Destinasjon 71° Nord (m 47 28 93 20; e mail@71-nord.no; w 71-nord.no) are the people to contact if you're looking for **tours and activities** while you're in Honningsvåg. They can offer boat trips to go fishing for king crab, ATV safaris, as well as tours of Magerøya. Alternatively, you could **hire a car** yourself and explore Magerøya under your own steam – 4 hours' rental goes for 1,500NOK, 24 hours costs 1,700NOK – worth considering if there's a group of you: AVIS (m 91 00 33 21; w avis.no) and Nordkapp Bilservice (✆ 78 47 60 60; w nordkappbilservice.no) are the main players.

NORTH CAPE

Here, at the end of the world, my longing also comes to an end, and I return home satisfied.

Francesco Negri, first tourist to reach the North Cape in 1664,
after a two-year journey from Italy.

The Sámi call Norway's northernmost island Máhkarávju or 'steep, barren coast', which has been Norwegianised into today's **Magerøya** and is home to around 3,500 people, three-quarters of whom live in Honningsvåg. As the E69 threads its way north towards the cape (it only opened in 1956), the island certainly lives up to its name as vistas of bare, windswept rock and tundra unfold at every turn. This Arctic landscape is Norwegian Lapland at its most elemental: a high treeless plateau edged by distant frost-shattered peaks and a coast that has been gnawed into countless craggy inlets by the unforgiving might of the Arctic Ocean. Seeking shelter from the ferocious storms, which sweep in from the sea with merciless regularity, the island's few settlements huddle at the head of fjords that slice deep into the heart of the land.

The English sea captain, Richard Chancellor, brought the North Cape to prominence. Searching for the Northeast Passage between the Atlantic and the Pacific, he sailed his ship, *Edward Bonaventure*, along this stretch of coastline in 1553 and used the North Cape cliff (307m) as a navigational landmark; its sheer face reaching up from the sea was certainly easy to spot. Although Chancellor failed to reach his destination, China, sea charts of northern Europe soon began to feature his name for the northernmost point in Europe, the North Cape, and the rest is history. However, the belief that the North Cape is the furthest extremity of Europe is one of the greatest geographical gaffes of all time. The gently sloping promontory, **Knivskjellodden**, just to the west of the cape, is the true top of Europe since it stretches 1,500m further north than the cliff. Content not to let the truth get in the

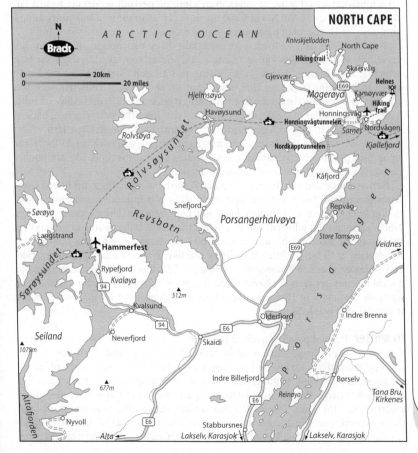

way of a good story, the Norwegian tourist authorities promote the North Cape (Nordkapp in Norwegian) as Europe's most northerly point with all their might – and succeed: 200,000 people make the considerable journey to North Cape Hall every year and pay handsomely for the pleasure (see opposite).

Once you finally reach the North Cape, it is worth taking stock of just where you are on the globe: at 71° 10' 21" of latitude you are considerably closer to the North Pole (2,093km) than you are to London, for example, and the Norwegian capital, Oslo, is a staggering 1,420km to the south. As a sign of how far north you are, there's **midnight sun** at the cape from 11 May to 31 July and **polar night** from 18 November to 24 January each year. There's certainly a tremendous sense of achievement in having made the journey to 'the very end of Europe' but at the same time, as Francesco Negri pointed out in his journal, *Viaggio Settentrionale* (see epigraph on page 214), it is also where curiosity reaches completion and the realisation sets in that you have an extremely long trip ahead of you – there's over 650km to go just to reach the Arctic Circle.

GETTING THERE

In summer For years it was possible to take a public bus from Honningsvåg to the North Cape, costing around 120NOK one-way, but this is no longer an option. In a much-criticised move to fleece even more money out of visitors to this far-flung corner, trips to the North Cape are now run as **organised bus tours** aimed, primarily, at Hurtigruten passengers – book online at w northcapetours.com.

Between May and October you essentially have two options if you are not travelling with your own car or taking a taxi: either you take the day-time tour which leaves Honningsvåg at 11.45, giving you 1 hour 15 minutes at the North Cape and arriving back into Honningsvåg at 14.30 (790NOK). Alternatively, you can take the evening departure from Honningsvåg at 22.00 (⊕ mid-May–Jul only; 1,395NOK) in order to see the midnight sun at the cape. This option arrives back in Honningsvåg at 01.00. Both prices include entrance to the North Cape Hall.

The fixed rate for a **taxi** from Honningsvåg to the cape and back is 1,350NOK for up to four people which includes 1 hour waiting time at the cape. You can book a taxi on ☏78 47 22 34 or e taxi@nordkapptaxi.no.

Between June and late August a popular Finnish bus operates to the North Cape **from Rovaniemi** bus station (departure 11.40) – a mammoth journey of 650km taking over 10 hours. Although local journeys between Honningsvåg and the North Cape are not allowed, you can board the bus at other points in Finland on its way to the North Cape, and you can take the service south from the cape (it leaves daily at 01.00) and ride it as far as you like: it runs via Lakselv, Inari, Ivalo and Sodankylä back to Rovaniemi, arriving at 17.30. Once again, you cannot make a local journey between the North Cape and Honningsvåg. Note also that this bus waits for 2½ hours in Honningsvåg before leaving again (at 05.10). There's more information at w eskelisen.fi.

In winter It is not possible to drive to the North Cape in your own vehicle when there is snow on the ground, roughly between November and April, though the exact period varies from year to year (check with the Honningsvåg tourist office for the latest information). Although the road may appear open, the last 13km section of the E69 between the junction for Skarsvåg and the North Cape is not ploughed; a barrier bars the road. To visit the North Cape during this time you must take the organised tour, which runs in connection with the arrival of the northbound Hurtigruten ferry, leaving Honningsvåg at 11.30. Coaches with snow chains then run up to the North Cape, closely following a snow plough, which opens the last section of the road for them to pass – quite something to experience. They then spend about 90 minutes at the cape before returning back to Honningsvåg for the ship's departure at 14.45. This trip costs 850NOK (including North Cape admission) and can be booked through North Cape Tours (**w** northcapetours.com).

WHAT TO SEE AND DO

North Cape Hall (Nordkapphallen; ****78 47 68 60; **w** visitnordkapp.net; ⊕ mid-Aug–end Aug 11.00–01.00; mid–late Aug 11.00–22.00; Sep–mid-May 11.00–15.00 daily; 285NOK, 180NOK without access to the panoramic cinema and exhibitions, pedestrians & cyclists free) A commerical pleasure dome designed to relieve you of as many kroner as possible in a short space of time. The hall, cut into the rock of the cape, is not without its critics either, who claim it is grossly overpriced and has destroyed the natural environment. Be that as it may, it would be churlish not to go inside having made the journey here. The main building is divided into two sections, which are linked by an underground tunnel. As you enter from the car park, you will find a souvenir shop selling seemingly everything your heart could ever desire, emblazoned with the Nordkapp logo; a café serving coffee and cakes; the Kompasset café and restaurant, offering superb views of the Arctic Ocean through its floor-to-ceiling windows and some of the most expensive à la carte dishes anywhere in Norway; and a red postbox for that all-important '9764 Nordkapp' postmark.

Take the stairs or lift down to Sub-level Three and you will find the impressive wide-screen **panoramic cinema**, which shows a regular free film about the North Cape and Magerøya in all seasons. Ignoring the tacky model of a bird cliff; beside the cinema entrance, make your way along the underground tunnel towards the edge of the cliff. A potted history of the cape is presented in a couple of glass display cabinets along the tunnel before you reach a chapel and more surreally a small museum, which commemorates the visit of King Chulalongkom of Siam to the North Cape in 1907 – he was so ill on arrival that he had to be carried up the cliff in nearby Hornvika Bay by stretcher. At the end of the tunnel you'll find the Cave of Lights where a tacky animation takes you on a journey through the changing seasons at the North Cape – sadly the lighting effects have all the sophistication of a school. Back in the main section of the building, on Level Two, you'll find the post office which will stamp postcards and letters (but not passports or books, etc) – with the North Cape postmark.

On the Entrance Level, you will find the exit to the outside viewing area (the wind out here can be particularly strong) and the location for the much-photographed steel globe, which has come to symbolise the North Cape. As you stare out to sea, you are looking at the scene of one of the northernmost naval encounters in history: the **Battle of the North Cape**. In heavy seas and a mounting snowstorm, the German battleship *Scharnhorst* sailed from its base in Altafjorden in December 1943 to intercept Allied convoys supplying Murmansk, but was fired on by Britain's Royal Navy, capsizing and sinking off the cape with the loss of over 1,900 lives. There's more information about the Murmansk covoys, including a scale model of the *Scharnhorst* on Level One, near the toilets.

Hiking to Knivskjellodden

Should your thirst for last places not have been quenched by Nordkapphallen and its tourist paraphernalia, you might want to escape the crowds and **hike** to the real northernmost point of Europe, Knivskjellodden. The start of the 16km (return; moderate) trail is signed from the E69 about 6km before the North Cape Hall and heads off towards the northwest; there's a car park here at the beginning of the trail. Don't underestimate how fast the weather can change out here on the plateau and before embarking on the hike you should make sure you are properly equipped; allow about 6 hours to make the return hike from the road. Perhaps in response to their critics, the North Cape Hall's operators, the Scandic hotel chain, urge visitors not to build cairns since they damage the soil and vegetation, and not to drive their vehicles off the roads provided.

MOVING ON FROM THE NORTH CAPE: TOWARDS KIRKENES

East of the North Cape, things get pretty remote and bleak. Once south of Olderfjord again, the E6 charts a long and lonely course via frightfully ugly Lakselv, Karasjok and Utsjoki (accessed from the highway by the bridge over the Tana River; page 169) towards **Tana Bru**, 180km or so east of Karasjok and the only crossing point over the Tana River for miles. Tana Bru, a dot of a Sámi village dominated by the suspension bridge over the river, is no reason to linger and it's better to press on and burn the remaining 135km to Kirkenes.

An alternative and slightly shorter route east from Lakselv, Route 98 follows a more northerly course than the E6, clipping past fjords and negotiating upland terrain on the shores of the Arctic Ocean. It approaches Tana Bru from the north, as opposed to the E6 which comes in from the west, both routes merging in the village to cross the river. Lakselv to Tana Bru via Karasjok is 255km; via Route 98 the journey from Lakselv is 211km.

From Tana Bru, northern Norway's final frontier comes into view: the **Varanger peninsula**, a forbidding, remote and alarmingly exposed, cauliflower-shaped butt of land, lost in the fog north of Kirkenes. Few people make it out here – and, to be frank, there's no real reason to stray from the E6 at Tana Bru to chug your way along the E75 around the peninsula's south coast to see essentially more of the same. (There's no road around the whole of the peninsula so you'll be forced to retrace your steps to Tana Bru should you decide to come.) So why mention the Varanger peninsula at all, then? Simply because this far-flung corner of Norway offers some of the most dramatic **aerial views** you'll see in Lapland – courtesy of the small turboprop planes which **Widerøe** operate all along the Varanger coast. So forget the car, and instead take the **plane ✷** which leaves Hammerfest every morning bound for Kirkenes via the Varanger peninsula, landing on the way at the fishing villages of **Berlevåg**, **Båtsfjord** and **Vardø** (Norway's most easterly town) as well as the administrative centre, **Vadsø**, which has historically had a large Finnish population and is also known by its Finnish name, Vesisaari. The plane flies exceptionally low for large parts of the journey since the flying time between the settlements is little more than 15 minutes – you simply stay on board each time the plane lands to allow passengers to either disembark or board. From the plane you'll have unsurpassed views of the remote, boggy hinterlands of the peninsula and will gain instant respect for the tough folk who live out here making a living from the sea. Flying from Hammerfest to Kirkenes will also save you a tiring drive of around 550km. Book tickets at w wideroe.no and be sure to choose a departure for Kirkenes which calls in at Varanger en route – some planes go direct.

KIRKENES

With street names in both Norwegian and Russian, rusting Russian ships in the harbour and Murmansk's nouveau riche trotting around town doing their shopping,

Kirkenes is quite unlike any other town in Lapland. A grubby port at the very end of the E6 and the Hurtigruten line, the place may be hard to like, but it does have a certain hard-bitten charm. That's just as well since it is a long way to come just to visit another Norwegian town with its familiar grid of modern anodyne streets. Once here, it is worth taking stock of just how far you've travelled – Kirkenes is as far east as Istanbul and Cairo, Oslo is a mind-boggling 2,480km away, whereas Murmansk is barely 243km, a mere stone's throw in these parts. Indeed, it is the town's proximity to Russia that helps keep the economy ticking over – local politicians are constantly dreaming up new initiatives to enhance all forms of cross-border co-operation in the Barents Sea region.

Kirkenes is named after the church (*kirke*), which was built in 1862 on the headland (*nes* meaning 'point' or 'headland' and cognate with English 'ness' in place names such as Skegness) where the town currently stands; previously the area had been known by the less than holy name of Pisselvnes (*piss* river headland). The town is also known as Girkonjárga in Sámi and Kirkkoniemi in Finnish.

During World War II, Kirkenes paid a high price for its proximity to Murmansk, the only ice-free port in the European part of the Soviet Union, which regularly received supplies and goods from the United States and Britain across the Arctic Ocean to help support Moscow. The Germans posted 30,000 troops in Kirkenes in

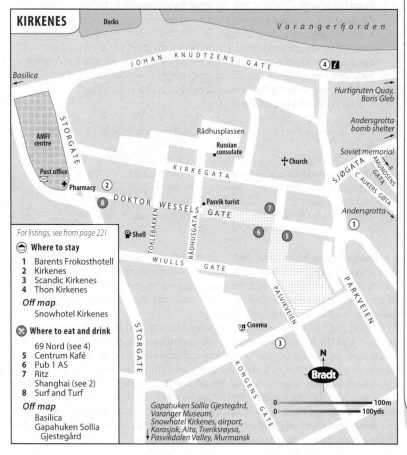

KIRKENES   Docks   *Varangerfjorden*

JOHAN KNUDTZENS GATE   ④ *i*

Basilica

Hurtigruten Quay, Boris Gleb

Andersgrotta bomb shelter

AMFI centre

Rådhusplassen

Russian consulate

Soviet memorial

Post office

STORGATE

KIRKEGATA

✝ Church

SJØGATA   AMUNDSENS GATA   C AUKERS GØTA   R AUKERS GATA

Pharmacy ②

⑧ DOKTOR WESSELS GATE

Pasvik turist

⑦

Andersgrotta

①

For listings, see from page 221

Shell

TOKLEBAKKEN   RÅDHUSGATA

⑥   ⑤

Where to stay
1   Barents Frokosthotell
2   Kirkenes
3   Scandic Kirkenes
4   Thon Kirkenes

WIULLS   GATE

PASVIKVEIEN   PARKVEIEN

Off map
  Snowhotel Kirkenes

Where to eat and drink
  69 Nord (see 4)
5   Centrum Kafé
6   Pub 1 AS
7   Ritz
  Shanghai (see 2)
8   Surf and Turf

STORGATE

🎬 Cinema

③

N

Bradt

KONGENS GATE

Off map
  Basilica
  Gapahuken Sollia
  Gjestegård

Gapahuken Sollia Gjestegård, Varanger Museum, Snowhotel Kirkenes, airport, Karasjok, Alta, Treriksrøysa, Pasvikdalen Valley, Murmansk

0   100m
0   100yds

THE POMOR TRADE AND 'RUSSENORSK'

The Pomors were Russian merchants from around the White Sea and the Murman coast of the Kola peninsula who sailed west every summer to the provinces of Finnmark and Troms in Norway to fish and trade with the Norwegians. This commercial activity off northern Norway became known as the Pomor trade and operated for over 150 years from the mid 1700s until the outbreak of World War I and the Russian Revolution. Against salted and air-dried Norwegian fish, the Pomors traded products which were much sought after in this part of Norwegian Lapland, far from the well-supplied towns and cities of the south: timber planks, flour, grain, milk products, hemp and sugar. It's widely claimed that Russian grain prevented starvation in northern Norway during the famine years at the beginning of the 19th century – the potato had not yet arrived in Lapland. In order to facilitate communication between the Russian merchants and Norwegian fishermen (they traded directly with each other – no middlemen were involved), a language developed based on Norwegian and Russian, though also incorporating words from Finnish, Sámi and Swedish: *russenorsk*, though local people also knew it as the '*moja-på-tvoja*' language ('I speak like you speak'). It is extremely rare for a pidgin (an artificial language which acts as a link between two completely different mother tongues) to survive for a century and a half without turning into a creole, ie: a new stand-alone mother tongue. The seasonal nature of the Pomor trade meant that *russenorsk* was only spoken during the short summer months and never had the chance to develop functionally and grammatically. The Pomor trade and, consequently, the continued existence of *russenorsk* ended in 1917 when the new Soviet government outlawed all private commerce.

A few examples of *russenorsk*:

Tvoja fisk kopom?	Will you buy fish?
Basiba	Thank you
Kak pris på tvoja?	What's your price?
Nogoli dag tvoja reisa på Arkangelsk otsuda?	How many days did it take you from Archangel?
Ju dovolna pjan	You're a bit drunk
Moja tvoja på vater kasstom	I'll throw you in the water

an attempt to take Murmansk. Sadly, much of the town, including the church, was destroyed during World War II, as Kirkenes's iron-ore mines became a target for Soviet carpet bombing. Indeed, the town was second only to Malta in the number of air attacks it received. Following 320 air raids and the Germans's scorched earth policy, only 13 houses remained standing.

During the Cold War, relations between Norway and Russia were sometimes strained and the border between the two countries close to Kirkenes was a place of tension; on several occasions soldiers and tanks lined up on either side of the border in a show of force. Today, as a member of the European Union's Schengen agreement, Norway maintains an active military base at Høybuktmoen, west of the town which is also the location for the airport, and is obliged to guard the border with Russia. Since there is passport-free travel throughout the Nordic countries, the agreement effectively makes the Norwegian–Russian border the outer frontier of the European Union, at least in terms of immigration.

GETTING THERE Arriving by **bus**, you will be dropped outside the AMFI centre, a modest shopping complex in the town centre one block inland from the harbour, which effectively serves as the bus station. Hurtigruten **ferries** terminate at the dedicated quay about 1km east of the centre from where a local bus runs into town. The **airport** (code KKN), 12km west of Kirkenes, is connected to town by a **shuttle bus**, Flybussen (20mins; **w** flybussen.no; 94NOK), which runs in connection with flight arrivals; a **taxi** into the centre costs around 350NOK. The bus between Karasjok and Kirkenes also calls in at the airport. Timetables for regular buses to and from Kirkenes are at the **w** snelandia.no.

TOURIST INFORMATION Kirkenes has no functioning tourist office. Instead, you'll find general information at **w** visitkirkenes.info. Otherwise, your best bet is to ask at local hotels or, for specific information about Russian visas and getting to Murmansk, visit Pasvik Turist at Doktor Wessels gate 15B (**w** pasvikturist.no) and see page 225.

Incidentally, despite Kirkenes's extreme location, as far east as Finland, the town keeps Norwegian time, rather than Finnish time.

CAR HIRE If you're intent on visiting Treriksrøysa and the Pasvikdalen Valley (page 132), you'll find it's much more practical to get there with your own transport. Car rental is available from all the outlets listed below:

🚗 **Avis** 🕿78 97 37 05; **e** res@avis.no
🚗 **Europcar** **m** 45 25 69 11; **e** reservations@ europcar.no
🚗 **Hertz** **m** 90 05 31 71; **e** kirkenes@hertz.no
🚗 **Sixt** **m** 46 44 26 66; **e** kirkenes@sixt.no

🏠 **WHERE TO STAY** *Map, page 219*

🏠 **Scandic Kirkenes** Kongens gate 1–3; 🕿78 99 59 00; **e** kirkenes@scandichotels.com; **w** scandichotels.no. The best that Kirkenes has to offer with comfortable, modern rooms, a swimming pool & sauna. Luxury at the end of the road, though, doesn't come cheap. €€€€

🏠 **Snowhotel Kirkenes** Sandnesdalen 14, Bjørnevatn; 🕿78 97 05 40; **e** info@ snowhotelkirkenes.com; **w** snowhotelkirkenes.com; ⏱ Dec–Apr. This impressive snow structure lies beside the Guhkesvuotna fjord in Bjørnevatn, 10km southwest of Kirkenes & offers igloo accommodation in rooms of snow & ice. €€€€

🏠 **Thon Kirkenes** Johan Knudtzens gate 11; 🕿78 97 10 50; **e** kirkenes@olavthon.no; **w** thonhotels.no/kirkenes. Modern, stylish &

efficient – in short, everything you would expect from Thon in this new, purpose-built hotel, plus great sea views & a pleasant outdoor bar overlooking the water. €€€€

🏠 **Kirkenes Hotell** Doktor Wessels gate 3; 🕿78 99 86 00; **e** kirkenes.hotell@yahoo.com; **w** kirkeneshotell.net. An odd complex that combines a hotel with a Chinese restaurant. Rooms are fine if uninspiring. If nobody is around at the hotel, try the Shanghai restaurant. €€€

🏠 **Barents Frokosthotell** Presteveien 3; 🕿78 99 32 99. A soulless modern block just off the main square with 14 rather dreary, though affordable rooms; half of them have private facilities. Popular with visiting Russians. €€

🍴 **WHERE TO EAT AND DRINK** *Map, page 219, unless otherwise stated*

🍴 **69 Nord** Johan Knudtzens gate 11; 🕿78 97 10 50; ⏱ 17.00–22.00 daily. The best restaurant in town belongs to the Thon hotel (see above): the inventive menu features a starter of reindeer carpaccio or pan-seared scallops & mains such as chicken confit with a purée of sweet potato or

a mouthwatering seafood platter of king crab, scallops, crayfish & mussels. €€€

🍴 **Gapahuken Sollia Gjestegård** [map, page 184] Storskog; 🕿78 99 08 20; **w** storskog. no; ⏱ late Jun–Aug 18.00–22.00 Mon–Sat, 15.00–19.00 Sun. Located 10km east of Kirkenes close to the Russian border, this rustic restaurant specialises in northern Norwegian specialities such as Arctic Sea salmon with cucumber salad & sour cream & is really worth the trip out here – the food is the best for miles. €€

✖ **Ritz** Doktor Wessels gate 17; ☏78 99 34 81; ⏲ 14.00–22.00 Mon & Tue, 14.00–23.00 Wed–Fri, 13.00–02.30 Sat, 13.00–22.00 Sun. Forget any resemblance to its famous namesake, though this is Kirkenes's best pizzeria, located on the 1st floor of the building. There's a large selection of pizzas – a medium, depending on toppings, will cost around 210NOK. Also take-away. €€

✖ **Surf and Turf** Doktor Wessels gate 2; m 46 44 52 45; ⏲ 11.00–22.00 Mon–Sat. Pleasant European-style bistro serving whale steaks, chicken breast, burgers, pasta, fish & chips & steamed cod. €€

✖ **Basilica** Verksveien 1; ☏78 99 50 05; ⏲ 10.00–20.00 Mon–Sat. For none-too-authentic Italian food, such as pizzas & pasta dishes, this cheap & cheerful place in the town centre is certainly good value with a range of burger & kebab dishes, too. €

✖ **Centrum Kafé** Doktor Wessels gate 18; ⏲ 10.00–17.00 Mon–Fri, 10.00–16.00 Sat. A no-nonsense daytime fast-food place with burgers, omelettes, chicken nuggets & salads. €

✖ **Shanghai** Doktor Wessels gate 3; ☏78 99 01 28; ⏲ 13.00–22.00 Sun–Thu, 13.00–23.00 Fri & Sat. Inside the Kirkenes Hotell, a good range of Chinese dishes such as beef in oyster sauce, duck in soy sauce & chicken fried rice. €

♉ **Pub 1 AS** Doktor Wessels gate 16. 13.00–01.00 daily. The most lively pub in Kirkenes opposite the main entrance to the shopping centre attracting a mix of locals, sailors & tourists. €

WHAT TO SEE AND DO Thanks to the unholy alliance of Soviet bombs and German fires during World War II, Kirkenes town centre is a frightfully drab place to explore: rows of modern concrete blocks befuddle the view at every turn. Instead, head down to the **dockside** on Johan Knudtzens gate for your first impressions of Norway's most remote town. Here, lined up against the quay, a contingent of Murmansk's most battered ships and freighters waits patiently to be patched up in the wharves operated by the ship-repair company, KIMEK; the three vessels you can see down here, all roped together, were confiscated by the Norwegian authorities for non-payment of taxes and have consequently now been abandoned by their Russian owners. Behind the adjacent AMFI shopping complex, the sight of ships hoisted up in the dry dock of the shipyard confirms Kirkenes's role as a strategic port for the Barents Sea area. The quay is usually busy with Russian sailors weaving to and fro, returning to their vessels after sampling the delights of Kirkenes's various watering holes.

Soviet memorial Kirkenes was liberated by the Red Army on 25 October 1944 – an event commemorated with the erection in 1952, on Roald Amundsensgate (head up Sjøgata from the church and take the second on the right), of a statue of a Soviet soldier, facing north and looking out over the Arctic Ocean. Generally, the plinth on which he stands is adorned with flowers and white, blue and red banners. The simple inscription written in Norwegian and Russian reads: 'To the Soviet Union's brave soldiers. In memory of the liberation of Kirkenes 1944.'

The Andersgrotta bomb shelter (w snowhotelkirkenes.com; ⏲ Jun–Aug 12.30 daily; 30min tour; 200NOK) For a further taste of what life was like in Kirkenes during World War II, check out Andersgrotta, a huge cave hidden away inside the hillside just to the east of the town centre on Christer Ankersgate, which served as a bomb shelter from 1941 to 1944. In addition to a short tour, a video is shown detailing the 320 air raids directed at Kirkenes which totally destroyed the town.

Russian market (w russianmarket.info) On the last Thursday of every month a popular all-day Russian market is held in the main square in Kirkenes. Russian *babushkas* make the journey from Murmansk to sell all manner of goods ranging from furs to wooden spoons from stalls which they set up in the square. The grannies then spend the night in Kirkenes before heading back to Russia by minibus with their takings.

Varanger Museum (Sør-Varangermuseet; ✎ 78 99 48 80; w varangermuseum. no; ⊕ mid-Aug–mid-Jun 09.00–15.00 daily; mid-Jun–mid-Aug 09.00–17.00 daily; 80NOK) From the town centre, a 15-minute walk south along Storgata, which becomes Solheimsveien, will bring you to the lake, Førstevann. Here, at Førstevannslia, by the water's edge, you will find **Kirkenes's main museum complex** containing the Borderland Museum (Grenselandmuseet), devoted to the history and nature of the border country hereabouts, and **Savio Museum** (Saviomuseet), which displays the work of local Sámi artist, John Savio.

The museum is dominated by a real-life single-propellor Ilyusin aircraft which crashlanded in Sennagress Lake on Jarfjordfjellet Mountain, outside Kirkenes, in 1944. The plane was on a mission to blow up the Elvenes Bridge near Kirkenes but was shot down. Restored to her former glory in Revda south of Murmansk, the aircraft returned to Norway in the mid 1990s, to take pride of place in the new museum built to house it. Around the aeroplane, you'll find collections of military equipment including rifles, grenades and gas masks, while upstairs, there's a potted history of Kirkenes's industrial past.

Back on the ground floor, the area of the museum known as Saviomuseet is dedicated to the short life of John Savio (1902–38) from Bugøyfjord, northwest of Kirkenes. At the age of 18 he attended art college in the Norwegian capital, Christiania (now Oslo), and received instruction from leading contemporary painter, Axel Revold. Although the museum mostly displays Savio's sculptures, he also produced a number of paintings that draw on the power of nature and Sámi themes for inspiration. Savio studied art in Paris where his work was exhibited, but he contracted tuberculosis in 1920; the disease returned later and tragically claimed his life at the age of 36.

Boris Gleb: boat trip to the Russian border Sailing from the boatyard off Fyllingsveien at the east of the town centre, this highly recommended 3½-hour boat trip runs down the Pasvikelva River, passing under the road bridge carrying the E105 at Elvnes, towards the small Russian enclave of Boris Gleb, named after two Russian Orthodox saints. The enclave is unusual in that it lies on the western bank of the river, which otherwise belongs entirely to Norway; the eastern bank and the town of Borisoglebskiy is in Russia. Because of its historical links, the village was awarded to Russia when the border was finally formalised in an agreement between Russia and Sweden in 1826. Boris Gleb has even belonged to Finland; from 1920 to 1944, it formed part of Finland's newly acquired Petsamo district until Soviet post-war reparations called for its return to the Soviet Union.

Annoyingly, because of visa restrictions the boat doesn't dock in Boris Gleb but does sail close enough to get a glimpse of Kirkenes's nearest neighbour. There's also a chance on the tour to walk along the eastern riverbank to the Norwegian–Russian border posts, though, importantly not to step over the demarcation line. Incidentally, the timber **church** you see in the enclave, across the river on the western shore, was built in the late 1800s and it is now the only church in Boris Gleb. However, until 1944, there were two churches here: an original, erected in 1565, which served as a place of worship for the local Skolt Sámi until it was destroyed in World War II, once stood alongside today's structure. Bizarrely, for just 59 days during the summer of 1965, the border at Boris Gleb was open to any

Scandinavian who wanted to cross into the Soviet Union to buy alcohol; it's been claimed the Soviets used this one-way tourist traffic to try to recruit Norwegian agents for the KGB. However, an American student, Newcomb Mott, decided he, too, should be allowed to visit the Soviet Union (although he wasn't Scandinavian and had no visa) and made his way around the border posts into the bar at Boris Gleb – he was promptly arrested. His tortured body was returned to the Americans five months later and the border at Boris Gleb was closed for good.

Departures are daily from June to mid-September at 09.00 and 14.00 (990NOK). Book with Barents Safari at Fjellveien 28 (m 90 19 05 94; e info@barentssafari. no; w barentssafari.no), who also operate a free pickup from the town centre 30 minutes before the departure: lunch is provided on the tour.

Kirkenes Snowhotel (℄ 78 97 05 40; e info@snowhotelkirkenes.com; w snowhotelkirkenes.com) Not to be outdone by Lapland's other icehotels, Kirkenes now has its very own snowhotel, which opens in early December and operates until late April. Built 8km south of Kirkenes at Jentoftbukta Bay on Guhkesvuotna fjord, the hotel consists of a series of igloo-style rooms of snow and ice and a sauna. A room for two people costs a steep 6,200NOK and includes dinner, breakfast and sauna.

Perhaps because of its remote location, this snowhotel does not compare favourably with all the other spin-offs of the Jukkasjärvi original; Kirkenes is indeed at a disadvantage in terms of attracting visitors because it is so far away. If you are here though in connection with a Hurtigruten cruise, it is certainly worth calling by for a look (if not spending the night here); tours lasting 90 minutes operate from the town centre at 13.00 and cost 790NOK per person.

SOUTHWEST FROM KIRKENES: TRERIKSRØYSA Contrary to popular belief, Lapland doesn't have one border post where three countries all rub shoulders – but two. The better known of the two is Treriksröset near Kilpisjärvi in western Lapland, where Norway, Sweden and Finland all meet (page 132). However, here in the east, there's another triangular border point, **Treriksrøysa**, located at the southern end of the Pasvikdalen Valley which runs southwest from Kirkenes down towards Finland, where Norway, Russia and Finland all meet. To get here, take Route 885 out of Kirkenes towards Nyrud, a distance of around 100km, which passes through the marshes and forests of the Øvre Pasvik National Park, a narrow tooth-shaped tract of wilderness home to bears and wolverines. From just before Nyrud (at a place called Gjøkåsen) a forest track leads further south to a point known as Grenseneset – the very last extremity of Norway. From here, a marked walking trail of around 5km leads northwest to the border post, Treriksrøysa. It is extremely important not to stray across the border into Russia at this point or you will be arrested.

The enormously useful **Øvre Pasvik Café & Camping** (m 95 91 13 05; e atle. randa@pasvikcamping.no; w pasvikcamping.no) in Vagattem rents out cabins (€) as well as canoes (250NOK/day), bikes (120NOK/day) and rowing boats (50NOK/ hr) and can help with advice on getting to the border post and also back to Kirkenes.

Getting there There is just one **bus** daily from Kirkenes (13.25 Mon–Fri) along Route 885 towards **Pasvik**, terminating in nearby **Vagattem**. The bus from Vagattem back to Kirkenes leaves at 07.20 (on schooldays, check w snelandia. no for the latest details). Alternatively, and much more practically, given the skeletal bus connections out here, consider renting a **car** in Kirkenes – see page 221 for details.

GETTING TO RUSSIA: KIRKENES TO MURMANSK Rules for getting a Russian visa are seemingly in a constant state of flux. Check w visatorussia.com for the latest details. It is not possible to get a visa to Russia at the border post.

There are daily **buses** between Kirkenes and Murmansk. Departing from outside the Scandic Hotel in the town centre, a bus leaves every day at 15.00 (14.00 Nov–Mar), arriving in Murmansk 5 hours later after travelling via Nikel. A ticket costs 350NOK one-way, or 600NOK return. For the return journey, the buses leave Murmansk at 07.00 (daily). There are maps of the exact departure point for the bus at w pasvikturist.no, and there's also an office at Doktor Wessels gate 15B (page 221).

MOVING ON FROM KIRKENES In addition to the buses to Murmansk mentioned above, a **bus** leaves from outside the AMFI shopping complex at 06.05 (Mon–Fri) and at 11.20 (Sun only) for **Hammerfest**, arriving at 15.35 (20.25 Sun); change at Lakselv for Karasjok. From Kirkenes it is 492km to Hammerfest, routing via Lakselv.

For **destinations in Finland**, the best bet is to pick up the painfully timed Finnish bus operated by Eskelisen Lapinlinjat (w eskelisen.fi) from Tana Bru (⊕ 03.20) for destinations towards Rovaniemi via Utsjoki, Inari and Sodankylä. Times from Kirkenes to Tana Bru are available at w snelandia.no.

UPDATES WEBSITE

You can post your comments and recommendations, and read feedback and updates from other readers online at w bradtguides.com/updates.

7

Appendix 1

LANGUAGE

Lapland has four official languages: Finnish, Norwegian, Sámi and Swedish. However, Sámi is not widely spoken, known by just 17,000 people of Lapland's 900,000-strong population (which includes Lapland's 66,000 Sámi people). Other than road signs in Sámi, you're unlikely to come into contact with the language and we have therefore excluded it from the vocabulary lists below. All Sámi are bilingual and many also speak English; there's more information about Sámi on page 17.

NORWEGIAN AND SWEDISH The Germanic languages Norwegian and Swedish are mutually comprehensible. Thanks to their common history through Old Norse, the languages have not greatly diverged from each other and share a common word base and grammar. Anyone with a knowledge of German should recognise a whole host of words. With a little practice English mother-tongue speakers should also be able to pick out a number of similarities: for example, *båten sprang läck och sjönk till botten* means 'the boat sprang a leak and sank to the bottom', and *han har en skruv lös* means 'he's got a screw loose'. The task is easier for speakers of northern English or Scottish dialects who will spot even more familiar words: *slänga ut* ('sling out'), *flytta* ('flit') and *leka* (Yorkshire dialect 'lake' meaning 'play') are just three examples. English is widely spoken and understood in Norwegian and Swedish Lapland.

Pronunciation Pronunciation in Swedish and Norwegian is tricky. Both languages are tonal and getting the tone wrong can change the meaning of a word. For example, Swedish *femton*, with stress on *fem-*, means 'fifteen'; with equal stress as *fem ton* it means 'five tons'. The resulting up-and-down rhythm produces the hurdy-gurdy sounds you're no doubt familiar with. Although it takes considerable practice to get the tones right, native speakers will usually understand what you're trying to say. In both languages vowels are normally long when followed by a single consonant, short when a double consonant follows. Unusual sounds are highlighted below.

Letter	English equivalent
Ä	like English 'eh'
Å	like English 'oh'
EI, EJ	like English 'ay'
J, DJ, GJ, HJ, LJ	as English 'y'
G (before i, y, ä, ö)	as English 'y'
HV (Nor)	as English 'v'
K (before i, j, ö)	similar to English 'sh'
Ø (Nor) Ö (Swe)	like English 'err'
RS	as English 'sh'

S	always 's', never 'z'
SJ, SKJ, STJ	similar to English 'sh'
TJ	similar to English 'sh'

FINNISH Finnish is quite different from Swedish and Norwegian. It is not related to either, or indeed to many other languages in Europe. Part of the Finno-Ugric (as opposed to Indo-European) language group, its closest relatives are Sámi, Estonian and, much more distantly, Hungarian. As a result there are very few words you will recognise. Take, for example, *pysähtyy vain matkustajien ottamista varten*, which means 'boarding passengers only'. Its grammatical structure is the stuff of nightmares with 15 cases alone to grapple with. Instead of prepositions, Finnish employs a complex system of suffixes – something which is further complicated by obligatory vowel harmony. Despite that, it's worth learning a few words of Finnish since English is not widely spoken in Finnish Lapland and you'll make things considerably easier for yourself. However, beyond the most simple of phrases, you will need a lifetime to make any real inroads.

Pronunciation In Finnish, words are pronounced exactly as they are written, with the stress falling on the first syllable. In the case of a compound noun, stress falls on each part of the word. Double consonants are both pronounced and double vowels lengthen the sound accordingly. Unusual sounds are highlighted below.

Letter	English equivalent
Ä	like English 'eh'
Å	like English 'oh'
J	as English 'y'
Ö	like English 'err'
S	always 's', never 'z'
U	like English 'oo'
Y	as in French 'eu'

ESSENTIAL VOCABULARY
Basics

English	Finnish	Norwegian	Swedish
Good morning	*huomenta*	*god morgen*	*godmorgon*
Good afternoon	*päivää*	*goddag*	*goddag*
Good evening	*hyvää iltaa*	*god kveld*	*god afton*
Hello	*moi*	*hei*	*hej*
Goodbye	*hei hei*	*adjø*	*hejdå*
My name is	*minun nimi on*	*jeg heter*	*jag heter*
I am from	*olen … (-sta)*	*jeg er fra*	*jag kommer från*
England	*Englannista*	*England*	*England*
America	*Amerikasta*	*Amerika*	*Amerika*
Australia	*Australiasta*	*Australia*	*Australien*
How are you?	*mitä kuuluu?*	*hvordan har du det?*	*hur går det?*
Pleased to meet you	*hauska tavata*	*hyggelig å treffe deg*	*trevligt att träffas*
Thank you	*kiitos*	*takk*	*tack*
Cheers	*kippis*	*skål*	*skål*
Yes	*kyllä*	*ja*	*ja*
No	*ei*	*nei*	*nej*
I don't understand	*en ymmärrä*	*jeg forstår ikke*	*jag förstår inte*
Do you speak English?	*puhutko englantia?*	*snakker du engelsk?*	*talar du engelska?*

Questions

How?	miten?	hvordan?	hur?
What?	mikä?	hva?	vad?
Where?	missä?	hvor?	var?
Which?	kumpi?	hvilken?	vilken?
When?	milloin?	når?	när?
Who?	kuka?	hvem?	vem?
How much?	paljonko?	hvor mye?	hur mycket?

Numbers

1	yksi	en	xett
2	kaksi	to	två
3	kolme	tre	tre
4	neljä	fire	fyra
5	viisi	fem	fem
6	kuusi	seks	sex
7	seitsemän	sju	sju
8	kahdeksan	åtte	åtta
9	yhdeksän	ni	nio
10	kymmenen	ti	tio
11	yksitoista	elleve	elva
12	kaksitoista	tolv	tolv
13	kolmetoista	tretten	tretton
14	neljätoista	fjorten	fjorton
15	viisitoista	femten	femton
16	kuusitoista	seksten	sexton
17	seitsemäntoista	sytten	sjutton
18	kahdeksantoista	atten	arton
19	yhdeksäntoista	nitten	nitton
20	kaksikymmentä	tjue	tjugo
21	kaksikymmentäykri	tjueen	tjugoett
30	kolmekymmentä	tretti	trettio
40	neljäkymmentä	førti	fyrtio
50	viisikymmentä	femti	femtio
60	kuusikymmentä	seksti	sextio
70	seitsemänkymmentä	sytti	sjuttio
80	kahdeksankymmentä	åtti	åttio
90	yhdeksänkymmentä	nitti	nittio
100	sata	hundre	hundra
101	satayksi	hundre og en	hundraett
1,000	tuhat	tusen	tusen

Time

What time is it?	mitä kello on?	hva er klokka?	hur mycket är klockan?
It's …	kello on …	klokka er …	hon är …
Today	tänään	i dag	idag
Tomorrow	huomenna	i morgen	imorgon
Yesterday	eilen	igår	igår
In the morning	aamulla	om morgonen	om morgonen
In the afternoon	iltapäivällä	om eftermiddagen	om eftermiddagen

Days

Monday	maanantai	mandag	måndag
Tuesday	tiistai	tirsdag	tisdag
Wednesday	keskiviikko	onsdag	onsdag
Thursday	torstai	torsdag	torsdag
Friday	perjantai	fredag	fredag
Saturday	lauantai	lørdag	lördag
Sunday	sunnuntai	søndag	söndag

Months

January	tammikuu	januar	januari
February	helmikuu	februar	februari
March	maaliskuu	mars	mars
April	huhtikuu	april	april
May	toukokuu	mai	maj
June	kesäkuu	juni	juni
July	heinäkuu	juli	juli
August	elokuu	august	augusti
September	syyskuu	september	september
October	lokakuu	oktober	oktober
November	marraskuu	november	november
December	joulukuu	desember	december

Getting around and public transport

I'd like …	sannko …	jeg vil gjerne ha …	kan jag få …
A one-way ticket	menolipun	et enkelt billett	en enkel biljett
A return ticket	meno-ja luulipun	et tur-retur	en tur och retur
When does it leave?	milloin lähtee?	når går den/det?	när åker den/det?
Timetable	aikataulu	tidsplan	tidtabell
Bus station	linja-autoasema	rutebilstasjon	busstation
Train station	rautatieasema	jernbanestasjon	järnvägsstation
Train	juna	tog	tåg

Signs

Entrance	sisään	inngang	ingång
Exit	ulos	utgang	utgång
Gentlemen	miehet/miehille	herrer	herrar
Ladies	naiset/naisille	damer	damer
Open	avoinna	åpent	öppet
Closed	siljettu	stengt	stängt
Push	työnnä	trykk	tryck
Pull	vedä	trekk	drag
Arrival	saapuvat	ankomst	ankommande
Departure	lähtevät	avgang	avgående

Accommodation

Single room	Finnish yhden hengen huoneen
	Norwegian et enkeltrom
	Swedish ett enkelrum
Double room	Finnish kahden hengen huoneen
	Norwegian et dobbeltrom
	Swedish ett dubbelrum

Share a dorm	Finnish *makuusalin sänkypaikka*
	Norwegian *ligge på sovesalen*
	Swedish *bo i sovsal*

Food

I am a vegetarian	Finnish *olen kasvissyöjä*
	Norwegian *jeg er vegetarianer*
	Swedish *jag är vegetarian*
The bill, please	Finnish *lasku, kiitos*
	Norwegian *regningen, takk*
	Swedish *notan, tack*

Basics

Bread	*leipä*	*brød*	*bröd*
Butter	*voi*	*smør*	*smör*
Cheese	*juusto*	*ost*	*ost*
Salt	*suola*	*salt*	*salt*
Pepper	*pippuri*	*pepper*	*peppar*
Sugar	*sokeri*	*sukker*	*socker*

Fruit

Apple	*omena*	*eple*	*äpple*
Banana	*banaani*	*banan*	*banan*
Orange	*appelsiini*	*appelsin*	*appelsin*
Pear	*päärynä*	*pære*	*päron*

Vegetables

Carrot	*porkkana*	*gulrot*	*morot*
Garlic	*kynsilaukka*	*hvitløk*	*vitlök*
Onion	*sipuli*	*løk*	*lök*
Mushroom	*sieni*	*sopp*	*svamp*
Potato	*peruna*	*potet*	*potatis*

Fish

Salmon	*lohi*	*laks*	*lax*
Arctic char	*pikkunieriä*	*røye*	*röding*
Herring	*silli*	*sild*	*sill*

SWEDISH HOME COOKING – *SVENSK HUSMANSKOST*

On many menus across Swedish Lapland, particularly at lunchtime, you'll come across the term: *husmanskost* (home cooking), which deserves a little clarification. At its best, *husmanskost* is a modern interpretation of classic, everyday dishes which were rustled up at home to fill empty stomachs. Examples include: meatballs with lingonberries; *Janssons frestelse* (a creamy potato bake with anchovies); *pytt i panna* (cubes of sautéed potato and ham with onion and egg); *Sjömannsbiff* (beef casserole) and *kåldomar* (cabbage rolls stuffed with meat). This is not intended to be *haute cuisine*; instead, it's simple fare which is still much favoured by Swedish families today.

Plaice	*punakampela*	*rødspætte*	*rödspätta*
Tuna	*tonnikala*	*tunfisk*	*tonfisk*

Meat

Beef	*nauta*	*okse*	*biff*
Chicken	*kana*	*kylling*	*kyckling*
Pork	*porsas*	*svinekjøtt*	*fläsk*
Steak	*pihvi*	*stek*	*stek*
Reindeer	*poron*	*rein*	*ren*
Elk	*hirvi*	*elg*	*älg*

Drinks

Beer	*olut*	*øl*	*öl*
Coffee	*kahvi*	*kaffe*	*kaffe*
Tea	*tee*	*te*	*te*
Juice	*tuoremehu*	*juice*	*juice*
Milk	*maito*	*melk*	*mjölk*
Water	*vesi*	*vann*	*vatn*
Wine	*viini*	*vin*	*vin*
Red wine	*punaviini*	*rødvin*	*rödvin*
White wine	*valkoviini*	*hvitvin*	*vitvin*

Appendix 2

GLOSSARY OF FINNISH, NORWEGIAN, SÁMI AND SWEDISH TERMS

áhpi (Sámi)	marsh	*joki* (Fin)	river
backe (Nor, Swe)	hill	*kåta* (Swe)	wooden tepee
berg (Nor, Swe)	mountain	*lávvu* (Sámi)	turf hut
boatka (Sámi)	mountain pass	*ö* (Swe)	island
bro/bru (Nor, Swe)	bridge	*øy* (Nor)	island
dal (Nor, Swe)	valley	*saari* (Fin)	island
duottar (Sámi)	low-lying mountains	*sjö* (Swe)	lake
fors/foss (Nor, Swe)	waterfall	*skog* (Nor, Swe)	forest
gákti (Sámi)	traditional dress	*tunturi* (Fin)	rounded hill
gieva (Sámi)	bog	*vággi* (Sámi)	broad mountain valley
järvi (Fin)	lake	*várri* (Sámi)	hill
jávri (Sámi)	lake		

Incidentally, *duottar* is the only Sámi loanword in English. Having passed via Russian into English, *duottar* is the origin of the English word 'tundra'. It is cognate with the Finnish word *tunturi*, 'rounded fell'.

GLOSSARY OF SÁMI REINDEER TERMS The Sámi language has hundreds of words relating to reindeer and reindeer husbandry, clearly showing the importance of the animal to the Sámi people. Some of the most enlightening are listed below.

Sámi	English
áldu	reindeer in its third winter
barfi	reindeer with antlers with many branches
biikasággi	reindeer with vertical horns
čaločoarvi	reindeer with skin peeling off its antlers
čearpmat	reindeer in its first winter
čora	small reindeer herd
čuoivvat	reindeer with white muzzle or sides
dápmat	taming a reindeer
gabba	completely white reindeer
heargi	castrated reindeer who pulls sleighs
jieva	white reindeer
luosttat	reindeer with white flanks
muzet	black reindeer
nálat	reindeer with its antlers cut off
nulpu	reindeer without antlers

ráidu	reindeer caravan
rávži	sick reindeer
rotnu	reindeer who has failed to calf
ruksesmiessi	reindeer calf while still red
ruovgat	reindeer grunting noise
sad-d-at	reindeer panting noise
siida	reindeer village or mountain camp
sivlá	reindeer corral
spágat	reindeer packsaddle
stáinnat	barren female reindeer
váibbat	exhausted, worn out reindeer
vuonjal	reindeer in its second winter

SEND US YOUR SNAPS!

We'd love to follow your adventures using our *Lapland* guide – why not tag us in your photos and stories on Twitter (🐦 @BradtGuides) and Instagram (📷 @bradtguides)?

Appendix 3

FURTHER INFORMATION

BOOKS English-language books on Lapland are remarkably scant. Those listed below are the pick of the meagre crop.

Non-fiction

Acerbi, Giuseppe *Travels through Sweden, Finland and Lapland to the North Cape in the Years 1798 and 1799* Adamant Media Corporation, 2001. A truly fabulous account of a trip to the North Cape and his encounters with the Sámi by an intrepid Italian traveller.

Beach, Hugh *A Year in Lapland* University of Washington Press, 2001. A fascinating account of an American student living with the Sámi of Jokkmokk in the 1980s.

Booth, Michael *The Almost Nearly Perfect People* Random House, 2014. A well-observed and at times hysterically funny critique of the Nordic peoples which claims to tell the truth about the Nordic miracle. His observations of the Swedes, however, are inaccurate.

Bryson, Bill *Neither Here Nor There* Black Swan, 1998. Beginning his epic journey across Europe from Lapland, Bryson sets out from Hammerfest and has some rather terse things to say about it.

Copp, DeWitt S *Incident at Boris Gleb: The Tragedy of Newcomb Mott* Doubleday & Company, 1968. A gripping account of the disappearance of American student, Newcomb Mott, inside the Russian enclave of Boris Gleb in September 1965 at the height of the Cold War.

Francis, Gavin *True North* Polygon, 2008. A readable, informative account of one man's wander-voyage across large parts of Lapland, blending historical and comtemporary narratives.

Goldstein, Robert M *Riding with Reindeer* Rivendell Publishing Northwest, 2010. Follow the author on an adventurous bike ride across Finland and Arctic Norway, all the way from Helsinki to the Barents Sea. The author's solitude in the far north is relieved by reindeer who become his constant companions.

Mann, Chris *Hitler's Arctic War: The Wehrmacht in Lapland, Norway & Finland 1940–1945* Thomas Dunne Books, 2003. The true extent of the devastation caused by Hitler's scorched earth policy becomes clear in this gripping account of World War II.

Ratcliffe, Derek *Lapland: A Natural History* Poyser, 2005. A rare and wonderfully detailed account about the flora and fauna of Lapland by an author whose passion for the region shines through.

Seurujärvi, Irja *The Saami: A Cultural Encyclopaedia* Suomalaisen Kirjallisuuden Seura, 2005. The leading authority on all aspects of Sámi life and culture. A tremendous resource and quite unique in its scope.

Fiction

Ekman, Kerstin *Under the Snow* Vintage, 1997. The death of a teacher in a small village in Swedish Lapland polarises the community. A novel by one of Sweden's leading authors, which brings the dramatic landscapes of Lapland to life on the page.

Niemi, Mikael *Popular Music* Harper Perennial, 2004. The enchanting tale of two boys growing up in Pajala in Swedish Lapland during the 1960s and 1970s.

Truc, Olivier *Forty Days without Shadows* Trapdoor, 2014. Translated from French and written by an author based in Stockholm, this book recounts a prize-winning tale about indigenous people fighting to preserve their identity and culture in the modern world. The novel centres on the theft of a priceless relic from Kautokeino in Norwegian Lapland just days before a UN conference on indigenous rights is due to take place. The plot thickens when a local reindeer herder is found brutally murdered nearby.

Language

Ahlgren, Jennie, and Holmes, Philip *Colloquial Swedish* Routledge, 2006. A thorough and accessible course to get you started in Swedish.

Bratveit, Kari, et al *Colloquial Norwegian* Routledge, 1994. A good first course in Norwegian.

White, Leila *From Start to Finnish* Finn Lectura, 2001. Undoubtedly the best beginners' course on the market. Available in Finland (ISBN 951 792 105 5).

Other Scandinavia guides For a full list of Bradt's Scandinavia guides, see w bradtguides.com/shop.

Evans, Andrew *Iceland*, 2020
Evans, Polly *Northern Lights: A practical travel guide*, 2017
Norum, Roger & Proctor, James *Svalbard: Spitsbergen, Jan Mayen, Franz Josef Land*, 2018
Proctor, James *Faroe Islands,* 2019
Proctor, James *West Sweden including Gothenburg*, 2018

WEBSITES
General

w **eng.samer.se** Detailed information about Sweden's Sámi community.
w **eskelisen.fi** Bus times for Finnish Lapland.
w **hurtigruten.no** Times and prices for the Norwegian coastal ferry, Hurtigruten.
w **laplandfinland.com** The definitive tourist site on Finnish Lapland.
w **matkahuolto.fi** Finnish bus timetables in English.
w **outdoors.fi** Masses of information about Finland's national parks.
w **samer.no** Exhaustive details on the Norwegian Sámi community.
w **santaclaus.fi** The big man's homepage including a webcam on the Arctic Circle.
w **sauna.fi** The definitive source of information on the Finnish sauna.
w **scandinavica.com/sami** Summary about the Sámi and Lapland.
w **shelandia.no** Bus and ferry times for Norwegian Lapland.
w **sj.se** Train times for Swedish Lapland.
w **swedishlapland.com** Tourist information for Swedish Lapland.
w **visitnorthcape.com** Information about Finnmark and the North Cape.

Weather conditions

w **fmi.fi/en** Finnish Meteorological Institute.
w **smhi.se** Swedish Meteorological and Hydrological Institute.
w **yr.no** Norwegian Meteorological Institute.

Index

Bold indicates main entries; *italic* indicates maps